The Berbers of Morocco

The Berbers of Morocco

A History of Resistance

Michael Peyron

I.B. TAURIS

LONDON • NEW YORK • OXFORD • NEW DELHI • SYDNEY

I.B. TAURIS
Bloomsbury Publishing Plc
50 Bedford Square, London, WC1B 3DP, UK
1385 Broadway, New York, NY 10018, USA
29 Earlsfort Terrace, Dublin 2, Ireland

BLOOMSBURY, I.B. TAURIS and the I.B. Tauris logo are trademarks of Bloomsbury
Publishing Plc

First published in Great Britain 2021
This paperback edition published in 2022

Cover design: Adriana Brioso
Cover image © Michael Peyron

A catalogue record for this book is available from the British Library.

A catalog record for this book is available from the Library of Congress.

ISBN: HB: 978-1-8386-0046-4
         PB: 978-0-7556-3935-9
       ePDF: 978-1-8386-0373-1
      eBook: 978-1-8386-0375-5

Typeset by RefineCatch Limited, Bungay, Suffolk

To find out more about our authors and books visit www.bloomsbury.com
and sign up for our newsletters.

Michael Peyron defended a Doctoral thesis at the Grenoble Institute of Alpine Geography on the Tounfit region as a result of extensive field work in the Eastern High Atlas of Morocco (1970–90). He subsequently lectured on Amazigh History and Culture at Al-Akhawayn University, Ifrane (AUI) and at the Faculty of Letters, Rabat, Morocco (1999–2011). His better known Berber-related publications include *The Amazigh Studies Reader* (2008), *Berber Odes* (2010) and *Mountains worth living for* (2019).

To Josiane, Caroline, Margaret, Maya and Yan

Also to Ayad Kerouach, Houssa Yakobi, Youssef Aït Lemkaddem, Assou and Khadija Lhatoute, Rkia Montassir, Khadija Aziz, Fatima Boukhris, Labha El Asri and many other Amazigh friends and acquaintances

In memory of David M. Hart, Berber fieldworker extraordinary, and alsoMohammed El-Manaouar from Asif Dadds, late member of IRCAM

Semi-nomads on the move, Tounfit, Ayt Yahya (Eastern High Atlas).

Contents

List of Illustrations and Maps   xi

Preface   xiv

Introduction   1

1   Berber Origins   5

2   From Carthage to Islam   9

3   Dynasts versus Heretics   15

4   Triumph of the Atlas Berbers   21

5   Makers of Mayhem: Beni Hilal and Ma'qil   27

6   Atlas Saints and Mountain Kings   35

7   Senhaja Revival   43

8   Scourge of the Berbers   51

9   Transition and Recovery   57

10   Berber Backlash   65

11   Dawn of the Great *Qayd* Era   79

12   The Foreign Threat   91

13   The Start of Morocco's "Thirty Years' War"   101

14   The Defense of Jbel Fazaz   109

15   Stemming the Tide in Southeast Morocco   115

16   Great *Qayd* versus Marabout   123

17   Between Oum Rbia' and Moulouya: Failure of the Marabouts   131

18   Bitter Battles Around Jbel Tishshoukt   139

19   The Rif War (1921–7)   149

20   Phoney War on the Atlas Front (1926–9)   161

21   Reckless Raiders Rule the Roost (1927–34)   179

22   The Opening Rounds of the Atlas Endgame: Ayt Ya'qoub to Tazizaout (1929–32)   197

23   Heroic Defense of Tazizaout   213

24   Atlas Endgame: The Closing Stages (1933–4)   225

25   Pacification Aftermath   235

26   Transition to Modernity: Protectorate and Independence   241

27   From Oblivion to Recognition   249
28   Conclusion   255

Notes   259
Bibliography   299
Index of Place and People's Names   313

Illustrations and Maps

Frontispiece: Semi-nomads on the move, Tounfit, Ayt Yahya (Eastern High Atlas). viii

1 Boumaln-Dadds: cubic, kasbah-style architecture typical of southeastern Morocco. 12

2 Village of Imlil n-Oughbar with the shrine to *mahdi* Ibn Toumert (Western High Atlas). 23

3 Camel-herding, High Moulouya Plain, Eastern Middle Atlas in the distance. 26

4 Agersaffen village, upper Seksawa Valley (Western High Atlas). 36

5 Village of Imi n-Wasif, upper Seksawa Valley (Western High Atlas). 37

6 An *ashelhiy* (Berber) man from the Western High Atlas. 42

7 Rooftops of Zaouit Ahansal and cliffs of Jbel Aroudan. 44

8 Ayt Hadiddou couple on the trail, Asif Melloul Valley (Eastern High Atlas). 45

9 Seventh lineal descendant of Bou Salim el-'Ayyashi, Zaouit Si Hamza. 46

10 Ayt 'Atta summer camp at foot of Jbel Azourki. 47

11 Cedar forest at the foot of Jbel 'Ayyashi. 54

12 Autumn scene, Berber village, Western High Atlas. 58

13 Village of Azgour and Jbel Erdouz, Guedmioua (Western High Atlas). 60

14 Nomadic encampment at foot of Jbel Maasker, Tounfit (Eastern High Atlas). 61

15 Sheep and cattle in upper Moulouya; Jbel 'Ayyashi in the background. 69

16 Zaouit Si Hamza, on the southern slopes of Jbel 'Ayyashi. 75

17 Village upstream from Amellago, Asif Ghriss gorge (Ayt Merghad). 76

18 Girl from Seksawa, with rope on a grass-cutting chore (Western High Atlas). 81

19 Woman from the Glaoua tribe near Tizi n-Tishka 89

20 Typical mountain Berber architecture, Ayt Bahammou, Seksawa (Western High Atlas). 91

21 Shrine of Sidi 'Ali Oulhousseyn, Anergui, at the foot of Jbel Kousser. 98

22   Girl from the Glaoua tribe near Tizi n-Tishka (Marrakesh High Atlas).   124

23   Men from Ayt Bou Gemmez brandishing vintage muzzle-loaders.   127

24   Villages in Ayt Bou Gemmez Valley (Central High Atlas).   129

25   The snow-covered Middle Atlas massif of Jbel Tishshoukt seen from the
     southeast.   137

26   Marmousha plateau on a fine winter's morning, Bou Nasser in the
     background.   137

27   Town of Shefshawn: evening view, looking west (Rif).   151

28   French 155 mm howitzers in action north of Fez (*L'Illustration*,
     summer 1925).   155

29   Spanish troops west of Melilla (1921 photo, Archive Vidal).   160

30   French AI officer on winter patrol with his bodyguards in the Middle
     Atlas (*L'Illustration*, winter 1923–4).   165

31   Jbel Tishshoukt, Middle Atlas citadel of Ayt Seghroushen (1923–6).   169

32   Village assembly, Qsar Arrwadi, deep in former "*Tache de Taza.*"   171

33   Tea-drinking Berbers, Qsar Arrwadi, near Oulad 'Ali.   174

34   Ploughing fields below a lone *tighremt*, Azilal area.   178

35   Jbel 'Ayyashi main ridge seen from Imtchimen.   187

36   Camels graze on esparto grass east of Amellago, with a fresh dusting
     of snow on the tops.   193

37   Berber family, Oul Ghazi, Asif Melloul, Ayt Sokhman.   195

38   Tighremt n Ayt Saïd, downstream from Imilshil, Asif Melloul
     (Ayt Hadiddou).   200

39   Ruined French outpost, Ayt Ya'qoub; Foreign Legion camp above
     qsar in right background.   204

40   Tounfit and Jbel Ma'asker (3,277 m), seen from due north.   205

41   Woman from Ayt Yahya, Ayt Bou Arbi clan, Tounfit region.   207

42   Sheep grazing at hamlet of Mshitt, behind Jbel Ma'asker, Tounfit region.   208

43   Woman from Ayt Yahya, Ayt Sliman clan, Tounfit region.   210

44   The Imilshil *mawsim*, trade fair of the Ayt Hadiddou, on Asif Melloul.   211

45   Ruined Foreign Legion fort, Tizi n-Ighil, Tazizaout left background.   215

46   Sidi Lmortada's grave on the left; Cedar Pinnacle, Tazizaout.   219

47 Ou Terbat and other Ayt Hadiddou villages east-southeast of Imilshil, aerial photo, *c.* 1932. 229

48 Jbel Hamdoun dominates the hamlet of Itto Fezzou. 229

49 North side of Jbel Baddou, seen from the stone parapets of the former *Tirailleurs'* camp. 230

50 Graffiti promoting Amazigh identity on rocks above Asif Melloul (2008). 252

Maps

1 West Barbary. 33

2 Marrakesh High Atlas. 64

3 Meknes-Fez, the Middle Atlas (Fazaz) and Moulouya region. 109

4 A rough sketch map of operations by General Theveney's column in the foothills of Jbel 'Ayyashi, including the fight at Tafessasset (May 1922). 135

5 General map of northern Morocco and the Rif. 149

6 Southeast Morocco. 183

7 Rough sketch map of Jbel Maasker and Bou Ijellaben. 196

8 Rough sketch map showing Berber encampments at the western end of Tazizaout ridge. 219

9 Ayt Yafelman country, Eastern High Atlas, corresponding to the area still holding out (1933). 223

10 Stage-by-stage conquest and main resistance areas, 1907–34. 234

NB – Unless otherwise stated, all photographs and maps are by the author.

Preface

This account of Moroccan Berber resistance down the ages initially drew principally on French sources. However, I was fortunate in having access to oral data, some of it personally collected, some of it on file at the Roux Archive in Aix-en-Provence—much of it in poetic form.[1] This material has proved invaluable as it has enabled me to portray events as much as possible through Berber eyes to obtain a more balanced picture of a given historical event, rather than from the pen of a French officer or a post-Protectorate revisionist historian. Thus have I drawn extensively on the better-known secondary sources, as well as the various volumes that have been devoted to the topic of Moroccan Berber resistance, not to mention certain archival sources. Despite the numerous inconsistencies that exist between accounts penned by medieval authors in Arabic, regarding early history an attempt has been made to keep the narrative coherent. The present work being designed as much for academics as for a non-specialist English-speaking readership, I have not hesitated to cite certain secondary sources in English—writers gifted with a fine turn of phrase, not necessarily professional historians. My numerous endnotes are intended to provide extra anecdotal material, further data and a bibliography on a particular item. Nothing quite like this all-encompassing historical survey has been attempted before in English.

Without aiming to be a definitive work, this book is intended to provide as detailed an account as possible of how over the centuries the somewhat mysterious Berber inhabitants of the Moroccan mountains have resisted various forms of outside encroachment. This includes primary resistance to Romans, Arabs, Portuguese, Spanish, and French, together with *jacqueries* and rebellions directed against the *makhzan*, not to mention secondary resistance to colonial/imperialist rule during the Protectorate period, and more recently cultural/ethnic resistance.[2] Events described in this book will embrace the Anti-Atlas, High and Middle Atlas, the Rif and the plains that lie at their feet. Barring some exceptions such as Marrakesh and Fez, Moroccan place names and family names will be spelled as per normal usage in that country, though the final 'e' will be dispensed with; viz. Mohammed for Muhammad; zaouia for zawiya, Tounfit for Tounfite, and so on. Where brief expressions in Arabic or Tamazight are included, they will be written as per scholarly usage in italic: for example *qur'an* for Koran. True, very little hard information in English is available, whether on their origins and early history, most of it shrouded in legend, or on their tribulations during the forty-four years of colonial rule as the French undertook protracted military expeditions to bring to heel the unruly hill tribes. This, of course, was where the French conquest was enacted over a period of thirty years in the twentieth century, with artillery, aviation, and machine-guns snuffing out the heroic age of the Berber hillmen.

My account of Amazigh resistance in the face of these campaigns thus constitutes the core of the book. Volumes of prose have been produced on this period, some of it colorful, most of it couched in the bombastic, high Imperial French style of the interwar years. That the whole process constituted something of an epic there is no doubt. But it was not only a French epic peopled by near-legendary characters which emerges from contemporary sources. More to the point, the swansong of the Berber tribesmen, pitting their puny strength against a vastly better-equipped invader, undoubtedly qualifies as an eminently Moroccan epic, a fact obscured for far too long by an unfairly selective, nationalist discourse. Thus shall we revisit Atlas history, in a manner that has perhaps never before been attempted, describing and analysing events against the broader backcloth of Moroccan history, without becoming overinvolved in the latter. Without underwriting any notional Arab–Berber dichotomy, this work intends to place the emphasis fairly and squarely on Morocco's mountain regions and the Imazighen rather than on the largely Arabic-speaking urban areas. Another purpose of this book will be to grant credit where it is due, not only by attempting to debunk popular misconceptions about the Amazigh as an uncouth, unruly bumpkin, but also rehabilitating the Berber contribution to Moroccan national resistance by reinserting it in the niche it so richly deserves to occupy in the country's history. In so doing I will place myself firmly in what I consider to be the post-revisionist camp of Moroccan history, a definition that requires elucidation.

Many post-independence writers on Morocco, through a natural reaction to the message imparted by colonial authors of the Protectorate period, conform to what I call the 'Post-independence Moroccan Vulgate'. By understandably distancing itself from the classic, pro-colonial attitude of many earlier researchers, a bevy of self-proclaimed revisionist authors emerged after the 1960s.[3] Half a century after the end of the Protectorate, I consider my stance to be resolutely post-revisionist, as I seek to shed the unnecessarily inhibiting, exaggeratedly anti-colonial bias that characterizes much of the above-mentioned writings. In this light it is refreshing to note that, although still to some extent subject to the influence of classic revisionists, recent French historians D. Rivet and J. Lugan tend to be moderately post-revisionist in outlook.

In publishing these Berber-related historical chronicles I hope to write off a long-standing debt of gratitude vis-à-vis the inhabitants of Morocco's Mountains that I have frequented over the past forty years: gratitude for their friendly hospitality, gratitude for their long-suffering patience as they helped me assimilate a basic knowledge of their beautiful language—Tamazight.[4]

Introduction

Despite the present vogue of adventure-trekking and mountain-biking, not to mention the success enjoyed by Gavin Maxwell's *Lords of the Atlas*,[1] few people speak of Morocco as a land of mountains, though the classic vision of snow-capped peaks above Marrakesh has become a cliché. It is also enshrined in a well-known Berber saying: 'In September look up to the mountains above, white as the plumage of a dove!' (*shuf adrar shutanbir zund atbir!*).

Rearing up like the crest of an angry wave, the age-old rampart of Atlas continues to resist attempts at quick analysis. While extreme summer temperatures are rarely high, spectacular thunder storms will spark flash floods, just as winter can bring heavy snowfall and unexpectedly bitter cold, alternating with crisp, sparkling days when finely frosted ridges will gladden the eyes of the beholder. Predictably then, overall conditions are similar to those obtaining in semi-arid ranges of the Mediterranean fringe, with grass thriving only in the immediate vicinity of springs and water channels, and noticeably strong contrasts between fertile northern slopes with snow-retaining qualities and a heavily eroded Saharan side.

On first discovering the Atlas, some early travelers have felt carried away to continents other than Africa. The vast steppe of the upper Moulouya and the gigantic mass of Jbel 'Ayyashi put one English traveler in mind of Central Asia,[2] while the British climber Wilfred Noyce was reminded of the Hunza Karakoram.[3] There are also similarities between the Atlas and Kurdistan, the Zagros and Elburz ranges of Iran, not to mention the more arid reaches of the Hindu Kush. Though there may be something of all that, the Atlas undeniably has its own sharply-defined character, which rarely fails to exert an overpowering attraction to those who approach it.[4] The human element undoubtedly accounts for much of this special allure. True, it is difficult not to develop a liking for the hardy, mountain-dwelling Berbers after long hours in their company, on the march, in camp, or on some mutton-eating and tea-drinking occasion in their snug little wood and stone houses.

If man has been in the ascendancy for centuries in the West, further east he has only left his mark in recent times and nature is relatively unspoiled. Scorching winds blow in from the desert in summer, fostering erosion and aridity. In winter, on the contrary, anywhere above 1500 m, temperatures may drop well below freezing point at least thirty days a year. These conditions naturally preclude fruit-growing, agricultural pursuits often being limited to a few meager barley-patches, thus obliging the locals to fall back on stockbreeding and tent-based transhumance centered on jealously-guarded upland pastures. Eastwards the valleys appear sparsely populated, villages being few and far between. Extensive tracts of cedar and pine still adorn the hills north of the main watershed, adding to the savage beauty of the scene. In this area, man is still up against the elemental forces of nature.

Just as snow-choked passes will remain sealed to pedestrian traffic for weeks, so will the advent of the spring thaw render narrow canyons impassable. However, man proves surprisingly cordial and hospitable in this harsh "neck of the woods." This is in open contradiction with a past marked by raiding, blood feud, close kinship ties, and inter-clan warfare, where defending one's honor, dagger in hand, was of paramount importance, and in which social life alternated between a neo-feudal, warlord culture and basic democracy enshrined in village assemblies and kinship solidarity. Added to this, the resultant fragmentation of the ranges contributes to the proudly independent nature of the Berbers, as well as noticeable nuances in custom, dress, habitat, and speech. Architecture, too, is varied, the medieval-looking stone fortresses of the Central High Atlas being more elaborate than the modest, less-inspired buildings of the terraced villages in the Marrakesh High Atlas.[5]

As far as mutual intelligibility is concerned, and contrary to widely-publicized misconceptions, tribesmen usually understand the vernacular of neighboring clans. Moroccan Berbers speak one of several related dialects: *tashelhit*, spoken in the southwest, *tamazight*, used northeast of an imaginary line between Beni Mellal and Qala'at Mgouna, with the *znatiya* dialect south of Taza, and *tarifit* among the valleys to the north looking out onto the Mediterranean. Actually, on the ground, linguistic frontiers are less perceptible. On the whole, widely-traveled individuals, having learnt to attune their ears, will have little difficulty adapting to whichever dialect is being used in the neighborhood.

Originally, Berber was spoken all across Africa north of the Niger and west of the Nile by the so-called Libyco-Berber group of peoples. Nowadays, it holds out in Algeria (Ahaggar, Aurès [*awras*], Kabylia, and the Mzab), certain pockets of Libya and Tunisia, over most of upland Morocco, and amid the sandy wastes of Mali and Niger. The sole surviving traces of a written language, *tifinagh*, are to be found in this last-named area, whose Tuareg inhabitants speak dialects (*tamasheq* and *tamahaq*) related to Moroccan Berber vernacular and commonly claimed to be the purest archetypal forms of the language currently available.[6]

These linguistic considerations inevitably lead to a far more complex topic: the problem of Berber origins. This problem is addressed in Chapter 1, myth and legend being carefully sorted from fact and archaeological and linguistic theories pointing to the Chamito-Semitic origins of the Imazighen, and the Nile valley as their probable ancestral home. Chapter 2 describes the primary resistance of local Mauri tribes to the Roman Empire, centering on the regional capital of Volubilis, its population subjected to both Punic and Latin language influences. The riddle of the kasbahs and their mud architecture is also briefly evoked.

Chapter 3 is devoted to the aftermath of the Arabic conquest, Maysara's anti-Arab revolt of 743 and the establishment of a first Berber dynasty, the Idrissids, around the city of Fez in the face of competition from the Senhaja princedom of Sijilmassa and the Berghawata heretics of the Tamesna plain, culminating in invasion by the Berber-speaking Almoravids from the Sahara. In Chapter 4 we witness the Almoravid decline in the face of an aspiring rival Berber group, the Almohads from the High Atlas, with their Unitarian creed of *ttawhid*. These fundamentalists conquered all of the Maghrib and most of the Iberian Peninsula as Morocco enjoyed something of a Berber dynastic heyday intellectually, militarily, and religiously. Worms, however, appear in the woodwork, as we see in Chapter 5, the Almohad Empire acquiring unmanageable proportions. The influx of Arabic-speaking Bedouin tribes, together with competition from a rival Berber group, the Merinids, led to decline and debacle. Chapter 6 describes a fragmented Morocco, with independent mountain princes in Seksawa, and Hintati overlords behind the throne, while the Ouattasid dynasty fails to face down the incoming Saadi *shurafa* ('sons of the Prophet'). Chapters 7 and 8 are devoted to the dynastic struggle between the zaouia of Dila'—the driving force behind the northwestern push of the Senhaja Berbers—and the Tazerwalt marabouts, with the 'Alawid *shurafa* coming out from Tafilalt to finally carry the day. Chapter 9 shows how the mountain Berbers gradually recover from the drubbing they have taken at the hands of the 'Alawids as the battle lines are henceforth drawn between sultanate and Atlas tribes. Chapter 10 marks the Berber backlash as a weakened sharifian state is seriously defeated at Lenda (1818) by Boubker Amhaoush, in an early example of *lquwama lughawiyya* ('linguistic resistance') to an Arabic-speaking *makhzan*.

In Chapters 11 and 12, Moulay Hassan I attempts to preserve Moroccan independence vis-à-vis colonial encroachment, appointing *qayd*-s to uphold his authority on the periphery. Pacification gets under way in Chapters 13 and 14 as Berber tribesmen give the French a bloody nose at Ksiba and El Herri, while the western Middle Atlas witnesses bitter fighting. In Chapters 15 to 18 the tribesmen more than hold their own in southeast Morocco, the Central High Atlas, Moulouya Valley, and around Jbel Tishshoukt. The Rif war arrives in Chapter 19, which seriously endangers France's position on the northern front, but overwhelming Franco-Spanish power ultimately brings Abdelkrim to book.

The tide turns in Chapters 20 and 21 as the Middle Atlas finally succumbs, though highly mobile raiders keep the Berber flag flying in the southeast. Chapter 22 witnesses the opening rounds of the Atlas end-game as the French win a Pyrhhic victory at Ayt Ya'qoub (1929). Chapter 23 is devoted to the heroic defense of Tazizaout (summer of 1932) by 1,000 Berber warriors pitted against three French divisions. Chapter 24 describes the closing stages of the Atlas campaigns, with bitterly contested battles at Bou Gafr, Msedrid, Kerdous, and Baddou, and the capture of Jbel Kousser marking the end of tribal resistance. Chapter 25 deals with the aftermath of pacification, an analysis of the causes of the failed resistance and *pax gallica*, leading up to the 'Berber dahir'.

Chapter 26 embraces the Protectorate period up to and including independence. Berber loyalties gradually switch from the French to the Nationalists as they indulge in secondary resistance to the Protectorate, but in independent Morocco their culture, seen as subversive, is swept under the carpet. After twenty-five years in the academic wilderness, however, the 1980 *tafsut imazighen* ('Berber spring') heralds the Amazigh revival. Chapter 27 traces ongoing secondary resistance to assert Amazigh identity in Morocco, and the fight against *hogra* ('neglect'). This meets with mixed success: although the Berber Institute is set up (IRCAM in 2001), and Berber officially comes of age as the second national language (2011), in practice it remains sidelined. Finally, the Conclusion analyzes the present situation, attempting to provide Amazigh identity with a road map for success, based on unity, patriotism, and confidence in the face of a substantial Salafist threat.

1

Berber Origins

Morocco has retained in the Atlas Mountains the largest reservoir of what one British writer called "the last barbarians of the white race left on the face of the earth."[1] More prosaically, in Morocco one finds the highest percentage of Tamazight speakers divided into several racial types, speaking different, though closely-related dialects— a fact which has been emphasized only in recent decades. Then why, the reader may be tempted to ask, is the term Berber generally associated with a given ethnic group?

The problem stated

The Romans labeled uncivilized nations "from beyond the Pale" as barbarians, hence *barbarii* in Latin, from which the name "Berber" was ultimately derived, although they were variously referred to as Libyans, Garamantes, or Numidians. Another explanation is put forward by leading medieval scholar Ibn Khaldoun, according to whom the locals were called Berbers by their Arab conquerors because of their loquacity.[2] Thus was the term "Berber," little used until the mid-eighteenth century, considered as representative of aboriginal North Africans. Berbers tend to reject this casually inflicted label, preferring the term Imazighen.[3]

Regarding Berbers it must be emphasized that the different racial characteristics among them point to varied origins.[4] Generally, the *shluh* of the Sous and Anti-Atlas are short, round-headed, their white skins sometimes tanned a healthy-looking brown, while the *tamazight-* or *tarifit*-speakers are usually fairer-skinned, tall, and spare, with long faces and straggly beards. Brown eyes are common to both groups, though blue eyes and/or fair hair are met with at times. Some early twentieth-century French visitors to Morocco imagined they had discovered descendants of *"nos ancêtres les Gaulois,"* while to quote one British traveler, the Vandals had apparently left "traces of their blond hair and blue eyes in dim recesses of the Atlas."[5] However, both the *tashelhit* and *tamazight* linguistic areas feature a strong sprinkling of dark-skinned elements, thus complicating the issue. These are to be found in greater numbers among the pre-Saharan oases, where they rub shoulders with their lighter-skinned cousins, especially in the Dra'a Valley, though colored people do not necessarily present Negroid characteristics. They are thought to be survivors of the original inhabitants of the Sahara, and have been tentatively identified as descendants of the Garamantes, or some early Ethiopians who moved northwest as the desert gradually became drier during the second millenium B C, which would appear to fit in with recent research.[6]

Myth and legend

Amateur speculation has led to various origins, some of them fanciful, being attributed to Berbers:[7] the Amerindians, the Basques, the Carthaginians, the Arabs, the Sumerians, the Turkic peoples of Central Asia.[8] Throughout the Middle Ages, theories on this much-vexed topic were aired, chiefly by Ibn Khaldoun, famous for his distinctions between first-race and second-race Berbers of so-called Himyarite stock who formed a proto-Arab race that mingled with African aborigines, thus becoming "Berberized."[9] This attempt to ascribe a Yemeni origin to the Berbers remained a favorite ploy well into the Middle Ages, especially with the Almoravids, probably due to the fact that quite a few Yemenis actually did come to Morocco at the time of the Arab conquest. Too numerous to be described in detail, different theories were expounded by Maghribian genealogists throughout North Africa and Andalucia.[10] Ibn Khaldoun claimed a Canaanite origin for the Berbers, described as descendants of Mazigh, while their leaders answered to the title of *jalut* (Goliath).[11] This was largely dictated by prestige-building and dynastic considerations, a fabricated oriental ancestry, especially with origins skillfully and convincingly traced back to the Koraïshi family and the Prophet, notably enhancing the pedigree of any local Berber kinglet.

Much of it, however, was incoherent propaganda, tending to depict Berbers in an unfavorable light, either as eternally disreputable underdogs, or as exiles forced to flee from Canaan, or even Arabia. In the latter case they could be demonstrated as having no specificity at all, having originally been Arabs who emigrated towards the Maghrib at an early period. This apparently convincing interpretation was the one that featured for long in official Moroccan history textbooks.[12] Thus were they conveniently stripped of their identity, as in the following gem:

> The Berbers are a nation of the offspring of Abraham. It is also said that they were descended from Japhet and from Gog and Magog who were shut up by *dhu l-qarnayn* (Alexander). A party of them came forth to wreck havoc and destruction on others. They remained and intermarried with the Turks and Tartars.[13] It is also said that they are from the land of *jinn* (*al-jayn*). A party went to Jerusalem and spent the night in a valley. In the morning they found that their womenfolk had been made pregnant by the men of that spot. They gave birth to them. They are a people who are by nature blood-thirsty, who loot and pillage goods and possessions and wage war.[14]

This is typical of the many falsehoods circulated for the sole purpose of belittling the Berbers. As will be immediately perceptible to the discerning reader, material of this kind alternates between twaddle and half-truth, would-be Arab affiliations being unashamedly politico-racist in motivation, though the supposed Sumerian connection is less foolish than it sounds. Indeed, Berber has distinct morpho-syntactical similarities with ancient Akkadian, both belonging to the Chamito-Semitic family of languages.[15]

Archaeological and historical theories

Among specialists and non-specialists alike, however, the main body of Berbers is held to have come from slightly further afield, either from the Nile Valley, or some notional circum-Mediterranean sub-stratum,[16] though differences in appearance and speech argue against their having shared a common homeland at any one time. The fact, however, that the *tashelhit* and *tamazight* dialects have a fair number of words in common does appear to suggest that the westward movement was a prolonged process lasting several decades, even centuries, during which the language would have gradually evolved through contact with the different linguistic areas of pre-historic, Libyco-Berber North Africa.

Archaeology gives credence to the above theory by tentatively suggesting that present-day Berbers may trace their origins back to snail-eating Capsian man (from Gafsa in Tunisia, where the first skeleton was found), whose ancestors earlier emigrated from the Black Sea region, or Nile Valley, some 10,000 years ago.[17] From the eastern Maghrib they subsequently moved westward in successive waves till checked by the unavoidable breakwater of the Atlas ranges.[18] That the whole of North Africa once shared what was basically a common culture and language there is little doubt.

Archaeological research on rock-drawing sites on the Yagour plateau and elsewhere in Morocco has opened windows on a fascinating past. The drawings tally with the style used by most Saharan rock-artists, depicting the usual gamut of animals, figures, and symbols, arguably belonging to the close of the "Cattle Herder" period, *c.* 2000 BC.[19] These include chariots, elephants and cattle, lions, snakes, and solar wheels. According to one researcher,[20] mountain-top worship fanned out from the eastern Mediterranean in the Neolithic Age and was linked in North Africa with the "Cattle Herder" migration away from the Sahara and into the Atlas as the former continued to dry up, around 2500–1200 BC.

Hence, it can be reasonably surmised that these "Cattle Herders" were the ancestors of most of today's sedentary Berber-speaking tribes in the Morocco. Others no doubt joined them from Iberia via the sunken land-bridge of the "Pillars of Hercules," if one is to lend any credence to a theory pointing to early links between Proto-Berbers and Iberians.[21]

These so-called Proto-Berbers appear to have developed an early civilization of sedentary small-scale stock-breeding peasant farmers living in dry-stone houses. Today, we may observe their descendants in the Western High Atlas, though, as one survey has shown,[22] this way of life was formerly prevalent throughout the more accessible mountain areas along the northern fringe of the Sahara as far as Ifriqiya (Tunisia), until the Beni Hilal nomads broke up their communities in the eleventh century. It remains unclear, however, whether these Proto-Berbers, who originally moved in from the east, were fair-skinned like most Atlas Berbers, or ark-colored like the present-day inhabitants of the Dra'a Valley. The likeliest theory is that the fair-skinned newcomers absorbed the dark-skinned elements, more or less holding them in thrall, a state of affairs that prevailed among pre-Saharan oases until the early twentieth century. At least one expert, summarizing the various theories expounded above, sounds quite categorical as to Berber origins:

> The Berbers [are] a population of Caucasian origin which had migrated through Arabia before crossing over to Africa in the 2nd millennium BC onwards. They swept through the continent as far west as the Atlantic.[23]

Thus, at a very early date, was Morocco in general, and the Atlas Mountains in particular, seen by and large as a Promised Land of milk and honey where the grass was greener, literally and figuratively, where the women were more beautiful, just as it is visualized today by Gulf Arab oil-sheikhs on a spending spree: both a terminus and a crossroads for the great migrations at the dawn of history.

From Carthage to Islam

Carthage was the first to leave her mark on the Atlas tribes. The Punic language became the language of art, culture, and government in the city's vast Berber-speaking hinterland. The eastern Maghrib also came under Hellenistic influences at this time, noticeably under the reign of the Numidian monarch Massinissa,[1] while the subsequent Roman invasion, far from killing off Punic, intensified its usage as Carthaginian refugees fled southwest. A more lasting contribution to Berber economy, however, was the introduction of agricultural improvements such as irrigation for fruit-growing.[2]

The Berbers and the *Pax Romana*

Although Rome barely penetrated the Atlas Mountains, she made her presence felt in depth over that part of the Maghrib that now corresponds to Morocco, peopled in those days by the Mauri and deserving inclusion in the contemporary pattern of organized, early Berber kingdoms. The province of Mauretania Tingitana, which she set up in the first century AD, while retaining Juba II's kingdom as a semi-autonomous state, had as its southern frontier a chain of fortified outposts running inland from the Bou Regreg estuary on the Atlantic coast, then skirting the northern rim of the Middle Atlas before curving back northwest towards Jbala country and the Rif coast. Yet her influence, chiefly through the ephemeral spread of Christianity, reached tribes well to the south, even in the heart of the Atlas. This is substantiated by Arab chroniclers who report the survival of Christian communities in the eighth century between the Atlantic plains and central Morocco.[3]

To anyone who has dabbled in *tamazight*, the Roman origin of a small number of words related to agriculture, not to mention the complete Julian calendar, will at once be apparent. That the Berbers should have referred to the French as *irumin* should come as no surprise. It merely suggests a twofold association with things Roman: peaceful notions connected with the plough, architectural innovations, and a unifying form of speech, together with a well-proven martial reputation calculated to command respect. Rome's intrusion was chiefly highlighted by the Jugurthine War. The actual conflict, however, did not affect Mauretania Tingitana proper, in so far as the military operations were limited to Numidia, yet passing mention must be made of an outstanding cult figure. Jugurtha, or Yugerten,[4] has remained to this day the archetypal Amazigh hero. Present-day Berber cultural associations make much of his skill as a guerrilla warfare leader, and of his epic stand against Rome, prefiguring subsequent resistance against Islam, and later, France.

However, by 106 BC, Jugurtha was sufficiently in trouble to look beyond the Mulucha (Moulouya) for help from Bocchus I, king of Mauretania. The resulting reinforcements, while contributing to prolonging the conflict, were to prove Jugurtha's undoing, in that, for political reasons, Bocchus eventually elected to hand Jugurtha over to the Romans.[5]

Occasionally, the legions would muster for large-scale operations. Following the murder of the Mauretanian king Ptolemy at the hands of the mad emperor Caligula, the Berbers under Aedemon rose in revolt, and quite rightly so, though this move heralded the loss of their independence. The subsequent punitive expedition by Suetonius Paulinus, sent in 45 AD to chastise these rebellious tribes, is the first recorded European crossing of the Atlas. Advancing up the Moulouya Valley, the Roman general crossed the Eastern High Atlas by a low pass. Once on the southern side, near present-day Boudenib, he supposedly reached Oued Guir, flowing through open, bushy country peopled by elephants, the African species still being quite numerous locally in those times. This sort of thrust far south may have temporarily impressed the mountaineers with Rome's military might, but as it was followed by a withdrawal rather than permanent occupation its effect was minimal.[6]

The riddle of the Kasbahs

Rome, though, would have left behind some outposts of the small, fortified *castellum* type. The French historian Terrasse[7] contends that this type of architecture directly inspired a subsequent small Berber fortress known as a *tighremt*, generally used as a defensive granary, its four, loop-holed corner-towers admirably suited for the task of repelling attackers in a land where insecurity was rife. The same writer also makes out a case for the *taddart*, a form of habitation peculiar to the Eastern High Atlas which, he claims, stems directly from the Roman house, complete with *impluvium*, or inner courtyard, the same applying to the fortified hamlets, or *qsur*,[8] of pre-Saharan Morocco. Though he acknowledges that "the castles of the Yemen are strangely similar to the Berber kasbahs, that the houses and mud-brick castles of Hadramaut also have pyramidal outlines," and argues in favor of a possible link between the two, he draws no conclusion from this similarity.[9] Terrasse concludes that a distinctive style of pyramid-like architecture is to be found along the belt of steppe-land that girdles North Africa and Central Asia, and that this form appears to survive in blind alleys like southern Morocco and Arabia.[10]

As for the intricate geometrical carvings—mostly chevrons and lozenges—that adorn these structures, Terrasse pronounces them to be probably Ancient Egyptian in origin. A British contemporary arrives at a slightly different conclusion:

> The first and only comparison that is certain to strike any person . . . is resemblance to the "skyscraper" buildings of the Hadramaut, in southern Arabia ... In the Hadramaut there is, probably, less reason than in the Atlas Mountains for structures

of defence ... the tradition must be one of great antiquity, going back to the old eastern empires, to Persia or Babylon in one place, and to Carthage, it may be, in the other. Such would seem to be the only possible explanation, alike of the Hadramaut and of the kasbahs of the Atlas.[11]

As the springs dried up, the pastoral peoples of the Sahara gradually sought refuge on higher ground unaffected by all-encroaching aridity. An animal specifically adapted to desert conditions became necessary, such as the one-humped dromedary. There were large numbers of these available in the southwest corner of Arabia, where their masters, the oasis-dwelling Himyarites, had evolved a camel-based economy. A restless, expanding people, they undertook the conquest of the almost empty Sahara at the beginning of the third century A.D.[12]

Some of them entered Africa by the Suez isthmus,[13] traveling eastwards by easy stages from oasis to oasis, while others ferried their camels across the Red Sea on large rafts, and journeyed onward via Ethiopia and the central Sahara. Once they had overrun a sizeable chunk of desert south of the Atlas, they settled down and attempted to recreate their traditional living conditions, erecting impressive castle-like structures to protect their families and property. Thus, if we are to believe Mazel, "in all likelihood, the origin of the kasbahs would appear to be linked with the arrival of the dromedary in the Western Sahara."[14] Attractive though this theory may sound, it is far from watertight; in fact Norris questions this view, going on to point out that:

> The flaw in this argument is now to be seen in the Arabic documentary evidence. This indicates that several respected Arab genealogists of early date dubbed all these south Arabian stories and epics as fiction, fabricated for purposes of lineal prestige and attributable to Yemenite authors whose writings had been diffused among the lettered Arabs in Africa.[15]

Whatever learned speculations were subsequently derived from these developments, the invasion of the Sahara by camel-driving nomads proved an epoch-making event. It came at a time (*c.* 450 A.D.) when the Berber inhabitants of the Atlas regions were in the process of ultimately rejecting both the Roman Empire and its by-product, Christianity, just as they declined to throw in their lot with the Vandals or, ultimately, the Byzantines. By and large, however, the Berbers had turned their backs on trans-Mediterranean influences. This was to have far-reaching consequences, as clearly emphasized by one observer:

> In the final analysis Barbary turned the other way. This great renouncement, by cutting her off from western Europe, by pushing her back into the African solitudes, by leaving her powerless in the face of further offensives, has influenced her entire history.[16]

It was indeed a turning-point. The reluctance of the Atlas Berbers to accept the spiritual and temporal authority of Rome may be accounted for by a possible lack of common interests with a race and culture from northern climes. Be that as it may, they were, in the event, soon to find new masters who would hold them in spiritual tutelage down to the present day. From the depths of Arabia invincible forces were being unleashed on the contemporary Mediterranean world. The new, expanding and combative faith of Islam, a simple egalitarian creed evolved in arid, semi-desert surroundings similar to their own, was calculated to appeal to the Berbers' democratic and warlike nature, and those who came into contact with the Moslem cult, however "stormy"[17] the relationship may at first have been, made surprisingly convincing converts. In fact, historians have remarked that while the initial Arab invasion of Morocco at the end of the seventh century AD was a small-scale affair—little more than raids, albeit fiercely resisted—by the beginning of the following century large contingents of freshly-recruited Berber levies, with a mere leavening of Arab cadres, were already pouring north into the Iberian Peninsula in the first flush of their Islamic zeal.[18]

The Arabs, essentially horsemen, felt understandably less at home among wooded hillsides and narrow valleys than out on open plains. In the event, they were soon to be driven from the country during the Kharijite flare-up, the Berbers subsequently being left largely to their own devices. Yet Islam survived in its strongly democratic and egalitarian form known as "kharijism," urging that Arab and Berber be recognized as equal.[19] This was soon branded as heresy by the Baghdad Caliphat, the more so as numerous Christians adopted it, especially in Jbel Fazaz.[20] Already *maghrib al-aqsa*, the "land of the furthest west," was asserting its own prickly personality. Under the Idrissid dynasty, conversion of the Berbers to the new faith was actively undertaken by their own recently-proselytized brethren. Thus Islam had come to stay, though it was but the

Fig. 1: Boumaln-Dadds: cubic, kasbah-style architecture typical of southeastern Morocco.

first stage on a very long road to full Arabization of the Moroccan population—a process that is far from complete today.[20] It is paradoxical, however, that the French military invasion of the Atlas in the early twentieth century should have enabled both Islam and the Arabic tongue to make such phenomenal progress in the boondocks.[21] Of the present *tamazight*-speaking population of the Moroccan Atlas, half are partly Arabized in that they have a smattering of *darija* which they will use once a week in foot-hill markets, or whenever they have dealings with officialdom.

Others, mainly women, neither understand nor speak a word of Arabic, and, in mountain villages, only seldom does the visitor find more than one or two persons who know it properly, usually the local headman, or *muqqadam*, and the preacher, or *fqih*, who acts as scribe and handles Koranic teaching for youngsters in the village mosque.[22]

Whereas in low-lying countries Islam had usually proved an adequate vehicle for enabling Arab culture and speech to make rapid headway, in the Atlas it was forced to reckon with the sheer physical obstacle of high mountains and the strong language barrier of the Berber tribes who long remained totally uncompromising on this issue. This explains why Tamazight was able to survive the way it has down to the present day. While this did not preclude intercourse with lowland areas, Jewish traders often fulfilling a useful middle-man role, these mountain communities remained, to all intents and purposes, Berber-speaking islands in an Arabic sea and, alternating between feud and truce, led their lives distinctly aloof from mainstream Morocco.

3

Dynasts versus Heretics

With time the Berbers became disgruntled on noticing that the democratic aspects of Islam were not strictly adhered to by their Arab masters. Capitalizing on a wave of discontent, Maysara, an obscure water-carrier from Numidia, headed the successful Kharijite revolt in 740. The movement was also a by-product of religious infighting in the Orient as to whether or not the imam should be descended from the Prophet Mohammed. The revolt culminated in the capture of Tangier and the murder of its governor, El-Mourtadi.[1] Yet Maysara's attempt to set up a caliphate in the Atlantic plain proved ineffectual and he was soon eliminated.

Some years later (788), a certain Idriss, a fugitive from the east and descendant of the Prophet, arrived at Oualili (Volubilis under the Romans) in Jbel Zerhoun, where, respectful of his sharifian status, the local Berbers spontaneously accepted him as leader. Anxious to spread the true religion, Idriss raised a substantial army from the Awraba and other tribes.[2] Taking the field in late spring, Idriss cut a long swathe of fire and destruction through the vast plains of Tamesna and Tadla, forcibly converting the local inhabitants. "These people were holding out in mountains and inaccessible fortresses yet the Imam ... seized their lands and fortifications. He slew those that refused to submit to Islam ..."[3] His campaign against the Berghaouata heretics, however, was less than successful.[4] A grandson of Idriss unfortunately weakened the Idrissid heritage through an unexpected exercise in devolution by sharing his territory in 828 with a brother, Ahmed, who received the Meknes and Tadla areas, together with a fair-sized portion of Jbal Fazaz.[5] It is interesting to record how Idrissid power spread southwest and south, both along the edge of the Fazaz, and over onto the Saharan side of the Atlas, actually acquiring some degree of permanence through the establishment of royal mints. These were at Tigrigra near Azrou, where coins cast in 836–48 have been discovered[6] close to the silver mines of Jbel 'Aouam; also at Waoumana near the Wansifen river on the Tadla fringe, and even in Todgha, near present-day Tinghir.[7]

These are clear indications that the dynasty was attempting to set up a sultanate worthy of the name and may be credited with creating a fledgling central government or *makhzan*. Significantly, the Idrissids have won lasting acclaim as Morocco's first dynasty, thus conferring upon anyone claiming descent from them an enviable aura of prestige by dint of their sharifian descent.[8] In 808 they had founded Fez, a Berber city that ultimately became Morocco's cultural and religious capital, its citizens notorious for being unwarlike and rabidly anti-Berber in outlook.

The Berghaouata

One of Maysara's companions, Tarif El-Berghaouati, himself a devout Moslem, had an equally pious son, Salih, who took upon his shoulders the mantle of prophet. In 742 he proclaimed himself *mahdi*, compiled an eighty-surah Koran in Berber, launching a formidable heresy destined to plague Moroccan affairs for four centuries. While Salih left for a protracted tour of the east, his own son Elias ruled over the Beni Tarif for fifty years, strictly observing the precepts of orthodox Islam. It was left to his grandson, Youns the visionary, to reveal Salih's mission as *mahdi*, and spread the newly concocted creed "by fire and by sword"[9] throughout Tamesna, Doukkala, and surrounding areas (842–84).

Thus "in the plain south of Casablanca the Berghaouata state by its adoption of a Berber distortion of Islam paid its own tribute to the influence of that faith while it rejected it."[10] This indigenous Maghrebian kingdom developed a significant military capability, surviving well into the twelfth century, thanks to interior lines of communication, skillful exploitation of terrain, and a 25,000-strong army, including a crack cavalry force recruited from among the Zenata tribes that formed the confederacy.[11] Contemporary accounts are unanimous in praising the Berghaouata for "their outstanding moral values, their fine appearance and bravery."[12] This fearsome fighting force was vigorously employed either to proselytize neighboring tribes, or defend the Berghaouata state from invasion, as in the epic Battle of Beht.[13]

By the mid-ninth century the Berghaouata state stretched from Rabat to the Wanfisen river (Oum Rbia'), and east across the Tamesna plain to the Oulmes hills and southwest spurs of Jbel Fazaz. Their interpretation of the Koran deviated somewhat from the parent religion: the pre-dawn call of the *mudden* replaced by cockcrow;[14] all important feasts occurred on dates different from the Muslim calendar; *ramadan*, the month of fasting, was replaced by *rajab*; unsuitably slaughtered fish, eggs, and animals' heads were pronounced unfit for human consumption; true Muslims were treated as infidels, while Judeo-Christian influences appeared in the form of a Messianic tradition whereby the *mahdi* would return the day before the resurrection to confront *al-dajjal*, the donkey-riding Anti-Christ.[15] Their god was referred to as *yakush*, also *bu itran* ("lord of the stars"). Neither the Zenata nor the Almoravids were able to quell these stubborn heretics who survived until the mid-twelfth century. Interestingly, some Amazigh militants have recently claimed that the Berghaouata princedom was the first organized Moroccan state.[16]

The Senhaja princedom of Sijilmassa

Immediately south of the High Atlas lies the oasis of Tafilalt. On the edge of this sea of date-palms stood a busy metropolis, Sijilmassa, founded against a background of strife in 757 by a local Kharijite leader. Capital city of a small Senhaja princedom, it drew its economic importance from being a terminus of Saharan trade routes and was ruled over by Miknassa Berbers of the Beni Midrar dynasty, established after 824 by Midrar El-Montassir. The Kairouan Fatimids, its absentee landlords, were anxious to profit from the revenue of the Sudanese caravan trade—gold, black ivory, and ostrich feathers—amassed in the Sijilmassa treasury:[17] an admirable arrangement whereby the local Midrarid rulers could sleep soundly so long as they remained staunch political supporters of the distant Fatimids.[18] In 967, however, a certain Mounadir El-Berbri unwisely switched alliances, granting his allegiance to the Oumeyyads of Cordoba. This inexorably singled him out for punishment by the irate Fatimids, so in 959 Sijilmassa was stormed by a mercenary army under Jawhar El-Roumi, one of the ablest field commanders of his day, the then ruler, Ibn Mimoun Ibn Midrar, being led away captive to Fez.[19] Meanwhile, the Beni Ifran, or Zenata of the mountains, who appear to have been incorporated within the bounds of a loose-knit Berghaouata confederacy, occupied the Tadla plain and neighboring heights of the Fazaz.[20]

An Atlas heretic stronghold: Qala'at El-Mehdi

Touli, leader of the Beni Idjfashi,[21] founded a citadel, Qala'at El-Mehdi, south of Azrou in Jbel Fazaz. The purpose was to create a fortified stronghold capable of holding at bay the strongest armies and setting up a secure trading post near the main trade route from Fez to Marrakesh. Many traders, principally of Judaic confession, took to using it as a convenient and secure warehouse for their goods. As we are told, "At the end of the tenth century, the *qala'* harboured a coalition of schismatics and Jews."[22]

Touli (or Tawala), founder of the citadel, appears to have been a wandering preacher from Mauretania,[23] who, on arriving in the Fazaz, immediately sensed that, given the proximity of the Jbel 'Aouam silver mines, the presence of Jewish traders and warlike Berbers, together with the ready money available from caravan dues, he could found a promising power base. The dynastic ambitions he nursed were perpetuated under his son, Mehdi Ibn Taoula Idjfashi, who, using the small army at his disposal, indulged in forays at the expense of other Meghraoua princes in the Meknes area.[24] However, this particular minnow in the Fazaz pond was shortly to attract the attention of a voracious pike. Before being gobbled up, however, it would give a good account of itself. By the latter half of the eleventh century during their campaigns against the Berghaouata, the *al-murabitun* (Almoravid) invaders under Youssef Ibn Tashfin moved up from the Sahara against the fortress. However, when distant dust clouds heralded the approaching cavalry, the Beni Idjfashi slammed shut the gates, then snubbed their noses at the invaders (1063–72).[25]

Try as they might, the Saharans failed in their attempts to storm the Fazaz citadel, only gaining access after a nine-year siege. The besieged eventually capitulated after negotiation, and the fortress became an Almoravid military establishment. Claims of an epic siege may sound preposterous, but from what we know of the assailants, it is hardly surprising. As nomad cameleers, the Almoravids were newcomers to siege warfare, totally lacking in mangonels and *ballista*, their investment of a besieged citadel being less than watertight, the rugged, wooded terrain of Jbel Fazaz and the accuracy of Berber archers and slingers hardly improving matters.[26] The actual site of Qala'at El-Mehdi proved something of a mystery until Berberist Arsène Roux concluded that the cliff-bound Tisigdelt plateau above Zaouia Had Ifran, between Aïn Leuh and Mrirt, was the likeliest spot. As one chronicler states, "Qala'at El-Mehdi is a very strong fortress, situated at the top of a high mountain; there are bazaars and various sources of wealth; the people there indulge in agriculture and animal husbandry."[27]

This description tallies with today: two-thirds of the Tisigdelt plateau[28] is given over to fields, irrigated by an intricate network of water channels that fan out from Aïn Tisigdelt. The central section, however, is set aside for grazing mules and cattle. Behind the spring, slopes thickly-wooded with evergreen oak and cedar forest rise some 200 meters to a col. On its northwest and northeast sides the plateau is bounded by limestone cliffs rendering it almost impregnable, while to the east and west, the slopes, though moderately steep, could be assaulted by a resolute foe. These approaches, however, were covered by an extensive outer stone wall, a portion of which is still standing on the northeast side.[29] All of which tallies with the observation that "In the Jbel Fazaz lies the stronghold named after El-Mehdi Ibn Touala Idjfashi; it occupies an extremely strong defensive position and resisted a seven year siege by the Almohads."[30]

Almoravid intervention

We must now turn to the reasons which had brought the Almoravids out of the desert and into the Atlas. Early in the eleventh century had begun that complex and continuous southeast–northwest push of the Senhaja Berbers which gradually gained momentum over the centuries as each successive clan or tribe headed for the heights in search of pastures new.[31] In those days, the Central and Eastern High Atlas were virtually empty, allowing unlimited grazing for all comers. Likewise, smoke rarely rose from campfires on the cedar-covered plateaux of Jbel Fazaz, as yet home to but a handful of wandering shepherds.[32] In contrast, the fertile valleys of the southwest ranges were already quite densely populated by sedentary farmers. The Senhaja oasis dwellers, however, could not emigrate *en masse* into the Atlas ranges, nor were they the sort of people to be meddled with lightly. Smarting from their recent reverses at the hands of the Meghraoua newcomers, they appealed for help to their southern cousins. These desert allies constituted a formidable mobile force ideal for operations in open country. Recent converts to orthodox Maliki Islam, masters of western Senegal and the upper Niger in the eleventh century, they were diligent wagers of the *jihad* against refractory tribes. Thus it was that in 1055:

> The *fqih*-s and saints of Sijilmassa congregated and drafted a letter to 'Abdallah Ibn Yassin, to amir Yahya and other *murabitun* sheikhs, calling upon them to come and rid the country of the vice, violence and injustice visited upon them by their amir, Mess'aoud Wanoudin El-Meghraoui.[33]

These tough Berber-speaking Saharans of the Lemtouna group of tribes have gone down in history as the Almoravids, a Spanish corruption of the name *al-morabitun*,[34] meaning "men of the *ribat*." Their imam was 'Abdallah Ibn Yassin, a peripatetic religious preacher from southeast Morocco, who had wandered all over northeast Africa in search of tribesmen to proselytize. The Almoravid *ribat* was a fortified monastery somewhat resembling a commando training camp, where these soldier-monks received religious instruction while undergoing a Spartan code of discipline including floggings for mild misdemeanor, and death for the most serious offences. This was in keeping with rules of conduct, enshrined in a primitive mix of Islamic (*shari'a*) and tribal (*'urf*) law, as laid down by Ibn Yassin.

Though monogamy was the order of the day, some measure of female sexual freedom was tolerated.[35] These then were the dour, saintly warriors who, in 1056, headed north under Abou-Bekr, linked up with their Senhaja cousins, and hounded the Meghraoua out of the oases. Recapturing Sijilmassa,[36] they went on to occupy the walled town of Taroudannt in the Sous. Striking north again from Taroudannt in 1058, they crossed the Atlas, probably by the easy pass of Tizi n-Bibaoun, occupied Aghmat, and advanced towards Tadla, in so doing killing Louqqout, the local Meghraoui amir, when they occupied the fortress of Day (Beni Mellal).[37] Following in the wake of the armies, 'Abdallah Ibn Yassin El-Jazouli pursued his purifying mission among the Masmouda Berbers of the area.

Overconfident of his charisma, of his ability to convert the still defiant Berghaouata deviationists single-handed, Ibn Yassin rashly left Aghmat towards the close of 1058 with a few companions and headed into the Tamesna plain. There his recklessness met with swift retribution, and he died fighting against the Berghaouata on the bushy banks of Oued Khorifla early in 1059.[38] Although Abou-Bekr arrived hotfoot with a large host to avenge his colleague and allegedly slaughtered myriads of Berghaouata, he failed to wipe them off the map, contrary to what is claimed in the *Rawd al-Qirtas*, and "this heresy was to blossom and bloom, and was yet to cause untold trouble under the Almohads."[39] Among the spoils of captured Aghmat, Abou-Bekr discovered a gem— Zineb bint Ishaq el-Nafzaouiyya, widow of the defeated Maghraoui emir.[40]

This beautiful Berber lady was well versed in magic, having by one account refused to wed any prince unless he ruled over the entire Maghrib;[41] a version at variance with the fact that, prior to Louqqout, there had already been at least one husband.[42] Abou-Bekr now married her. Their nuptials, however, were to prove short-lived. Recalled to Mauretania in 1061, Abou-Bekr relinquished both command and bride to his cousin, Youssef Ibn Tashfin. The former, however, is famous for having started work on the city of Marrakesh, around which his successor, Ibn Tashfin, planted an extensive palm grove to remind himself of the desert oasis of his boyhood. Meanwhile, before he finished with besieging Qala'at El-Mehdi, Ibn Tashfin scored some signal successes. In 1069 he stormed Fez before sweeping south to the Moulouya and occupying Aoutat (Midelt) in 1071.[43] Crossing over into the Iberian Peninsula, Ibn Tashfin restored the waning fortunes of Islam in a successful campaign against the Christians, thanks to the fact that his army had been readapted to suit the exigencies of warfare in the Maghrib and *al-andalus*. Camel-mounted warriors had been replaced by horsemen, and his infantry was made up of large numbers of blacks and Berbers armed with crossbows, pikes, and javelins.[44] Many renegades, among them Reverter the Catalan, joined Tashfin's standard and contributed invaluable expertise.

Once in Spain he set to work cleaning the Augean stables of the refined, profligate Moorish kinglets whose military shortcomings and lax morals had jeopardized the Muslim cause. Rebuking these sovereigns (*Reyes de Taifas*) for their lukewarm faith and overall inefficiency, Ibn Tashfin waged war on the worst offender, El-Mou'atamid, king of Sevilla, seizing his city and placing him under house arrest in Morocco.[45] Surprisingly, his first place of enforced residence proved to be Qala'at El-Mehdi in Jbal Fazaz, a little-known fact, as revealed in the following account:

> ... El-Mou'atamid was exiled there; that prince thus sadly refers to his captivity: "Due to violated treaties was I sent to a town built of wood, inhabited by Jews and with monkeys for next-door neighbours!" True, most of the population consisted of Jews, traditional shop-keepers, whose trade naturally urged them to find refuge in such a stronghold where their goods would be in safety.[46]

Later, El-Mou'atamid was sent to cool his heels in the more congenial surroundings of Aghmat (near present-day Marrakesh), in which Atlas foothill town that unhappy prince was to die in 1095. Thus was el-Mou'atamid, the poet-king, buried in the shadow of *adrar n-dern*, below whose peaks a new creed was being preached: the unifying Almohad movement, a harbinger of change soon to be launched by Ibn Toumert and destined in good time to humble the haughty Almoravid conqueror.

Triumph of the Atlas Berbers

West of the Tizi n-Test, the High Atlas takes on a more hospitable aspect where man has achieved an unusual degree of harmony with nature. In those far-off days of the late eleventh century, extensive forests of juniper, oak, and cypress still clothed the mountainsides almost to the summits.[1] Within their high valleys, the sturdy Masmouda mountaineers tilled their barley patches, harvested their walnuts, and waged guerrilla warfare against their upstream neighbors whenever the latter cut off their water supply.[2] Thus were there frequent opportunities to defend their honor with bow or dagger, though such conflicts as did occur were usually nipped in the bud by local marabouts. Each village-republic constituted a self-contained unit generally centred on a fortified granary, known as an *agadir*.

It was fortunate for the Masmouda Berbers that the land from which they eked out an often precarious living possessed the unique quality of imparting an element of greatness and sense of leadership to its chosen sons, making of them a fertile breeding ground for those numerous saints the Atlas has always nurtured. As one British writer has observed, "these wild, gaunt regions close to desert areas are apt to produce great warriors and great saints, single-minded, dynamic men who sweep through territories and souls with a terrifying intensity."[3] Such a man was Moulay Bou'azza,[4] who lived in the eleventh/twelfth centuries, and who spent his boyhood as a shepherd among the mountains north of Tinmel.

Moulay Bou'azza, who later became one of Morocco's most revered medieval holy men, though endowed with *baraka* ("divine effluvium") and other saintly qualities required of a major religious figure, was essentially a pacifist.[5] Meanwhile, the centuries-old rivalry between sedentary folk and nomad resumed, the more so as the Almoravids were perceived as crude barbarians. Harassing raids were launched against the intruders, this being one of the reasons for which Ibn Tashfin had chosen the site of Marrakesh, hopefully out of reach of marauding hill men.[6] As one historian explains, the Masmouda "could not contemplate for long without anger and envy these aliens dominating their country and accumulating in their new capital Marrakesh the revenues of the whole empire."[7]

As they enjoyed the fruits of victory and became exposed to the culture of Andalucia, the Almoravids lost much of their pristine Islamic purity and piety. Women were allowed to bare their faces in public, the veil remaining the privilege of the reigning warrior caste, while anthropomorphism and wine drinking were tolerated. A reaction was bound to set in.

Ibn Toumert hailed from the Hargha country in the northeast of the Anti-Atlas. As a young man he had spent his time in mosques reading the scriptures. A lively character with a strong personality, he soon received the nickname *asafu*.[8] He was "small and misshapen, his eyes sunk in their orbits beneath a protruding forehead, there emanated from him an irresistible force."[9] He had lost no time traveling east to visit the fountainheads of Islamic learning, meeting the great theologian El-Ghazzali, who actively encouraged him in his quest.[10] An orthodox Sunnite, Ibn Toumert sought to develop the egalitarian principles of early Islam calculated to appeal to his fellow Berbers. To this end, he conducted an exhaustive analysis of the Muslim faith. As he journeyed homeward through Barbary, stopping at times to preach in wayside towns, he gradually gathered a small band of disciples, one of whom, 'Abdelmoumen, from Bejaïa, would be his successor.[11] On returning to Morocco, Ibn Toumert took to preaching in marketplaces, upbraiding the Almoravids for their dissolute morals, suppressing sinful practices in keeping with the Ghazzali doctrine, tantamount to an early form of fundamentalism. Censuring all forms of licentiousness, he would break up wedding parties, smashing musical instruments or wine jars and separating men from women.[12]

In Meknes he was bastinadoed; in Marrakesh during a theological debate in the amir's very presence, he held all the learned men at bay, astonishing them with his knowledge of Arabic.[13] One of 'Ali Ibn Tashfin's chief scientists warned the amir against the grave danger posed by this adventurer: "Clap him in irons! Else one fine day his drum-beat will resound in your ear!"[14] Ibn Toumert, who had found refuge at Tinmel,[15] in the upper Oued Nfis Valley of the High Atlas, was by now convinced that he had been placed on earth by divine providence, and that he was the long awaited *mahdi*; that the time had come to turn militant in the name of Islamic unity. Thus did he commence preaching to the Berbers; theirs would be the priceless privilege of unsheathing their swords in the fight for Islamic renovation and reunification, in the name of the doctrine of *ttawhid* ("unity"), hence the term *al-muwahidin*, or "unifiers," by which his followers were known.[16] A shrewd judge of his fellow-countrymen's character, he gave their natural blend of credulity and superstition time to do its work, being helped not a little by the local penchant for saints and old legends:

> Ibn Toumert led an extremely austere life. He fed simply, wore plain and old clothes ... Religious duties were enforced with a severity equal to that of the early Almoravids; the believers were taught to listen to lengthy sermons; absolute obedience was exacted from the rank and file, to the extent of killing their own relations if so ordered ... In his teaching he emphasized the speedy coming of the promised *mahdi* ... until one day his followers by a sudden illumination exclaimed, "You ... are the *mahdi*, the one exempt from sin."[17]

His important decisions were made after consultation with a "Council of Ten" consisting of 'Abdelmoumen and his most faithful followers, the *ttelba*. Next in line, for dealing with matters of less moment, sat a council of fifty sheikhs and other bigwigs hand-picked from the five tribes that formed his power base: the Hargha, Tinmel, Hintata, Guenfissa, and Guedmioua.[18] Below them was a more popular assembly. Military

Fig. 2: Village of Imlil n-Oughbar with the shrine to *mahdi* Ibn Toumert (Western High Atlas).

tactics were simple and effective: based on the spontaneous tribal muster, each contingent occupied a specific place in the order of battle, and once the fighting was over, received its allotted share of booty.[19]

Deviants were pitilessly done away with. In commenting on these instances of "precautionary murder," one researcher has attributed Ibn Toumert's ruthlessness to the very values of North African society in which notions of treason and violence are dissimilar from those that obtain in the West, the notion of pre-empting grave future complications excusing actions of this kind, a feature of segmentary societies, especially in "sedentary settings."[20]

From their capital in Marrakesh, the Almoravids ruled over an empire that spread east to central Maghrib, north beyond *al-andalus* to Aragon. In the latter area the military achievements of these simple, Saharan barbarians were outstanding; in fact one observer claims that their action retarded the *Reconquista* by some two centuries.[21] To some extent, however, they found themselves overextended, with long, vulnerable lines of communication. To govern this far-flung empire a prototype *makhzan* had been set up, partly based on a simple legal system, inspired by Maliki Islam, while their coinage, especially a magnificent gold *dinar*, was in general circulation. Nevertheless, simultaneous with their greatest military advances, the socio-political climate had been deteriorating at home since the death of Youssef Ibn Tashfin. His son 'Ali, an *amir al-muslimin* of irreproachable piety, granted excessive importance to scholars of Holy Law and other notables, ultimately neglecting affairs of state for matters of religion, while the rulers of *al-andalus* gradually turned aside from these uncouth, veiled savages whom they despised anyway, added to which women took a hand in social life; licentiousness, wine drinking and prostitution became widespread.

Meanwhile, in the capital, the fact that Christian mercenaries were charged with maintaining law and order made the regime increasingly unpopular. Simultaneously, the people of the *adrar n-dern* (High Atlas) were paying increasing attention to the siren calls of Almohad propaganda.[22] Before launching an all-out campaign against the anthropomorphists, Ibn Toumert conducted a tour of the surrounding valleys.[23] In 1128–9, the Almoravids took the initiative and marched south into the Atlas for a direct thrust at Tinmel, but their army fell foul of the entrenched meanders of the Nfis Valley and the mountaineers repulsed them easily.

Following up their success a little too impetuously, the Almohads ventured out onto the Haouz plain with an army of 40,000 foot soldiers armed with spears, bows, and swords, but only 300 horsemen. This at once gave the defenders the whip hand because of their superiority in crossbowmen, cavalry, and battle-hardened Christian renegades, enabling them to make a victorious sortie.[24] 'Abdelmoumen, who was wounded in the battle, had some difficulty extricating his command.

Shortly afterwards, the *mahdi* passed away.[25] To his successor, 'Abdelmoumen, the lesson was clear. To defeat the enemy still too powerful in open country, his Almohad zealots would have to consolidate their gains locally. They would then advance northeast along the Atlas fringe, sticking to the high ground and eliciting help from other Berber tribes on the way. Only when they could muster sufficient military strength, and when the disparity in mounted troops had been reduced, could they stake their fortunes in a set-piece confrontation. First, in 1132, the Almohads subdued the Oued Dra'a region, south of the Great Atlas.[26] There are traces of 'Abdelmoumen's passage on the south side of Jbel 'Ayyashi, where a sheer-sided, flat-topped hill bears his name, as he was able to use it as a stronghold against the Almoravids. As he was passing through the broad valley that lies between 'Ayyashi and Jbel Afaday, 'Abdelmoumen was outmaneuvered by a strong Almoravid force that had taken advantage of the open nature of this terrain, better suited to their type of camel-mounted warfare. Surrounded on all sides, the Almohad prince turned to his local Berber allies and, thanks to them, succeeded in gaining access to the nearby hill under cover of darkness.[27]

In 1139, 'Abdelmoumen commenced a protracted period of military campaigning by advancing eastward along the edge of the mountains.[28] The Almohad army first occupied Demnat after the inhabitants had declared in favor of the newcomers, then moved onto Waouizaght on Oued La'abid, before defeating the Almoravids in the mountains. This occurred at a critical time for the Almoravids as, in 1142, 'Ali Ibn Youssef was to die and was succeeded by Tashfin, who spent most of his short reign leading armies in the field.

The *azaghar* and Day (Beni Mellal) were soon invested. The Almohads followed Tashfin, defeating his Almoravid army at Tizi Tazgart, then following the River Wansifen and entering the strategic town of Azrou. A short side-show ensued, involving Qala'at El-Mehdi, garrisoned by the Almoravids under a certain Yahya Ibn Sir.[29] The Almohads secured this strategic fortress as it commanded the environs of the vital Jbal 'Aouam silver mines, which they were anxious to lay their hands on.[30]

In the meantime, in Azrou, 'Abdelmoumen was receiving delegations from the surrounding Senhaja tribes of Jbel Fazaz and the Moulouya as they rallied to his cause.[31] The *al-muwahidun* army then swung south for a lengthy campaign through the Atlas valleys, and thence back to Azrou via the Moulouya Valley.[32] Upon the resumption of the campaigning season in 1141, the Almohads left Azrou and first sacked the town of Sefrou, then making for Beni Yazgha territory, east of Fez.

At this point, Reverter the renegade, who was in Fez with amir Tashfin, emerged from the city and defeated an Almohad force under Yahya Aghoual, killing him and sending his head to Tashfin![33] The Almohads thereupon moved further east through the land of the Beni Mkoud, finally reaching the Ghiata hills south of Taza, which 'Abdelmoumen occupied.[34] 'Abdelmoumen's strategy appears to have paid off. By the early 1140s he was powerful enough to commit his force to the open plains and win some decisive encounters.[35] In 1144, Tashfin retired towards Tlemcen and occupied a hill fortress near that town. The place was soon besieged and Tashfin attempted a night escape on horseback but fell over a cliff; with him perished the last hopes of Almoravid success.[36] The Almohad army now surged back through Morocco, first occupied Fez in 1146 and took Marrakesh by storm in 1147, indiscriminately massacring its veiled Senhaja defenders.

The Almohads followed this up with a vigorous campaign against the heretics that settled the Berghaouata problem once and for all.[37] Thus do the Almoravids pass from the scene. Their reign had lasted but eighty years and, despite being Berber-speakers, they had chiefly suffered from being visualized as unrefined, alien Saharans. With the Masmouda and the dynasty they now set up, there was a different story to tell. They, at least, could lay as fair a claim as any to being indigenous Moroccan Berbers. However, as subsequent chapters of the Almohad epic encompass *al-andalus* and most of the Maghrib, those particular developments need not concern us here.

Suffice to say that, apart from having consolidated the existing *makhzan* and ruled over a united Morocco within boundaries similar to those of today, 'Abdelmoumen eventually held sway over the greatest ever Muslim-Berber empire, extending from the Atlantic to the Gulf of Gabès, from the Guadalquivir to the Saharan marches. The triumph of the Atlas Berbers was complete. All empires rise and wane and that of the Almohads was no exception to the rule, yet the years 1143–1268 were to prove as near to a "Golden Age" as Morocco ever experienced. Apart from spectacular military conquests and architectural achievements, this period proved a heyday for science, arts, and letters,[38] with a galaxy of great names including Ibn Toufail, Ibn Roshd, El-Baidaq, and Ibn Tunart, the latter famous for his Arabo-Berber lexicon compiled in 1145.[39] This points to a partly bi-lingual population:

> While the mass of Almohad supporters were Berber-speakers,[40] there was a greater proportion of educated persons; that is people with a good Arabic culture, in the higher levels than there had been among the Almoravids ...
>
> This was the beginning of an epoch in which the learning of Muslim Spain ... was diffused in Morocco also.[41]

Indeed, Ibn Tunart's famous lexicon[42] was designed for judges, merchants, physicians, and scribes, to facilitate everyday transactions with the Berber-speaking rank and file of the population. Thus did a twelfth/thirteenth century Sharifian state, while

Fig. 3: Camel-herding, High Moulouya Plain, Eastern Middle Atlas in the distance.

acknowledging Arabic as the language of officialdom and religion, freely admit the existence of a vernacular language, and made commendable efforts to accommodate it. A sensible lesson in pragmatism and tolerance that, in Morocco today, many would be well advised to heed!

Makers of Mayhem: Beni Hilal and Ma'qil

Now that the entire Maghrib had been united, with the Islamic faith seemingly restored in its pristine purity, the stage seemed set for a long period of stability and prosperity. But it was not to be; barely 120 years later the Almohad Empire was to experience decadence and disintegration. The mountain Berbers had thrown away a unique opportunity to establish their power for all time. There are several reasons for this. The first explanation is the familiar tale of conquerors losing their initial zeal and falling by the wayside. As with their Almoravid forbears, contact with the laxity and profligacy of Andalucia proved fatal. Also, Sultan 'Abdelmoumen compromised his Messianic image by founding a dynasty—the Mouminids—earning for himself the suspicion of the Masmouda and sowing the seeds of ultimate decay. Above all, the Almohad Empire, consisting of two chunks of mainly mountainous land, separated by a stretch of sea, had acquired unmanageable proportions.[1] The rebellious nature of many of his feudal vassals meant that once the Almohad sovereign was busy in Spain, armed revolt was liable to flare up behind his back.[2] For example, during the reign of Amir Youssef, there were three recorded instances of uprisings in the Rif between 1163 and 1166, all of which were suppressed with unmitigated ferocity entailing beheadings and crucifixions galore.[3] However, the Almohad's attempts to stem the *Reconquista* in Spain led them to neglect Morocco, now threatened with Arab invasions compounded by Merinid encroachments.

The Beni Hilal nomads, who had first appeared in Tunisia *c.* 1050, made their presence felt in Morocco a century later. After defeating these Arabs in the central Maghrib in 1152, 'Abdelmoumen used them as cavalry for subsequent expeditions into Spain and allowed some of them to settle in Morocco. But the plan backfired as many of the newcomers banded together with former Almoravid supporters, causing anarchy and unrest.[4] Although the Muslim faith had spread to most areas of the Atlas as of the ninth century, the Arabic language had initially but little affected the widespread use of Berber. The relative importance of the Arab invasion has become a debatable issue among historians, with the revisionists attempting to downplay the matter and branding the writing of colonial historians as racist.[5] The point made was that De Slane, Ibn Khaldoun's translator, was blatantly anti-Arab in outlook.

Contemporaries such as Gautier and Terrasse followed suite, later emphasizing the dichotomy between nomad and settled folk, so that matters came to a head at the close of the 1960s, with feathers flying and an exchange of robust prose between rival protagonists.[6]

Almohad decline

Over thirty years later there seems little cause to doubt Ibn Khaldoun's word. Whether labeled "Arab" or "Bedouin," the difference is academic. There is no escaping the fact that these new arrivals made inroads into use of the Berber language, also causing unmitigated disaster of a socio-economic nature. Putting things quite mildly, "the unfortunate result was the introduction of nomad destructiveness into a hitherto settled agricultural area." The Berber point of view is more forcibly expressed. Apparently, shortly before his death, Amir Ya'qoub El-Mansour admitted that having allowed Arab tribes from Ifriqiya (Tunisia) into the Maghrib was one of the three things he regretted most, because "I then came to realise that they cause nothing but sedition."[7] One would be hard put to find a more scathing indictment.[8]

That these invasions occurred and caused profound change, there is little doubt; the issue appears to be whether they were the work of only a few thousand individuals, or whether it was a case of gradual infiltration. Marçais introduces some common sense into the debate when he points out that in Ifriqiya alone did the Beni Hilal resemble a "flight of locusts." Those Arabs that were sent to Morocco, whatever trouble they may have caused later, went there as defeated, displaced persons.[9] An interesting point is made regarding these nomads: "it was as mercenaries that they played a leading role in the disintegration of the [Almohad] empire."[10] Sufficiently whitewashed by some to assume a position of respectability in history, demonized and vilified by others as barbarian invaders, the Beni Hilal will divide scholars for some time to come. Far more serious was the thirteenth-century invasion by the Beni Ma'qil, coincidental with Almohad decline.

Of possible Yemeni origin, they reached eastern Morocco from the desert areas of Touat and Gourara and occupied the Moulouya and Ziz valleys. In fact, to this day, two of their clans still lead the life of tent-dwelling nomads in the area.[11] It will be shortly demonstrated to what extent their arrival was to have a knock-on effect vis-à-vis the Senhaja tribes of southeast Morocco.

Worms in the Almohad woodwork

Meanwhile, for the Almohads, the writing was on the wall. Apart from the loose-knit nature of their empire and the general disenchantment with *jihad* in Andalucia after losing the vital Battle of Las Navas de Tolosa in 1212, rivalry between descendants of Ibn Toumert and the Mouminids, bickering between Beni Hilal and Beni Merin mercenaries, between the caliph's councillors and the ambitious sheikhs of the "Council of Ten"—all these factors gradually enfeebled the fabric of state. Add to this a general disenchantment with the unifying doctrine of *ttawhid* coupled with a correspondent rise in Sufism and you have it all.[12] Rebel chiefs such as Saïd El-Fazazi and Hadi Ibn Hanin, who reoccupied Qala'at El-Mehdi, had had to be put down and eventually killed, generally by public crucifixion after capture.[13] Regarding that specific area, though, the ruined fortress of Qala'at El-Mehdi somehow symbolized the Fazaz Berbers' independent nature. It was also close enough to the emerging Merinids to warrant attention from them also, as in 1223, when Amir Abou Saïd 'Athmane Ibn

ʿAbdelhaqq mounted a successful foray into Fazaz to chastise the turbulent Zenata nomads of the area and "put an end to their acts of brigandage and other exactions."[14]

In Morocco itself the decadent Almohads were facing two foes: the Merinids, Zenata nomads usually wandering between Agerssif and the Tafilalt, and their bitter rivals the ʿAbd el-Ouadid, a kindred group of former loyalist Zenata Berbers, who, with some Arab elements, had occupied Tlemcen and the gateway city of Sijilmassa. If early Almohad emirs had been able to check the Merinids, after Yaʿqoub El-Mansour the rot set in and a fractured Almohad sultanate proved no longer equal to the task. The newcomers accordingly went from strength to strength till their final success in 1270. Dependence on Arab elements, however, was a grave mistake as it merely reinforced the influence of the newcomers in the land. As a result, "the mountains, into which the Bedouin never penetrated, were more and more severed from the plains and almost escaped the dynasty. The country of the unsubdued, the *blad siba*, from then on became one of the great realities of the country."[15]

In 1220, attempts by Yaʿqoub El-Mansour's son, Idriss El-Maʾmoun, to restore some dignity to the Almohad dynasty had had the reverse effect. Heavily influenced by boyhood contact with Christian princes in Spain, himself wed to a Christian, he rode down to Marrakesh with a bodyguard of 12,000 Christian mercenaries, defeated the army of his nephew, Yahya Ibn Nasser, and occupied the capital. He then astounded all and sundry by solemnly denouncing the basic tenets of the Almohad doctrine and formally did away with Ibn Toumert by declaring in the Marrakesh mosque that the only impeccable one was Sidna ʿIsa (Jesus)! This astonishing pronouncement was followed by other measures that threw society into disarray, such as the construction of a church for his mercenaries to worship in and a purge of some 4,000 sheikhs, whose heads ended up on the ramparts. When the local inhabitants complained of the stench, El-Maʾmoun callously replied:

> This is but an excuse on the part of those who mourn those severed heads, whose rottenness should do them so much good. The smell of a loved one's corpse has the fragrance of perfume; only enemies' bodies give off a foul stench.[16]

Unsurprisingly, this half-demented despot's reign was a disaster, marred as it was by unrest, brigandage, and civil war with his nephew Yahya, who usually found refuge in the Atlas near Tinmel, and also with the new sovereign of Andalucia, Ibn Houd. Things hardly improved during the brief reign of his successor, El-Rashid, obliged to pursue operations against rival claimant Yahya in a ding-dong campaign fought out between Marrakesh and Sijilmassa. As for the unfortunate Yahya, in 1235 he finally ran into some Arab elements near Taza and his head was despatched at once to his kinsman in Marrakesh.[17] El-Rashid fared little better, managing to drown whilst bathing in a Marrakesh pool.[18]

Almohad debacle

For five years, one of El-Maʾmoun's sons, Saïd, attempted to stop the rot. Bedeviled by dissension and intrigue at home, he first had to neutralize one of the principal mountain sheikhs, the Hintati Mohammed Ibn Wanoudin. Squaring accounts with the Merinids was his next priority, so an army of 20,000 cavalry—Almohads, Arabs, Christians, and Haskouri Berbers—was gathered for this specific purpose and sent north. The rival armies clashed outside Fez at a place called Al-Sakhrat Abi Riyash. Desperate fighting ensued from sunup to sundown and ended in a defeat for the Merinids, whose emir, Abou Ma'arouf, perished during the battle. His horse killed under him, he had been despatched rather unsportingly, as he lay on the ground, by a Christian Almohad mercenary. Meanwhile, the debris of the Merinid force fled to the safety of the Ghiata hills above Taza (1244).[19]

The same year, however, Saïd had treachery to contend with in Marrakesh, where another great Atlas sheikh, El-Guedmioui, was causing a commotion. In this instance, a punitive expedition had to be mounted against the city of Sijilmassa, where his brother had sought refuge, before things quietened down again. The sheikh was beheaded.[20] In April 1248 Amir Saïd contemplated a major expedition to the furthest reaches of his worm-eaten empire in a final bid to reaffirm Almohad supremacy in places where it was now boldly challenged. Something of a forlorn hope, the Almohad host, with its motley combination of Arabs, Berbers, and Christians, tramped out of Marrakesh. Contrary to all expectation, all went well at first. The news that the army had reached Oued Beht was sufficient for the Merinid amir, Abou Yahya, to abandon Fez and withdraw to Taza. Meknes and Fez were occupied and Abou Yahya sent in a deputation to pay homage to Saïd, who headed east towards fertile, hill-girt Tlemcen, "pearl of the Maghrib," which Yaghmourasn evacuated.

The 'Abd el-Ouadid prince retreated with army, harem, and treasure to the fortress of Temzezdekt which Saïd now invested. During siesta time on the fourth day of the siege, as Saïd was rashly reconnoitring the enemy position over very rugged terrain with a few companions, he was ambushed and killed by Yaghmourasn himself and two horsemen.[21] Thus in a brief affray with lance and scimitar did the last Almohad sultan worthy of note vanish from the scene. However, there was an element of poetic justice about his death, as Yaghmourasn, a somewhat Quixotic figure, amply demonstrated some noble Berber qualities. As his opponent lay mortally wounded on the ground he alighted from his steed and did his best to comfort him, regretting that events had taken such a turn. He later prepared a lavish funeral and treated the amir's wives and sister, Princess Ta'azzount, with great courtesy, eventually having them escorted back to the Dra'a region.[22]

Saïd's other territorial gains were thus canceled at one blow, the Merinids reoccupying Taza, Fez, and the Moulouya forts (1249), Amir Yahya significantly visiting the 'Aouam silver mines in Jbel Fazaz.[23] Under Saïd's successor El-Mortada, an attempt to repeat Saïd's success against the Merinids failed ignominiously when his army of 24,000, including Almohad and Aghzaz cavalry, Christian mercenaries and Andalucian crossbowmen, was routed at Beni Behloul outside Fez (1255).[24] Unsuccessful in quelling rebellions in the Sous, El-Mortada had better luck with Sijilmassa which his troops temporarily repossessed in 1257.[25] In 1262, however, a Merinid army came south and defeated the Almohads under Yahya Ibn Wanoudin on the Oum Rbia' river, but failed to press home their advantage in the direction of Marrakesh. Nevertheless, two years later, the Merinid amir Ya'qoub Ibn 'Abdelhaqq besieged the city and Almohad fortunes plummeted. Fortunately for them, though, in one sharp little encounter, the Merinid heir to the throne was killed. Chivalrously, El-Mortada sent his opponent a message of condolence and the siege was raised forthwith.[26] Disaster for El-Mortada ultimately came from within. One of 'Abd el-Moumen's grandsons, Abou Debbous, a tall, freckled, blue-eyed ruffian, discovered one day that his royal cousin meant to have him done away with. He accordingly absconded and placed himself under the protection of the Haskouri sheikh, Mess'aoud Ibn Gelidasen, south of the Great Atlas. Finally, making his way to the Merinid court in Fez, he was made welcome by the amir, Ya'qoub Ibn 'Abdelhaqq, with whom he struck a bargain whereby his host was to help him recover Marrakesh. Abou Debbous headed south with a treasure chest and 3,000 Merinid cavalry, made a long detour via Haskoura-land to recruit friend Mess'aoud and his tribal levies, and then marched on Marrakesh, worsted the loyalist forces at Aghmat and, without any further ado, entered the capital by one gate as El-Mortada fled by another (October 1266).[27]

The hapless fugitive sought a safe haven in the Gedmioua region of the Atlas, before making for Azemmour where his father-in-law resided, only to be betrayed and handed over to the usurper's assassins. When Amir Ya'qoub Ibn 'Abdelhaqq heard of his protégé's victory, he naturally sent him messengers reminding him it was time he delivered on his side of the bargain. Abou Debbous's recent success had apparently gone to his head, though, and he sent the Merinid ruler an extraordinarily ungrateful and defiant letter.[28] Mindful of the dire consequences that would result from issuing such a challenge, Abou Debbous now made overtures to Yaghmourasn, offering an alliance through a letter he sent to that prince's son, Yahya, then governor of Sijilmassa.[29] This was immediately accepted and the stage was set for a three-sided campaign. In 1267, after recuperating in Fez, the Merinid amir marched east to reach a conclusion with Yaghmourasn. The two armies met on the banks of Oued Telagh, near Tlemcen, and though many Merinid warriors fell, they were finally victorious and Yaghmourasn retreated, having lost one of his sons in the fighting. The Merinid amir now had his hands free to deal with Abou Debbous. In 1269, near Oued Aghfour, came the final bloody reckoning between Merinid and Almohad, the victory going to the former. As the reckless Abou Debbous attempted to flee to the safety of Marrakesh, he was intercepted, pierced by a pike, fell off his horse, and beheaded in next to no time.[30]

Thus had the Almohad empire-builders ultimately failed. Unable to capitalize upon early successes, its elitist nobility riven by bickering, incapable of imposing *ttawhid*, or keeping together the fabric of empire, the Almohad administration gradually allowed large territories to slip through their fingers, or fall under the sway of tribal chiefs or rival dynasts. As French historian Terrasse aptly puts it, "While the empire was everywhere falling to pieces and needed devotedness from all, the unworthy descendants of the great Almohad leaders quarrelled like mean, greedy peasants over what remained of the government and the revenues of the last provinces still under their rule."[31] Whereas the commercial significance of such permanent institutions as the A'ouam silver mines and Sijilmassa emporium remained unimpaired, from the regional point of view, the fall of Marrakesh implied that the focus of power in Morocco had now turned away from Tinmel, the Atlas Mountains, and the sedentary Masmouda south in step with the north's newfound legitimacy centered on the city of Fez and its

Merinid incumbents of nomadic Zenata origin. This strategic shift accordingly left the inner valleys of the Atlas and their inhabitants somewhat out of the limelight. It will be interesting to see, in the following chapter, how they would react in the face of this new dynasty and its freshly organized *makhzan*.

Exit the sedentary Masmouda Berbers, then; enter the nomads from eastern Morocco. The Merinids mainly concentrated on the central Maghrib as they dreamed of recovering the lost Almohad Empire, and did enjoy a measure of success against Tlemcen.[32]

Satisfaction proved but short-lived, however, as Abou l-Hassan's subsequent march to Ifriqiya ended with a humiliating defeat in 1348 at Kairouan (Qayrawan).

Nomad takeover

With the death of Abou Inan (1358), strangled by one of his *wazirs*, the Merinid dynasty slowly subsided. Their chief weakness undoubtedly lay in their being nomads from eastern Morocco without a strong ethnic power base. On the credit side, however, they achieved much for the state: the *makhzan*, during their long tenure, came of age, the country acquired the frontiers she would keep for centuries, and there were achievements in the realms of architecture, science, arts, and letters. By the mid-fifteenth century the Merinids were eased out of office by their near-cousins, the Beni Ouattas, like them Zenata Berbers from eastern Morocco, many of them having risen to prominence in the ranks of the *makhzan*.

Theirs was fated to be an undistinguished century in the riding seat; in fact, historians have tended to be rather unkind to them, especially Terrasse, who dismisses them somewhat summarily.[33] Recently, fresh interest has been aroused, with one French historian finding far more to say about them,[34] while an American researcher has emphasized their contribution to the "gunpowder revolution" and spirited defense of some Moroccan coastal towns against Iberian encroachments.[35]

True, the advent of gunpowder had not immediately resulted from its widespread use in the field. By the fifteenth century, however, crude stone-throwing cannon, usually termed "bombards," suitable for operations on both land and sea, were to be seen in Spanish and Portuguese service. Soon, some found their way into Morocco, followed during the next century by the first hand-held guns, cumbersome culverins and early matchlocks, though the actual gunners were usually Christian renegades and Turks. Unfortunately the rate of fire of these new-fangled devices was so woefully slow that the bow and crossbow were still favored by many fighters. In this respect, let it not be forgotten that the *rrami*, or Berber village sharpshooter, famed for his skill with musket or rifle, was originally an archer.[36] These various considerations affecting general Moroccan history have led us somewhat off-course, so to the Atlas Imazighen we must now return.

Marginally more accurate map of Morocco by James G. Jackson (1820).

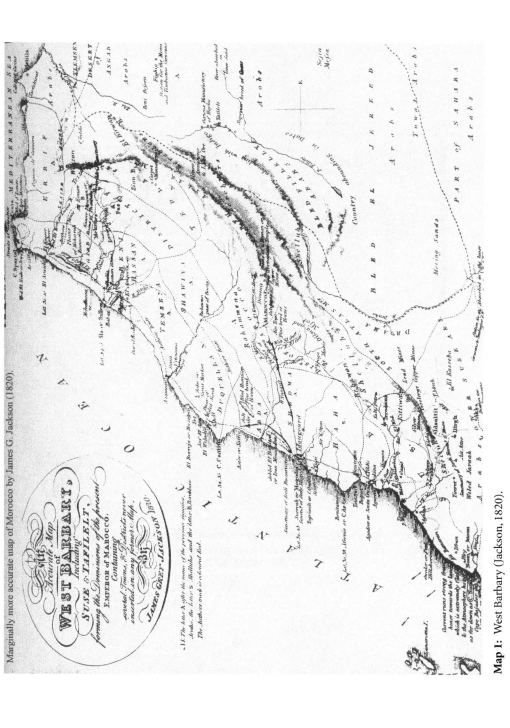

Map 1: West Barbary (Jackson, 1820).

Atlas Saints and Mountain Kings

In 1269–70, Zenata Berbers of the Beni Merin hunted down and killed Ishaq, the last Almohad prince, at Tinmel among those very hills whence his forebears had once drawn their strength.[1] This ignominious event ushered in four centuries of strife and turmoil in the Atlas with a turning inward of the Masmouda Berbers and a corresponding expansion of their Senhaja cousins to the east. It was a murky period with few salient features emerging from a labyrinth of endemic warfare, religious agitation, and interpenetration by rival peoples.

Start of the northwesterly push

Under pressure from Arab tribes, several groups of Zenata Berbers moved from the Atlas into the Atlantic plain and intensified their attacks on the tottering Almohad Empire.[2] Likewise, various Senhaja tribes joined the northwesterly movement into and across the main range. Thus did the important Beni Mguild tribe[3] appear in the Atlas during the twelfth century. Later, the Ayt Ouanir (Ayt 'Atta) are reported as despatching herds in summer to the northern slopes of the Atlas.[4] During the thirteenth century, the rugged mountains near Anergui witnessed the arrival of the ancestors of the Ayt Sokhman.[5] Thus was unleashed the northerly push of the Senhaja Berbers which was to continue unabated from the twelfth to the seventeenth centuries.

The Western High Atlas also became affected by successive waves of immigrants from the south as the Anti-Atlas and the Souss became overpopulated or fell into alien hands. Their imagination fired by reports of lush pastures on the north side of the Atlas ranges, the tribes would depart, lock, stock, and barrel. Pushing forward on their own or under pressure from behind, "through droughts, famines, bad harvests and epidemics,"[6] these various groups briefly occupied focal points, then passed on, sometimes leaving isolated communities in their wake. As the Atlas relapsed into secular unrest and anarchy, so did chroniclers find less leisure to record facts, and a veil descends over these "Dark Ages" of the Atlas Berbers.

The Masmouda Berbers had undoubtedly shot their bolt. The declining years of their epic, turning from victory to a protracted ordeal, had left them exhausted. However, that propensity for greatness which had sparked off the Almohad movement lingered at the foot of the rugged peaks. In the valleys of Seksawa the candle lit by Ibn Toumert flickered on.

Seksawa heyday

Although he never set foot there, Ibn Khaldoun paints an enchanting, if somewhat exaggerated, picture of this mountain region and its people: "The mountains they inhabit are among the highest in the Atlas and provide them with a sanctuary that hill-forts, steep rocks and bold peaks render inviolable. Their tops reach to the heavens and conceal, behind a mantle of clouds, summits ringed with stars."[7] Despite their proximity to Tinmel, the locals had only maintained tenuous links with the Unitarian movement. Unlike most of their fellow Masmouda, they were less eager to jump onto the Almohad bandwagon,[8] nor were they prepared to pay lip service to the incoming Merinids. They had merely been content to acquire a modicum of civilization while quietly biding their time. Their strength intact, they now felt in a position to step forward as champions of Berber independence.

Their achievements, however, limited to the Atlas, the Haouz, and the Souss, were a far cry from the imperial forays of the Almohads. At the head of this tiny state we find an ancient line of kings: the Seksawa dynast Haddou Ben Youssef was the son of Youssef Ibn Tashfin.[9] Little is known of this first kinglet, who came to power during the closing years of the Almohad regime, but his son, 'Amr ou Haddou, better known as 'Aomar Seksawi, who succeeded him in 1281, acquired a certain measure of fame, actually taking upon himself the royal title of *agellid*.[10] Thanks to the warlike qualities of his subjects, he carved himself out a small mountain fiefdom between the Nfis Valley and Tizi n-Bibaoun, with some overlapping onto the surrounding plains. Northward,

Fig. 4: Agersaffen village, upper Seksawa Valley (Western High Atlas).

Fig. 5: Village of Imi n-Wasif, upper Seksawa Valley (Western High Atlas).

he succeeded in fending off efforts by the Merinid sultan, Abou Thabet, to invade his mountain domain (*c.* 1305).[11]

Thus did 'Aomar establish the Seksawa as a force to be reckoned with in and around the High Atlas. As skillful with the pen as with the sword, 'Aomar Seksawi rapidly earned a reputation as lawyer, philosopher, even magician, his Moslem orthodoxy at times questioned as a result of frequent intercourse with rabbis. As for his well-stocked library, it told its own tale of the degree of civilization an allegedly uncouth mountaineer could attain. The greatest Seksawi monarch, his reign, reputed to have lasted 100 years, is remembered to this day among his self-styled descendants—the Ayt Haddious—on whose land stands his shrine.[12]

As for his legend, it spread well beyond Seksawa tribal territory, the neighboring Mentagga and Ida ou Mahmoud also cherishing the memory of Sidi 'Amr ou Haddou.[13] His son 'Abdallah, similarly versed in magic and alchemy, trod in his father's footsteps for a while, making the Merinid sultans tremble more than once in their Marrakesh palaces when he threatened to sweep down from the hills and destroy their iniquitous mosques. By a combination of intrigue and cautious enterprise, 'Abdallah skillfully avoided a decisive encounter with the Merinids, who at this time had other fish to fry. True, Abou Inan, usurping the throne of his father, Abou l-Hassan, had forced the unfortunate sovereign to seek refuge among the Hintata Berbers in the Marrakesh High Atlas. Cowed into submission by his son's army, Abou l-Hassan was to die from misery and hardship in the inhospitable mountains as Abou Inan stepped into his sandals.[14]

The new Merinid sultan had strong views on the subject of rebellious hill tribes. If they could not be flushed out of their valleys, he would seal them off to avoid further trouble. Thus did he build the fortress of El-Qahira to block the Seksawa outlet onto the Haouz.[15] His shutting them up within the cramped confines of their valleys precluded their northerly expansion, particularly possible designs on Marrakesh which might have led to a fresh imperial venture. Henceforth, the Seksawa, for all their skill at war, turned aside from the mainstream of history to become a rowdy little backwater.

Lalla 'Aziza and 'Amr Hintati

As usual, age-old anarchy—a compound of cupidity and apparent disunity—had a hand in the local power game. Taking a hint, as it were, from Sultan Abou Inan, 'Abdallah's own son rose against his father and expelled him from Seksawa country. The dethroned kinglet had to call in his powerful neighbor, the great Sheikh 'Amr Ibn Mohammed Hintati, to restore him to the throne with an army of well-paid professionals. Meanwhile, Abu Inan having come to grief, the Merinids went into decline. Quick to seize the opportunity, 'Amr Hintati was on the brink of achieving paramountcy in the south.

After defeating and killing his rebellious son, 'Abdallah Seksawi himself was murdered, and the Seksawa line of Ayt Haddou Ben Youssef succumbed in a welter of disorder. A firmer hand might well have taken advantage of a weakening Merinid dynasty to bolster up the Seksawa as a rampart of Berber independence, instead of allowing the tribe to subside into internecine warfare. As Berque observes, "this decadence sums up Seksawa history, rather their decline from mainstream XIVth-century history to sordid local mountain intrigues."[16] Fortunately for the hillmen, the power vacuum left by the disappearance of the Seksawa *caudecillos* did not last long enough to enable 'Amr Hintati, by now governor of Marrakesh, to invest their valleys with his 6,000 mercenaries, as he had done in Ourika and Guedmioua country.[17]

Their ability to throw up saints like magicians' rabbits once again proved their saving grace. In the person of Lalla 'Aziza, arguably the most famous woman in Atlas history, they found spiritual guidance every bit as effective in their dealings with the enemy from the plains as the temporal power formerly wielded by the defunct 'Abdallah.

Legends make her out to be essentially a saintly shepherdess, others claiming she was a direct descendent of Sidi 'Amr ou Haddou. This genuine daughter of the Atlas would miraculously find sufficient grazing for her sheep on barren slopes above Ouanchrigh, halfway up the Seksawa Valley. Unsurprisingly, her beauty had half the youths in the village yearning for her, though one of them got the surprise of his life one day when, after cornering his quarry on the edge of a precipice, she vanished into thin air. Her fame having spread to Marrakesh, the sultan summoned her to his court.

Shunning the glitter and pomp, Lalla 'Aziza remained meek and mild, impressing everybody in her entourage with her goodness and pious simplicity. Eventually becoming jealous of her influence on the people, the sultan decided to do away with her and had repeated efforts made to serve her poisoned food. Finally, her faithful servant was ordered to offer her the fatal dose and this time she accepted resignedly, but requested that after her death her body be embalmed, placed on a mule, and wherever the beast stopped, there should her grave be dug. Her final wishes were respected and the mule bore away the sacred corpse. The patient animal plodded into the mountains and finally stopped short of the narrow portals where the Seksawa river breaks through the last gorges to the lowlands. Marveling at this miracle, the locals raised a shrine there at Zinit, above the tomb they made for her, and there to this day she sleeps.[18]

In 1362, Lalla ʿAzizaʾs namesake, ʿAziza Seksawiya, was seen in flesh and blood, by a Muslim scholar, Ibn Qounfoudh, at the border fortress of El-Qahira, where she had come to parley with ʿAmr Hintati who wished to reduce the Seksawa to vassalage. Interceding on behalf of her people, she sent the Hintati a letter guaranteeing Seksawa fealty, an empty promise sufficient to make him back away. Indeed, subsequent invasion attempts never got past her shrine at Zinit, and we shall see how her spiritual power played a major part in the later history of the area.[19]

Saints and robber barons

Meanwhile, young Merinid sultan ʿAbd el-ʿAziz forsook the pleasures of Fez and headed south to bring to book his powerful Hintati vassal. Pursuing him into the mountains, he surprised the skeptics by conducting a winter campaign regardless of the Atlas snows and capturing El-Hintati by the spring of 1370. The proud amir was brought back in triumph to Marrakesh where he was whipped to death.[20]

Two years later, however, the promising young king died, and in the confusion that characterized every change of sovereign in the old Morocco, the Hintata amirs strengthened their grip on southern Morocco, remaining its uncrowned monarchs until early in the sixteenth century.[21] Meanwhile, heralding a fresh chapter in Berber resistance, the Portuguese (*burtgiz*) had started harrying the coasts, setting up outposts like Santa Cruz and allying themselves with the Berber tribes, especially near Safi, where local chieftain Yahya Ben Taʾafuft threw in his lot with them. The Portuguese also foraged deep inland, sometimes as far as the Western High Atlas, though never actually endangering Marrakesh.[22] In the Berber south, the signal failure of the Merinid and Ouatassid dynasties both to stem the *Reconquista* and curb the Christian invader led to a strong nationalistic reaction based on xenophobia and spiritual fervor. Local saints, possessors of *baraka*, referred to as marabouts,[23] thus cropped up all over the Atlas to catalyze latent Berber energies and mastermind these martial tribes. At times acting individually, at others, these saints would band together in some out-of-the-way zaouia[24] to form religious brotherhoods extolling the virtues of Sufism "based on a partnership of spiritual emotion with God."[25]

Initially, "maraboutism" resulted in a formidable upsurge of Islamic mysticism throughout Tamesna, also in inner Morocco, in which the superstitious Berbers established a happy medium between their own ancient saint-worship—a survival of the pagan cult of sacred grottoes, mountains, trees, springs, and rocks[26]—and strict Muslim orthodoxy.

Not content with working miracles such as levitation among their faithful parishioners beneath Atlas peaks, marabouts branched out into neighboring areas.

Their zaouias became regular institutions, part-monastery, part-hostel, and part-school, perhaps holding sway over several tribes and possessing the necessary authority to unleash thousands of warriors on the path of *jihad*. Masters of humbug, many would claim descent from some earlier sultan of Morocco, or even the Prophet Muhammad, given the enhanced prestige conferred by sharifian descent. Their authority was all the greater if they censured the sultan's incompetence in terms of waging war on the *burtgiz*. Every year, on an appointed date, the hallowed sanctuaries where they were buried attracted a vast concourse of pilgrims and other devotees.

Typical of such gatherings is the great *almuggar*, dedicated to Sidi Hmad ou Moussa, which takes place in the Tazeroualt region on a westerly spur of the Anti-Atlas. This *agwerram*, famous as the patron saint of the jugglers and acrobats who grace the festivities with their presence, led an exemplary life (1460–1563) and founded the Semlali[27] zaouia which galvanized the resistance of the Souss Berbers against the *burtgiz* at the time of the earlier Sa'adi sultans.

Saints of this line later preserved the independence of the Tazeroualt district more or less continuously until the end of the nineteenth century. One of Sidi Hmad's most famous sayings was that "the land of the Igezzouln and the Doukkala both produce saints just as grass sprouts from the earth."[28] This was no overstatement, the far west of Morocco having been a nursery of holy men, especially during the so-called "maraboutic crisis" of the early sixteenth century, largely prompted by the political anarchy then rife in southern Morocco.

A typical situation prevailed in the Marrakesh area where one sheikh, more or less Portuguese-backed, mulcted the inhabitants of that city, while his cousin, Moulay Driss Hintati, had declared himself king of the mountains, and, from a castle on Asif Lmal in the Atlas foothills, lorded it over both Masmouda mountaineers and lowlanders. Their feudal tenure, chiefly based on the Tadla and Haskoura tribes, was brought to an abrupt halt in 1524 by the arrival on the scene of the Sa'adi,[29] a new breed of Arabic-speaking *shurafa* ("descendants of the Prophet"), who had crossed the Atlas from the Dra'a valley to participate in a *jihad* against the *burtgiz*.

The Sa'adi sultans

The Sa'adi sultans mark a turning-point in Morocco's chequered past. Quick to see their opening, they proclaimed themselves standard-bearers of the local Berbers in the fight to oust the *ayt burtgiz*. At first, the Masmouda welcomed them with open arms; however, the speed with which the newcomers set about collecting taxes rapidly dampened their enthusiasm. The Souss was soon up in arms (1542), with ripple effects spreading to the High Atlas.

The following year, a humble village preacher and magician, 'Abdallah, claiming descent from the Almohads, raised the standards of rebellion high up in the Seksawa valleys, and it took a sizeable army of Christian mercenaries to cut him down to size. A few years later, various other independently-minded mountain sheikhs from the Damsira and Seksawa tribes declared their reluctance to pay taxes. Retribution was not slow in coming. Tricked into accepting a parley with the authorities, eleven of them were enticed down into the plain, captured, taken to Marrakesh, and promptly decapitated (1547) *pour décourager les autres*.[30]

During the reign of Ahmed Mansour, desultory tribal warfare and discord in the Western High Atlas thus persisted unabated, except around Toubkal, which appears to have been administered on the Sa'adi monarch's behalf by *qayd* El-Mezouari, an Ayt Waouzgit Berber from the south side of the High Atlas, also with an Almohad pedigree. An able, long-serving governor, yet another precursor of the twentieth-century *grands caïds*, he would appear to have been a learned scholar in his own right if his well-stocked library—containing a claimed total of 50,000 volumes—is anything to go by.[31]

Unsurprisingly, *mrabtin* continued to galvanize the hill tribes, to put more zest into anti-Christian resistance. For much of the seventeenth century, in southwest Morocco, marabouts were to call the tune. As if ordained by fate, the Seksawa hills once more provided a refuge for yet another line of saints—the sons of Sidi Saïd ou 'Abdnaïm. In the sixteenth century, Sidi 'Abdallah ou Saïd, having incurred the wrath of the reigning sultan, left his lowland home and established a zaouia in the shadow of the higher peaks. In fact, three of his descendants are said to have been buried among the Ayt Haddious, a prominent highland Seksawa clan.[32]

"Bum Hully," the would-be *mahdi*

This fresh bid for power occurred in the opening years of the seventeenth century, by which time the ailing Sa'adi kings had become mere clay in the "maraboutic" potters' hands. Any *mahdi* who cared to do so could make a bid for the sultanate, such as Ahmed Ibn 'Abdallah Ibn Abou Mahalli,[33] a pious Sufi scholar from the Saoura area southeast of the Tafilalt. He had devoted his life to study, spending time with the chief *murabit*, Ibn Abou-Bekr, at the zaouia of Dila' in the Middle Atlas.

After a theological disagreement with his mentor, Abou Mahalli headed south to the Tafilalt and proclaimed himself *mahdi*. By dint of inflammatory speeches censuring the recent surrender of Larache (1610) to the Spanish, he raised an army and captured Sijilmassa, before taking Marrakesh. During his short-lived triumph in that city, a local man criticized the vanity of his quest and announced his forthcoming demise: "Your fight will have amounted to a squabble for a mere *shrawit*, a ball of rags!" Whereupon Abou Mahalli, stung to the quick, burst into tears.[34]

Meanwhile the Sa'adi incumbent, a clever character and lover of poetry named Moulay Zidan, unavailingly sent a scratch force to oppose Abou Mahalli, before fleeing to safety in the coastal town of Safi. To restore the situation he appealed to Sidi Yahya Abou Zakary, the master of the Western High Atlas. It was a wild gamble, which, in the event, paid off. In a battle near Imi n-Tanout, Sidi Yahya's clansmen made mincemeat of Abou Mahalli's undisciplined rabble, and the false *mahdi*'s head was nailed to the ramparts of Marrakesh.[35] Eventually, after Sidi Yahya had decided against claiming the sultanate for himself, the undeserving Moulay Zidan recovered his throne.[36]

This serves to show that the cleavage between Berbers and central government was becoming more pronounced between their tribal areas, known as *blad as-siba* ("unsubdued territory") as opposed to *blad lmakhzan*[37] ("government territory").

Fig. 6: An *ashelhiy* (Berber) man from the Western High Atlas.

Thus, if the "Dark Ages" of the Western High Atlas had witnessed several abortive attempts by *caudecillos* to achieve something grander than mere local supremacy, by the mid-sixteenth century it had become obvious that this form of undertaking was far from the ideal blueprint for success. This was due to the difficulty the various candidates had in achieving the proper mix of spiritual and worldly authority, or proving competent war leaders when the chips were really down. Ultimately, for a combination of reasons, none passed the acid test. Perhaps mystical saintliness and military strategy made poor bedfellows, or excessive worldliness invariably led to ambition, avarice, and, in the final analysis, to despotism. In either case, this proved a recipe for disaster.

Senhaja Revival

The pattern of resistance was set for the next four centuries, with the Berbers constantly striving to recover that supremacy which they had previously enjoyed over the whole country. Exhausted by their imperial epic, not to mention subsequent attempts to retrieve their fortunes, the Masmouda had not yet fully recovered. To the east, however, their Senhaja cousins had been in the doldrums since Almoravid times. Most of them had been dragged into the migration of their nomadic brethren northwestward across the Atlas. Again we encounter one of those "foggy patches" in Atlas history. What is clear, however, is that in the fourteenth century the Ayt Iseha of lower Oued Ahansal were staving off attempts by the northward-thrusting Ayt Ouallal to displace them from their cliff-lined, pine-scented valley, while the Imelouan and Ishqern occupied the southern foothills of Jbel el-'Ayyashi about this time.[1]

The role of Zaouit Ahansal

As in the Western High Atlas, local saints (*igwerramn*) had played a pivotal role in these tribal migrations. Among the most celebrated were those of Zaouit Ahansal, who were often consulted by rival groups on disputes over grazing rights. At the head of the Ahansal line of saints was Sidi Saïd el-Hansali (Dadda Saïd), hailing from the Souss.[2]

One account makes out Dadda Saïd as having lived in the seventeenth century, and another stating that he belonged to the twelfth, which might be more compatible with further references to the Ahansal marabouts in the sixteenth century.[3] The location of his shrine at an Atlas crossroads is typical of the out-of-the-way places in which these saints chose to live. The bird's-eye view of Zaouit Ahansal, as one descends on it by the rough track from Ayt M'hammed (Ayt Mohand), is one of the finest in Morocco. Red-brown, turreted kasbahs and groves of poplar and walnut line a white-water torrent, conveying an impression of cool fertility after the miles of dusty ravines and stunted boxwood bushes the traveler has encountered. A semi-circle of gaunt cliffs, from whose very depths Asif n-Ouhansal gushes forth, lines the southern horizon. Huddling at the foot of the seemingly impenetrable barrier of Jbel Timghazin, Zaouit Ahansal is a kind of *ljent ushkan* ("lost paradise"), the last stopping-place, as it were, before a mysterious world of gigantic precipices and deep canyons apparently leading nowhere. That inter-tribal competition was keen for possession of the best pastures is evident from a decree, dating back to 1436, whereby the Ahansal *igwerramn* regulated access to the Amdghous grasslands on Oued

Fig. 7: Rooftops of Zaouit Ahansal and cliffs of Jbel Aroudan.

Ghriss. In the fifteenth century a Yaflman tribe, the Ayt Merghad, had reached the source of Asif n-Imdghas. Numbering some 600 families at the time, they were to become one of the most powerful and warlike tribes of the Eastern High Atlas.[4]

Their Ayt Hadiddou cousins acquired a similar reputation; in fact the two tribes were frequently at loggerheads over water rights in this early period, and could not resist the temptation of raiding each other.[5] Of all the Senhaja tribal groups, they are among the most traditionally-minded. Both tribes claim Imdghas as their home turf; both are semi-nomadic *qsur*-dwellers resorting to tent-based pastoral migration in summer. There are three main Ayt Merghad clans—Ayt Mesri, Ayt Youb, and Irbiben—not to mention their nomadic cousins, the Ayt 'Isa Izem. Allied to the Ayt 'Atta up to the sixteenth century, the Ayt Merghad eventually broke away and became members of the Ayt Yaflman alliance,[6] expanding into the Ghriss Valley between Asoul and the Semgat district. To this very day, the Ayt Merghad are among the most radical in the fight for Amazigh culture and Berberness (*timuzgha*).

Historically, two sub-divisions of the Ayt Hadiddou are mentioned: the Ayt Hadiddou n-Zoulit and the Ayt Hadiddou n-Midoul.[7] They are famous for their sheep and the beauty of their womenfolk, strikingly tattooed, with their conical head-dresses and dark-striped woolen cloaks. According to oral tradition, one of their clans, the Ayt Y'azza, are of Portuguese descent, this being part of those nebulous legends whereby the *burtgiz* penetrated the innermost recesses of the Atlas.

As for the proud Ayt Brahim, renowned as respecters of tradition, they are allegedly of royal line, the only group worthy one day of producing a sovereign.[8] Make no mistake, the Ayt Hadiddou know the meaning of the word "honor."[9] The Ayt Hadiddou also fought against other neighbors, expelling the Ayt 'Ayyach from the southern slopes of Jbel 'Ayyachi in 1520. In so doing, they obliged an Idrissid sharif, one Sidi Mohammed ou-Bou-Bker, to seek refuge in the *qsar* ("fortified village") of Tazrouft, near the spring of a fast-flowing Oued Ziz tributary, some miles from which he founded Zaouit Si Hamza, destined to become a great seat of learning.[10]

Fig. 8: Ayt Hadiddou couple on the trail, Asif Melloul Valley (Eastern High Atlas).

I had the good fortune, in May 1969, to visit the zaouia and drink mint tea with the seventh lineal descendant of the marabout, who gave his name as Bou Salim El-ʿAyyashi,[11] perpetuating the memory of his illustrious ancestor. He lives in a peaceful oasis at the foot of the snow-capped southern slopes of ʿAyyashi,[12] whose meltwaters fertilize a neatly laid-out patchwork of barley fields and poplar-lined irrigation ditches. This lofty seat of intellectuality boasts a famous library.

To revert to the Ahansal marabouts, a significant role awaited them in the power game for access to the Central High Atlas pastures. In 1588, one of their number, Sidi Lahssen ouʿAtman, confronted by the Ayt Ouassar confederation, cunningly purchased a large strip of grazing land between Ayt Bouguemmez and the upper Dadss.[13] He then turned it over to the Ayt ʿAtta, destined to become the most faithful clients of Zaouit Ahansal. Such was to be the impact of this super-tribe on Atlas history that they deserve more than a mere footnote.

Fig. 9: Seventh lineal descendant of Bou-Salim el-'Ayyashi, Zaouit Si Hamza.

Driving force behind the Senhaja push

Before becoming the driving force of the Senhaja Berbers, the Ayt 'Atta constituted a hotchpotch of tribes strung out between the bend of the Dra'a and the Tafilalt palm groves. The medieval Arab invasions left them reeling.[14] The founding father of the tribe, Dadda 'Atta, who licked them back into shape, appears to have been killed while fighting against some "unspecified Arabs,"[15] probably in the early seventeenth century. Regaining their composure, the Ayt 'Atta established their main stronghold among the jagged peaks and parched, sun-baked valleys of Jbal Saghro, from which they dislodged tribal groups such as the Zemmour, Beni Hassan, and Gerouan, which are now found far to the north, near Meknes.[16] Thus was born a confederation that became specialized in the mercenary protection of oasis dwellers and conducted seasonal transhumance from Jbal Saghro up to Izoughar, Talmest, and other High Atlas pastures, while their southernmost clan, the Ayt Khebbash, specialized in long-range camel warfare, eventually giving the super-tribe a strategic reach encompassing far-away Touat and other Saharan waterholes, expansionist tendencies that a later writer would describe as "Berber imperialism."[17]

For now, however, their eyes were turned northward, obsessed as they were by those fabled grasslands north of the range, the thought of which was enough to make any Saharan's mouth water. Three lines of advance lay open to them: the Dadss and Ahansal valleys in the west and that of the Ghriss in the center, the lower part of that last-named valley constituting the main route in the east.[18] In the western sector they were largely successful, largely due to their good relationship with the Ahansal *igwerramn*. Every year, the pastoral clans would follow the River Dadds to Oussikis and over the High Atlas to the lakeside Izoughar pastures dominated by the sacred mountain of Jbel Azourki. There, to this day, one can admire their camels, dark goat's-hair tents, and stone enclosures decorating the slopes once the snows have withdrawn before the sun's onslaught.[19] Access to the upper Ghriss was denied to the Ayt 'Atta by the Ayt Merghad, with a similar lack of success in the face of the uncompromising Ayt Izdeg—distant relatives and backed by the Dila'yin *igwerramn*—on the middle Ziz. Yet, in this area, the Ayt 'Atta do appear to have made headway beyond the Asif Melloul–Oued Ziz watershed, as oral tradition speaks of an abortive attempt to take over the Tounfit area in the eighteenth century.[20] A later expedition, to the Berkin area in the Eastern Middle Atlas, is also reported, with the Ayt 'Atta again heavily overextending themselves.[21]

Failure in those two areas, however, was offset by success in the west, while the lethal surgery practiced on their neighbors, by eliminating and/or or displacing less powerful groups, contributed to the dynamic northward movement of the Senhaja Berbers. Most of the credit in engineering the Senhaja revival is attributable to the marabouts of Dila', especially their leader, Abou-Bekr ben Mohammed El-Mejjati Es-Senhaji. This religious confraternity had founded their zaouia in 1566 at the village of Ma'ammar near Ayt Shaq in a fertile bowl amid wooded hills. As champions of the Jazouli doctrine, they won themselves a reputation for honesty and justice when reconciling feuding

Fig. 10: Ayt 'Atta summer camp at foot of Jbel Azourki.

factions, thus drawing many tribes of Jbel Fazaz and the Moulouya into their orbit. By the turn of the seventeenth century, their zaouia had become a noted pilgrim center, a seat of Koranic learning and rural, Arabo-Berber intellectuality.

The zaouia of Dila'

This fact is not fully appreciated. Observers of the Arabo-Islamic school tend to equate erudition and learning with Fez and the Qarawiyin, conveniently forgetting that, in seventeenth-century Morocco, southern cities like Marrakesh, Taroudannt, and Sijilmassa witnessed intense scholarly activity which made up with its dynamism what it may have lacked in finesse. In fact Amazigh culture at that time, especially among the Igezzouln of the Western High Atlas, continuing a rich tradition inherited from the Almohads, included a galaxy of erudition that reads like a contemporary Berber "Who's Who." Similar to the Zaouia Si Hamza, the Dila'yin lodge thus attracted contemporary celebrities, acting as it did as a halfway house between seats of learning in the south and the pre-eminent center of Fez. The famous scholar El-Youssi, himself a Berber from the Moulouya, subsequently author of the *Muhadarat*, after studying with great masters in the south, established his residence for some time in Dila', rubbing elbows with the likes of El-Jazouli, Mohammed ben Saïd El-Marghiti the famous astronomer, and Mohammed el-'Arabi El-Mesnaoui, then only a child but who would later make his name as an author of prose and a preacher at the *madrassa* Bou'inaniya.[22]

To set the record straight—and this is an important point—this was no collection of *tamazight*-speaking yokels, but bilingual scholars proficient in Arabic, with Koranic teaching figuring prominently on the Dila'i syllabus. Significantly, the Dila'yin marabouts were able to muster a large force of skilled fighters, a development that eventually led to their nursing dynastic ambitions. Thus was one of the chief actors in the drama of the Sa'adi succession ready to move center-stage.[23] This notable policy change at Dila' occurred after 1637, under Mohammed ben Bou-Bker Dila'i, partly due to calls for help from his client-tribes around Oued Ghriss, who were being bullied by the forces of a rival marabout, Sidi 'Ali Abou Hassoun of Tazeroualt.[24]

Matters came to a head over the *qsar* ("fortified village") of Tabou'samt, in Tafilalt, a pawn in a three-cornered power struggle between Tazeroualt, Dila', and the up-and-coming 'Alawid *shurafa* of Tafilalt. As it was, no armed clash occurred with Tazeroualt though the Dila'yin reinforced their influence in the High Atlas with a treaty signed at the zaouia of Sidi Bou Ya'qoub (Asoul) in 1645, to which the Ayt Merghad, Ayt Hadiddou, and other Yaflman tribes were signatories.[25]

True, Morocco at this time was suffering from chronic disunity, with the ailing Sa'adi kingdom of Marrakesh barely acting as a buffer state between the zones of influence of the Tazeroualt and Dila'yin marabouts. The penultimate Sa'adi sovereign, Mohammed esh-Sheikh, rashly sought a conclusion with the Dila'yin on the battlefield in 1640, but was defeated. In the following year the Dila'yin won fresh spoils when they destroyed the power of a rival marabout, El-'Ayyashi, the pickings including most of northern Morocco, including the city of Fez, which they made their capital. On the strength of these successes, the Dila'i chief, Abou 'Abdallah Mohammed Lhajj, attempted to found a new Senhaja dynasty.²⁶ He also moved to occupy the village of Tabou'samt in Tafilalt.

This brought him into collision with a formidable rival—the 'Alawid *shurafa*, who had settled there in the thirteenth century in the wake of the Ma'qil invasion.²⁷ After an initial attempt by 'Alawid Moulay Mohammed, son of Moulay Shrif, to expel Dila'yin sympathizers from Tabou'samt, the village came under the personal protection of Sidi 'Ali of Tazeroualt, anxious to retain some of his influence in the area.

However, the oasis dwellers appealed to the 'Alawid *shurafa* for help, so one dark night in 1637/8, Moulay Mohammed captured Tabou'samt with 200 chosen followers.²⁸

Sharifian contenders: The 'Alawids

Taking this fracas as a personal slight, Sidi 'Ali of Tazeroualt declared war on the 'Alawid *shurafa* and captured Moulay 'Ali Shrif. He sent his captive back to his capital of Iligh, in the Anti-Atlas, and confined him there in a hilltop *agadir* ("fortress"), granting him the companionship of a female slave to alleviate the tedium of solitary confinement. The most significant by-product of this captive union was a male child, later to become the fearsome Sultan Moulay Ismaïl. As Justinard puts it, tongue-in-cheek, "the gun was loaded"!²⁹ Meanwhile, his captor, shading himself beneath the confiscated yellow parasol, was having himself proclaimed sultan in the Souss. Sidi 'Ali's glory was to be short-lived.

In 1638, Moulay Mohammed ransomed his father at a stiff price before setting about extending 'Alawid influence around the Tafilalt. Then, moving west, he broke Sidi 'Ali's hold on the Dra'a valley (1640). In March 1646, however, when the 'Alawid attempted an armed foray into the Moulouya Valley, they were crushed at Lgara by the Dila'yin, who followed up their victory by crossing the High Atlas and capturing Sijilmassa.³⁰

Four years later, the 'Alawids came close to reaping full revenge when they responded to a call for help from the citizens of Fez, in open revolt against the Dila'yin, and actually occupied the city for a brief period. But their time had not yet come. Unable to withstand a vigorous Dila'yin counterstroke the 'Alawids were again defeated and forced to accept terms by which Jbel 'Ayyashi was fixed as their northern boundary. Complacently reclining in his palace at Fez, Abou Mohammed Lhajj Dila'i seemed more firmly ensconced than ever. A scathing epistolary exchange that now occurred between the rival would-be suzerains is interesting because of the light it sheds on Arabo-Berber sentiments. According to the recent truce between 'Alawids and Dila'yin, it was stipulated that the latter were to retain their hold on Moughfir in the Oulad 'Isa (Retteb). Naturally, when the 'Alawid *shurafa* elected to attack this locality, Mohammed Lhajj wrote a letter to Moulay Mohammed, accusing him of "treachery and of breaking his word."³¹ Here is a startling excerpt from the 'Alawid leader's reply.

> You are notorious in the whole Maghrib for the large dishes of *'açida* [crude barley *kus-kus*] that you serve your guests . . . You are nothing but an Anti-Christ in our

land, your power shall be broken ... You and your kind are but the bastard off-spring of a prostitute, while your ancestor Abou Isir was none other than Goliath. Your young men are pansies ... As for you, you are little better than a monkey; in actual fact you are the tick that clings to the fur of a mangy dog.[32]

Scourge of the Berbers

His fief restricted to the Souss, Anti-Atlas, and Oued Noun, Sidi 'Ali of Tazeroualt made overtures to the last Sa'adi monarch, Mohammed XIII, and gave him one of his daughters in marriage (1647).[1] Among the 'Alawids, a dynastic problem further obscured a none too rosy outlook. On Moulay Shrif's death in 1659, his succession by Moulay Mohammed was challenged by his second son, Moulay Rashid, who, leaving Tafilalt, took to the Atlas in search of solace and support among the Atlas tribes.

For a few years, both literally and politically, Moulay Rashid wandered in the wilderness.[2] In the words of one historian, "after various and possibly legendary adventures, in which the recurring themes are treachery and ingratitude, he collected an army in the north and marched against his brother."[3] The inevitable outcome of this fratricidal affray was that Moulay Mohammed died on the battlefield, while his entire army rallied to his brother's standard. For the Dila'yin marabouts, the writing was very much on the wall.

Dila' destroyed

Moulay Rashid, however, was too clever to risk a premature encounter, opting rather for a gradual build-up. Some successful campaigning in the Rif and Tafilalt enabled him to test the mettle of his troops, before turning against Fez, by now under only the nominal rule of Dila'. Fully exploiting the garrison's internal dissensions, he made short work of the city's defenses (1666). Thus did the first 'Alawid sultan enter the intellectual and spiritual capital of Morocco, an epoch-making event. His dynasty's hold on it has never since been relinquished.

When the 'Alawid sultan sortied into the countryside south of Meknes, he ran into a large contingent of the Ayt Ouallal, liegemen of the Dila'yin, who adopted the time-honored tactic of the feigned retreat. Once Moulay Rashid had tired of the chase and turned his horse's muzzle in the direction of its Meknès stables, the Berbers rallied and vigorously assailed his rearguard, only leaving off when darkness fell, a tactic they would repeat on many an occasion against the French. In 1668, Moulay Rashid felt it was time to conclude matters with the Dila'yin and marched on their zaouia, which he reached after decisively defeating his opponents' army at Batn El-Roumman.[4] He destroyed the place, but proved unable to remove the memory of Dila' from local Berbers' minds.[5]

As for the local Imazighen, "From that time onwards they became irrevocably hostile towards the new dynasty."[6] In fact, if the Rif tribes' opposition remained anti-Iberian, in the Atlas Mountains the focus of Berber resistance was henceforth on the 'Alawids who had shattered their dreams of hegemony. In 1669, the new sultan gave the Atlas Berbers a foretaste of things to come when he chastised the Ayt 'Ayyash of the upper Moulouya.[7] The following year he came down on the Souss with fire and steel, and besieged Iligh. Despite desperate resistance, the place was stormed by the sultan's overwhelmingly superior forces.[8] Of the many Tazeroualt leaders, Sidi 'Ali was captured, later to be poisoned in a Fez prison,[9] while his younger brother, 'Ali Ben Haïdar, was lucky enough to escape through the back door to the Sudan.[10] Shortly afterwards, Moulay Rashid fell off his horse and killed himself, being replaced by his brother, Moulay Ismaïl.

Enter Moulay Ismaïl

In Moulay Ismaïl, sometimes known as the "Black Sultan," the Imazighen of Jbel Fazaz were to meet their nemesis. The ruthless determination with which he scoured their tribal areas, and the large, well-equipped army he used for this purpose, were his main assets.[11] Wasting no time in attempts to win them over through diplomacy, he resorted to brute force.[12] Not content with butchering and decapitating as many Berbers as he could catch hold of, he confiscated their horses and weapons, and had fortresses built and garrisoned with his Black Guard at strategic sites throughout the Berber marches. Behaving with uncharacteristic leniency on other occasions, a troublesome tribe would be deported with bag and baggage from its usual area and dumped some hundred miles or so to the north and instructed to hold other tribes in check.

Subsequent French empire-builders derived substantial satisfaction from the fact that Moulay Ismaïl's approach to the problem was "that of the firm hand as pioneered by Rome and later renewed in our times by Bugeaud in Algeria and Lyautey in Morocco, but with less barbarous and more efficient means."[13] Whatever the ethics of Moulay Ismaïl's Berber policy, it had the merit of putting an effective damper on Senhaja expansion, at least in his lifetime. It took several campaigns in difficult, mountainous country to crush the obdurate hill tribes of Fazaz and the upper Moulouya, but those of the High Atlas and the pre-Sahara, secure in their inviolate sanctuaries, he never subdued.[14]

Attempted Dila'yin revival

Though the zaouia at Ma'ammar had been sacked, the actual fighting ability of the neighboring tribes was little impaired. Never at their best when defending a walled town, the Middle-Atlas Berbers had taken this reverse with characteristic resilience. Far more important was the fact that the victorious enemy had left the area without committing further ravages. This was enough to make them spoil for fresh battles with their foe, a tactical situation that would be repeated in 1914. It is thus hardly surprising that by the autumn of 1674, Moulay Ismaïl felt compelled to punish the Berber tribes near Dila'.[15] Not only had they been raiding the Tadla and Meknes plains, but, not content with refusing to pay their taxes, had murdered the royal tax collectors, individuals mostly bent on receiving gifts of chickens and/or eggs.[16]

Confident of success, 13,000 of them took up a strong position in the foothills of Fazaz. In vain did the sultan's forces attack. Then Ismaïl outflanked them, took them in the rear, and the Berbers fled the field, some 6,000 of their womenfolk and children being massacred. Of course, massacring women and children was "definitely not cricket" in an engagement prompted by such a trivial matter as unpaid taxes! According to the code of honor of these Senhaja Berbers, the fighting should have been limited to a gentlemanly exchange of shots followed by some parleying to reach an amicable settlement!

However, serious trouble brewed in the summer of 1677 in the Dila' area. Ahmed ben 'Abdallah Dila'i, grandson of old Mohammed Lhajj, had returned from his pilgrimage to Mecca with the promise of Turkish support. On arriving among his people "he was enthusiastically welcomed as a second Abou-Bekr sent from God to deliver the country from the hands of the tyrant." He set about rebuilding the zaouia, and soon mustered a large but undisciplined force of Senhaja Berbers.[17] Underestimating the attempted Dila'i restoration, Moulay Ismaïl twice despatched his *mhalla* ("armed expedition") against the rebels without personally taking the field. On each occasion, his military commanders were routed.

Smarting with indignation at these reverses, the sultan finally gathered a force of seasoned veterans. This time he was eminently successful, largely due to the support of a battery of cannon which struck terror into the hearts of the Berbers. Some 3,000 mountaineers were killed in battle and 700 severed heads were presented to the victor.[18] Again, no mercy whatsoever was shown to captured women and children, but the Berbers still had a lot of fight left in them, and it would take several more campaigns to subjugate them.[19]

Ismaïl's confrontation with the Ayt 'Atta

The following year, 1678, the Imazighen enjoyed a brief respite from the attention of their formidable sultan. Leaving his plague-stricken capital of Meknes, he had taken up summer quarters in the relatively cool upper Moulouya Valley, whence he could keep an eye both on the Berbers of Fazaz and on his troublesome kinsmen in Tafilalt—a wise precaution as two of his brothers were plotting to raise the whole Ayt 'Atta confederation against him. As soon as he got wind of this mischief, the sultan crossed the Atlas, harried all the way by neighboring Berber tribes. Having dislodged his rebellious brothers from Tafilalt, he then moved against their powerful ally, the Ayt 'Atta.

After an initial skirmish in January 1679 on the open plain south of the High Atlas in which the Berbers with their arquebuses and bows and arrows were worsted by the sultan's black musketeers and swordsmen,[20] the fight was carried up into the heart of Jbel Saghro. To give their womenfolk time to get their flocks and other possessions out of the way, they tricked Moulay Ismaïl into believing they would accept his peace conditions, which was also standard Berber practice.[21] By now firmly entrenched within their rocky citadels, they gave battle on their own terms. Terrasse claims the *makhzan* won a "difficult victory," whereas local legends are adamant that the Ayt ʿAtta smashed the sultan's *mhalla*.[22] Even the official *Istiqça* chronicle admits that "the Fez troops lost 400 men in Ayt ʿAtta country."[23] This is corroborated by Moulay Ismaïl's English biographer.[24] The well-proved Berber practice of harrying an enemy's rear in rugged country had more than paid off. To add insult to injury, Sultan Ismaïl was forced to accept humiliating terms before being allowed to leave Ayt ʿAtta country. Meanwhile, provisions were becoming scarce, while a number of his men were deserting to hunt for treasure[25] on their own account among the castles of the Dadds Valley.

The sultan had to plan his next move. Returning to Meknes via his outward route was out of the question because recent snowfall had blocked the passes and because the Amazigh tribes were sure to gather in strength to dispute his passage. There remained the shorter route via the Tizi n-Telouat linking the Draʾa Valley to the Marrakesh. After bribing the Glaoui sheikh, doorkeeper of this strategic col, into letting his army pass

Fig. 11: Cedar forest at the foot of Jbel ʿAyyashi.

unmolested, the *mhalla* ran into a snowstorm. Part of his army was lost in the blizzard, while warriors from nearby villages picked off stragglers: "3000 tents, including twelve covered with costly velvets and brocades, had to be left behind. Finally, the slaves bearing gold and silver, which Moulay Ismaïl had looted, refused to advance another step, and were immediately put to death."[26]

The circular route the sultan followed was interesting in that it became the pattern for many a subsequent *mhalla* which his successors undertook on similar attempts to bring to book dissident tribes on the periphery.[27] Moulay Ismaïl had been taught a bitter lesson in mountain warfare by Berber tribes whose very inviolability proved that he was far from master in his own house. Nearer home, however, Ismaïl was determined that Dila'yin client-tribes such as the Ayt Oumalou, and other groups of Fazaz, should no longer be allowed to flout his authority with impunity. After disarming all the plains Berbers, he lunged deep into Jbel Fazaz in 1683/4 and hounded rebellious elements as far as the foot of Jbel 'Ayyashi. He then operated along the Moulouya till winter.[28]

Meanwhile, he had kasbahs built at Azrou and Aïn Leuh. Garrisoned with *'abid* ("black guard") contingents, 1,000 in Azrou, 500 in Aïn Leuh,[29] they were designed to make life uncomfortable for the Ayt Idrassen in their winter migration towards the *azaghar*. However, the bulk of the Senhaja Berbers continued to defy the sultan from their mountain hideouts and, for the moment, felt little inclined to surrender. It would take another three major campaigns over the next twelve years to temporarily subdue them. Sultan Ismaïl began in 1685/6 by tackling the Berber bastion at its eastern end.

Heading south from Sefrou, he laid waste the country down into the Moulouya, the foothills of mighty Jbel 'Ayyashi, again marking the southern limit of his foray.[30]

Showdown in the Fazaz

The sultan took advantage of this campaign to establish a kasbah at Aoutat (Midelt) and "remained on the spot, accepting the submission of tribes that were prepared to hand over horses and weapons."[31] To strengthen his hold on the area, Ismaïl disarmed the tribes and built a chain of forts along the middle Moulouya and Oued Gigou, including Qsar Beni M'Tir, Aoutat, and Lqsabi.[32] In this last-named position he left a permanent garrison of 600 hand-picked members of his *'abid* guard.[33] Thus were most of the dissident areas cordoned off, or at least neutralized. This left the final Ayt Oumalou strongholds of Fazaz to deal with. Situated near the sources of Wansifen (Oum Rbia'), this cold country of stony plains, bushy ravines, and magnificent cedar forests has nurtured as hardy a breed of fighters as ever emerged from the Atlas. Well aware that they would prove a tough nut to crack, Ismaïl proceeded by easy stages. Acting according to his usual tactics, the sultan sent a large force of press-ganged Zemmour and Ayt Idrassen under *qayd* 'Ali ben Ishou Aqebli deep into the Ayt Oumalou heartland to restore the ruined Almoravid fortress of Adekhsan, not far from present-day Khenifra. This would make an excellent advanced base.[34]

Meanwhile, 5,000 men were marooned there for the winter,[35] their mission being to prevent the Berbers from effecting their seasonal migration from the heights on the

Wanfisen/Moulouya watershed towards the warmer lowlands west of Adekhsan. By sealing them off in the mountains, he not only forced them to spend a highly uncomfortable winter, but was confident that the cold would decimate the tribesmens' livestock. By hitting them where it hurt most, the sultan hoped to blunt their fighting spirit and cow them into an early submission. After thus compelling the Ayt Oumalou to spend a couple of winters in conditions of extreme hardship, he decided that the plum was ripe for the picking.

Half-starving, their flocks famished and reduced, their wives taunting them for their apparent cowardice while lamenting the high death rate among their babes, the Ayt Oumalou warriors must have longed for the final battle. By now better equipped, many of them fondled intricately-carved, long-barreled matchlocks, which they could fire from the saddle or from behind a bush with innate skill. But when it came to the rough and tumble, there was no weapon better than the curved dagger. Firearms of any sort were an object of contempt, enabling a coward to kill a brave man, whereas it took courage to wield the knife![36]

From their hilltop redoubts on Jbel Fazaz, they impatiently awaited the sultan's onslaught (1692). The monarch was in a grim, no-nonsense mood. A formidable army, divided into three contingents, converged on Jbel Fazaz from three directions. The main body under the sultan's command, and comprising 2,500 of his regular troops, headed up Oued La'abid from Kasba Tadla to take the Ayt Serri in the rear. Two other groups homed in on the rebel enclave from the north. One of them, consisting of Ayt Idrassen and Ayt Yoummour tribal levies under 'Ali ben Barakat, occupied Tinteghallin south of Adekhsan. The third included Zemmour and Beni Hakem tribesmen, under 'Ali ben Ishou Aqebli, and a contingent of Spanish renegades from Larache dragging a battery of cannon on which Moulay Ismaïl was relying to bludgeon the Berbers into submission.[37]

There is also evidence of limited Ayt Yaflman participation in the campaign: "The sultan sent messengers to the inhabitants of the Todgha, Ferkla and Ghriss, also to the Sebbah, ordering them to come in arms and join 'Ali ben Ishou"[38] at the actual battlefield. It proved more of a massacre than a martial encounter.[39] The mountaineers had not yet acquired that capacity for withstanding bombardment that they were to display in the twentieth century. Blown to bits by artillery fire, 12,000 of them were slaughtered and their heads lined up so *qayd* 'Ali ben Ishou's men could count them.

According to the official chronicler, "Here and there, in the ravines and valleys the sultan's forces hacked the Berbers to pieces, flushing them out of caverns and grottoes."[40] Thus did the peace of death descend on Jbel Fazaz, while the monarch busied himself with other matters of state. The deeply resentful Amazigh survivors were then left to their own devices under the surveillance of a network of forts, the sultan doing nothing to win over the local population, which was to prove a decidedly short-sighted policy, as will soon be illustrated.

Transition and Recovery

Meanwhile, though advancing years precluded his personally resuming operations against the Atlas Berbers, Moulay Ismaïl's minions and successors made sure they were regularly kept under surveillance, even broken in, as and when dictated by circumstances. In the aftermath of conquest, maintaining subject peoples under the yoke required a blend of vigilance and severity. Several episodes typical of this transitional period, marked by a gradual recovery of the Berber tribes, occurred, the first one in the Western High Atlas.

Fiercely independent, contemptuous of the central government, and wary of any outsiders from the plains, the Masmouda mountaineers owed allegiance to none but their yearly elected *jemma*', or "council" of graybeards; and also to their marabouts. The power wielded by these holy men, especially as arbiters of inter-tribal conflict, was considerable.[1]

Although war remained something of a choice pastime, it was rarely allowed to get out of hand thanks to an ingenious system of alliance which divided the tribal chessboard between large coalitions (*leffs*) of practically equal strength, and which automatically squared off against each other in the event of hostilities. As a prelude to action, a signal fire, a *tamatert*, would blaze from a nearby col, summoning one's *leff* brothers to the scene. The system's main purpose was to ensure that the weak were not devoured by the strong. Thus, in a given valley, left-bank villages might belong to one *leff*, and righ-bank villages to another. Likewise, Seksawa clans answered the call of the Indghertit, except for the Ayt Lahssen who belonged to the Imsifern.[2] As an insurance policy against total war, it was repeatedly brought into application.[3] Quarrels over grazing rights, however, rarely escalated to a higher level of confrontation, so that the sacrifice of some animal could usually bring proceedings to a satisfactory conclusion. Thus did similar considerations, doubtless under the aegis of the local marabouts, put a stop to a squabble over access to the Tishka plateau between two Seksawa clans who reportedly buried the hatchet in 1701. A *modus vivendi*, also involving the Ida Gerioun clan, was drawn up whereby the plateau was out of bounds to flocks from the period of winter snows to early July. A fine would be levied on any trespasser, an arrangement typical of Berber pastoral practice throughout the Atlas Mountains.[4]

Fig. 12: Autumn scene, Berber village, Western High Atlas.

The marabout of Tasaft

Typical of these High Atlas marabouts, undisputed leaders of the mountain men, was the *agwerram* whose zaouia lay at Tasaft, not far from the dilapidated mosque of Tinmel on the upper Nfis. Claiming descent from the Idrissid sharif Moulay Driss Zerhoun, as indicated by his name, Lhajj Brahim ben Mohammed ez-Zerhouni[5] was a man who combined love of the mountains and their tranquility with a deep mistrust of the reigning sultan, Moulay Ismaïl. His philosophy vis-à-vis the monarch is perhaps best portrayed in the lines of a statement contained in his book of travels, or *rihla*: "Even if granted an official pardon the wise man trusts not in the word of princes!"[6]

The sultan, having learned of the marabout's influence over tribes that specialized in brigandage, summoned him to court. Unsurprisingly, the marabout declined this invitation to leave his safe retreat in the hills. The saint now qualified as a rebel; therefore the recently-appointed pasha of Marrakesh, 'Abdelkrim ben Mansour, was ordered to take appropriate action against him (1713). An ambitious upstart, the pasha had spent his early years in the cloth trade, plying regularly between Marrakesh and the Nfis Valley on his donkey.[7]

Proclamations were accordingly read out in Marrakesh marketplaces, calling for volunteers for the *mhalla* which the pasha was planning to lead "up Oued Nfis and through the mountains against whomsoever rebelled against Sidna's authority."[8] Attracted by the prospect of loot, numerous volunteers came forward. While his forces were gathering, Pasha 'Abdelkarim sent his emissaries into the Atlas to suborn a few *imgharn* ("sheikhs") into provoking a massive confrontation between the *leffs* to weaken the highland clans before he attacked. This was no more successful than a personal message to the marabout at Tasaft: "If you refuse to follow this course and choose the path of rebellion, you will have cause to remember my words. I place the matter in God's hands."[9] Another pasha supported his Marrakshi colleague, accusing the marabout of sedition: "We know that you have strayed from the straight and narrow path of virtuous marabouts and even now are stirring up rebellion among the *ishelhayn* ["Berbers"], and inciting them to ambush and loot caravans, thus causing bloodshed."[10]

On mule-back, at the head of a large retinue of Guedmioua tribesmen, the pasha reconnoitered a route which should have taken his forces with relative ease over the main Atlas ridge, past Jbel Erdouz and down into the Ogdemt Valley, within striking distance of the upper Nfis. What he saw curbed his enthusiasm. There was no question of leading a large *mhalla* over such rugged terrain, every inch of which would be as familiar to its defenders as their own kitchen-gardens. Discarding plans for a northern approach, as winter was approaching, he opted to reassemble his army at a later date.

This prompted the marabout to send a message to Marrakesh protesting his friendship and peaceful intentions—a typical, time-saving Berber ploy! The pasha quashed this overture with thinly-veiled threats: "We have received your apologies for which we thank you. Send a *hediya* [gift] of five healthy mules as proof of your sincerity. Thus shall we know that you submit to the *makhzan*. Otherwise, we shall know which course to adopt!"[11]

Winter came and went. On the eve of the month of Ramadan, there was a vast concourse of Berbers at Ijoukak marketplace. According to the rumor mill, the pasha of Marrakesh had gathered a fresh *mhalla* in the Souss to descend on the upper Nfis and put the entire population to the sword. A whole day's palavering ensued, while treachery hovered in the air. "They talked, and the talk between them was unending . . . as is the custom among undisciplined Berber rebels,"[12] the marabout told his son. When the tribesmen heard that their enemy would be crossing the Atlas by Tizi n-Ouichden, they stationed some warriors at this high col (2,700 m). The traitors in their midst, however, did such a thorough job of it that mere token resistance was offered. On the first morning of Ramadan, from their zaouia at Tasaft, the marabout and his son heard a roll of drums followed by a ragged fusillade up at the col. Grabbing a few belongings, they escaped up the valley into the wooded gorges of Aghbar, where they ran across other fugitives fleeing from the pasha's wrath.

Reaching the village of Imlil n-Oughbar, the marabout and his suite noticed that people steered clear of them with frightened glances as if they had been lepers. Even deeper in the mountains, in Ijanaten country, the fugitives were at first coldly received at a notable's house, until his wife (a Seksawiya woman) reminded him of the laws of hospitality. "She followed us along the path and swore by her right hand that we would not pass without stopping. And I marvelled at the magnanimity of this woman, far nobler a person than her husband," recalled the marabout's son.[13] Confident that he had reached a secure hiding place, Lhajj Brahim stayed there for three weeks. But the pasha was not giving up his man so easily.

Learning of his whereabouts, he sent a letter to the Janati notable inviting him to pay tribute and hand over the marabout and other refugees, "or else the army will come

Fig. 13: Village of Azgour and Jbel Erdouz, Guedmioua (Western High Atlas).

down on you from all sides, and great will be the slaughter among you."[14] Hoping to make good his threat, the pasha assembled his troops on a hillock above Tasaft, whence distant views were to be had over the mountains of the Nfis headwaters. "From what he could see of these mountains, he realised that his soldiers were not men enough to tackle such difficulties." Reverting to psychological warfare, he despatched a further letter to the marabout: "How have you come to refuse obeisance to *sidna*? You have caused the loss of your own land and property ... A drawn sword shall ever remain between us!"[15] Not wishing to cause trouble for his hosts, Lhajj decided to leave Ijanaten country and cross over to the Ida ou Msattog, a clan on the sunny side of the Atlas, where he was sure of a good welcome.

Even from that distant haven, however, the vengeful pasha sought to dislodge him. As long as the marabout held out in the hills there could be no respite. Moving back over onto the Souss side of the Atlas by a flank march, he ran into a large concentration of tribesmen at Tizgui and took a drubbing.

Undaunted, pasha 'Abdelkrim marched on till he reached the Ida ou Msattog border. From his camp, he made the usual threatening noises, insisting that the Ida ou Msattog drive out the marabout and "ravage any territory where he might seek refuge." To which the tribesmen, loyal to their guest and respectful of the laws of hospitality, turned a deaf ear.[16] The pasha and his henchmen were convinced they were in the right and merely executing their duty in attempting to bring the lost sheep in the hills back to the fold of allegiance to *sidna* ("sultan"). Conversely, the marabout and his supporters were equally adamant in their spirit of independence, protection of their interests and their guests, and abhorrence of constraint. To show the pasha that they meant business, 300 chosen Ida ou Msattog stalwarts staged a successful night attack on his bivouac. 'Abdelkrim rallied his men with difficulty and withdrew as best as he could while the tribesmen looted his abandoned camp. Never again would the pasha venture into the Atlas at the head of a *mhalla* to subdue the marabout.

Shortly afterwards, doubtless softened by declining years, Moulay Ismaïl granted the marabout his pardon. However, shrewd as ever, Lhajj preferred to reside peacefully at Amgernis with the Ida ou Msattog for the rest of his life. His aloofness brought a final reprimand from the pasha, who observed disdainfully that "you feel compelled to hide in the hills, to resort with rebels."[17]

There were economic and political reasons for *makhzan* frustration over this failure to bring to book a mountain marabout. There was typical *makhzan* nervousness at allowing yet another Masmouda power base to emerge within a stone's throw of Tinmel, a potentially dangerous development that revived fears of a possible Almohad-style comeback.[18] That said, pasha 'Abdelkrim died in 1717, to the delight of Atlas mountaineers: "How could it have been otherwise?" pleads the marabout's son, for "he [the pasha] had wrought havoc throughout the Souss with his army and his misguided antics."[19] Nor were his successors to make any more headway against the troublesome Berbers of the Western High Atlas. In his palace at Meknes, the ageing Moulay Ismaïl would have given little weight to this reverse at the hands of Berber warriors of one of his armed detachments if and when he heard of it. The implication that victory was about to change camps could not have occurred to him. Berbers, especially those of Fazaz, as we have seen, had had good reason to dread his name. Rarely were they to encounter such a harsh taskmaster. As a contemporary English writer so aptly observed, "Moulay Ismaïl ... tamed the natural savageness of his subjects by showing himself still more savage than they."[20]

Fig. 14: Nomadic encampment at foot of Jbel Maasker, Tounfit (Eastern High Atlas).

Thus had the sultan shown skill at containing and punishing unruly Atlas tribes. Since the destruction of Dila', the Senhaja had undoubtedly lost the initiative. Almost overnight, they were now to recover it. Ismaïl's death, in 1727, was the signal that unleashed chaos and rebellion throughout the sultanate. Taking advantage of the situation, the mountain Berbers slowly switched from internecine squabbling to active anti-*makhzan* aggression. In this interlude, the focus shifts to central Morocco. Prominent among the local tribes, the Ayt Yoummour appear to have occupied the environs of Asoul until the early seventeenth century. They were then dislodged from the Ghriss valley through having incurred the wrath of an incoming marabout, Sidi Bou Ya'qoub, also due to pressure from neighboring tribes; shortly after, we hear of them battling with the Ayt Sokhman along Asif Melloul. By Moulay Ismaïl's time we find them along the northern foothills of the Atlas, from Tagzirt to Tounfit. After the sultan's 1693 campaign they were concentrated north of Aghbala in the Eastern High Atlas under *qayd* 'Ali Ou-Barka,[21] as a *jaysh* contingent.

Qayd Ou-Barka and the Ayt Yoummour

In this capacity, they received weapons from the *makhzan* the better to contain potentially hostile Atlas tribes, should the latter be tempted to tramp north from Asif Melloul. Once in place, the Ayt Yoummour had to settle down under their new *qayd*. The subsequent relationship lasted thirty years, and seems, at best, to have been a prickly one.[22] A typical, feudally-minded pro-*makhzan* Berber, out to work the system to the best of his ability, Ou-Barka proved a zealous authoritarian, ever anxious to keep his parishioners from raiding, playing at highwaymen, or making secret deals with their "untamed" brethren in the Atlas anxious to spill over northwards.[23] Actually though, through Yoummouri connivance several tribes gained fresh ground on the *amalu* ("shady") slopes of the Atlas.

This went well beyond their border-guard brief. Worse still, part of the Ayt Yoummour stationed near Ksiba actually joined in the worst outburst of rebellion that followed on the heels of Moulay Ismaïl's death (1729–30). At this point, when a rebel delegation came to parley with Ou-Barka, he made as if to welcome them, then had them slaughtered out of hand.[24] Unwittingly, he had dug his own grave. Among those killed were kinsmen of his own nephews, the sons of Aïcha Termoun, who, incensed at what they deemed to be outright treachery on the *qayd*'s part, waylaid him near a lonely ford on Oued Srou and chopped his head off.[25]

Thus was removed from the scene yet another of those border barons that the Atlas Mountains have so frequently nurtured. For their prominent part in the disturbances subsequent to Ou-Barka's assassination, Sultan Moulay 'Adallah had the Ayt Yoummour promptly deported to the Meknes area. As they continued to stir up strife, however, they were eventually exiled to the Haouz, where, to this day, they are still to be found, constituting a small, *tamazight*-speaking island in an Arabophone sea.[26] Thus do they pass out of the limelight. Meanwhile, this history of the Atlas Berbers would have been incomplete without further documentation from an unexpected quarter.

An English renegade at large in the Atlas

Thanks to Magali Morsy, a gifted Anglophile French researcher, a little-known volume, destined to cast fresh light on operations against Atlas Berbers at the end of Moulay Ismaïl's reign and its immediate aftermath, was saved from relative oblivion in the early 1960s.

Being the memoirs of an Englishman captured by the notorious "Sallee rovers," it was enticingly entitled *The History of the Long Captivity and Adventures of Thomas Pellow in South-Barbary*.[27] Though purportedly "written by himself," the story was probably dictated to a professional writer—hence the charmingly deformed Moroccan names with which the book is studded. Pellow was lucky to have escaped the usual hazards attendant upon captivity in Barbary, and served in the sultan's army under renegade status. He thus found himself in the unique position of visiting parts of the Atlas, albeit as a soldier, where no European had ever set foot, all in the course of no fewer than eight campaigns.

However, Pellow's share in suppressing a major rising in the Tadla, probably in 1730, under Moulay Ismaïl's successor (Moulay 'Abdallah) is his most revealing achievement. His account clears up the mystery surrounding Sidi Youssef, then head of the Zaouit Ahansal, who is thought to have died about this time "under suspicious circumstances ... during the troubles following death of Moulay Ismaïl [1727]."[28] Pellow's force joined the main body in Kasba Tadla, where he "found Moulay 'Abdallah diverting the time plundering the country and murdering his subjects." That these Sharifian activities were not entirely gratuitous there is little doubt, as "Joseph Haunsell, a noted conjurer, [had] stirred up rebellion in and about Tedlah, [he] having before them shown many magic pranks ... [claiming he was] invulnerable from Moulay 'Abdallah"s shot."[29]

This refers to the influential marabout Sidi Youssef Ahansali, who, despite earlier association with the *makhzan*, had now fallen from grace with the present sultan and was in open revolt, which reflects the relative importance of Zaouit Ahansal at this time. Its spiritual leader was seen by many as having inherited the legacy of Dila', and fulfilling henceforth a leadership role among the Senhaja Berbers. Unwise counsels appear to have prevailed in Sidi Youssef's entourage, effectively compromising his chances of success. Throwing tactical caution to the wind, he was prevailed upon to venture down onto the Tadla plain with a scratch force of some 200,000 Berber tribesmen, rarely at their best away from their hills, only to find further progress blocked by the *mhalla*, some 80,000 strong (according to Pellow) under 'Abd es-Salam Doukkali.[30]

The result was a foregone conclusion. Once the rabble had scattered like chaff they were relentlessly pursued by the sultan's forces up into the mountains—no doubt Jbel R'nim—where "we by the sword and musket killed vast numbers in a very little time."[31] Youssef Ahansali himself was captured, probably with the help of some Ayt 'Attab tribesmen collaborating with the *makhzan*,[32] and taken into custody, no doubt aware of the fate that lay in store. Sure enough, after his hands and feet had been cut off, he was put out to die on a dung heap and his body was eventually devoured by dogs.[33]

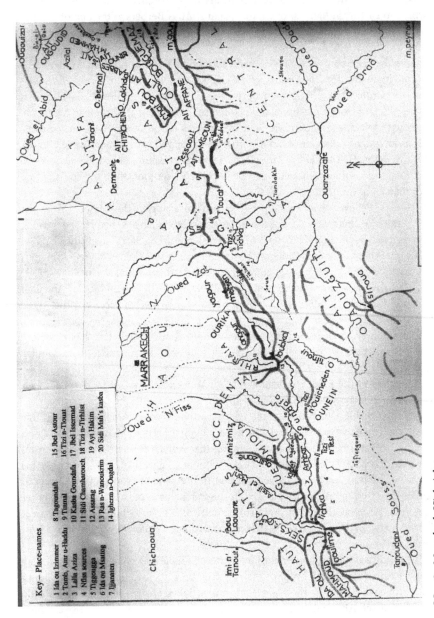

Key – Place-names

1 Ida ou Izimmer	8 Tagoundaft	15 Jbel Asatour
2 Tomb, Amr u-Haddu	9 Timnal	16 Tizi n-Tlouat
3 Lalla Aziza	10 Kasba Goundafa	17 Jbel Issermad
4 Nfiss sources	11 Sidi Chamharouch	18 Tizi n-Tirhlist
5 Tiggougga	12 Assarag	19 Ayt Hakim
6 Ida ou Mantog	13 Ras n-Wanoukrim	20 Sidi Mah's kasba
7 Ijjanaten	14 Ighcrm n-Ougdal	

Map 2: Marrakesh High Atlas.

10

Berber Backlash

As we have seen, hardly had Moulay Ismaïl's death become common knowledge than the country erupted into violence and civil war, with the Black Guard, to all intents and purposes a state within the state, powerful enough to play a major political role. This state of affairs accounts for the startling series of palace revolutions, engineered by these king-makers, which saw successive sons of the great sultan whisked in and out of office at disconcerting speed. Over the years 1727–57, Moulay 'Abdallah, although deposed five times, was to prove the most consistent performer in this startling game of musical chairs.[1]

Black goats and white rams

Taking advantage of the collapse of *makhzan* authority, *'abid* deserters and levies from the Arab *jaysh* tribes organized themselves on semi-military lines and had the free run of the Atlantic plain.[2] In the meantime, isolated and abandoned, most of Ismaïl's border fortresses fell into disrepair, their unpaid garrisons left to forage for supplies in the surrounding countryside, incurring the wrath of local tribes, or allowing themselves to be absorbed into the *tamazight*-speaking environment.[3]

Needless to say, the mountaineers, taking time by the forelock, seized this opportunity to recover their freedom. Involved in ceaseless broils and upsets, however, the central authorities were in no fit to state to oppose them effectively, as became evident when two columns, sent into Jbel Fazaz from the fortress of Adekhsan, were overwhelmed and beaten back, the soldiers sent home as naked as the day they were born.[4] That leaving an adversary alive but destitute would impress his companions more than actually killing him was a broadly accepted truism among mountain Berbers.[5] Meanwhile, after each brief sojourn in his royal palace, Moulay 'Abdallah would find refuge with the Berber plains tribes at the foot of Jbel Fazaz and elicit their support to restore him to the throne. Now he would reside among the Zemmour, now near El Hajeb with the Gerouan. Gradually finding himself in the position of cat's paw between the "black goat" and the "white ram" (*'abid* guard versus Berber tribesman), he soon learnt how to play one off against the other.[6] During this period of extreme peril, the 'Alawid dynasty was fortunate in that the usual feuding and raiding between tribes prevented the Senhaja Berbers from uniting to retake Fez and Meknès.

This lack of cohesion had to be cultivated, such as when the sultan hired the services of Mohammed ou 'Aziz, paramount *qayd* of the Ayt Idrassen, as a makeweight against rival Berber groups.[7] The age-old principle of *divide ut regnes* seldom had greater significance than at this time. Another powerful confederation, the Gerouan had crossed the Moulouya and penetrated Jbel Fazaz where they clashed with the Ayt Idrassen. Through Machiavellian diplomacy, the sultan not only saved face and throne, but managed to keep the cauldron sufficiently on the boil to weaken both contenders, thus preserving a precarious balance of power among those warlike communities.[8] However, the sultan's brinksmanship could not conceal the fact that, in the final analysis, it was a sad reign, with the burden of misery lying heaviest upon the common people, their sufferings being sufficient "to whiten the hair of infants at the breast."[9]

Henceforth, "divide and rule" would be the grand Sharifian watchword. The sultan had to detect the chink in the Berber armor, for only at this price could he hold his would-be attackers at arm's length. For example, early on in the next reign, that of the more sagacious Sidi Mohammed ben 'Abdallah (1757–90), intermittent fighting between Idrassen and Gerouan had built up to a climax, the former being worsted. Later, the Beni Mtir, briefly aided by the sultan's 'abid guard against the Gerouan and Oudaïa, were seen as having outlived their usefulness, whereupon, by a sudden reversal of alliances, they were brutally dislodged from the Tigrigra and Gigou valleys in the Middle Atlas.[10]

Moulay Yazid and the Imhiwash

Meanwhile Moulay Yazid, the sultan's eldest son, was becoming a thorn in his father's flesh. As headstrong as he was generous, and an excellent horseman to boot, this dashing prince, "brilliant but half-mad,"[11] had become such a favorite with the Fazaz tribes—especially the Gerouan—that his father accused him of championing rebellious Berbers. So adept had he become at causing trouble that, in 1770, fearful of the parental wrath, he sought refuge at the remote zaouia of Ayt Ishaq in Ayt Oumalou country,[12] where the marabout, Sidi Mohammed ou Nasser Amhaoush,[13] welcomed him with open arms. This is the first reference we find to the Imhiwash lineage of saints, as successors of the Dila'yin. They appear to have achieved untold influence over the Senhaja Berbers, reuniting them largely by dint of their magnetism and charisma, miracle-working, prophesying, and sheer quackery, rather than by their skill at leading Berber warriors to battle.[14]

In fact, through their ceaseless intrigues, coupled with undoubted leadership qualities, the Imhiwash were the ones who really put a sting into the long-delayed Berber backlash. The presence in the Atlas of a member of the royal line, though, somehow crystallized latent ambitions to switch from the spiritual to the temporal and stage a rerun of the Dila'yin venture. Thus, succumbing to the blandishments of the marabout and his client-tribe, the Ishqern,[15] and encouraged also by the Gerouan, Moulay Yazid had the crown handed to him on a platter.

To punish them for having incited his son to rebel, the sultan raided the Gerouan encampments near Azrou, killed 500 of them, and deported to the Meknes area those he had made prisoner. Upon seeking his father's pardon, Moulay Yazid was ordered forthwith to make the *hajj* ("pilgrimage") to Mecca to keep him from further mischief. His son out of the way, Sidi Mohammed made a commendable effort, on both the domestic and foreign fronts, to restore the country's unity and dignity to a semblance of the conditions obtaining under his grandfather, Moulay Ismaïl. His hands full with curtailing the more disruptive efforts of *al-fitna al-barbariya* ("Berber tribal chaos"), he was the first in a line of Moroccan sultans whose chief occupation was to effect periodic military excursions to collect taxes and suppress revolts, and who, "the existence of *blad as-siba* henceforth accepted as an inevitable fact,[16] ... had to spend part of their lives trotting around with their camp and imperial parasol in the more inaccessible regions of their kingdoms."[17] In so far as his expeditions all concern Berber tribal areas, a summary of the principal ones is called for.

Anxious to stage a repeat performance of his grandfather's exploits against the Ayt Oumalou of Jbel Fazaz, who had been steadily reconsolidating their power, he had marched south in 1187H./1772–3 with high hopes, his army divided into three detachments. A battle plan that had worked under the mighty Ismaïl could only enjoy a successful second innings if sufficient, seasoned forces were mustered. This was not the case. The army that Sidi Mohammed was taking into the field was a mere shadow of its former self, thereby exposing each of its relatively weak columns to piecemeal defeat. On reaching Adekhsan with the main body, only to find the country empty of inhabitants, the sultan was reluctant to advance deeper into the Fazaz on hearing that the rest of his forces had come to grief. The Ayt Idrassen contingents under *qayd* Ould-Mohammed Ou-'Aziz had in fact been defeated at Tansmakht, near the sources of Oued Gigou, while another detachment, sent to the neighborhood of the former zaouia of Dila', had shamefully capitulated to local tribesmen.[18] For the mountain Berbers, revenge must have seemed all the sweeter. This was the first in a series of serious reverses suffered by the 'Alawid sultanate at the hands of Fazaz Berbers.

Sensibly deciding that his forces were not equal to such stern encounters, Sidi Mohammed now switched his attention to the Atlantic coast, founding Mogador (Essaouira) in 1765. He also devoted time and energy to keeping the peace between the more unruly Arab- and Berber-speaking plains tribes. Thus, in 1781, did the restless Gerouan again experience the pendulum-like swing of his tribal policy when they were hustled back into the mountains for their pains, while the year after, the Ayt Idrassen, now back in favor, were sent to curb a revolt of their Zemmour cousins.[19]

In H.1196–7/1783, Sidi Mohammed's parasol followed in Moulay Ismaïl's footsteps along the Berber trail for the last time. Just as his grandfather headed for the Tafilalt to put down sedition, so did he now have to repair to the very cradle of the dynasty, where his uncle, the Sharif Moulay Hassan ben Ismaïl, at loggerheads with the *shurafa* of Sijilmassa, had allied himself with the Ayt 'Atta and Ayt Yaflman—a most formidable combination if ever there was one. On this particular expedition the sultan achieved some measure of success and "forced the Berbers to evacuate the *qsur* and sent his uncle off to house-arrest in Meknes." The *Istiqça* chronicler then claims, though failing to mention which specific 'Atta and Yaflman components were concerned, that the sultan put an end to their depredations, appointing as governor to rule over them one of his most trusted *qayds*.[20]

Moulay Yazid and the power vacuum

Returning to the Gharb by the same circuitous route as that followed by his illustrious forebear, Sidi Mohammed likewise made extremely heavy weather of a November crossing of the Tizi n-Telouat, losing part of his *mhalla* in a snowstorm.[21] In 1790, Sidi Mohammed died and was succeeded by his unsatisfactory son, Moulay Yazid. By now well into middle age and with his wild oats presumably safely behind him, he might have been expected to have matured sufficiently to discharge his duties as monarch.[22] Not two years had elapsed, however, before he was slain in a skirmish with his brother, Moulay Hisham, who had set himself up as sultan in the southern capital of Marrakesh. And yet, for a few intoxicating weeks after Sidi Mohammed's death, prospects of an Amazigh-friendly sultanate were no doubt foremost in peoples' minds in Jbel Fazaz. As one man, the Ayt Oumalou, in more or less open revolt for the past decade, had declared for Moulay Yazid and, headed by their ambitious leader, Amhaoush, converged on Meknes to swear allegiance to the new suzerain. "To Amhaoush the sultan gave 10,000 douros and 100,000 to those that had accompanied him" as a generous handout in exchange for loyalty past and present.[23]

Times had indeed changed for hitherto irreconcilable highland Berbers to be involved in such a spontaneous demonstration of fealty to a reigning monarch who would undoubtedly favor their long-standing designs on the coveted lowland grazing-grounds of the *azaghar*. Fate decided otherwise. The former governor of Tafilalt, Moulay Sliman, succeeded in having himself proclaimed in Fez, though it took him five years, a period highlighted by feuds and competition between rival claimants to the throne, before the south acknowledged his suzerainty. The new sovereign soon asserted an attitude to refractory, semi-*jahiliya* ("pre-islamic") non-tax-paying tribes in marked contrast to that of his predecessor, the emphasis being on incessant punitive expeditions.[24] The Fazaz Berbers, though confident they could handle anything he cared to throw at them, decided this new ruler was a man to watch.

Turmoil on the Atlas marches

The balance of power had, in fact, shifted away from the shade of the imperial parasol in Meknes to the "land of the shadow"—Jbal Fazaz and its northward-facing valleys. Concurrently, fresh reshuffles on the tribal chessboard, having their genesis in the very bowels of the Atlas, were adding momentum to that centuries-old, dynamic northwesterly push of the Imazighen, for which the Ayt 'Atta were still "acting as the rearguard and south-eastern propeller."[25] As we have already seen, however, the rival Ayt Yaflman confederation, possibly in conjunction with some astute brinksmanship on the part of the 'Alawid *shurafa*, had succeeded in containing the 'Atta along Asif n-Imdghas and the Ghriss Valley.[26]

Nor had the northwest push of the Saharan nomads been slowed down by force alone. Internal dissensions, periods of epidemic and starvation, following hard on the heels of drought, especially during the period 1776–82,[27] had taken their toll. Throughout this period the Ayt 'Atta maintained their combat efficiency up to scratch through constant duels with the Ayt Merghad for the possession of the Todgha and Ferkla oases. Their way further north more or less blocked, they were thus consolidating their power in the foothills of the Saharan side of the High Atlas. A further development in this particular process came in 1818, when they succeeded in occupying the Tafilalt district and taking over the main terminus of the Saharan caravan trade.[28] By this time Sijilmassa lay in ruins, its role as caravan terminal usurped by a rival location—the *ssuq* at Abou 'Aam. Henceforth, dictated by new circumstances, the main 'Attaoui thrust, spearheaded by the desert-ranging Ayt Khebbash, would be southeast towards the oases of Gourara, Touat, and Tidikelt.[29]

Their sworn enemies, the tent-dwelling Ayt Yaflman, obliged to make do with sparse grazing on the less fertile south slopes of the Eastern High Atlas,[30] were beginning to feel the pinch as a result of over-pasturing. Informed by spies of a favored land of relatively cool forests, lush meadows, and snow-fed torrents north of the divide, the Ayt Yahya, for example, were waiting for the right moment to emigrate from the Todgha/ Kerdous area to the region north of Jbel Ma'asker. Likewise, the Ayt Sokhman, a southwesterly neighbor of the Yaflman, had expanded from their home turf on Jbel Kousser and Anergui[31] towards the oak and cedar forests around Aghbala and the grazing grounds of Azaghar Fal. Further east, the Ayt Izdeg were, like their Yahya kin, awaiting the first opportunity to cross Tizi n-Talghemt into the upper Moulouya.

To the thirsty nomad who had resolutely turned his back on the Sahara, the high Moulouya plain must have appeared as a promised land. Among these boundless reaches, where time and space seem to merge into some new, intangible dimension, he was to find more congenial territory. From the foothills on each side of this wedge of alfa-covered steppe, water descends in innumerable streams, or gurgles up from resurgent springs, fertilizing tracts of rich pasture land. From the rounded, gray-brown hills of Fazaz in the northwest to the snow-crested heights of Jbel 'Ayyashi[32] looming along the southern horizon, the eye of our Saharan migrant could travel through the clear air for over sixty miles. The first wandering clans to cross the Atlas invariably turned west, following the Moulouya[33] up over higher ground to its sources at Jbel Toujjit.

Fig. 15: Sheep and cattle in upper Moulouya; Jbel 'Ayyashi in the background.

Struggle for the upper Moulouya

To cope with extremes of temperature and heavy snowfall, for which their goatskin tents were totally inadequate, a low, flat-roofed house of mud-brick, stone, and cedar planks was developed, the offspring of the Saharan fortified dwelling house adapted to colder climatic conditions.[34] Further east amid the semi-desert expanses of the middle Moulouya, an architectural style reminiscent of the Saharan *qsar*, with massive mud walls, ornamented corner towers, and fortified gates, was retained by others. This, then, was the heart of inner Morocco, for possession of which the Senhaja tribes were vying as the curtain rose on the nineteenth century. It is difficult to unravel the confused sequence of events, the more so as oral accounts differ dramatically from those of the official chronicles.

Of these tribes the Ayt Ihand occupied a rugged, wooded strip of land near the Moulouya sources, to the north of which lay the territory of their Beni Mtir allies. To the east, the Ayt 'Ayyash extended from Talialit up Asif n-Ounzegmir to the *triq al-kbir* and 'Ayyashi foothills, which they shared with the Ayt Oufella. Further east, around Boula'joul, were the Beni Mtir, while the powerful Ayt Youssi tribe held the country along the vital Tafilalt–Fez lifeline, or *triq as-sseltan*.

The Ayt Idrassen constituted a substantial tribal alliance occupying a strategic area astride the main Atlas caravan routes, yet the sands were running out for them, their power soon to be eroded by the sultan, their lands coveted by rivals.[35]

Moulay Sliman: A peripatetic sultan

The new sultan crossed the Fazaz on several occasions at the head of his *mhalla*. Moulay Sliman, however, in the words of Terrasse, "wore himself out on rounds of pacification."[36] No less than six times did the dust clouds of his marching columns herald his approach to the waiting Berbers.[37] Despite his incessant activity, though, he was unable to make any lasting impression on the tribes. His armies, no longer of the same quality as those that Ismaïl had led into the fray, proved a poor match for their sturdy opponents, who, hardened by constant practice, had developed their own brand of warfare based on night infiltration, swift raid, feigned retreat, and lethal ambush. Oral tradition has retained a somewhat confused record of Moulay Sliman's expeditions:

> The first sultan whose campaigns are remembered here is Moulay Sliman. But recollections of him are hazy. The only campaign of his which the Moulouya tribes can relate in detail is the one he undertook in Ayt Ihand country;[38] whereas, in actual fact, Moulay Sliman attempted on several occasions to subjugate the mountaineers, abandoning each attempt after the defeat of his armies.[39]

Vague and inaccurate though these reports may be, Moulay Sliman's campaigns were obviously of a repetitive pattern, while the tactics employed by both sides underwent little evolution. The unwieldy *mhalla*, with its Black Guard nucleus, Arab levies, and contingents from lowland Berber tribes, occupied several acres of countryside, as, preceded by outriders and scouts, and renegades dragging a battery of cannon, it looted its way across the land. Its impending arrival was understandably bad news for any homesteads or villages that had the misfortune to lie in its path. In this respect, an old Moroccan proverb reminds us that there are three unstoppable things in life: fire, flood, and the *makhzan*. Even if village elders fearfully sent out presents in cash and kind, then, in the Sharifian presence, struck attitudes of servility, they were never sure of emerging unscathed from the ordeal. Once the *mhalla* had moved on, the sultan's host might, in the best of circumstances, merely leave the village poorer by a few poultry, sheep, girls, or bags of grain; in a worst case scenario, there would be smouldering ruins and headless corpses to bewail.[40]

True, the *mhalla* on the march with the monarch in its midst, incarnated *dar al-mulk*, the "house of power," and being perceived as an instrument of "grace and terror" combined,[41] was both respected and dreaded. Naturally, faced with a scorched earth policy, the usual Berber plan was for the tribes to abandon their villages and take refuge in secluded bolt-holes: forested ravines, deep caves, and/or rocky hillsides. For all the *mhalla*'s advantage, it was a hard game for the sultan to play, especially once the Berber hills were reached and the initiative then lay with a nimble foe who rarely failed to exploit the least tactical advantage.

Meanwhile, a sea change had occurred within the armed forces. From 1792 to 1798, Idrassen components such as the Zemmour and the Beni Mtir formed the mainstay of the lowland Berber contingents of the Moroccan army. Two notables of the last-named tribe, in fact, achieved prominence: Mohammed Ou'aziz and Ibn Nasser el-Mtiri, the latter becoming "the effective commander-in-chief of Moulay Sliman's forces."[42]

However, the arrangement was too good to last, given the sultan's habitual penchant for a policy of compromise. Once pacification of wayward tribes in the Tadla had been achieved, as far as the sultan was concerned, dependence on this *amazigh* tribe was no longer necessary. He correspondingly recruited large numbers of men from the Cherarga, Ouled Jama, and Beni Hassan tribes into his *jaysh* contingents, an emphasis on Arabic-speakers that "tended to involve [the sultan] in tribal antagonism which opposed some of the Arab tribes to the lowland Berbers."[43]

A first expedition against the Ayt Oumalou, under *qayd* El-Hakmaoui, reached Adekhsan in 1800/1, only to be lured into the nearby wooded hills, encircled, and forced to surrender. The Berbers returned the *qayd* to his sultan, without touching a hair of his head.[44]

Come 1803, Moulay Sliman took the field in person, determined to cut the Idrassen down to size. Apart from a desire to protect his communications with Tafilalt from the depredations of brigand bands, appointment of an unpopular *qayd* had yet again antagonized the Idrassen, who set up their own man, a certain Bou'azza Ibn Nasser.[45] Directing his actions mainly against the Ayt Youssi, the monarch utterly defeated them near Ahlil, on Oued Gigou, and allotted a tract of their territory to the devious Gerouan. A Sharifian *razzia* ("pillaging expedition") along the upper Moulouya then accounted for most of the Ayt 'Ayyash livestock, while some elements of the tribe were carted off to the plains near Fez.[46]

Now that the crumbling Idrassen confederation had been dealt another blow, their Ayt Oumalou neighbors, especially the Beni Mguild on the high moors around

Aghbalou n-Serdan, sat up and took notice. Initially on friendly terms with the Idrassen, the Beni Mguild had been cutting their neighbors' lines of communication and interfering in their seasonal migration.

Matters came to a head in 1810. A full-size cavalry confrontation between the rival confederacies, near Sidi 'Ayad on Oued Tanfit, resulted in a disaster for the Idrassen contingents, the brunt of the defeat being borne by the Ayt 'Ayyash. The limbs of this once powerful tribal body were scattered far and wide,[47] between their Anzegmir *qsur* and their brothers in exile near Fez.[48]

Making a tardy appearance on the scene, Moulay Sliman hypocritically offered his mediation. To prove that their victory over the Idrassen had been no trick of fate, the Beni Mguild, especially their Irklaoun section, smartly escorted the *mhalla* away from the Moulouya.[49] By indirectly conniving at weakening the Ayt Idrassen, Moulay Sliman had all but eliminated his front line of defense against the mountain Berbers, now strengthened by the adhesion of the Gerouan[50] and Ayt Youssi to the Ayt Oumalou ensemble. Having, as it were, "shot himself in the foot," the sultan had to retrieve the situation at any cost, and headed up to Azrou.[51]

Also called "the Azrou affair," although the actual fighting took place in the environs rather than in the town itself, another account mentions a two-day action (28–29 April 1811), with the sultan, worsted on the first day, and the Ayt Yoummour and Idrassen arriving on the second day to put matters right.[52] The *'abid*s of Moulay Sliman's rearguard badly mauled, the Arabic speakers in his ranks jealous and suspicious of their "tame" Berber comrades who had saved the day,[53] it was a demoralized *mhalla* that struggled back to Fez.

In the interval, various developments paved the way for that inevitable confrontation. In April 1814, when Bou-Bker Amhaoush, anxious to keep up the pressure on the *makhzan*, sent his Ayt Oumalou to attack Meknes, they were stopped by *qayd* Mohammed Oua'ziz and his tribal levies. The ensuing encounter encompassed the further discomfiture of the Idrassen, their *qayd* being killed in the debacle. The Ayt Yoummour and Beni Mtir were permanently weakened, but the Zemmour, initially on their side, and who fled the battlefield, were to emerge shortly as the strongest component of the lowland Berbers, their leader, Ibn el-Ghazi, becoming warlord, king-maker, and honorary *qayd* of the Fazaz Berbers at one fell swoop.[54] In all likelihood, this unscrupulous schemer established contact with Bou-Bker Amhaoush about this time, probably through their both being active members of the *tariqa darqawiyya*—an ascetic religious brotherhood that, under Moulay el-'Arabi ed-Darqawi,[55] had become powerful in Morocco, with a widespread following among the Fazaz Berbers.

The brotherhood was now in the throes of a "traditionalist revival,"[56] the focus of their action simultaneously switching from the spiritual to the temporal. There is evidence that its chief, Moulay el-'Arabi, incited Bou-Bker Amhaoush to launch the Ayt Oumalou against the sultan's *mhalla* at the first opportunity;[57] the indications are that the Zemmouri, Ibn el-Ghazi, was also privy to the plot. In the meantime, although the Ayt Oumalou were left to their own devices, the Moroccan sovereign did everything in his power to pressure them. An economic blockade of the Fazaz was thus rigorously enforced, with fines inflicted on traders caught smuggling grain to the uncouth hillmen. Undaunted by this unprecedented campaign of discriminatory oppression, the latter maintained the tempo of the northwest push on their lowland cousins, as harsh winters increasingly forced them to send their flocks into the *azaghar*.

Meanwhile, in the wake of earlier epidemics and an economic slowdown attributable to the Napoleonic Wars, came famine, and in 1818, the plague. Thus, against this unfavorable politico-economic background, the stage was set for the Battle of Lenda. Firm in his resolve to subdue the Fazaz tribes, Moulay Sliman mustered an army of some 60,000 for this fateful expedition.

In May 1819, a two-pronged advance was planned. As suggested by *qayd* Ibn el-Ghazi, crown prince Moulay Ibrahim with the main body, including the *'abid* Guard and levies from Arabic-speaking *jaysh* tribes, was to head south from Fez, cross the Fazaz, and join his father, who would have come up from Marrakesh with the Haouz tribes, near Adekhsan. This was an awe-inspiring deployment of military strength, complete with artillery, though many of its components, affected by recent privation and illness, were little more than a demoralized rabble, nursing a paranoid distrust of the Amazigh elements in their midst.[58] Moulay Ibrahim, who had been his father's regent in Fez, now took the field. Through olive groves to Sefrou tramped the cumbersome force, along the *triq as-sseltan* to the uplands of the Gigou Valley before following the foot of the Fazaz range to Timhadit. When the Berbers heard that the imperial army was on the way, they rallied from all points of the compass.

The Battle of Lenda (or "Zaïan incident")

Up to this point, the *mhalla* would have been safe from surprise attack, the soldiers thankful to enjoy the fresh mountain air. West of Timhadit, however, the Fazaz range reaches 2,400 m in Jbal Hayyan, separated from Jbel Koubbat by Tizi L'afit.[59] This was the first high pass the army had to negotiate to reach the wooded knoll of Ras Tarsha, overlooking the Bekrit hollow in the heart of Beni Mguild country.

Afterwards, escorted by Ayt 'Arfa guides from Agerssif,[60] they continued to Senoual, before descending towards Adekhsan by a succession of long cedar-clad spurs, interspersed with deep-cut valleys and gorges, through which race the headstreams of Wansifen (Oum er-Rbia'). Somewhere along Oued Srou, the *mhalla's* nemesis lay in wait. At the instigation of Bou-Bker Amhaoush, a large irregular force of eager warriors was gathering.

To an observer stationed near the Tinteghalin pass, the scene is at once harmonious, peaceful, and verdant. On the right, Oued Srou meanders lazily from the gorges of Talat Oukidar; in the center foreground stretches the green, fertile plain of Lenda, backed by a further sweep of green reaching up to stately cedars on the far northern skyline. Moulay Sliman, who had arrived from Marrakesh, was plundering the fields along the Wansifen and its tributaries, literally inviting attack. Unsurprisingly, the Fazaz tribes rallied to defend their bread basket. At this juncture, Moulay Ibrahim's army emerged unimpeded from the Oued Srou gorges and linked up with the Marrakesh contingents under his father, encamped at Lenda. The stage was set for a famous fight.

The Zaïan were the first to react, descending from the hills to interfere with the destruction of their fields. Moulay Sliman despatched his lowland Berber forces to head them off and there was an indecisive skirmish. Under cover of darkness, *qayd* Ibn el-Ghazi contacted the Zaïan and it was agreed that the Berbers serving with the Sharifian army would only fire blank rounds at their Ayt Oumalou kin. The next day, the Arabic-speaking elements in the *mhalla* suffered numerous casualties at the hands of the Ayt Oumalou, while their Amazigh colleagues indulged in innocuous powder-play with their "wild" counterparts.[61] At this point, Bou-Bker Amhaoush sent a message to the sultan, suggesting that the *mhalla* leave the area without further ado: a three-day truce was decided upon and, initially, all was peaceful. This, however, went counter to Moulay Sliman's determination to capture the rogue marabout who had proved so conspicuously successful at federating the Fazaz tribes. The last thing the sultan needed was a Dila'-style reunification of the Berber bloc.

Now occurred a despicable incident destined to bring events to a dramatic conclusion. A delegation of Berber women, children, and elderly men arrived at the Sharifian camp to beg the sultan to leave them in peace and depart. The monarch impatiently fobbed them off on his son, Moulay Ibrahim, who, apparently acting on *qayd* Ibn el-Ghazi's recommendation, had the whole party shot out of hand. Such was the impact of this unspeakable deed on both "tame" and "wild" Berbers that negotiations were immediately resumed between them, the former intimating that they would join the latter in the event of a resumption of hostilities.[62]

The following afternoon, incensed by this massacre, leaders from among the mountain Berbers selected their best horsemen and staged a surprise attack on the *mhalla*.[63] Doubtful of the loyalty of his lowland Berber contingents, Moulay Sliman ordered forward his Arabic-speaking levies. No sooner had the shooting started than the Zemmour and Idrassen elements, under *qayd*-s Ibn el-Ghazi and Hassan ou Hammou, decided to change sides. All afternoon the battle raged, the Arabic-speaking divisions losing heavily. By nightfall, the *mhalla*, as a combat force, was reduced to the Oudaïa and Black Guard component, while Prince Moulay Brahim had been mortally wounded. The end came before midnight: the *'abids* melted away into the darkness and the sultan was taken prisoner, while his camp offered a haul of booty that far exceeded the plunderers' wildest expectations. Three of the army's cannon were captured, one of them being dragged over the mountains to faraway Tounfit.[64]

The Fazaz Berbers had won hands down. They refrained, however, from cutting off the sultan's head. Though captured, Moulay Sliman received the red-carpet treatment from tribesmen, mindful of his spiritual authority as *amir al-muminin* ("Commander of the Faithful"). One account claims that the royal captive's flight was facilitated by a single Berber "who still retained a semblance of respect for the sultan,"[65] or perhaps he saw the monarch as the ultimate bargaining chip? An English writer observes that:

> Berber respect for their Imam led his captors to treat him with great respect, even though they had been fighting his armies. The women crowded round to kiss the hem of his garments; the men begged his pardon, and escorted him back to his capital, Meknes.[66]

According to oral tradition, the sultan managed to flee in the general rout, and was saved by the Ayt Bou Attia, a section of the Ayt 'Arfa, who for long kept a slipper lost by

Fig. 16: Zaouit Si Hamza, on the southern slopes of Jbel 'Ayyashi.

Moulay Sliman as he was mounting his horse. On returning to Meknes and finding a new-born son, he called him Moulay Srou in memory of the disaster that had befallen his army.[67] The tribesmen ran amok as far as the walls of Meknes, their enthusiasm and lust for loot fired by this decisive success.

Their ardor became all the stronger on learning that Moulay Sliman, smarting from his recent defeat, had lured scores of Idrassen notables within the walls of Meknes with promises of handouts and forgiveness, only to place them promptly under lock and key.

With the capital now hard pressed by hordes of victorious mountaineers, acting in total concord, the sultanate seemed to be on its last legs.[68] Through the mediation of *murabit* 'Abdallah Ibn Hamza el-'Ayyashi (from Zaouit Si Hamza), the prisoners were released early in 1820, though Berber pressure on Meknes persisted unabated. Worse still, unrest in Fez urged the sultan to head there in a rash night march, the *mhalla* harried every inch of the way, despite the presence of the above-mentioned Hamzaoui marabout.

Once in Fez, Moulay Sliman managed to restore some semblance of order. His exactions against the Berbers, however, knew no let-up and "acquired a tinge of racial antagonism."[69] Advised by one of his counsellors to reside in Marrakesh, a humiliated and dispirited sultan accordingly moved to his southern capital. Yet trouble flared up in Fez again shortly after, aided and abetted by Bou-Bker Amhoush who, together with the Sharif of Ouazzan and Moulay el-'Arabi Darqawi, had decided to overthrow the

'Alawids. These dignitaries drew up a document destituting Moulay Sliman and replacing him with a certain Moulay Brahim, son of Moulay Yazid who had earlier unsuccessfully attempted to establish a Berber-backed sultanate. Interestingly, the three conspirators claimed Idrissi descent, "the plot thus assuming the proportions of an Idrissi revolt, with, arguably, an unavowed attempt to install a new dynasty."[70]

By a stroke of luck, Moulay el-'Arabi Derqawi, head of the *tariqa darqawiyya* in Morocco and ringleader of this dynastic conspiracy, was captured by *makhzan* soldiers, thus placing a trump bargaining-card in the sultan's hands. Bou-Bker Amhaoush was informed that dire misfortune would befall his colleague unless the sieges of Meknes and Fez were raised. Bowing to necessity, the maraboutic leader headed back into the hills.[71]

No doubt *qayd*s Ibn el-Ghazi and Hassan ou Hammou shared little common ground with Bou-Bker Amhaoush. Inspired, according to one observer, by a form of "right-wing regionalism,"[72] they appear to have been anxious to recreate a *makhzan* more in keeping with their own personal ambitions, while Amhaoush was more concerned with apocalyptic preoccupations, prophesying the rebirth of a resplendent Lenda, heralding the countdown to Doomsday in which needy mountaineers would acquire wealth.[73] Concerning their rank and file, brilliant tacticians though the Fazaz Imazighen may have been, they were out of their element when it came to siege warfare, walled towns, and the finer points of negotiation and diplomacy. Nor were they any more successful as king-makers: two successive puppet-sultans, nephews of Moulay Sliman, were proclaimed in Meknes, but proved equally short-lived, the latter being finally banished by his uncle to Tafilalt.[74]

Fig. 17: Village upstream from Amellago, Asif Ghriss gorge (Ayt Merghad).

The Battle of Lenda set the seal on Moulay Sliman's military ambitions, while understandably granting exaggerated importance to a perceived Berber threat to the peace and quiet of the 'Alawid sultanate. Throughout the next two reigns, the mountaineers were quietly permitted to consolidate their gains, as their resistance vis-à-vis the sultanate marked time, as it were, rendering the sultan's communications between Marrakesh and either of his two northern capitals sometimes precarious.

11

Dawn of the Great *Qayd* Era

Fortunately for the 'Alawid sultanate, the Fazaz Berbers, united for a fleeting moment under the aegis of Bou-Bker Amhaoush, gradually frittered away their strength in futile rivalries. Tribes such as the Beni Mtir, which had been fortunate enough to gain a toehold on the longed-for plains north of Fazaz, guarded hard-won gains against the encroachments of their expansion-minded kinsmen. They even openly sought the sultan's support.

On the face of things, the price the sultan charged for his help amounted to little more than their acknowledging his nominal suzerainty through the supply of gifts (*hediya*) and contingents of *mujahidin* to oppose Christian incursions as and when wanted. There was, however, a significant development: the nomination, by sultan Moulay 'Abd er-Rahman (1822–59), of three *qayds* to be his official representatives among the Beni Mtir, an important tribe close to Fez.[1] Each of these *qayds*, duly authorized and backed by the sultan, could be expected to act in a Trojan Horse capacity, whereby the *makhzan*, even in its most diluted form, would seep through to the innermost citadels of *blad siba*.[2] Results did not always live up to expectations. None the less, the appearance of these dignitaries must, in some cases, have been unwelcome to freedom-loving Berbers, upsetting as it did their basically democratic clan structure which had survived for over two millennia.

From village chief to village bully

Each tribe, each clan, each section entrusted its assembly of graybeards (*jemma'*) with the running of its day-to-day affairs according to Berber customary law (*izerf*), the assembly being presided over by a sheikh (*amghar*), elected on an annual basis from among its more prominent members. His role might be purely administrative, or, possibly, combined with such noble tasks as organizing defense against and/or raiding neighboring groups. Some tribes would elect a paramount *amghar* in wartime; others, such as the Ayt Yahya of Tounfit, appointed two separate chiefs: one, the *amghar n-teqbilt*, solely concerned, as his name implies, with summoning tribal gatherings, and the *amghar n-tzemalt*, or chief of the war camp, whose duty it was to lead tribal warriors into battle. Whatever the *amghar*'s functions, his tenure was usually limited to one year. Writes Captain Guennoun in his authoritative description of the Ayt Oumalou:

> The Berbers consider that privileges must never be awarded to any man or group, and insist on the yearly renewal of the *amghar*'s mandate, thereby preventing him

from achieving a position of predominance. Apart from a few exceptional cases, he is never required to stay in office for an extra year.[3]

The assemblies were chiefly concerned with keeping the chief's power within manageable limits according to their egalitarian principles.[4] In this case, however, some newly-appointed qayds, often ambitious opportunists to boot, were presuming to lord it over them in the sultan's name. Would not the temptation be to take advantage of the situation for the furtherance of their interests? Until he had built up his little coterie of loyal followers, however, the new qayd had to be both quick-witted and smooth-tongued to explain how and why he had accepted the appointment, whenever the assembly questioned his status and pointed out its incompatibility with the normal workings of a village-republic. As the aspiring tyrant's power base grew stronger, residual criticism would be silenced by more drastic means,[5] until one day, the jemma' would find itself playing second fiddle to an assertive individual who would only be paying lip service to the sultan. He would feel free to help himself from the community's livestock and harvest, any girl he fancied would be his for the taking, while an assembly of yes-men would tamely knuckle under to his arbitrary rule.

Thus did the sultan's attempts to retain at least nominal control over the remoter tribes of his far-flung empire nurture a bizarre brood of self-centered satraps, the most successful of whom are generally referred to as the "great qayds" (les Grands Caïds). From this odd assortment of tribal chieftains, some, such as Moha ou Hammou Zaïani, were eventually promoted to an exalted niche in Moroccan history. Some, such as El-Glaoui, experienced a quick drop from the Capitol to the Tarpeian Rock; others, like El-Mtouggui and Taïb Goundafi of the Western High Atlas, gently subsided into decline after a prolonged heyday, while yet others barely got off the ground in their giddy-minded attempts to reach the top.

Of the three dignitaries appointed by Moulay 'Abd er-Rahman over the Beni Mtir near Lhajeb, by the time Sidi Mohammed (1859–73) inherited the throne, qayd Mohammed ould-Chebli had managed to elbow his way upwards till his fief included not only all of the Ayt Idrassen but most of the other tribes that had found a home on the azaghar rim. Typically, however, he saw to it that the sultan intruded as little as possible in tribal affairs, which was hardly to the monarch's liking. If the man he had put in place failed to keep his side of the bargain, unless his tribe occupied relatively impenetrable country, which was not the case with the Beni Mtir, he could expect retribution sooner or later. Sure enough, qayd ould-Chebli's hour of reckoning would come during the reign of Moulay Hassan I.

As the last independent sovereign of the old Morocco, Moulay Hassan I has won near universal praise both for his sense of regal dignity and for the unstinting efforts he undertook to check tribalism and foreign interference. Painfully aware that since Moulay Ismaïl's time, most of the Atlas Mountains and Berber south had been enjoying a period of unquestioned and defiant independence, he did his utmost to restore the balance in the makhzan's favor. He first exercised his talent south of the Western High Atlas.

Fig. 18: Girl from Seksawa, with rope on a grass-cutting chore (Western High Atlas).

Bringing to book tribes and marabouts

A fresh wind was stirring the date palms of the Souss. The Semlali marabouts of Tazeroualt were moving back into the limelight under Sidi Lhouseynn and living on good-neighborly terms with the nearest *makhzan* official, *qayd* ʿAbdallah ou-Bihi in

Taroudannt. But the 'Alawid dynasty, uneasy as ever at the renaissance of earlier rivals, were determined to hold them in check, the more so as an old prophecy ominously warned, "In the beginning were the Filala; ultimately will come the Semlala!"[6] During an expedition to the Souss in 1864 to establish his father's nominal suzerainty, Moulay Hassan camped with his army on the borders of Tazeroualt territory and summoned Sidi Lhousseyn to appear before him to pay homage. To which the marabout replied, "I give you three days to go back whence you came!" The indignant prince replied in kind: "Well, I give you three years to yield!"[7] This piquant exchange concluded, he marched back over the Atlas in high dudgeon.

In this particular incident, *qayd* 'Abdallah ou-Bihi's attitude towards the *makhzan* had been judged highly suspicious by the sultan. Not only had he failed to use his influence with the marabout to bring him to his senses, but he was actually suspected of being in cahoots with him. Sure enough, shortly afterwards, the *qayd* welcomed Sidi Lhousseyn to Taroudannt with great pomp and friendliness and, instead of arresting him, entered into an alliance with the marabout against the *makhzan*. This scandalous flirtation proved the last straw. 'Abdallah ou-Bihi was summoned to Marrakesh by Sidi Mohammed and accused of plotting treason with the enemies of the realm. The choice given was a grim one: either the cutting edge of the executioner's scimitar or—as in Ancient Greece—poison. The *qayd* accordingly accepted a lethal glass of tea and then was taken back to die in his home kasba of the Haha country, north of the High Atlas (1868). His disappearance was to leave a vacuum in the area between Mogador and the Souss, soon to be filled by another great tribal chief, El-Mtouggui.[8] Apart from this shrewd stroke, Sidi Mohammed made no further attempts to interfere in local Berber affairs before the end of his reign.

Moulay Hassan was representing his father as *khalifa* in the Oued Noun area, when he heard of his death. Losing no time to assert his lawful claim to the throne, he dashed north to Marrakesh to have himself proclaimed sultan. Then, having gathered a small force of loyal troops, he marched on Meknes via the Atlantic plains, rightly expecting to meet with fierce resistance from the Berber-speaking tribes. For some centuries now, Meknes had come to be considered as the Berber capital of Morocco; the tribes, while not actually holding the city, exerted strong pressure on it by virtue of their occupation of the surrounding countryside. As usual, an Amazigh-elected candidate to the throne had been put forward, and the tribes had risen to oppose Moulay Hassan's advance. This time around, however, there was no charismatic leader at their head. The successors of Bou-Bker Amhaoush, falling on hard times and temporarily losing their Messianic touch, had withdrawn from Ishqern territory to Aghbala, a mountain-girt location well to the south.[9]

While the new sultan was doing his devotions at the Idrissi shrine of Moulay Idriss Zerhoun, a first unsuccessful attack was launched on the sultan's camp near Volubilis by a large Berber *harka*.[10] Moulay Hassan then entered the city of Meknes, and his army, while encamped outside its walls, repelled another vigorous onslaught. The sight of his vanguard pursuing the retreating tribesmen towards Lhajeb proved sufficient to cow the local Beni Mtir and Imejjat into subjection. However, those that the sultan demonized as "devils and riff-raff, the Berbers of the Beni Mguild," retreated deep into the Fazaz, defiant and unrepentant, and refused to come down and pay tribute.[11]

Moulay Hassan was by now on his way to Fez to win over a city habitually sympathetic to the 'Alawid sultanate. This delicate task satisfactorily concluded, he was able to take stock and consolidate. By giving government troops their first taste of victory in years, the new sultan had achieved no small measure of popularity with his army which he now endeavored to reorganize along modern lines. Modern rifles[12] were ordered from England and military instructors recruited in France, these improvements giving the Sharifian *mhalla* a decisive edge in firepower and combat-worthiness over rebellious Berber tribesmen still mainly equipped with swords, daggers, muzzle-loaders, and bayonets lashed to staves.

Having left his mark on the Imazighen around Meknes, it was against the renascent power of Tazeroualt that Moulay Hassan left Marrakesh in 1882 at the head of 40,000 men. Within a week or two, Sharifian control was re-established over the coastal strip as far south as Oued Dra'a, an area in which British traders Donald Mackenzie and James Curtis, not to mention Spanish gunrunners, who had no business to be there, had been particularly active of late.[13]

Though sending one of his sons with *hediya* to the sultan's camp as a gesture of appeasement, Sidi Lhousseyn sagaciously refused to leave the shelter of his *agadir* at Iligh. With an eye, no doubt, to keeping the marabout pent up indefinitely in the Tazeroualt hills, Moulay Hassan founded a garrison town at Tiznit, a little south of Oued Massa on the site of a former *makhzan* fortress.

Towards midsummer, sultan and marabout appear to have reached some sort of gentlemen's agreement. Partly out of respect for the Tazeroualt leader's piety and great age (eighty-four), partly through fear of a prestige-impairing setback should he attempt to reduce Sidi Lhousseyn by force, the sultan had opted in favor of diplomacy rather than violence. His southern marches secure, Moulay Hassan decided to take the "royal road" back to Fez via the Tadla and Fazaz—a feat which had not been accomplished since the 1730s. Unlike his less fortunate forbears, Moulay Hassan had a touch of greatness about him that enabled him to win laurels.

The rise of Moha ou Hammou Azayyi

Advancing past Kasba Tadla along the edge of the Atlas in the intense heat of late August, Moulay Hassan attacked the foothill tribe of Ayt Messat and forced them to pay tribute. The rumble of his approach reached the ears of a cunning, expansion-minded young chieftain, Moha ou Hammou, recently established at Khenifra. Since his brother Saïd was killed in battle in 1877, he had become *amghar* of the Imhazan clan, Ayt Harkat section, of the Zaïan (*izayyan*) tribe. When they were not campaigning to bring other Zaïan sections into their bailiwick, they earned a living from the toll they levied on travelers crossing the river.

Now Moha had far-reaching ambitions. Fully aware of the present disunity of his people and of their inability to contest a determined attack by the sultan's troops, he counted on being appointed *qayd* if he were to submit, with all the benefits such a position of power would bring him in the future. Accompanied by his cousin Bouhassous, he hastened down to the Tadla region, where the local population were being plundered by the Sharifian soldiery, and sought out the Sultan's camp. Introduced into the royal presence by his friend Sidi Ben Dawd Sherqawi, he knelt at the monarch's feet, while two Black Guardsmen held him down by the hood of his cloak. The sultan was favorably impressed by this spontaneous act of homage coming from the representative of an Ayt Oumalou tribe who also gave his liege lord a glowing account of the way he had been forcibly federating the clans around Khenifra.

The sultan is reported to have presented Moha with a fine black cloak, but he came away with more than that. Not only did he bear home in his *shukara* ("satchel") the regal document confirming his appointment as *qayd* over the Ayt Ya'qoub half of the Zaïan, but a detachment of 300 Sharifian infantry, under *qayd* Zouggati, marched back with him. This force would spearhead Moha's attack on any clan that failed to acknowledge his suzerainty.[14] Moulay Hassan had thus saved himself the expense of a costly campaign in Ayt Oumalou country, while the new *qayd* could be relied on to keep the peace among the Zaïan. In exchange, he would have to provide contingents to aid the sultan against the Zemmour tribe, next on the list for breaking in. Moha now possessed the necessary striking power to ensure his supremacy over the entire Zaïan confederation, while the monarch could flatter himself on having successfully neutralized one of his most formidable potential enemies.

In the higher interest of *divide ut regnes*, however, he simultaneously bestowed upon Mohammed Agelbi, one of Moha's rivals to the north, the *qayd*ship of the Ayt Sgougou.[15] As an exercise in *realpolitik* it deserved full marks.

Punishing unruly tribes

Like a thunderbolt, Moulay Hassan now fell on the Zemmour tribe, devastating their fields and collecting tax arrears. Marching on to the Meknes area, he headed up to Lhajeb on the Middle Atlas escarpment to cane the unfortunate Beni Mtir for having pillaged some Arabic-speaking communities in the *azaghar*. In the spring of 1886, the tireless monarch once more made for the Souss, which had erupted into revolt the year before. Many of the tribesmen were using Martini-Henry and Remington rifles that British traders Curtis and Mackenzie had been selling them. Now that the Tazeroualt marabout had joined in the *makhzan* game plan, the expedition achieved all its aims, reaching down as far as Tarfaya, chastising the rebellious tribes and forcing the gunrunners to re-embark and sail home. On its way back north, the *mhalla* had a skirmish with the Ida ou Tanan, an Atlas tribe above Agadir.[16]

The time had come for Moulay Hassan to tackle the dynasty's arch-enemies, the Fazaz Berbers. Thanks to his diplomacy, the Zaïan, whom Moha ou Hammou was busy uniting under his banner, could be relied upon for a little cooperation. Not only had the Beni Mtir, Gerouan, and most of the Ayt Youssi rallied the *makhzan*, but they could also be expected to send their quota of warriors to reinforce his *mhalla*.

This left only the powerful Beni Mguild to oppose his advance into the forested fortress of Fazaz. Deaf to the sultan's overtures, they intended to give Moulay Hassan as hot a welcome as possible. Then, once he had reached the headwaters of the Moulouya, the sultan would enter into the orbit of his most implacable foe, Sidi 'Ali Amhaoush, grandson of Sidi Bou-Bker. Moulay Hassan had an old score to settle with the Imhiwash marabouts. The story goes that Sidi 'Ali had come to Fez for his religious studies early on in Moulay Hassan's reign, but had hastened home after a fortnight on learning that the new sultan intended to make him atone for the insult inflicted on Moulay Sliman by a previous Amhaoush.

"The sultan of the mountains"

Sidi 'Ali Amhaoush is one of the most outstanding figures in Atlas history. Inheritor of the divine *baraka* that had already made his forebears famous, this astute politician, prophet, saint, miracle-worker, and womanizer rolled into one was the object of quasi-mystical veneration on the part of countless Atlas Berbers. The spiritual domain of this "Sultan of the mountains" extended from Ksiba in the west to Tounfit in the east. For the Ayt Ouirra, Ayt Sokhman, Ishqern, Ayt Ihand, and most of the Ayt Yahya, his maxim—"There is but one God, and no other Master!"—was the very expression of their creed of liberty, untrammeled by any restraining secular authority.

This spiritual descendent of the Berghaouata and Dila'yin could be confidently expected to champion their cause against overambitious *qayd* or meddling monarch. Among these wild hills where each man was a law unto himself, his was the supreme authority. Even the various village assemblies heeded his counsel, or accepted his mediation in time of conflict.[17]

Sidi 'Ali's activity centered on Aghbala n-Ayt Sokhman, the local marketplace where tribesmen from the surrounding heights would throng to buy and sell their wares. There might be some dispute to settle, some children or, more likely, women anxious to touch the hem of his garment and benefit from his *baraka*. Should he find one to his taste, the comely creature might be lured back to his residence at Bou Wattas. Sidi 'Ali was a great ladies' man, a trait he shared with his inveterate rival, Moha ou Hammou, chastity not being a prerequisite for saintliness in an area where sexual laxity sometimes prevailed. More in keeping with his role, on other occasions such as in 1888, when Moulay Hassan's great expedition was impending, the warriors would require exhortation, so Sidi 'Ali would give vent to prophetic utterances about the forthcoming discomfiture of the sultan's forces.[18]

The wheat fields around Fez had ripened to a rich, golden hue when the *mhalla* marched off into the mountains. This time, the monarch was taking no chances. First came the battle-tried Black Guards, the Oudaïa and Cherarga *jaysh* detachments, together with some companies under French officers equipped with repeating rifles, the *tabur al-'araba*, and the five guns of the artillery battery. Then came levies from the Haouz and Souss plains, men of doubtful fighting value, and finally, Berber levies, skilled enough at the type of warfare that lay ahead, but of unpredictable loyalty. Following Oued Feqran up to Agouraï, and Adaroush, Moulay Hassan then angled round to the deserted Tigrigra grazing land. Rather naïvely expecting to entrap him deep in the Fazaz in a rerun of Moulay Sliman's blunder, the pick of the Beni Mguild awaited him on the wooded knoll of Ras Tarcha.

Giving the forested country a wide berth, he kept to the open plateau, skirted Timhadit, and continued up the Gigou Valley, through the defile of Foum Kheneg without mishap. Lured down from their strong position on Ras Tarcha, the Beni Mguild harassed his column and staged a major attack against his rearguard at the cedar-girt Tarzeft pass. The Berbers were beaten off, and the *mhalla* emerged unscathed onto the broad vistas of the upper Moulouya. This show of strength favorably impressed the tribes, who sent numerous delegations to visit Moulay Hassan's camp at Tamayoust to pay tribute. All, that is, except for the kasbah of Ayt Oufella, whose inhabitants had to be bombarded into obedience. By and large, however, the Moulouya *qsur*-dwellers appeared only too willing to show their loyalty to the sultan whose visit might herald the return of law and order to a region too frequently at the mercy of predatory hill tribes. The campaign was developing into a military promenade. From Itzer, the *mhalla* moved to the market-center of Aghbalou n-Serdan, where it sojourned for a fortnight, giving the surrounding tribes time to prove their allegiance.

Many of the locals, who had fled on hearing of the sultan's approach, sent emissaries to sue for peace while the Beni Mguild came to terms with Moulay Hassan when he reached Alemsid, near the Moulouya source, on Sidi 'Ali's doorstep. By this time Ayt Yahya envoys from Tounfit had also arrived at his camp.[19] This latest development allowed the sultan to recover one of the antiquated cannon his grandfather had lost at Lenda. All this was particularly galling to Sidi 'Ali Amhaoush, the more so as the *mhalla* had camped with complete immunity near a certain *kerkur* ("cairn") which had not collapsed as the marabout had prophesied it would. We can picture the marabout, seated chin in hand under a cedar on Jbel Toujjit, from where he could spot the sultan's camp at Alemsid, pondering over this blow to his prestige and planning the next move.[20]

So far, Moulay Hassan's campaign had gone forward without a hitch. Apart from his own forceful determination, Moha ou Hammou's benevolent neutrality had undoubtedly deprived the Beni Mguild of support from the Zaïan, thereby proving instrumental in their recent reverse. The Zaïan chieftain, however, counseled the utmost caution in any dealings with Sidi 'Ali Amhaoush, whom he deeply mistrusted; a timely warning, it unfortunately went unheeded.

Amhaoush and the Aghbala ambush

No tribute had been forthcoming from the Ayt Sokhman, so, from Alemsid, Moulay Hassan despatched his uncle Moulay Srou—born, it will be recalled, shortly after the disaster at Lenda—with a 200-strong cavalry detachment to levy a fine and set up a *qayd* at Aghbala. The track runs straight from Alemsid to the edge of the plateau, through dense oak scrub at Tizi n-Tighanimin and down the Aghbala slope, affording countless opportunities for any would-be attacker. Somewhere along the way, Moulay Srou, by then a very old man, and undoubtedly born under an unlucky star, met his fate. Dragged off his horse, he was knifed by a Berber, while other members of the detachment were ruthlessly slaughtered.[21]

Compensation for this dastardly deed was never obtained. For some obscure reason, the sultan refrained from launching his avenging *mhalla* on Aghbala. More likely than not, his military advisers, especially Moha ou Hammou, dissuaded him from involvement in a tricky campaign over difficult terrain. Closer at hand were the Ayt Ya'qoub ou 'Isa, a section of the Ishqern tribe who could now be made to pay for their fidelity to Sidi 'Ali Amhaoush.

Thus, one tragic morning, did sword and torch bring death and destruction to the unsuspecting Ayt Ya'qoub ou 'Isa. As the *mhalla* sliced through their territory, according to one account, "young girls were raped and mothers with child disembowelled."[22] Rape has long been standard procedure, observed by invading armies the world over, but the disemboweling of pregnant woman introduces a fresh dimension of warfare to the surprised reader.[23] According to the reasoning of the time, however, this apparently excessive savagery may have been seen as a fitting act of retribution for the cowardly manner in which a Sharifian prince had been done to death with his escort. It was merely the Ayt Ya'qoub ou 'Isa's misfortune to have been selected as scapegoats.[24]

Although *makhzan* prestige had been restored by this blow of exemplary severity, recollections of his uncle's death, with vengeance as yet unvisited on his murderers, must have continued to badger the sultan's conscience. Something had to be attempted to make the Ayt 'Abdi answer for their crime. It is not clear from the chronicles when this occurred, but it was probably towards the close of the 1888 campaign that a punitive expedition was mounted from Takbalt, north of Ksiba.[25]

Moulay Hassan did not lead it in person. While Moha ou Saïd, newly-appointed *qayd* of the Ayt Ouirra,[26] was sent on ahead, Si Mohammed es-Sghir, the sultan's *wazir* in charge of military matters, found himself saddled with the unenviable task of seeking out the marabout and his henchmen in their mountain fastness. This entailed taking the *mhalla* south of the Tadla through a maze of rocky, wooded hills, cut up by innumerable ravines and gorges. Bent on mischief, the *mhalla* headed over the Tizi n-Ayt Ouirra and east up Oued L'abid while the inhabitants melted away into the hills. Having torched his own Aghbala house, Sidi 'Ali made for the heights with *qayd* Mohammed Ou-Lbaz and some 150 armed men. For a month they held out in some hilltop hideout. Meanwhile, an advanced guard of cavalry of Ayt Ouirra from the sultan's army had advanced unopposed as far as Boutferda. By then, of course, the Ayt 'Abdi, the true culprits, had gone to ground in cliff-side bolt-holes such as Ighrem n-Tihouna n-Ouwejjal, near Boutferda, or else in the deepest recesses of the Asif Melloul gorge.[27]

Eventually, the cavalry pushed on towards the Isrouta plateau where they were ambushed by the Ayt Sokhman and driven back in disorder to the *mhalla*'s camp at Ahnou, causing uproar and confusion.[28] Shortly after, the retreat was sounded, but not before Sidi 'Ali, in a token gesture of submission, had sent *qayd* Ou-Lbaz to the royal camp with four sacrificial *ta'argiba* bulls.[29] This had been done to remove the pressure on the mountaineers, who were beginning to feel the pinch of hunger.

Thus did Moulay Hasan's campaign against the Ayt Oumalou end on a note of disappointment: while the Beni Mguild had been brought back into the fold, the highland Ayt Sokhman remained obdurate and defiant. Around 1891, however, a second attempt was made to punish the Ayt 'Abdi. This involved a mixed force, again built up around irregular cavalry under *qayd* Moha ou Saïd, apparently with the sultan's full backing. While the Ayt Ouirra lunged straight for Aghbala, another *harka* under *qayd* Bel Moudden crossed Oued L'abid, headed over the wooded, panther-haunted plateaux for Tingerft, setting fire on the way to Imi n-Ferouan and other Ayt Sokhman villages. The attack on Aghbala achieved little; the second, however, including loyalist Ayt Sokhman elements under *qayd* Ou-Aïsha ou-'Ali, succeeded in killing twenty-seven Ayt 'Abdi and, in time-approved fashion, sending their heads back to the sultan's court in Fez! The other Ayt 'Abdi, however, entrenched on Jbel Imghal, put up a stout resistance, dissuading Bel Moudden from pushing onto Anergui. With this partial atonement for the Moulay Srou massacre then, the sultan had to be content. Shortly afterwards the Ayt 'Abdi sent him a propitiatory *hediya* and the matter was settled.[30]

Anxious to visit his ancestors' tomb in Tafilalt before his death, the sultan planned to pacify the Moulouya and Oued Ziz tribes on his way. Thus did he set out from Fez across Jbel Fazaz. Neglecting the *triq as-sseltan*, he headed instead via Timhadit, Foum Kheneg, and Tizi n-Taghzeft.[31] Soon Kasbat al-Makhzan on the Moulouya was reached, while from his vantage-point on Jbel Toujjit Sidi 'Ali Amhaoush mustered his expectant tribes. That an imperial force should venture for a third time in six years into the Berber heartland was a momentous event. It soon became clear, however, that their particular neck of the woods was to be spared the sultan's attention. "The time is not yet come. I have not seen the fateful signs," the marabout reassured his tribesmen as he sent them back to their villages.[32] To the credulous locals, Sidi 'Ali, by dint of his very magic, had diverted the *mhalla* from their area.

Moulay Hassan's last campaign

Marching to Aoutat (Midlet), Moulay Hassan secured the allegiance of the Ayt Izdeg tribe. He listened to their protestations of loyalty and apologies for earlier acts of rebellion against the *makhzan*, instigated, so they said, by the obstreperous Derqawi marabout Mohammed el-'Arabi El-Medghari. The sultan, however, was angry with them for not having come to his camp earlier, and inflicted a stiff fine, which was levied on the spot.

He then crossed the Tizi n-Talghemt into the Ziz Valley and continued through the Ti'allalin district, accepting submissions and homage on the way, even from some usually reluctant Ayt Hadiddou elements.[33] Before reaching Ksar es-Souk, he made a side-trip to Tadighoust and the Medghara district to secure the rebel sheikh 'Ali Ibn Yahya el-Merghadi, the Derqawi marabout's successor, and send him away under escort to a Marrakesh prison.[34]

Nevertheless, heat and skirmishes with rebellious Berbers took their toll, not to mention sickness in the *mhalla*'s ranks, so that winter was impending by the time the palm groves of Tafilalt finally hove into sight. After visiting his ancestors' tomb and his innumerable Filali cousins, their unceasing quarrels irksome to his ears, Moulay Hassan felt it was time to head for home. Rather than retracing his steps due north to Fez, he chose to follow the southern route to Marrakesh via the Ghriss, the Dra'a, and Tizi n-Telouat, knowing he could expect a warm welcome form the local *qayd*, a certain Si Madani el-Glaoui.[35] Only recently had this family achieved prominence. Towards the close of the previous sultan's reign an insignificant Glaoui chieftain, nicknamed

Fig. 19: Woman from the Glaoua tribe near Tizi n-Tishka (Marrakesh High Atlas).

tibibit ("little sparrow"), had amassed a fortune from the local salt trade. After evincing a potential rival he made himself paramount chief of the Glaoua tribe and gatekeeper of the strategic Telouat pass.

Shortly after, from the sultan's palace in Marrakesh came the offer of a government-approved *qayd*ship. This was accepted with alacrity. In 1886, his ambitious son Si Madani took over and at once embarked on a program of southward expansion.[36] A Glaoui chief was established in the Taourirt kasbah at Warzazat by stealth and guile, while Si Madani strengthened the walls of his grim Telouat fortress, also boosting the capacity of its dungeons. They would become hideously famous as places of detention and slow, lingering death for decades to come. This, then, was the bivouac the sultan had chosen for his troops. Thus towards Telouat and its barren cordon of snow-peaks did the exhausted *mhalla* wend its way in the face of a mid-winter gale, "struggling upward through the snows under a canopy of ravens and vultures and with a rearguard of jackals and hyenas."[37] Si Madani extended a hearty welcome to his sovereign. There ensued a brief stay at Telouat castle, during which the sultan's praises were sung by

Berber *ahwash* dancers in the fire-lit courtyard, while the troops outside dined on roasted mutton. Before leaving, Moulay Hassan presented his host with a significant gift: a small Krupp cannon and a consignment of breech-loading rifles, ostensibly to uphold *makhzan* authority in the area.[38]

In fact, at one blow, the sultan had totally upset the balance of power on the southern side of the Great Atlas. No tribe would be able to stand up against Si Madani's firepower; no castle would be safe from his cannon shells. Thus did the first of the great *qayd*s appear on the scene, and thus were the foundations laid for the Glaoui Empire, destined to hold sway for half a century over south Morocco. Little did Moulay Hassan dream that he had just armed the very hand that would come within an ace of destroying his own dynasty!

It was a weary, dispirited sultan who passed through Marrakesh before taking the long road back to Fez via the Tadla region. Not far from the Oued L'abid ford in the Tadla region, however, he passed away. His death was attributed by superstitious Atlas Berbers to a *jinn* ("spirit") in the shape of a queen bee that the sultan had found near Oued Ziz, north of Ksar-es-Souk, and had carried about with him for the rest of the campaign in a reed tube.

On crossing Oued L'abid, he wished to free the creature. The *jinn* assured his majesty that this was all in good order. Once out of its tube, however, the *jinn* fatally wounded Moulay Hassan, who, though kept out of sight by his retainers, passed away in his camp.[39] After five days, chief *wazir* Ba Ahmed finally acknowledged the sultan's death, having kept the event secret so as to ensure Moulay 'Abd el-'Aziz's succession.

Once the news was out it unleashed the usual welter of insurrection across the land.[40] Kept in check for twenty years by Moulay Hassan's firm hand, lawlessness and vendetta returned in strength, thus denting Morocco's reputation as the nineteenth century drew to a close. Little did the Imazighen imagine that the weakening of *makhzan* authority was actually jeopardizing their own freedom, laying them open to attack by outside forces. In 1860, there had been the Tetouan episode during the war with Spain and military defeat that had underscored Morocco's vulnerability and forced it into a crippling debt vis-à-vis Great Britain to pay off reparations to Spain.

Now, after gobbling up several autonomous sheikhdoms and oases in southern Algeria, France looked poised to invade to invade Morocco's southeastern marches. Never before had Morocco's age-old Tamazight culture been threatened in this way, not to mention its social and linguistic unity; soon, the French columns (*lkunnur*) would march.

The subsequent period of armed resistance would usher in the final years of the Heroic Age of the Imazighen. There would be Homeric, Wagnerian episodes marked by great deeds, sometimes even instances of chivalry. At others, Berbers would bicker between themselves over breadcrumbs while the confident, outside enemy was knocking at their very gates, flying over their territory, shelling their villages with long-range artillery. In courage they would never be wanting, yet overpowered by superior force and technology they would finally succumb.

The Foreign Threat

As had often happened on previous occasions, the sultan's death witnessed the sudden appearance of a myriad of ambitious, self-centered chieftains bent on strengthening their personal power in their own particular nook of the Atlas. Such was the distance from Fez or Marrakesh that this variety of local chief, part-brigand, part-warlord, a bizarre blend of rapacity and dignity, intrigue and panache, emerged whenever the *makhzan* showed signs of weakening. Some lasted no longer than that ephemeral carpet of grass and flowers that stems spontaneously from Moroccan spring rains; others prospered and thrived.

We have already mentioned Ou-Bihi, the Hahi chief from the hills west of Marrakesh, whom sultan Sidi Mohammed had forced to drink a poisoned potion as

Fig. 20: Typical mountain Berber architecture: Ayt Bahammou, Seksawa (Western High Atlas).

punishment for blatant treason. His disappearance from the scene had left a power vacuum that a certain Sidi 'Abdelmalek El-Mtouggui proved only too anxious to fill. From his kasbah at Bouaboud,[1] near the Tizi n-Bibaoun over the western end of the High Atlas, this wily fox soon carved himself out a feudal domain southwest of the Haouz plain, becoming the second of the "great *qayd*s."

Meanwhile, deep in the forgotten valleys of the Seksawa and Guedmioua, whose inhabitants used to be as skilled as any when it came to playing power games, appeared several similar characters in an episode typical of Berber politics. The first, *amghar* Mokhtar el-Seksawi of the Ayt Lahssen, had gained power over his tribe around 1880 by means fair and foul, including murdering his chief enemies at a banquet and remaining El-Mtouggui's ally only as long as it suited him. Independent to the end, however, he later broke with El-Mtouggui, became an unappointed *qayd* in his own right and enjoyed tremendous prestige till his death in 1925.[2]

The second was Lhajj Moulid, *muqqadam* of the Ayt Haddious fraction and a native of Tassa in the upper Seksawa Valley, who, anxious to keep his powder dry the better to defend his home turf, rose to power around 1890. Thanks to his skillful diplomacy during summer transhumance camps up on the Tishka plateau, he gradually forged a small local confederacy whose policy was to avoid falling into the clutches of any of the emerging great *qayd*s, whether Glaoui, Goundafi, or Mtouggui. His son Hmad ou-Moulid succeeded him in 1900 and eventually became the last independent chief in the area to surrender to the French in 1925. He was famous for his simple generosity, offering a sheep to any well-wisher that came by his house on the day of Aïd el-Kbir.[3] Typically, however, his power base was built up around a hard core of ruffianly outsiders, a Praetorian guard of trigger-happy tribesmen from the neighboring Ida ou Izimmer. Not far to the east, the venerable chief, El-Goundafi, could pride himself on having eliminated his most dangerous rivals through a lethal combination of fire, steel, and flintlock musket. After subduing the surrounding tribes he was now safely ensconced in his eagle's nest at Tagountaft, dominating the north–south trade route over the Tizi n-Test.

His son, Sidi Taïeb, was proving a worthy successor.[4] Ten miles down the track from Tagountaft, at Talat n-Ya'qoub, stood the imposing Kasba Goundafi. In 1897 this was where a somewhat eccentric British traveler attempting to reach Taroudannt via the Tizi n-Test, Robert Cuninghame-Graham, was taken after being arbitrarily arrested by the chief's men. He was detained for twelve days in miserable conditions before being released. Obviously, traveling through the Atlas in those days could be a hazardous experience for foreigners, who were less than welcome! One member of the party even got stung by a scorpion while changing into his pyjamas.[5] As long as Moulay Hassan reigned, El-Goundafi was wise enough to bide his time. When the youthful Moulay 'Abd el-'Aziz came to power the three mountain potentates were at each others' throats. In 1907, conveniently sinking their differences, the threesome threw in their lot with Moulay Hafid in a bid to wrest the throne from Moulay 'Abd el-'Aziz.[6]

Then, tired of dunning their impoverished parishioners, each *qayd* turned against his neighbor. Thus El-Mtouggui, initially in agreement with El-Glaoui to side with Moulay Hafid, unexpectedly welshed on the deal and marched on Marrakesh. Thinking better of this, he then answered Hafid's summons to Fez, while, behind his back, El-

Glaoui helped himself to half of his territory. When El-Glaoui fell from grace in 1911, Mtouggui, in turn, won back his lost acres and even more. Thus had plunder, intrigue, and alliance-switching, playing both sides against the middle, the usual unmeritorious assets of Berber feudal warfare, become the order of the day among unscrupulous Atlas warlords.[7] That was the usual rule of thumb in the Atlas Mountains.

At Tounfit, in the upper Moulouya region, no single *qayd* survived, whether self-appointed or *makhzan*-backed. All were killed or evicted by their own tribesmen, or else they fell in battle. By 1914, among the Ayt Yahya, not one of these local bullies was to be found.[8] Further north, as we have seen, the Beni Mtir tribe was divided between three *makhzan*-appointed potentates who, eventually, quietly distanced themselves from the sultanate.

This was the turmoil that paved the way for *rogui* ("pretender") Bou Hmara ("the man on the she-donkey"). This strange character, posing as one of Moulay Hassan's sons, enjoyed an unexpected run of success, defeating several Sharifian armies sent against him and even threatening Fez from his nearby base in Taza. Here, backed by Algerian dissidents (including 'Abdelmalek) together with Beni Mtir, Beni Ouaraïn, and Ayt Seghrouchen tribesmen, he had set up a rival *makhzan*. His stand against a possible Spanish invasion of the Rif, implying by Spain in the Rif, had won many a fence-sitter over to his side.[9] 'Aomar Youssi, one of the last loyalist *qayd*s, took the field in vain against the rebel. However, his prestige was impaired after the fruitless 1903 expedition against Bou Hmara, and he finally fell while fighting the Sidi 'Ali section of the Ayt Seghroushen near Tazouta, north of Jbel Tishshoukt.

For a while, then, the fortunes of war appeared to smile on the Pretender, thus consolidating his prestige, as shown by this excerpt from a contemporary Berber ballad:

O Bou Hmara! Power is henceforth in your hands,
As for Moulay 'Abd el-'Aziz, long past is his time.
O Bou Hmara! O mighty *sharif*,
Raise high your standards, lead on to victory![10]

Morocco in peril

The action of Bou Hmara's failed epic developed mostly in the Rif. However, after holding out some seven years in Taza, and later at Selwan near Melilla (1905–9), he was finally discredited when it was heard that he had reached an agreement with the Spanish, while in the field French military advisers tipped the scales in favor of Moulay Hafid's *makhzan* forces. The pretender was captured, brought to Fez in a cage and eventually done to death after being half devoured by lions in the imperial zoo.[11]

A characteristic of the reigns of the last two pre-Protectorate sultans was that the *makhzan* was constantly being challenged by a puppet sultan together with a rival *makhzan*: Bou Hamara under Moulay 'Abd el-'Aziz; Moulay Hafid had to contend with two—Moulay Hai el-Kettani among the Beni Mtir in 1909 and Moulay Zine, Hafid's brother, a short-lived sultan declared by the Berbers (1911).[12] On each occasion, the notion of an anti-sultan was duplicated by that of anti-*makhzan*. At the provincial level, power inevitably fell into the hands of feudal overlords such as the aforementioned great *qayd*s of the Atlas, or their Middle Atlas counterparts Moha ou Hammou and Moha ou Saïd, not to mention a bevy of small-time imitators. Throughout the land, arbitrary privilege, personal gain, graft, and intimidation held an undisputed sway.[13] As ever, the Moroccan people sought strength in examples from their own historical past. In desperate situations such as this, traditional spiritual leaders alone retain some credit and provide a credible alternative to temporal leaders. This period was to prove no exception as some outstanding *murabitun* came to the fore, commanding as much respect as their forerunners from the time of Sa'adi decadence.

Down south in the sands of Seguiat El-Hamra, famous saintly leader Ma El-Aïnin, after half a lifetime spent resisting their encroachments, was dislodged from his zaouia by French and Spanish troops. Of Berber origin and a skilled politician, parallels have been drawn between Ma El Aïnin's northerly venture and the eleventh-century Almoravid invasion.[14] There is no doubt that he derived considerable prestige from his father, prominent marabout Mohammed El Fadel, a renowned Saharan Islamic leader. With a deputation of "Blue Men," Ma El-Aïnin traveled up to Fez in 1902 in a vain attempt to elicit Sharifian support from Moulay 'Abd el-'Aziz against the foreign imperialist threat, a move dictated by the marabout's patriotic feelings rather than by sheer xenophobia. However, disappointed by the sultan's attitude vis-à-vis the colonialist threat, in May 1910 he moved north with a small army, hoping to reach Fez with help en route from Moha ou Saïd and Moha ou Hammou, won over the Souss to his cause, crossed the passes to Marrakesh, then advanced up the Oum Rbia' into the Tadla. As the French were concentrating a powerful force to head him off, Ma El-Aïnin climbed into the hills, winning support from the Ayt 'Atta n-Oumalou, the Ayt Bouzid, and other clans till he had about 5,000 men. These he launched against a French column in the Sidi Salah region, but was beaten off in a bitter confrontation, being wounded in the action. He returned home via N'tifa territory and Demnat.[15]

Ma El-Aïnin, who had earlier been forced to evacuate his capital Smara, subsequently remained in Tiznit till his death at the end of 1910. The next year, his son El-Hiba started from the same town on his abortive expedition north to Marrakesh in what was to prove to be the last serious attempt by traditional Morocco to turn back the clock of fate. The El-Hiba episode (or *hibaya*) was a curious affair, with the great *qayd*s playing a dubious role of brinkmanship. After capturing Taroudannt, El-Hiba's ragtag army crossed the Atlas at its western extremity, passively aided by El-Mtouggui. Once the pretender had entered Marrakesh to a warm welcome, although the Saharans' plundering activities made them unpopular, the other two mountain *qayd*s attempted to curry favor with El Hiba, making a show of support by sending in armed tribal contingents. Predictably, once the "Blue Men" had been butchered by Mangin's column at Sidi Bou 'Atman and El-Hiba,[16] the "Man of the Hour" had fled across the Atlas and the time-servers switched alliances. Thus had this sincere, grass-roots reaction to foreign imperialism failed dismally. Worse still, El-Hiba's defeat guaranteed a long-time French presence in Marrakesh and shortly afterwards paved the way for the unwritten pact between Lyautey and the great *qayd*s, ensuring peace at the same time as it firmly established arbitrary, despotic power in southwestern Morocco.[17]

Saints and warriors

In the Middle Atlas, however, two religious leaders would be in the forefront of resistance to the French. Strangely enough, another strong character, in the person of Zaïan chief Moha ou Hammou and self-appointed leader of *jihad*, would also play a leading role in the resistance. True, his consistent opposition to French military penetration from Tadla up to the Middle Atlas earned him considerable prestige, but the only trait shared by Moha ou Hammou and Sidi 'Ali Amhaoush was that both were womanizers, otherwise the two had been at loggerheads for twenty years.

Thus could there be no cooperation between the dashing Zaïan horseman and mighty warrior, and the scheming, venerated saint of central Morocco,[18] who would often galvanize his followers with words such as, "Make gun-powder, practice horsemanship and prepare for *jihad*!"[19] But when the marabout suggested they join forces against the French in the Boudenib region in 1908, the Zaïan chief answered, "Why should I bother to help? What gratitude can I expect from those Saharans?" Nor had Sidi 'Ali fared any better: when his tribesmen met with fleeing fugitives who spoke of French artillery fire near Boudenib decimating the Amazigh ranks, they had turned tail.[20] In return, the marabout never involved himself in operations around Khenifra, the Zaïan fief, though some of his Ishqern fighters participated in the Battle of El-Herri (1914) and he did later allow himself to be talked into an unsuccessful attack on a supply column. Subsequently commenting on his failure he observed, "God punished me for acting before the appointed time!"[21]

Yet there is no denying that these two men had a decisive influence on the opening gambits of the lengthy Atlas campaigns to come. If the French were kept confined in their cramped Khenifra outpost, if the western part of the Middle Atlas remained uncompromisingly hostile, this was due to the unflagging efforts of Moha ou Hammou. If the Zaïan chief was more active in deed than word, Sidi 'Ali Amhaoush's action was complementary in every way, if unwillingly so. The aura of mystical authority that emanated from his person coupled with a ceaseless anti-French discourse won him the unflinching respect and support of client-tribes. No wonder they proved almost impervious to propaganda from French Native Affairs officers.[22]

So long as such die-hard characters survived, any hope of denting the local carapace of suspicion and xenophobia remained illusory. By a trick of fate they both died around the end of the First World War. Sidi 'Ali Amhaoush passed away in 1918 at Ta'adlount in the heart of the Atlas, of suspected poisoning.[23] As for Moha ou Hammou, defiant to the end, he died a hero's death when, one fine spring day in 1921, a stray bullet laid him low at Azlag n-Tzemmourt during a skirmish with a detachment of pro-French Zaïan fighters. That doughty warrior's demise caused consternation for miles around, even though most of his sons, in order to hedge their bets, had by then gone over to the French. Thus were two separate destinies united in death.[24]

Beyond the Zaïan plain, on the austere plateau of the Beni Mguild and Ayt Youssi, at the foot of the arid Seghroushen and Marmousha hills, one name was on everybody's lips: Sidi Raho ou Mimoun. Here was another dyed-in-the-wool mountain *agwerram*, a fascinating figure, much respected by some French officers.[25] For seventeen years (1909–26), Sidi Raho was to become the heart and soul of the resistance in the area, succeeding, when French forces first occupied Fez, in grouping a large coalition of tribesmen, whom he led against the city walls.[26] Far from being a hard-hitting cavalryman like Moha ou Hammou or Moha ou Saïd, here was a quietly-spoken, simply-dressed leader of men whose spiritual aura won him universal acclaim and respect.[27]

After an attack on a French fort outside Sefrou in which he had lost two brothers, Saïd and Hassan, some of the local inhabitants were shot in reprisal, while his kasbah at Annosser in the Amekla district was destroyed by French forces, whereupon he retreated deep into the barren hills behind Tazouta at the head of two clans of the Ayt Youssi.[28] Thus, yet again, faced with the failure of her traditional *makhzan* leaders, from whom they had learnt to expect little enough in the past, rural Moroccans turned to their religious chiefs, the only ones who had kept their noses clean, the only ones fit to lead them against the invader. This was a widespread feeling, often vented in contemporary poetry:

> Slap my face and pluck my beard, O Christian,
> Our monarch to your king has sold us!
> Adversity and melancholy are my daily lot,
> O fellow-Muslims, whence will deliverance come?[29]

History in dispute

Much has been written about the exact nature and significance of the stiff resistance to colonialism by Morocco's Berbers; even more has been left unsaid. Between the two somewhat opposing stances adopted by historians, given the sum of bias and misinformation, perceiving the truth has become an arduous task. According to General Guillaume, the Berber fighter, a lukewarm patriot at best, was a mere dissident ready to get himself slaughtered only if his home turf was threatened.[30] Should his neighbors come under attack, he would turn a blind eye. Split up into innumerable clans, Berber fighters selfishly prioritized defense of home and hearth without sparing a thought to over-all cohesion. This is the classic notion of *al fitna al barbariyya* ("Berber anarchy"), a negative social manifestation that had to be contained, at best stamped out. At the same time there is no denying the importance that the Amazigh attaches to freedom, displaying a willingness to fight if need be.[31] The focus of post-colonial researchers, whether Moroccan or otherwise, runs counter to the above.

The battles of a century ago are analyzed, examined from different angles, to determine to what extent there may have been a national resistance to colonialism, based on cohesive game plans, interaction between various groups, and a semblance of unified command. Members of the Istiqlal, on the other hand, will claim that there was actually no national resistance before 1934, a negationist stance that merely aims to legitimize their own anti-French urban action. Others will claim that Fez as of 1911 was the starting-point of a *jihad* movement running counter to French *Pacification*.[32] That some of these experts fall into the trap of attempting to reinterpret past events in the light of contemporary ideology there is little doubt. Yet others emphasize that Berber *imjuhad* ("Holy War warriors") were motivated not by xenophobia but by an unwavering attachment to the inhospitable hills from which they eked out a living.[33]

To many observers of the colonial era, national unity was conspicuous by its absence when judged by Western standards. In the post-independence era, however, in a revisionist orgy of self-flagellation, many Western scholars opted for the opposite view: that put forward by the Istiqlal, whereby Morocco was certainly not the "sick man" of the Maghrib racked by tribal strife that colonialist writers were anxious to depict. Some, supporters of a supposed *makhzénisation*, that may or may not have been under way, have pointed to late nineteenth-century attempts at reform affecting the armed forces and the *makhzan*[34] as proof that the country was making progress in the right direction until the process was arrested by France's unwelcome interference; a situation best summed up by a late twentieth-century view:

> Protectorate period historians stressed the development of "dissidence" and regional division. It should be pointed out that if some tribes refused to pay taxes or rebelled against *qayd*-s appointed by the sultan, at no point was his authority contested: the sultan was universally acknowledged as the supreme head of the community, the country's representative in dealings with foreign powers and the source of all power. Even in traditionally dissident tribes *qayd*-s sought investiture by the sultan as a guarantee of legality. There was nothing rigid about the notions of *blad makhzan* and *blad siba*; at no time was the country's unity at risk. The *makhzan*'s actual power was to be measured in terms of the sultan's energy: under Moulay Hassan, the whole country was at peace. The development of dissidence and widespread disorder on the eve of the Protectorate were directly linked to colonial intrigue aimed at conquering the country.[35]

Of course, when reconsidering the conflicting viewpoints stated above, one is immediately struck by attempts at oversimplification, or expressions of political correctness dictated by the dominant ideology of the 1970–80 period. If, on the one hand, it is too facile to attribute Berber dissidence to xenophobia and religious fanaticism, trying to make a case for a unified national resistance is a historical non-starter. Again, trying to claim that the sultan could not travel between his capitals for fear of capture by rebellious Berbers is as fanciful as attempts to deny that these selfsame Berbers ever constituted a threat to the country's unity, or that all the tribes had submitted to Moulay Hassan!

This would too obviously disregard anti-*makhzan* resistance by the Dila'yin, Ahansal, and Imhiwash marabouts, not to mention events described in the previous chapter, ultimately amounting to historical denial. Likewise, the breakdown of law and order throughout Morocco should be visualized as the result of a gradual internal process, with the erosion of *makhzan* authority on the periphery matched by the rise of petty tyrants and influential *igweramn*, as much as it can be laid at the door of "colonial intrigue."

Let us accept that, in the context, the latter phenomenon acted as a catalyst, certainly, to the exclusion of supposed direct links or active conspiracies. Historians should attempt objective analysis rather than acting as time-servers toeing the line of contemporary official-speak. Another aspect of the problem lies in the slanted colonial French vision of Morocco colored by notions of society and exercise of power, based on a national sentiment cemented by conscription, education, justice, newspapers, postal services, and railways. In the old Morocco, equipped only with dirt tracks and devoid of stagecoaches, news could not travel as fast as in Europe. Nevertheless, it was common knowledge that the Christians would come one day; even the old Imhiwash prophesies said so: *yan wass irumin ad ffghen ghurun*.[36] Psychological preparation for the inevitable continued, the newcomers usually being caricatured as lecherous, pork-eating, and wine-drinking monsters. The religious side of this preparation was obviously emphasized, yet the marabouts well knew how to play on simple notions of patriotism, of which they were unwittingly the principal agents in the country.

However, attempting with the advantage of hindsight to reinterpret Berber dissidence in terms of overall national awareness and loyalty, though commendable from the political angle in post-colonial Morocco, is not matched by the piecemeal resistance that actually occurred on the ground at the time. That an Ou-'Abdi from remote Jbel Kousser should have desperately defended his native hills was clearly understandable. That he should have felt directly threatened by the French occupation of the Touat oasis or Beni Iznassen territory is arguable.

When the Ayt 'Abdi were finally subjugated in 1933, a French interpreter well recalls how one tribesman told him after surrendering, "We won't have anything to do with the sultan in Rabat! Is there one, anyway, now that the French are here? And, if so, what's his name?"[37] Again, *à propos* of the Ayt 'Abdi, when I asked an Ou-'Abdi why he failed to respect Forestry Commission regulations on collecting firewood, I was told, "Why should I bother with the *makhzan*? What do they do for me? Can I send my

Fig. 21: Shrine of Sidi 'Ali Oulhousseyn, Anergui, at the foot of Jbel Kousser.

children to hospital, or to school? Do we have our own weekly market [*ssuq*]? No, we have to travel two days to visit Msemrir, Anergui or Zaouit Ahansal, all far beyond our territory!"[38] In a country fraught with communications problems, where news circulated haphazardly, one is hard put to find more than the glimmers of national feeling. Yet such a feeling did exist at times, as we shall show in the subsequent account of the Atlas campaigns. Strangely, among the *imdyazn* ("wandering minstrels") up in those secluded valleys, their very profession enabled them to gain a global view of their country:

> To Lhajeb and Agouraï telephone lines ascend the slopes,
> They make for Sefrou, O Berber women, lost is the Atlantic plain!
> To the Qarawiyin mosque did I journey and to Jbel Zerhoun too,
> The Koran is read no more, the Christian has appropriated our world!
> May you know sadness, Bab Ftouh; wear mourning, Bab Lgissa;
> Shame on you, O place of prayer, the Christian has defiled you![39]

Had there been a genuine feeling of national solidarity no doubt the Moroccans' warlike ardor would have thrown the invader into the sea as in Sa'adi times. Actually, this was not the case; rather the opposite, as some historians have pointed out. Since independence,[40] official-speak has served both to rework recent Moroccan history and emphasize national unity, as any country is entitled to do in the interests of domestic harmony and political expediency. As we revisit the various stages of what amounted to a traumatic Moroccan version of the Thirty Years' War,[41] we shall endeavor to outline the fact that, while the fighting was mostly highlighted by spectacular, individual actions, contrary to earlier suggestions there are several examples on record of attempts at a concerted action between the various hill tribes.

The Start of Morocco's "Thirty Years' War"

The early twentieth-century Moroccan crisis ended with French troops racing to Fez and the dithering of Moulay Hafid, last sultan of the old Morocco, prior to his abdication and the setting up of the Protectorate.[1] Blending chronological description of Berber resistance with analysis and synthesis, our account of the Atlas campaigns, or *Pacification de l'Atlas*, will for the sake of convenience be divided into two main phases. The first embraces the period 1908–23; the second covers the years 1924–34. Defined as "the indecisive years," the first phase indicates that the issue remained in doubt throughout that period. After easy French military excursions based on Casablanca into the plains of Shawia, Hawz, the east and southeast, Berber resistance stiffened noticeably once the enemy invested the Atlas.

At Ksiba (1913) and El-Herri (1914) the mountaineers gave the French military a bloody nose. It was an edifying experience, inculcating as it did a healthy respect for the Berber combatant and giving rise to *le prestige de la montagne* ("prestige of the hills"), a myth born of these two defeats that injected an exaggerated element of caution into French military strategy thus prolonging operations for some twenty years. To appreciate the end-result, suffice to say that it took seven years to bring to book the Zaïan after El-Herri, while the Ksiba hinterland only succumbed after eighteen years of protracted campaigning.[2]

Elsewhere, operations achieved disappointing results. Whereas the Azrou–Midelt axis was successfully opened up via Tizi n-Taghzeft over five years (1912–17), it failed to bring about the disintegration of the Middle Atlas Berber bastion. For one thing, communications proved vulnerable to ambush, while setting up the nearby Bekrit outpost, far from rallying the Beni-Mguild to the French, resulted in little else than bitter fighting, extremely costly in human lives. More to the point, so long as the First World War lasted, French occupation forces were too weak to bring to bear sufficient military strength to crush resistance by the mountaineers.[3] While enjoying unquestioned military superiority, French forces were at a disadvantage when facing a brave, determined enemy on some of the most rugged terrain in North Africa in a situation typical of asymmetrical warfare. The Berber fighters' unimpaired morale and confidence in the outcome of *jihad* gave them a further edge. Had a charismatic national leader come forward at this point he might have been victorious. Yet, while Ma El-Aïnin and his son had failed in the southwest, on the southeastern marches two similar characters, religious leaders both, had got off to a good start.

Ultimately though, neither Moulay Lahssen es-Sbaï nor Moha n-Ifrouten es-Semlali proved equal to the occasion. Instead of using their numerical superiority and maneuverability to wage guerrilla warfare, they frittered away their strength in stand-up firefights with the *irumin*, only to be butchered by cannon and machine-gun fire. For a brief spell, however, the French were in serious trouble when, during the winter of 1918–19, the tribes rose as one man in answer to the Semlali's call, besieged all the outposts along the road to Tafilalt, and actually forced the enemy to abandon the last-named region for nearly fourteen years.

Meanwhile, Resident-General Lyautey launched another operation to secure the south side of the Taza corridor from possible attack. It was to take ten years of very tough campaigning to subdue this area, commencing with an indecisive battle at Skoura, north of Jbel Tishshoukt, and ending up among the cedars on Jbel Bou Iblan with the final surrender of tribes that had never really bowed to any sultan. In the Tadla area, French forces similarly made little headway. The real stars of the show were modest *igwerramn*, like Sidi Raho ou-Mimoun in the Middle Atlas, or Sidi Mah el-Hansali, who, with his cousin Si Lhousseyn ou-Temga, resisted tenaciously for years along the northern flank of the Central Atlas. Given the scant financial means and primitive logistics available, it is a wonder they lasted so long. Somewhat less successful, though they did go down fighting, their colleagues belonging to the *tariqa darqawiyya* in the Aghbala/Tounfit region, riven by squabbles over women, were unable to unite the tribes or deliver on promises that the Christian would soon be vanquished.[4]

Prestige of the hills: 1) Action at Ksiba

This first section will take us up to 1924, a quiet year on the Atlas front pending the *dénoument* of the Rif war. True, although substantial territorial gains had been made by the French, the Berbers still controlled large areas. They would prove tough nuts to crack so long as gunrunners could keep them supplied with arms and ammunition via the dissident corridor from Seguiat el-Hamra, over the Jbel Bani and up Oued Dra'a. Mangin's walkover at Sidi Bou 'Atman had given him a false appreciation of the Moroccan tribesman's fighting ability. The same applied to his second-in-command, Commandant Picquart, who had merely to charge straight in front of him to scatter his foemen like chaff. The Mangin–Picquart tandem was obviously spoiling for further action.

A risk-free victory, however, amounts to a lackluster triumph. In the early summer of 1913, as they rode easily and confidently across the scorching Tadla plain, little did our two swashbuckling gentlemen dream that they were about to deal in serious matters. The hardy Ayt Ouirra tribesmen, who lurked in those wooded foothills on their right, had so far paid scant attention to peaceful overtures and, so the French military fondly imagined, would soon be on the receiving end of a sharp, well-deserved lesson.[5] Their chief was Moha ou Saïd, a former Makhzan *qayd* and wily sixty-year-old veteran, whose "ardent patriotism," in the words of one contemporary observer, "should be measured in terms of his efforts to keep himself and his subject tribes totally independent."[6]

His capital, Ksiba, nestling in the first folds of the Atlas, lay a mere ten miles from the Tadla plain.[7] Well before dawn on the morning of June 8, 1913, Picquart, with his

Spahis and mounted Arab tribesmen, led the way up delightful wooded ravines drained by babbling brooks. The column must have been detected fairly rapidly, for at daybreak it came under fire. After a heated exchange involving artillery, the first assailants were repulsed. Picquart then charged off after them with his eighty *Spahis* and eventually reached a col between Ksiba and Moha ou Saïd's kasbah. As they came under attack from swarms of armed tribesmen, he ordered his troopers to retire to a more favorable position. Knifed, shot at close range from a tangle of bushes and large rocks, the detachment was quickly decimated, Picquart himself being killed; events thus described by a Berber bard:

> O colonel, in a thicket, like a dog were you done to death!
> O jackal, rejoice, of the pig's meat partake—'tis yours!
> God rewards you, thus are exterminated the unbelievers.
> O jackal, the brave Berber horsemen do offer you this feast![8]

The survivors had trouble joining up with the rest of the column. Before retiring, Mangin marched back and destroyed Moha ou Saïd's kasbah with high explosive. The second day the French camp itself came under harassing fire from the Berbers. Smarting from this reverse, the third day (June 10) Mangin returned undaunted to the fray. Though the Berbers occupied the heights in large numbers, they were outflanked by the cavalry and the French gained access to Ksiba, which was sacked and torched. The charred corpse of Commandant Picquart was recovered from the marketplace and Mangin led the column back down towards the Tadla plain. As he was retiring through the Foum Taghzout Valley, however, his command came under repeated onslaught from exceptionally brave Berbers. In savage hand-to-hand fighting, the French lost 100 men killed on that day alone; a further fifty on the other two days.

The Berbers had given a superb demonstration of their tactical skill, their eye for the country. It had, however, been a costly victory. Out of 3,500 fighters, two-thirds of them armed with guns, the rest with knives, about 600 had been killed, including some Ayt Sokhman who had come down to lend a hand. In compensation, though, their armament[9] received a considerable reinforcement in the shape of approximately 300 rifles and carbines scavenged from French dead and wounded on the battlefield. The so-called *affaire de Ksiba* came as something of a shock to the French and their arm-chair strategists. Lyautey was understandably furious and had his gung-ho field commander transferred to France, though Mangin's aide, Colonel Magnin, claimed that everyone knew that in Morocco, the closer you got to the hills, the more warlike its inhabitants.[10] Unfortunately, the same lesson would have to be painfully relearnt the following year, at considerably greater cost.

Prestige of the hills: 2) Battle of El-Herri

Having received no help from his rival Moha ou Hammou Azayyi during the Ksiba episode, Moha ou Saïd abstained from interfering when enemy columns converged on Khenifra in June 1914. Far from enticing the Zaïan to submit to the French, the capture of Khenifra seemed to have hardened their resolve. If the French went no further, it meant they were incapable of doing so—a sign of weakness.[11] Far from dominating the neighborhood, cooped up behind their barbed wire, the Khenifra garrison found themselves surrounded by a flexible line of pickets beyond which danger threatened. Otherwise, relief columns would be sent to keep the outpost fed and supplied with ammunition. On July 1, a major sortie by the garrison on the Oulghes plain came under heavy attack from Berber *imjuhad* who had infiltrated the French position. This led to a fighting retreat towards Khenifra, in the course of which over 100 soldiers were killed.[12] In August there was another furious action, costly in lives to both sides, in connection with the arrival of a supply column, in the course of which the Zaïan made massive use of their vaunted cavalry.

All this should have served as a warning that these fighters were not lightly to be trifled with. There then ensued more than two months of relative peace on the Atlas front. Moha ou Hammou was under the impression that a form of tacit truce had been declared and behaved accordingly. Less frequently did he harass the Khenifra garrison with small-arms fire or with ineffectual shots from an old bronze cannon that Moulay Hassan had left him. Some of his people even took to visiting the infirmary for medical treatment. Unfortunately, the French commander, Colonel Laverdure, was champing at the bit, the more so as inaction was making inroads on the morale of the garrison. A veteran West African colonial campaigner with scant respect for native opponents, he was itching to bring matters to a head with the Zaïan chief. Encouraged by unreliable advisers, he decided to attack the Zaïan encampment some ten miles southeast of Khenifra.[13]

In the small hours of November 13, 1914, the ebullient colonel rode out of Khenifra at the head of forty-two officers and about 1,200 men, mostly Senegalese, armed with repeating rifles, Hotchkiss machine guns, and a battery of field artillery. Moha ou Hammou's camp near El-Herri was reached shortly before daybreak and easily occupied and pillaged as the Berbers scattered. Two of Moha ou Hammou's wives were killed, the others captured, the contents of his tent rifled by looters. His felony accomplished, Laverdure ordered his detachment to withdraw towards Khenifra across a line of low-lying hills—perfect terrain for the Berbers. Having recovered from their initial surprise, large numbers of tribesmen occupied the surrounding ridges, crept down the ravines, and zeroed in on the retreating French force. Though the soldiers inflicted heavy losses on their assailants, the column came close to annihilation in a couple of hours, the survivors fleeing in disorder, many of them hunted down among the oleander bushes that line Asif Bouseqqour, which allegedly ran with blood:

> Thus spoke Bouseqqour stream: "He who came
> Of my waters to drink, found not their erstwhile purity.
> See, 'tis with gore that the river was reddened!"[14]

The French gunners had barely enough time to spike their field-pieces before going under; as it was, ten machine guns and some 700 rifles were captured by the victorious Berbers. Five officers and some 500 men straggled painfully back into Khenifra. It was the worst defeat ever inflicted by Moroccan Atlas Berbers on a French force, though because of the excessive number of dead among the Berbers, El-Herri proved a day of mourning:

> Art weak today and almost lifeless, O fighting field of El-Herri,
> Where nought is heard but the owl's mournful wail![15]
> From the hills came the destructive Christian, ere the
> Break of day; ere we had time to say our prayers![16]

In terms of lost French prestige, however, the effect was disastrous, as their onslaught was seen as foul play, coming as it did during what was seen by the Zaïan as a truce. Furthermore, the propaganda value of the prizes of war was tremendous since swords, uniforms, and rifles were subsequently displayed on souks throughout the mountains as visual tokens of the Christians' discomfiture.[17] Now that Moha Azayyi had this armament it was hoped he would use it to good purpose:

> O Zaïani, heed your country's call, face the foe!
> Art not lacking in arms to destroy the swine!
> O Zaïani, victor of the Christian, art not lacking in
> Guns or horses; what price your victory at El-Herri!?[18]

At this stage, his neighbor and rival Moha ou Saïd was chiefly concerned with surviving, counting mainly on positive fallout from a French defeat in Europe to further his cause. Thus did the mountain chiefs, jealous of each other's prestige, exchange messages in guarded terms, also writing to their colleagues in southeast Morocco. Little, however, was achieved. Strategically speaking, El-Herri was a fruitless victory, with Moha ou Hammou and his Amazigh fighters nursing their wounds in the hills, while the garrison held on grimly. Throughout the First World War it would remain encircled and "Khenifra became a logistic liability for the French as maintenance of supply lines to it invited constant attacks by the Zayans."[19]

Prestige of the hills: 3) The Khenifra convoys

Until 1917, when a proper dirt road was built, the slow Khenifra supply convoys from Azrou or Kasba Tadla suffered severely from incessant harassment by Berbers. Indeed, there were some epic encounters in the mist and snow of January 1916 and February 1917.[20] On each occasion the Berbers proved brilliant at using every scrap of cover and displaying proficiency with the knife at close quarters; they were also crack shots. The *imjuhad* were getting to appreciate their foemen. Of the Legionaries (*laliju*) they used to say, "They fire slowly and shoot to kill; they never seem to be in a hurry, nor do they bunch together to give themselves a false sense of security." As for the Senegalese troops (*saligan*), "those slaves have no back-bone to react against the basic survival instinct. They often turn tail for no good reason ..."[21] However, Berbers despised artillery and aircraft as weapons unworthy of brave men as they enabled a coward to kill from a distance. Amusingly, though, Berbers told the French, "Explosions from your artillery are a nuisance . . . they chiefly frighten our horses . . . the smell is abominable"![22]

Once the Berber attacks had been repulsed and before reaching the safety of Khenifra, the French had to file past Jbel Bou Hayati. Every time a lone marksman, affectionately dubbed "the Zaïan gatekeeper," would subject the supply column to long-range harassment. This kind of gesture was a typical trait of Berber bravura. On numerous other occasions in the Atlas campaigns there would be reports of lone snipers "taking pot-shots" at French camps.[23] The Khenifra convoys enjoyed improved conditions in 1918–19. Now there was a dirt track, and trucks, horse-drawn carts, and heavily-laden camels made light of the relatively hard going, while unwieldy Farman and Bréguet 19 biplanes operated out of an airstrip near Khenifra. As they buzzed overhead it became that much harder for the Berbers to mount ambushes, though there was one last glorious shindig around a convoy in October 1919, when some maverick Zaïan elements under Mi'ami Oul-Tfassiyt and Ou-Laïdi charged with drawn sabres, trading shots and insults with pro-French Zaïan auxiliaries, all to no avail.[24]

One factor that was taking the sting out of Zaïan resistance was the disarray that prevailed in the ranks of the Imehzan, chief Moha's numerous kith and kin. His son Bou'azza was the first to rally to the French cause in December 1917. A dashing, first-class horse soldier, albeit a likeable rogue, he was a great asset. In the following year, anxious to hedge his bets, came his elder brother Hassan, supported by uncle Amharoq, together with many of their followers—a move denounced by the Zaïan diehards, who, their herds depleted, their families famished, continued to hold out in the comfortless hills with chief Moha. Among other Zaïani relatives were cousin Ou-Laïdi, together with Moha's son, Mi'ami Oul-Tfassiyt (outlawed by the Protectorate authorities for murdering a French officer).

Ou-Laïdi, a tall, skinny, fifty-year-old opportunist whose ambition it had long been to lord it over the Zaïan confederation, was supported by his nephew Moha ou 'Aqqa and a distant relative, Mi'ami Ou-Lhajj Haddou, with help at times from the outlaw, Mi'ami Oul-Tfassiyt.[25]

The irreconcilables who were anxious to establish closer links with Moha ou Saïd in the Tadla and with Sidi Raho ou-Mimoun in the north also listened avidly to reports of France's forthcoming defeat in Europe, of Moha n-Ifrouten's imminent arrival in the area at the head of his victorious *harka* ("army"). Of vain rumors that, first Moulay 'Abd el-Aziz, and later, Moulay Hafid, would stage a comeback with German backing and head the *jihad* to restore Moroccan independence.[26] In the meantime, Hassan's people on one side, Ou-Laïdi's followers on the other, continued to lay siege to each others' kasbahs. The latter, continually harassed by Bou'azza's cavalry detachment, finally surrendered to the French in December 1919. As for the treacherous Miami oul-Tfassiyt, he escaped across the Atlas to Ayt Merghad territory.

Shortly after Ou-Laïdi's surrender there was an amusing episode over a young woman whom Hassan (eldest son of Moha) had inherited as part of the spoils of war. "Never shall I return her to him!" said Hassan. "Having vanquished Ou-Laïdi I had to sign a truce instead of squashing him like a fly. This woman is all I have to show for my victory. What would be left to me if I gave her up?" As edifying a statement as was

Ou-Laïdi's reply: "Let him keep the captive. If ever I lay hands on her again I'll have her flayed alive!"[27]

Meanwhile, the sands were running out for Middle Atlas resistance. The great uprising called for by Moha n-Ifrouten had failed, while the news from Europe spoke of French victory. "Morocco's Thirty Years' War" had reached a turning-point. By early 1920, supply convoys were circulating unopposed across the Middle Atlas. Shortly afterwards, the last recalcitrant Zaïan group, the Ayt Bou Haddou, threw in the sponge and Moha ou Hammou was reported killed in action, an event that caused consternation throughout the Fazaz. Little remained after seven years of tough campaigning in the bitter winter cold and sultry days of summer; equal courage had been shown on both sides. The French none the less felt admiration for their valiant foes.[28]

14

The Defense of Jbel Fazaz

In days of old, sultans crossing Jbel Fazaz used to prefer the Sefrou–Boulman–Enjil route to reach the Moulouya, chiefly because of the usually snow-free Oum Jeniba pass. Now that the area was under the surveillance of recalcitrant tribes united under Sidi Raho this was no longer feasible. There remained the tougher Lhajeb–Azrou–Timhadit–Tizi n-Taghzeft route, which was the one the French planned to follow. This had required considerable preliminary work, since the Beni Mtir, who held the plateau south of Lhajeb, had been making nuisances of themselves since 1912. Despite their resistance, the French had subdued the Beni Mtir, dislodged them from Ifran, and established an outpost at Itto overlooking the Adarouch plain, with a second one at Azrou, in April 1913.[1]

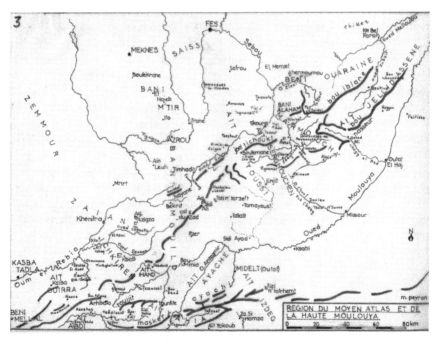

Map 3: Meknes-Fez, the Middle Atlas (Fazaz) and Moulouya region.

It was obvious to the Berbers that not only had the *irumin* come to stay, but they also intended to penetrate the cedar forest and brave the grueling, windswept miles across the plateau that stretched to Oued Gigou and Jbel Hayyan—the pasture land of the Beni Mguild, an abode of snow in winter and the coldest spot in the region. This alarming news did not deprive the Berbers of their sense of humor. When the Beni Mtir learnt that a French captain had made a reconnaissance up there, thus did they taunt their Beni Mguild neighbors:

> Praise be to God! The unfortunate Beni Mguild with fear tremble when
> They hear that towards Hayyan Mountain the French *qebtan* has ventured![2]

Actually, there ensued a brief respite as war had broken out in Europe, so it was not until 1915 that operations resumed. The Berbers were surprised to see the French march across the cedar forest to the foot of an old volcano overlooking Oued Gigou. At the top of this hill they established an outwork with views for miles over the surrounding country of the Beni Mguild. The very warriors would come by night to fire a few shots at the outpost, or more discreetly, creep up and knife a sentinel! Even more surprised were the Berbers, when winter came, to see some of the garrison using skis to fetch the mail from Almis n-Gigou. Timhadit was the name given to this hilltop fort.[3]

Colonel Poeymirau's plan to establish a link with the Moulouya Valley via the Foum Kheneg canyon and Taghzeft pass was put on ice, such was the threat posed by small Berber war parties (*djiwsh*) operating in their own backyard—never mind full-scale *harkas*, under Sidi Raho's command, known to be active in the vicinity. If the marabout had difficulty achieving unity between the Beni Mguild, Ayt Youssi, and Ayt Seghroushen, he did manage to maintain anti-French feeling at a high pitch in their ranks. In June 1916, Sidi Raho again took the field, this time further northeast on the *triq es-sseltan*, where the French had built a fort at Taghzout near Jbel Tishshoukt.

One night, he launched 2,000 of his men against this vital outpost held by a French-led force of 250 Goum irregulars and Senegalese riflemen. Though the battle raged non-stop for forty-eight hours, the Berbers inflicting heavy casualties on the defenders (and taking quite a few themselves), on the second day, the Taghzout outpost was still in French hands. Then the cavalry arrived from Meknes, in the shape of Colonel Poeymirau's rescue force.[4] The Berbers' failure was due to their lacking support weapons (machine guns, grenade launchers, etc.) and tools for hacking their way through barbed wire, while the outpost's heavy weapons gave the defenders a decided advantage. This would be the rule throughout the Atlas campaigns: with one or two exceptions, no French outpost ever fell to the Berbers, contrary to what happened in the Rif.

Bekrit beleaguered

Another Berber area was attracting French attention. West of Timhadit was hill-girt Bekrit, held by the Ayt 'Abdi (Beni Mguild). This group, then, had to be neutralized before the trans-Atlas route could be declared safe. Such an expedition would have the advantage of preventing German arms and ammunition, sent by 'Abdelmalek in the northeast, from reaching the Zaïan around Khenifra, and the best way to achieve this, apparently, was to occupy Bekrit itself.[5] At the end of May 1917, Colonel Poeymirau led a force that established an outpost on a low hill protruding from the Bekrit hollow. To the east lay a wooded hill, the Ras Tarsha; northeast stood the steep-sided Koubbat hills and cedar-studded Jbel Hayyan, the direction from which the supply columns would have to come.

With its clear fields of fire on all sides, the post would be difficult to capture; the rugged terrain to the northeast, however, had immense tactical possibilities—all of which the local Berbers took in at a glance. During the night of 18–19 June 1917, in poor visibility with rain and hail, a group of the Ayt Sgougou clan made an attempt on the outpost, only to be stopped in their tracks by machine-gun fire. Their war chief, Aqebli, was killed. Despite this setback, not one Berber rallied to the French flag.[6] The occupation of Bekrit was developing into a costly fiasco—yet another case of Lyautey's underestimating "the topographical obstacles and the ability of the un-subdued populations to sustain the hardships of refuge in the mountains during the winter."[7] The French were never able to evaluate adequately an unexpected Moroccan ability to accept suffering as the price to pay for freedom and honor. Contemporary poetry contains ample evidence of this:

> Still possess mules to transport bag and baggage,
> Also tea to drink; wheat to keep the wolf from the door.
> Shall remain among those who their pride have retained![8]

The Berbers soon understood that during the day, out of gunshot from Bekrit outpost, they could go about their pastoral business undisturbed. At night there were splendid possibilities for young bloods to prove their valor by infiltrating the French camp, stealing a rifle here, stabbing a sentry there. They were past masters at this sport and especially skilled at escaping detection. No wonder the garrison rapidly developed a siege mentality! Inevitably, morale would sink to its lowest point in winter, with repeated snowstorms and freezing weather barely relieved by the croaking of overflying ravens. Meanwhile, warmly draped in their homespun woollen cloaks, the Beni Mguild had been patiently observing the outpost from the fringe of the great cedar forest. Sooner or later a column would come to resupply Bekrit, giving the Berbers opportunities for ambush and assault.

Away from their fortifications, the *irumin* would be vulnerable to the classic Berber attack launched at close quarters over rugged, wooded ground: a sporting, man-to-man business with none of this firing-from-behind-parapets nonsense.

Ras Tarsha and the Koubbats

The resultant fighting certainly lived up to their expectations. In 1920–1, once the big early summer convoy had got through unscathed, their safe return passage was only secured at the price of desperate free-for-alls in bushy ravines, or bayonet charges through the cedars. Yet the June 1920 supply column had a smooth run in and things went perfectly on the way back—until Timhadit was almost in sight. Then Sidi Raho's men attacked and there was a short, sharp action.[9] Likewise, at the end of August 1920, the Beni Mguild allowed the relief column to resupply Bekrit unopposed. But once it headed for home it came under heavy fire from Berbers concealed in the cedars on Ras Tarsha. During the afternoon, as the column skirted the Koubbat hills, the Berbers came down like fiends on a disciplinary detachment of the unpopular *Bataillons d'Afrique*[10] and handled them very roughly indeed, throwing one of their wounded officers over the edge of a cliff.[11]

Meanwhile, Lyautey himself acknowledged that "the occupation of Bekrit had not yielded the expected results."[12] So, in 1921 the French returned to the fray in greater strength, planning to build a proper track in order to secure the Bekrit area and cow the local Berbers into submission. However, on June 25, 1921, unlike previous years, the column from Timhadit had to fight its way to Bekrit. The Berbers managed to delay the French for three hours of bitter fighting on Ras Tarsha. Leaping out from behind bushes, dropping from trees, there were Amazigh fighters everywhere. In the words of one officer, "our troops had to clear each rocky ridge at bayonet point and not without taking casualties. On the surrounding hill-sides, epic battles raged between opposing groups using dagger and bayonet."[13]

Once the French artillery had joined in, Ras Tarsha was finally occupied in strength. That night, however, the position suffered two terrific onslaughts from about 1,200 Berbers, the French gunners coming off second best in hand-to-hand work with knife and bayonet.[14] French losses that day amounted to approximately fifty killed and 100 wounded. Although there had been heavy casualties among the assailants, the French were amazed at their adversaries' courage and at their ability to press home lethal attacks in spite of their lack of heavy weapons.

The next day the French fared little better. They needed to occupy the Koubbat hills so as to protect the northern flank of their navvies, who were busy building the dirt road towards Bekrit. No sooner had the detachment reached the rocky summit plateau, full of cracks and crevices, of the Northern Koubbat than it was thrown back by a large Berber force. Subject to infiltration and outflanking moves, the detachment extricated itself with great difficulty. Again, some of their wounded were cast from the cliffs. Later, the Berbers on Jbel Hayyan were dispersed by an artillery supported counter-attack. Thus ended a particularly bloody episode: losses on both sides had been heavy and French prestige had suffered accordingly. In the final analysis, Bekrit had certainly not been worth such sacrifices in men and money.[15]

End of play in Middle Atlas

On the ground, the French had made rapid gains. In June 1921 their irregular Zaïan horsemen had reached the cedar-girt lake of Agelmam Azigza and, soon after, the very springs of the fast-flowing Wansifen (Oued Oum er-Rbia'). More significantly, in September, their flocks decimated as much by the rigors of winter as by bombardment, their stomachs empty, the Ayt Sgougou surrendered. Bekrit and its distant, dismal hollow were safe at last for the conquerors, thus guaranteeing free circulation along the trans-Atlas road. A significant group of Beni Mguild and Ishqern irreconcilables, however, refused to surrender and broke away southwards, seeking refuge in the Tounfit area.[16]

After ten years (1912–21) of intense effort the French had achieved what no Moroccan ruler had done since Moulay Ismaïl, that is bring to heel the unruly Fazaz tribes in the sultan's name. The Berbers had certainly not been wanting in courage. As long as warfare remained asymmetric in nature, their intimate knowledge of the cedar-covered hills in the Middle Atlas had enabled them to hold their own. But when their high-tech foe was able to bring to bear superior equipment, artillery, and aircraft—and thanks also to his communications and military training—they had been decisively outperformed. It now remained to be seen to what extent their equally warlike neighbors in southeast Morocco had fared against French incursions into the demanding environment of desert and palm grove.

Stemming the Tide in Southeast Morocco

Down in the southeastern border area near Algeria some of the best fighters from the Atlas and the desert had, for several years, been actively retarding the French advance. In this region, the resistance was as fierce as it was well organized. Already in 1889 a German ethnologist, commenting on the oases of the Dra'a, Tafilalt, and southeast, had observed that:

> The few travellers who have sought to explore this corner of northwest Africa have been considerably hampered by the fanaticism of the inhabitants, and even more by the suspicion that visitors are political agents and Christian spies seeking to infiltrate the country in some disguise or other. These people live in perpetual fear of annexation by France.[1]

This fear had already led to a delegation of chiefs from the Saharan oases Touat and Saoura traveling to Fez to lay their case before the sultan and implore his protection. Since around 1870, the most warlike tribe of the Moroccan southeast, the Ayt Khebbash, had borne French Algerian troops a serious grudge for attempts made to limit their nomadic movements. At home in the wide open sandy spaces, they were the real masters of the southeastern marches; highly mobile, living for days off a few dates with only buttermilk to quench their thirst, they were skilled raiders specialized in lengthy forays into the sand sea.

For some time now, they had become the most dynamic element of the Ayt 'Atta super-tribe. Blocked in the north, they had diverted their energy towards the desert in an attempt to gain a foothold in the southern Algerian oases. "If the French hadn't stopped us, we'd have gone right through to the Mzab," one of them told an American researcher.[2] When the French occupied these areas in 1901–2 this expansionism was somewhat curtailed. As a breeding ground of mysticism and saintliness, these arid reaches had produced outstanding characters, including Abou Mahalli and, now, Moulay Lahssen es-Sbaï, leaders of men able to preach the *jihad* against *irumin* invaders. Highly sensitive over this question of territorial integrity, intolerant, xenophobic even, the inhabitants of southeast Morocco were to react very strongly against *la Pacification*.

The Moroccans of today can be rightly proud of this area's contribution to the resistance effort. With the possible exception of the struggle in the Rif, nowhere else in the country did the invader come up against such highly organized resistance. Indeed, the local war effort here transcended the limits of village or clan. This wide open country of mud fortresses, grass-covered steppe, *artemisia* scrub, and stony plateaux produced fighters of a caliber more than equal to the invader. Most belonged to the Ayt Khebbash, supported by other elements from Ayt 'Atta and their neighbors, the nomadic Ayt Hammou Bel-Hsseyn.

These formidable raiders were usually dismissed by the French as mere looters, at best as *bandits d'honneur*.[3] In fact, they were genuine Moroccan patriots, having taken the field against the French since around 1900. At the beginning of that year 1,800 Ayt Khebbash had defended the Aïn Shayr palm grove against an incursion from Algeria, only retiring after putting one-eighth of the attacking French force out of action. They even took the war to the enemy, when, in February 1901, 1,500 cameleers amongst them and armed with "Remingtons and antique muzzle-loaders," they crossed the sandy wastes undetected to attack the French post of Timimoun, an oasis of the Touat region, deep in Algeria.[4]

The year 1908 witnessed the rise of Moulay Lahssen es-Sbaï, a religious figure from the Ayt Seghroushen of the upper Oued Guir and an indefatigable preacher of unconditional resistance. In May, he and his men stoutly defended Boudenib. After this, he retired up the Guir Valley to Toulal and spent a month recruiting men for the *jihad*. By mid-June a *harka* of 20,000 warriors had mustered, "armed with everything from Lebel repeaters to knives and clubs,"[5] the largest concentration of all the Atlas campaigns. Moving downstream to Tazouggert, they pitched camp at the outlet of the gorge slightly upstream from Boudenib.

Just before the attack on Boudenib on September 1, 1908, there occurred an incident which amply illustrates the sense of honor and courage prevalent among this warrior people. Knowing that their forces were not equal to storming the ramparts of Boudenib fort without artillery, the Moroccans sent the outpost commander a message by runner (*arekkas*) requesting a clean fight in the open, away from fortifications and defensive weapons.[6] For the official French commentator this was sheer insolence,[7] though there was, of course, no question of the garrison complying. To have done so would have been suicidal.

The next day, when the Moroccans attacked, they concentrated their efforts on a small blockhouse, held by eighty men and situated on a knoll. Try as they might all through the night, intense artillery and machine-gun fire broke up their successive charges. The following morning, decimated by bullets and splinters, the *harka* retreated to their war camp (*tazemmalt*) at Tazouggert, leaving some 170 dead on the field.[8] Shortly afterwards a French relief column arrived from Colomb-Beshar and on September 7 there was yet another confrontation at Djorf, with the Moroccans charging in close order, only to be chopped up and dispersed by cannon fire, losing another 300 men. "The *harka* disintegrated and most of the warriors headed into the mountains or down the Ziz valley."[9]

Again, *imdyazn* of the times had a first-class theme, if a tragic one, to enlarge on:

At dawn towards us the Christians did march,
From gigantic cannon unleashing havoc.
At the war-camp many who heard the guns' distant

Thunder turned and fled, their hearts filled with dread.
Some lost their way, climbed towards the peaks,
Others across the plain did roam, racked by thirst.
All was lost: tents, bag, baggage and cooking-pot,
Dire defeat did we suffer at the Christian's hands.
Long is the road to Tazouggert's fateful field
Where by the hundred our men were felled![10]

Reinforcements despatched by Sidi 'Ali Amhaoush reached the upper Ziz Valley as the shell-shocked survivors from the battle were retreating in disorder. At this sight the men from the Middle Atlas turned back, appalled by accounts of a devastating artillery bombardment. It had been a massacre; few families in the area had been spared.

Relative calm now returned to the area until 1911, when the Ayt Hammou's nomadic existence in the Gourrama/Talsint region was disrupted by French troop movements, forcing them to head southwest near to the Tafilalt.[11] In so doing the French had unwittingly stirred up a hornet's nest: the Ayt Hammou were soon to become their most pitiless and irreconcilable adversaries. In February 1914 the French set up an outpost at Gourrama, this event causing agitation in the area. Moulay Lahssen, who had heard how the French had been bested at Ksiba, resumed the call for *jihad*. A large *harka* gathered round him near Foum Asefti northeast of Gourrama, but the insufficiently prepared *imjuhad* were dispersed at the first sortie from the outpost, after which the region remained calm for another year or so.[12] On March 10, 1916, however, Moulay Lahssen scored a signal success when 200 of his followers mounted an ambush in the Kadoussa gorge of Oued Guir on a column bringing supplies to Gourrama and killed about eighty soldiers.[13]

Biding his time till the snow had melted on the summits, Moulay Lahssen once again called for *jihad*. As from May, about 2,000 warriors heeded his summons and grouped together on Oued Ziz between Rish and Kerrando. On May 30 they unsuccessfully set about a French column at Foum Zabel, and retired, first towards Ksar es-Souk, then to the Meski palm grove where they dug themselves in. The position they established was a formidable one, with some two and a half miles of entrenchments on the left bank of Oued Ziz, defended by 8,000 men equipped with rifles, bayonets, and hand grenades. In this exercise the Berbers had been fortunate in that some of their own French-trained folk, either on furlough or deserters, had passed on their trench-digging expertise.

They had also learned a lesson: rather than launch mass cavalry charges, wait for the invader to come and dislodge them. On a warm July morning came the first French assault on the right flank of the position. At first, the Moroccans counter-attacked with cold steel in groups of 100 or 200 men till the enemy gunners opened up and high-explosive shells yet again forced them back. The main *qsar* of Meski was burned and the *harka* retired, losing approximately 500 men.[14] Despite this reverse and the number of lives lost, Moulay Lahssen gathered another force with which he threatened Boudenib, cutting its line of communication with Algeria. Again defeated in battle near Talsinnt at the end of July, he escaped towards the Moulouya and finally surrendered a few days later.

On the credit side there was Moulay Lahssen's matchless energy in exhorting the local population to resist; on the debit side, however, apart from his one success at Kadoussa, all other ventures had proved spectacular failures. As one observer has pointed out *à propos* of these marabouts: "If his plans come to nothing, if his *baraka* appears doubtful or inadequate, he is put to death without hesitation."[15]

His brother, Moulay 'Abdallah ou Sbaï, nevertheless carried on the fight, concentrating his efforts on Tafilalt and occupying Aoufous with 10,000 warriors. After French artillery fire had flushed him out of this position, he and his men made a stand further south at El-Ma'adid on the northern fringe of the great palm grove. In mid-November 1916, undismayed by artillery bombardment, they stood off an assault by Senegalese riflemen for seven hours till El-Ma'adid and Jbel Erfoud were occupied, when they finally retreated, having lost more than 600 *imjuhad*.[16] This battle rounded off the 1916 campaign.

When one considers that more than a thousand Moroccans of the Ziz and Guir valleys had given their lives in one year, there can be but praise for their patriotism and spirit of sacrifice, a fact which was somewhat tardily acknowledged in official Moroccan circles—in the autumn of 1971 to be precise.[17] Moulay Lahssen and his brother had managed to achieve cohesion among clans occupying some 120 miles of country between Talsint and Tafilalt—no mean feat in Berber country, where all is allegedly anarchy and division.

Enter the adventurers

However, where Moulay Lahssen had failed, two other religious chiefs were destined to travel yet further along the same road, confounding the skeptics, those that remain convinced of the Berbers' supposed chronic disunity. True, these two figures were perhaps not wholesome individuals, a mixture of humbug and ruthlessness to say the least, yet there is no denying their substantial contribution to the cause of national resistance. Known under various nicknames including "the limper," or "the stork," Belqasm n-Gadi, from the Oujda region, was about fifty years old when matters in Tafilalt came to a head.

> A small, gaunt, weedy, yellow-skinned individual, he wears a short black beard while two locks (*nwadr*) cover his temples. His speech has a nasal twang. Of an inconsequential nature, he frequently changes his mind; letters are his weak point, but he is very religious and a bit of a fanatic. Some say he's slightly mad ... A veteran adversary of the *makhzan* he once served the pretender Bouhmara in the Taza region.[18]

This politico-religious agitator settled in Tafilalt towards the end of 1917, and learned that among the Ayt 'Atta of the Regg Valley, a marabout was preaching *jihad*. The individual in question was actually an impostor. A small-time preacher from Ida ou Semlal in the Anti-Atlas, he called himself Moha n-Ifrouten es-Semlali, though his real name was Mbark ould Hsseyn (aka Mbark ou Shettou). He had ended up in the Regg Valley after lengthy wanderings through the Sahara.

Shrewdly surmising that subsequent to the reverses of Aoufous and Ma'adid the area's *imjuhad* would be in search of a new leader, Mbark claimed he was the reincarnation of a long-dead Idrissid *sharif*, Moha n-Ifrouten, whose tomb in the Regg Valley was regularly visited by pilgrims from among the Ayt 'Atta. "I am the saint in person, brought back to life by the grace of God and his Prophet Muhammad to rid Tafilalt of the infidel!" were his words to the credulous multitudes. Thanks to his "gift of the gab" together with some simple exorcism and humbug, he soon gathered a small, miscellaneous band of "300 or 400 plunderers and other wretches, gaol-birds from every corner of 'Atta-land."[19] In fact, a few Ayt Khebbach and Ayt Y'azza joined him, and at their head, he toured through the Saghro, Tazzarin, Todgha, and Ferkla regions, practicing witch-craft and stirring up the local populations. In the spring of 1918 they gathered at the *qsar* of Mesissi, pending a move on Tafilalt, whose inhabitants had signaled for help against the French,[20] no doubt in these terms:

'Tis you whom we call to the rescue, Sidi Mohand n-Ifrouten, O green lion,
When with fire the Christian strikes, thunder echoes among the precipices![21]

Sensing his opportunity, this was the moment chosen by Belqasm n-Gadi to join up and be gratified with the command of the *harka* the bogus *sharif* had just formed. The Tafilalt palm grove was now invested, the sultan's local representative, Moulay El-Mehdi, soon being shut up inside his *qsar*, while another important local saint was murdered.[22] Meanwhile, French troops called up from Boudenib had relieved El-Ma'adid and brought supplies through to Tighmart, on the edge of Tafilalt, which had hitherto been subject to unceasing harassment.

In May, Lieutenant Oustry, the post's interpreter, was assassinated by an Ou-'Atta tribesman from the Regg, actually avenging a catalog of abuse and misdeeds. The dashing Frenchman, so it later transpired, apart from commandeering all the Berber carpets in sight during his visits to local villages, had meddled once too often with the local beauties and thus paid the supreme price! Finally, a strong French force attacked Tafilalt on August 9, 1918.[23]

Checkmate in Tafilalt

Whereas the main *harka* under Belqasm was obliged to abandon the southwest corner of the Tafilalt palm grove under a hail of bombs and shells, an entire battalion of Senegalese under Colonel Doury contrived to lose its way in the heart of a sandstorm near Gaouz. Taken by surprise at close quarters by large groups of Moroccans, the detachment were slaughtered to a man, the defenders helping themselves to rifles and ammunition recovered from the dead.[24]

His prestige strengthened by this victory, Moha n-Ifrouten went on the rampage throughout Tafilalt, having various traitors executed for their previous links to the French at Tighmart. Attempts by the French to retrieve the situation proved ineffectual. Although Lyautey despatched the energetic Poeymirau, he was unable to take proper action, his men being weakened by an epidemic of Spanish influenza. To make matters worse, in September Belqasm's men diverted the waters of Oued Ziz so that they began to lick at the base of the Tighmart fortifications, threatening to undermine them.[25] As the position was becoming untenable, the French retreated to Erfoud on October 15 and set up a fort there, strongly armed with cannon. For fourteen long years the French sentinels would gaze southwards in frustration to the immense green palm sea, a perpetual reminder of a reverse intolerable to a proud nation that had only recently triumphed in the Great War.

Meanwhile, weakened by the abandonment of Tafilalt, French prestige had suffered a severe blow. A number of decapitated heads, including those of ten officers killed at Gaouz, were paraded triumphantly from one oasis to another, even up into the Atlas, as unmistakable signs of a great victory over the *akhenzir* ("swine"). Bearing letters from the Tafilalt *sharif*, messengers raced north to alert their brethren in the Middle and High Atlas. From his Tounfit zaouia, Sidi Mohand ou-Lhajj passed on the message to the Beni Mguild of the Moulouya; further north, Sidi Raho urged the Ayt Seghroushen and Marmousha to sharpen their daggers and prepare their ammunition. Even Ou-Laïdi, holding out in the freezing Zaïan hills with a handful of followers, received an encouraging letter which announced Moha n-Ifrouten's imminent arrival in the area, after which they would join forces in an attack on Fez, from which they would march on the coastal towns and eventually on Algeria![26]

The Great Rebellion

All this inflammatory propaganda worked wonders; the time was ripe for *jihad*. Answering Moha n-Ifrouten's call, 12,000 warriors invested French outposts between Erfoud and Ksar es-Souk and severed the imperial road between Oued Ziz and the Moulouya, isolating the Boudenib garrison. Early in December, although the outer defensive line was initially swamped, the El-Ma'adid outpost survived a desperate assault. At Erfoud, the Berbers failed to penetrate the perimeter wire after which both sides settled down to a three-week siege. In the meantime, at Ksar es-Souk, several determined attacks occurred as the garrison were sitting down to their Christmas dinner.[27] In the Upper Ziz Valley and Moulouya most of the main posts were hard-pressed. In the meantime, Ayt Hadiddou and Ayt Merghad fighters surrounded Rish, the Beni Mguild closely invested Midelt and Itzer, while the Marmousha and Ayt Seghroushen came down on Ksabi from their icy plateaux for a two-month siege.

At no other time since El-Herri had the situation been so precarious for the French in Morocco. The resistance had staged such a spectacular recovery, contaminating the entire *blad as-siba*, that the invader appeared in real danger of losing the eastern mountain regions and desert fringe. All that was missing was a true leader. Now, unfortunately, Moha n-Ifrouten lacked the fiber of some of his predecessors. Although able to whip up the crowds into a fighting frenzy, there was an element of grandeur, of saintliness lacking in his make-up—that little extra something that marks the truly charismatic leader.

In her hour of need, France called on her ally, El-Glaoui, who obliged by sending a punitive expedition of 10,000 men to the Dadds and Todgha valleys on the rebels' western flank. Just after New Year's Day, Lyautey came to Boudenib and sent forward his best man, Poeymirau, to attack Moha n-Ifrouten's *harka* at Mesissi. The energetic general's troops acquitted themselves with valor and stormed the oasis, though unfortunately for him, he was maimed by the premature explosion of a 65 mm shell from one of his own mountain guns.[28]

Several weeks elapsed before his replacement arrived—a General Théveney, hitherto in charge of the Tadla region. By then, Moha n-Ifrouten, who had meanwhile proclaimed himself sultan,[29] had dug in amid the palm trees around Tizimi. At the end of January 1919, he was nevertheless evicted from that oasis after the usual artillery barrage. By now totally discredited, Moha n-Ifrouten was forsaken by the Ayt 'Atta and obliged to flee southwards with only 400 faithful followers.[30] To the north, however, the Berbers still had several French posts totally encircled and, at first, given the atrocious weather with heavy snowfall and *pistes* becoming mudbaths, little could be done. Ksabi, which had suffered heavy casualties from attacks by the Marmousha and Ayt Seghroushen, was eventually relieved on February 26, the sieges of Midelt and Itzer being raised some ten days later.[31]

After lying low for three months, Moha n-Ifrouten bounced back in May 1919, apparently none the worse for his recent adventures, having fully recovered his fluency and credit among the local inhabitants. After touring the Todgha and Ferkla regions, he launched a series of attacks on various French-held *qsur* in the vicinity of Erfoud. Though unsuccessful, he eventually planned a major expedition against Erfoud on October 23. This never materialized for, in the meantime, the two rebel leaders had quarrelled; as Moha made as if to draw a pistol, Belqasm shot him without any compunction.[32]

Belqasm's arbitrary takeover

Regrouping the *harka*, Belqasm took command on the spot and returned to Rissani. Claiming to be a *sharif*, he set up a pseudo-*makhzan*. During his thirteen years' dictatorship he showed himself every bit as cruel and despotic as Moha n-Ifrouten had been. Moha's death was a serious body blow to the resistance movement as it put paid to his repeated attempts to coordinate offensive action with other leaders. Belqasm's leadership appeared lacklustre by comparison: apart from a limited counter-attack on Oued Ziz in September 1921, he retained a defensive posture around Tafilalt. His first move was to win the Ayt 'Atta over to his side, getting them to recognize him as their lawful chief and defender of Islam. Above all, they were to weed out all unreliable elements, especially marabouts likely to set themselves up as rivals or those suspected of gathering intelligence for the enemy. With help from the Ayt 'Atta he seized the Derqawa zaouia of Sidi el-Aousan in Ferkla and brought back as prisoner to Rissani its highly respected saint, Sidi El-Houari. Belqasm had the venerable old man blown from a gun, rather like the British did during the 1857 Indian Mutiny. Belqasm justified this barbaric execution on the grounds that the saint had been in touch with Sultan Moulay Youssef's pro-Christian *makhzan*. Belqasm later had another holy man murdered by the Ayt 'Atta: Sidi Hmad ben Bou-Bker, respected chief of the important zaouia of

Tamgrout on Oued Dra'a. He also did away with various agitators who had come to Tafilalt to stir up trouble against him. Jews requesting French help, whose mail had been intercepted, were likewise put to death.[33] This was not unusual practice in a society where using *hartani* ("blacks") for rifle practice, or not respecting protection pacts vis-à-vis Jews, had sometimes been considered in good taste.[34]

No wonder most commentators have little to say in praise of this despot and the reign of terror he imposed on Tafilalt. More significantly, however, he was able to prevent the French authorities from setting foot in an important strategic region. For many years his name would ring in their ears as an unwelcome reminder of their earlier setback and ignominious retreat from Tafilalt. The Moroccan resistance would no doubt have been happier with a less unsavory character, but there was no denying his actual contribution to the resistance.[35]

Great *Qayd* versus Marabout

Whereas from Demnat to Taza mountain tribes blindly obeyed their religious leaders' call to resistance, the Marakesh High Atlas at this time was relatively quiet, thanks to the influence of the great *qayd*s. However, with time, what should by rights have been a short-lived experiment had gradually been allowed to develop into a permanent institution, allowing feudal despotism to hold sway. By the early 1920s, outshining his Mtouggui and Goundafi rivals, wily El-Glaoui had managed to become an essential part of the French system in Morocco. There was now no question of reforming his rule in any way. He had become one of the pillars of French native policy in the country, where, in the name of law and order, certain traditions should not be disturbed. As one French official pointed out:

> The great *qayd*s render a signal service in a country where banditry is such a well-rooted pastime that the aristocracy which it generates is equal to any other. Under our tempering hand, and on our account, these former plunderers of caravans know how to handle the natives, who in turn fully appreciate the situation, thus keeping the peace in areas where their authority receives our full backing.[1]

Hajj Thami eventually inherited the Glaoui Empire from his elder brother Si Madani. Since his formal investiture as Makzan *qayd* under Moulay Hassan, the former had set about bringing the surrounding tribes under his rule. Well served by its position near a low-lying pass in the range between Adrar n-Dern and the limestone central High Atlas further east, his citadel at Telouat dominated the entire region. Si Madani was the first incumbent to specialize in levying caravan dues on the trade route from Marrakesh to Tafilalt.[2] If on the *amalu* ("shaded") side of the range he could pose as a champion of Berber independence, on the south slopes, by keeping the peace in the sultan's name, he acted the part of the dutiful *makhzan* agent.

He was quite a character. Despite his occasional cruelty and unscrupulous treachery, he had the makings of a real statesman. Taking advantage of the *makhzan*'s weakened position, he had achieved supremacy in the south and felt that if he handled the French cleverly, he would obtain a free hand to operate throughout the tribal areas of the Atlas and Transatlasia. Glaoui expansionism had first cleared the road towards Ouarzazat in 1901. One of his most embarrassing rivals, *amghar* 'Ali of Tamdakht, had been an early victim. Si Madani's *harka* laid siege to his turreted kasbah, unlimbered their small Krupp cannon, and soon breached the walls. As his fortress fell, *amghar* 'Ali desperately

Fig. 22: Girl from the Glaoua tribe near Tizi n-Tishka (Marrakesh High Atlas).

sallied forth at the head of a small group and was rapidly neutralized, captured, and beheaded.[3]

Beyond Warzazat lay the Ayt 'Atta confederation. At first all went well, El-Glaoui acting as arbiter in their inter-clan disputes and protection racket directed at the oasis-dwelling communities of Oued Dra'a. Advancing west at a leisurely pace, the Glaoua easily crushed feeble village resistance and reached as far as Assarag on the upper Tifnout. Then, in 1913, among the flower-studded upland pastures and basaltic towers that surround the old Siroua volcano, decisive battles pitted musket-wielding Waouzgit tribesmen against Glaoua mercenaries armed with breech-loaders. Soon, the smoke of burning fortresses climbed slowly into the sky to shouts of frustrated rage from their Waouzgit defenders, outgunned by their attackers. The Ayt Waouzgit, however, later formed the backbone of many of El-Glaoui's expeditions.[4] Nevertheless, in the event of capture, nothing but destitution and death awaited headstrong tribesmen who, refusing to submit, took to the hills: either immediate demise at the hands of the headman's sword, or a slow, lingering agony, chained to the walls of a lice-ridden dungeon in Telouat fortress.

Tribal warfare on the Glaoua marches

Eventually, the entire Demnat backcountry, dominated by lofty, castellated Jbel Rat, came under Glaoui rule. Ayt Bou Wlli, Ayt Mgoun, Ayt 'Abbas—these previously independent tribesmen were forced to bow to the tyranny of the lord of Telouat. All, that is, except for the Ayt 'Affan, an out-of-the-way clan who hold the narrow cleft of the Tassaout gorge between 12,000-foot peaks.

As we have seen, at the end of 1918, Moha n-Ifrouten's great uprising had enabled El-Glaoui to reach through to Todgha, building a fine kasbah at Tinghir and others on Oued Dadds upstream from Boumaln. This actually proved the high-water mark of his imperial expansion; events were under way which would shortly result in El-Glaoui's first serious setback. The *igweramn* of Zaouit Ahansal had already been in the limelight in the early eighteenth century as champions of Berber resistance. This important religious confraternity, famous for its *baraka*, had a broad sphere of influence in the Atlas. Going from north to south, their domain ranged from the limestone cliffs of Jbel R'nim and the peak of Tasemmit above the Tadla plain right down to the fast-flowing streams of the Imdghas, Ousikis, and other Dadds tributaries.

Beyond lay Jbel Kousser and yet more plateaux, split by the vertical gashes of huge canyons, through which race white-water streams bringing to the parched Tadla plain a sizeable percentage of Atlas snow-melt. This Morocco of the heights was famous for its distinctive architecture best typified by the graceful wood and stone *tighremt*, a stout red tower-like defensive structure directly linked to the requirements of chronic vendetta. A social set-up such as this obviously required the presence of skilled arbiters, which was why the Ahansal marabouts had acquired great influence over the area's mountain clans. Thus, the chief occupation of Dadda Saïd's descendants was to settle disputes likely to arise in summer between semi-sedentary clans and the newly-arrived southern shepherds with their innumerable herds. Whichever their clan, all these men had recourse to the judgment of Sidi Mah El-Hansali, undisputed highland chief.[5]

He was, according to one observer, a small, authoritarian-looking man of thirty-five–forty years of age with a straggly beard and piercing eyes. French officers mention his generosity, his humor, his intelligence, his gay, playful nature and sense of diplomacy. He enjoyed sitting down with other trenchermen to a feast of roast mutton. He apparently behaved more like a trickster or a clever sorcerer than a saint, being scarcely proficient at saying his prayers, while his superior intelligence held the highlanders in thrall, probably due to his unquestioned *baraka*.[6] Sidi Mah's time was divided between his main Ahansal lodge at Zaouit Ahansal beneath the 11,000-foot cliffs of Timghazin and Aroudan, and his four-turreted *tighremt*[7] on Asif Bernat. Berber tradition has it that Sidi Mah's favourite stunt was to jump from one of these corner-towers, holding a tea-tray in his right hand with several glasses on it, and land without breaking a single glass.[7] Sidi Mah's authority was contested by three rival lodges: Zaouia Temga at the foot of Aghembo n-Mestfran's slab-faced, conglomerate pyramid;[8] the zaouia of Sidi 'Ali ou Hsseyn at Anergui; and finally, the near-rival Zaouia Asker under Si Housseyn ou Temga, a cousin of the elder Ahansal branch. These academic subtleties should not prove embarrassing to our reader, who will recall that the real Zaouit Ahansal is the one at Agouddim.[9] Events now shaping up on the Atlas front would soon curtail this internecine rivalry and Sidi Mah's undoubted political skills would be needed to meet the common threat:

O Sidi Mah, come help me do!
O *agwerram*, where have you been?
Your young men nowhere to be seen!
In God's name march with your *harka*,
That we may descend on the plain.
Let them come if any warriors remain!
People in the know do claim
The man with the *képi* is losing heart.[10]
The Senegalese are ready to depart.
Of supplies the enemy is bereft—
No guns, no bullets left.
Sunk, his ships lie on Ocean's floor.
O young men, onward to war!
Onward to take the outpost!
Despite the shells stand steadfast.
We'll capture the officer's horse,
We'll capture the French fort.
O warriors of Zaouit Ahansal,
Come and vanquish the Christian,
That in peace I may sleep again![11]

A blow to Glaoui prestige

From April 1916 the local Berbers had to defend the area from encroachment by the French, assisted by their proxy, Si Madani el-Glaoui. East of Demnat, the Atlas gateway town, Beni Mellal, was occupied on one hand, while a *harka* of hillmen proved unable to defend the access to Azilal, a strategic foothill staging-point on the trans-Atlas route. In October the enemy established a strong-point, with artillery, around its old castellated kasbah just in time to drive off a vigorous counter-attack by local tribesmen.

A strange phenomenon was observed in connection with these operations: the apparently cordial relations that pervaded between mountain peasants and invading troops. The day after the Azilal battle, the souk at Lrba' Ayt 'Attab took place among the olive trees in a cheerful atmosphere as local traders offered dates, turnips, oranges, and lemons to the French troops. Others were even parting with their beautifully decorated muskets and daggers. There were many women around, too, some selling home-baked bread, a few plying the oldest trade in the world beneath the leafy covert of a nearby wood.[12]

Throughout 1917–18, Sidi Mah displayed unflagging energy, exhorting the mountain tribes to resist the Christian invader, also threatening his line of communications between Demnat and Azilal. In the summer of 1918, the French and their Glaoua allies moved towards his residence on Asif Bernat, forcing him to muster a large force, including some Ayt 'Atta that he was fortunate enough to recruit. Nearby, on July 30, during the indecisive Battle of Bou Yahya, Si 'Abdelmalek, Si Madani's son, was fatally wounded as he charged with characteristic dash at the head of the Glaoua

Fig. 23: Men from Ayt Bou Gemmez brandishing vintage muzzle-loaders.

cavalry.[13] A grief-stricken Si Madani soon passed away, never recovering from losing his favorite son, and his mantle passed to brother Hajj Thami. For the next two years the latter quietly took over his brother's estate, dispossessing his nephews. He also consolidated his gains in the Dadds Valley, scoring some successes over the Ayt 'Atta,[14] though his influence in the Todgha and Ferkla regions remained weak so long as Belqasm Ngadi held Tafilalt.

In 1922, Hajj Thami el-Glaoui, pasha of Marrakesh, took the field near Azilal with a *harka* of more than 8,000 men. He planned nothing less than to crush the Ayt Bou Guemmez and Sidi Mah, sack Zaouit Ahansal and then march victoriously north to Waouizaght on Oued L'abid, by which time that too would have fallen into French hands. He rather naïvely set great store by the hoped-for intervention on Sidi Mah's southern flank of friendly Ayt 'Atta contingents,[15] forgetting that many elements of that super-tribe, highly suspicious of El-Glaoui anyway, were already on the marabout's side.

A French journalist who followed the French column has left us his impressions of that year's campaign. The proceedings opened in September with a parade at Tanant in the foothills, where a loyalist *qayd*, a certain Ou-Chettou, was present with his 1,200 N'tifa tribesmen: "A picturesque horde they were, clad in grimy, tattered cloaks . . . like heroes straight out of the pages of Homer. A warlike bunch, all of them anxious for the first whiff of powder, with red rags tied around their heads to distinguish them from the dissidents."[16]

Even as they moved out of Tanant, further to the south in the heart of the Atlas, more fighting was in the offing. Up in Bou Guemmez the locals had heard that the lord of

Telouat was bullying his way through the valleys. About 2,000 tribesmen had accordingly gathered near Ayt Hkim, in the upper part of the valley, their ranks reinforced by men from the Ayt 'Atta. They were now busy digging trenches and erecting stone parapets under the watchful eye of Sidi Mah. This was the real thing—no small-time mountain *barud* over some niggling grievance. Several thousand well-armed mercenaries, accustomed to easy laurels, were heading their way. Few observers would have been prepared to put their money on the defenders: "A ragged rabble in well-worn robes, armed with ornate, long-barrelled flint-lock muskets"[17]—the *taku*, as the Berbers called these weapons because of their characteristic sound, useful at close quarters but outranged by the modern rifle. One thing, however, gave them an edge over their assailants: they were fighting on home territory. On September 4, 1922, El-Glaoui's cavalry charged across the fields, their cloaks streaming in the wind. However, the tribesmen's musketry at close range from behind cover was excellent and broke this and a second charge. By nightfall, El-Glaoui sounded the retreat, having lost thirty-four killed and over seventy wounded.[18]

On the morrow a truce was declared, allowing a party of Ayt 'Atta finally to reach the Glaoui camp. But instead of arriving via Izoughar to take Sidi Mah in the rear, they had crossed by Tizi n-Ayt Imi, a move of far less tactical interest.[19] When the futile fighting resumed on the morrow, El-Glaoui's *harka* further failed to impress the assembled hillmen. So, on September 8, it was accepted that Sidi Mah's *baraka* had won the day and a ceasefire was negotiated between chief Mou Haddach and an Ayt 'Atta *amghar* in the opposing camp, Moha Ou-Daoud. The pasha of Marrakesh and his *harka* rejoined the French at Bou Yahya a few days later, having suffered a serious loss of face.

Fighting had meanwhile taken place around the kasbah of Bou Yahya, defended by a local tribal *harka*. Beaten by French-led Goums, they retreated into the winding, bushy canyon of Asif Ouabzaza. The French force and its Glaoua allies now resumed their march westward towards the mountain town of Waouizaght. They were not unopposed. Some Berbers put the rocky, tree-covered terrain to good use. Others, firing from wall-slits in their stout, wood-and-stone kasbahs, fought on till artillery shells brought the ceiling tumbling about their ears. French journalist Babin comments on the sublime courage of a lone rifleman who continued shooting even as his little fortress was catching fire.[20]

From Azilal to Waouizaght

The Tharaud brothers witnessed similar destructions of kasbahs at this time, also collecting a verse version of these desperate happenings as seen through Berber eyes:

O *jihad*, earnestly did I long for you!
O cartridge, indeed you were mine!
Had gun-powder in abundance.
Came the man with the big guns.
The proud Glaoui, too, was there.
The chatter of the *taraka* did sound.[21]
'Tis a mere piece of metal—said I.
O Doho, but we were forced to flee!

All our jewellery they did take,
Gone, all my garments were lost;
Better by bullets to be obliterated
Than to surrender by God be forced![22]

Where was Sidi Mah in the meantime? Certainly not at Zaouit Ahansal, which was ineffectually bombed on September 20 by a squadron of ten biplanes. No, he was among the tribesmen west of Azilal, urging them not to give in; promising that cousin Housseyn ou Temga would soon send the mountain clans to lend a hand. On the 26th, one group attacked from Tillouguit way; another, 3,000-strong, debouched from the Oued L'abid gorge, but pro-*makhzan qayd* Ou-Chettou and his irregulars, who bore the brunt of the assault, were equal to the occasion and the *imjuhad* came off second best, though shells and bombs were chiefly instrumental in causing their discomfiture. Waouizaght was captured shortly afterwards, thus concluding the 1922 campaign.[23]

Meanwhile, heralding the approach of winter, the first snows had fallen on Ighil Mgoun. Feelings were mixed among the Ayt Bougemmez: some youngsters knew they could get safely married, knowing that, thanks to Sidi Mah, they had been saved from El-Glaoui's timeless tyranny. Even the widows who mourned husbands, sons, or lovers killed at Ayt Hkim knew their menfolk had died bravely, musket or dagger in hand.

For the homeless around Azilal, however, the prospects were somewhat grim, though the invader proved unexpectedly generous, actually helping them rebuild their homes. Sidi Mah could not resist the French indefinitely, this he knew. The hillmen had been severely weakened by a year of tedious campaigning, yet he had, for sure, put a

Fig. 24: Villages in Ayt Bou Gemmez Valley (Central High Atlas).

stop to El-Glaoui's expansionist designs. Though visualized by the French as the lesser of two evils, they would eventually bring to bear their superior military machine and, if he wished to spare the mountain villagers famine and bombardment, not to mention subsequent plunder, Sidi Mah needed to decide on a plan of action. Perhaps he could count on the *irumin*'s leniency. Their Native Affairs officers, men like Lieutenant Spillman whom he had met on one occasion,[24] appeared approachable, open, and just.

When operations resumed in 1923, Sidi Mah and the clans around Azilal would put up token resistance. To hedge his bets, however, the cunning marabout decreed that the Agouddim, Temga, and Anergui lodges of the Ahansala brotherhood should not surrender just yet. By keeping a foot in the other camp Sidi Mah was taking precautions against any unexpected shift of fate. Accordingly, at the end of June 1923, after a short show of resistance, Sidi Mah emerged from his fortress at Bernat and came to offer his services to the French-supported *makhzan*. Thanks to his timely surrender, the hills between Azilal and the upper Dadds Valley escaped the horrors of modern warfare. Despite his subsequent total loyalty to France, Sidi Mah kept in touch with Zaouit Ahansal and, in 1933, played a major role in negotiating the final surrender of the dissident clans. In the mid-1920s, trans-Atlas trips by small French parties escorted by Sidi Mah would yield a rich harvest of geographical knowledge, without ever meeting so much as a single hostile *jaysh* fighter,[25] a fact that speaks volumes as to Sidi Mah's authority in the area, exercising in some measure as significant an influence as that of El-Glaoui in the Marrakesh High Atlas.

Whereas all was now quiet on the Azilal front, an interesting situation was developing north of Waouizaght, up on the rugged flanks of Jbel R'nim, haunted by recalcitrant bands that refused to admit they were beaten. Towards the close of May they were energetically preparing for combat, as it was obvious the *irumin* were about to attack upvalley to secure the strategic Sgatt plateau overlooking Oued L'abid. On this occasion, Sidi Housseyn ou Temga gathered a strong *harka* on Tizi n-Islit, the col between R'nim and Tasemmit, and, on May 26, 1923, came down like a wolf on the fold, inflicting some seventy casualties on the French camp. After a lull of two months, the French climbed towards the col to establish an outpost. This led to a week's fighting around Almou n-Tarselt. Biplanes from Beni Mellal had to be called in to strafe the tribesmen as they launched desperate attacks on French positions.[26]

A situation of uneasy stalemate finally emerged: the Berbers failed to capture any of the outposts, while the French were just as clearly unable to make further headway. Instead, they clung precariously to the flanks of Jbel R'nim, with vulnerable lines of communication. The operation had been a decided flop, with nearly 200 casualties to show for it.[27] Not only were the bulk of the Ahansal saints still firmly in the dissident camp, but they had successfully blocked the prospects of an immediate French advance up the Oued L'abid Valley. The confidence of the local tribesmen in their ability to fight off the French in future engagements had thus received a much-needed shot in the arm. The *irumin* had perhaps gained a foothold on the ridge dominating the Tadla plain, but the backcountry, its fighting potential practically intact, remained uncompromisingly hostile. This was nowhere more the case than in the upper Moulouya, with its aggressive mountain saints, an area on which we must now focus our attention.

Between Oum Rbia' and Moulouya:
Failure of the Marabouts

Since Colonel Mangin's column had been badly mauled in 1913 none of his colleagues had attempted to climb the heights above Kasba Tadla. Painful memories of that ignominious occasion had much to do with this, especially so long as the invader's attention was focused on reducing Zaïan resistance around Khenifra. A specialist in brinkmanship, Moha ou Saïd had managed to keep out of harm's way by alternating between diplomacy and a more radical attitude towards the French. With the onset of age he became downright careful. If in 1920 he had sent bogus sultan Belqasm Ngadi presents on hearing of his success in the southeast, he passed on to the Kasba Tadla outpost the latest letter announcing France's imminent defeat received from El-Hiba's brother, Merrebi Rebbo, still holding out in the southwest. In 1921, Moha ou Saïd advised his son to submit to the French though he himself retired deeper into the hills, biding his time till death came to claim him.[1]

Thus with the two Mohas, temporal leaders both, gone from the scene, there was a serious power vacuum on the Tadla/Fazaz borderlands. This was compounded by the fact that no spiritual leader had stepped into Sidi 'Ali Amhaoush's slippers. Of his sons, Sidi Sheikh was reputedly brave but young, while the heir presumptive, Sidi Lmekki, an able enough preacher, was rather too much of a womanizer, even by local standards. In fact, neither had the aura, the charisma of the departed "sultan of the mountains." From their zaouia at Bou Wattas near the Moulouya source, they barely managed to retain the clientele of the eastern Ayt Sokhman; many of their father's other parishioners escaped their control.[2]

In-fighting among the marabouts

Already, in 1917, there had been dissension in the Imhiwash ranks. After a row over some womenfolk, their cousins, the Oulad Sidi Taïbi, had broken away, with many of their parishioners in tow. Of the three Taïbi brothers, two were destined to play an important role: Sidi Mohammed Taïbi, who reigned on the southern Ishqern from his residence near the Moulouya source; and 'Abd el-Malek Taïbi, living further west at Naour and exerting greater influence on the tribesmen once Moha ou Saïd had passed away.[3] As for the eastern part of Sidi 'Ali's ex-territory, it was taken over by his former *fqih*, Sidi Mohand ou-Lhajj. Passing himself off as Sidi 'Ali's legitimate heir, he brought the Beni Mguild of the Moulouya and the Ayt Yahya, together with the *igwerramn* of Sidi Yahya ou Youssef and the Tounfit zaouias under his banner. An active anti-French propagandist, he maintained links to other resistance leaders such as Sidi Raho or Belqasm Ngadi, but at first refused to have anything to do with Sidi 'Ali's sons.

A clever sorcerer, well known for his long, unkempt hair, there was nothing Mohand ou-Lhajj liked better than showing off on market days, consorting with ladies, dispensing justice, or exhorting Muslims to battle. Thus would he harangue the crowd: "When fighting the Christian who has invaded our land and is preparing to advance further, no mercy can be shown."[4] Should he suspect someone of dealings with the nearest French outpost, he would admonish him in these words: "Material things are as nought compared to eternal felicity in heaven. Better die poor as a Muslim than lead a life of dishonour through contact with those dogs beyond Oued Srou!"[5] On another occasion he had denounced the defeatist atmosphere at a meeting of the local council of graybeards: "You want to surrender whereas fewer than ten of you have been killed. You want some helpful spirit to emerge from these very stones, yet you are powerless to defend yourselves!"[6]

Brave words these, though necessary if the fight was to go on. Given the gravity of the situation, most rival marabouts were resigned to sinking their differences; the Taïbi brothers had come to Bou Wattas to meet the sons of Sidi 'Ali, in an attempt to paper over the cracks and define a common policy.[7] Now that the enemy was attacking the Amazigh homeland, the time had come to show a bold front: trenches were dug around "front-line" villages like Kebbab, while the saints fixed certain limits, marked by *ikerkurn* ("stone cairns") beyond which the French should, under no circumstance, be allowed to advance.[8] Thus did the marabouts, amid protestations of undying friendship, persuade each other that bygones were bygones, that under their inspired leadership the Berber fighters would repel the pork-eaters. The invader's planes, known as *ibukha* ("insects"), would be changed into storks, the very bullets from their rifles would go wide of the mark.

"Thus it is," Guennoun reminds us, "that from time to time the Berbers will indulge in wishful thinking, only to sink back into despondency."[9] As the saints knew all too well, if their *baraka* was found wanting, if their tall stories were disproved, they would need to show the assembled multitudes a clean pair of heels. Luckily, these smooth talkers were rarely at a loss. Thus one market day at Tounfit did Mohand ou-Lhajj hoodwink the crowd into believing that an overflying French aircraft had been frightened away by his own magic arts!

Meanwhile, the marabouts spared no efforts. Sidi Lmekki issued the direst warnings against any of his people who were lukewarm Muslims or showed any inclination towards surrender. An atmosphere of frenzied commotion now reigned amidst the Atlas foothills throughout that spring of 1922. As flower carpets decorated the meadows, alive with newborn lambs learning how to walk on wobbly legs, endless processions of caterpillars ascended the cedars, while from Kasba Tadla to Tounfit the tribes were mobilizing.

Long files of market-goers would converge from all points of the compass on a typical upper Moulouya *ssuq*: a vast concourse of white-robed tribesmen, hawk-faced men wearing daggers, wielding long-barrelled muskets and breech-loaders. Drinking tea, dipping bread into dishes of *tajin*, they would talk for hours of the *irumin* and the imminent prospects of further fighting. The invader had not crossed the line of cairns; surely he must be impressed by the mountaineers' fighting ability. How else could one explain the Christians' comparative inaction over the past ten years since those days near Ksiba when they had proved such easy game! All this while, armorers and blacksmiths were working overtime, bartering grain for cartridges, sharpening knives and bayonets, replenishing empty cartridge-cases, or recalibrating Martini-Henry and Lee-Metford rifles so they could take the regulation 7.15 mm round as fired by the standard issue French '86-'93 Lebel. Far in the background, pearly-white against a peerlessly blue sky, lay the master mountain of the area, Jbel el-'Ayyashi, "beyond which lived the Ayt Hadiddou who feared nought but God," so men said.[10]

Zaïan cavalry versus mountain tribesmen

When operations resumed in April 1922, the Ayt Ouirra were the first to suffer. On the 9th, a column finally reached Ksiba and the French flag was hoisted above Moha ou Saïd's former capital. The same day, however, the dissidents evened the score by roughly handling a detachment of 700 Zaïan cavalry that tried to reach Ksiba from Zaouit ech-Cheikh. Caught in unfamiliar, rugged, and wooded terrain they were easy targets for the home team. There followed a genuine intertribal battle with ragged volleys of musketry, hand-to-hand fighting with daggers, and even Ayt Ouirra women throwing stones and encouraging their warriors with piercing, ululating cries.[11] The Zaïan finally retreated, booed by their adversaries.

This easy success over the Zaïan traitors was obviously good for Ayt Ouirra morale. They were now ripe to help Si 'Abdelmalek Taïbi in his attempt to storm the French post at Dechra el-Oued overlooking the Oum Rbia'. On the night of April 16–17, equipped with long ladders, they came with a rush and tried to scale the walls only to be repulsed by the garrison's use of hand grenades. They fled, leaving behind fifty dead.[12] This reverse thoroughly disappointed Si 'Abdelmalek, who retired to Naour with a few faithful followers.

In mid-May some 1,500 Ishqern were gathered round the fateful cairn on the bushy hill of Tinteghallin awaiting attack by Zaïan irregulars on the French side. A long and bloody brawl ensued as the fighters exchanged insults and blows, working off ancient tribal rivalries. At the height of the battle a mysterious flag-waving, white-cloaked horseman attempted to rally the Ishqern. Was this the Deliverer foretold by ancient prophecies? As the panic-stricken Zaïan wavered, Bou'azza, son of Moha ou Hammou, denounced the impostor and charged at the head of his cavalry. It took little more to rout the Ishqern, who had already suffered heavy casualties.[13]

The Tintaghallin *kerkur* had been violated in spite of their saints' prophecies that "Never shall the Imazighen be decisively defeated; vengeance can come when least expected."[14] The Ishqern were demoralized by the loss of 150 men at Tinteghallin.

At Tinteghallin pass did many a hero fall,
'Ali Oubaoui went down, on whom can we call?

See the master of the tent joyfully welcomes the
Stranger; then enters the butcher our ewes to take!
Lost for ever our finest givers of milk,
How distressful, left us naught but orphaned lambs!
O enlightened one, tell us the cause of our woe,
Buried our wise men, accursed be our line![15]

Rather death than dishonor

By the end of May the French were astride the Moulouya–Oued L'abid watershed at
Alemsid, where they built an outpost. Soon, shells were falling on Aghbala, former fief
of Sidi 'Ali Amhaoush. On June 20, 1922, the French column (*lkunur*) retired eastwards,
carefully monitored from the cedars of Jbel Toujjit, where the *igwerramn* had gathered
some 3,000 *imjuhad*.[16] The previous evening they had participated in a daring night
attack on the French bivouac at Alemsid; in the face of machine guns and grenade
launchers, several of them had got through the wire, slaughtered a few sentries and
stolen weapons from the tents.[17]

They were now poised to attack an apparently retreating enemy. During the
subsequent Battle of Tafessasset, General Théveney's column came close to disaster.
According to Guillaume, Théveney was "going to reconnoitre the site of another
outpost" when he moved east from Alemsid in the direction of Tafessasset. Voinot, for
his part, mentions a return to Azerzou, in other words a withdrawal, and that was how
the Berbers saw it. At 7 o'clock in the morning they started harassing the rearguard,
composed of a Foreign Legion (*laliju*) unit and Guillaume's Goum of native levies. As
the French conducted a fighting retreat from one low hill to another, covered by their
artillery, the Berbers would close in on the column, resulting in French bayonet charges,
"to prevent their dead and wounded from falling into enemy hands."[18] After five hours
of this running fight, Théveney's detachment reached the safety of Azerzou outpost. It
is clear, however, by reading between the lines, that an El-Herri-style disaster had been
narrowly averted.[19]

For their part, the *imjuhad* had spared no effort, pressing home their attacks in the
face of intense artillery and machine-gun fire. Among the Imhiwash, Sidi Sheikh and
Sidi Mohammed Benasser were killed as they headed a mass cavalry charge, together
with the Ayt Yahya *amghar n-tzemmalt* ("war-chief") and some hundred or so fighters.
Their grief-stricken wives had but one consolation: their men had perished like heroes
on the battlefield. Had they not sung, that very morning:

O spouses who lay with us and now are gone,
O men who prefer *barud* and forget our embrace,
O men, ne'er shall the Christian defeat you!
Fight courageously like you promised to.
In shame return not lest a yet more
Shameful welcome await you![20]

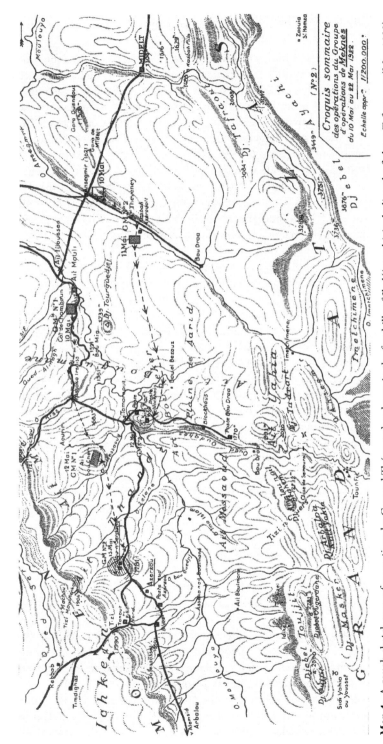

Map 4: A rough sketch map of operations by General Théveney's column in the foothills of Jbel 'Ayyashi, including the fight at Tafessasset (May 1922).

Inaccessible Tounfit

In addition to Alemsid, a post had been set up at Tafessasset, likewise equipped with 75 mm field artillery and 65 mm mountain guns for interdiction fire-missions to prevent the Berbers from using their Moulouya grazing land. On July 12, as long-range shells started falling on the Ayt Yahya capital, Tounfit, Sidi Mohand ou-Lhajj learned that the French were moving up Oued Oudghes and immediately despatched 500 local warriors to oppose them in the gorges north of the town. These occupied commanding positions on a couple of strategic hills, and a lengthy fusillade followed. Desultory fighting lasted a fortnight while an outpost and airstrip were established at Bou Dra'a, after which the French column withdrew towards Midelt. The powers that be had decided Tounfit was too tough a proposition for that year; the Ayt Yahya would be taken care of later.[21] No wonder the tribesmen imagined they could taunt the French with impunity, as portrayed in this saucy poetic couplet:

> O frog-eater, sure of yourself as ever, follow the river-banks up
> To Tounfit; see how its people will give you a good thrashing![22]

As summer gave way to autumn, some extra space had to be found in Yahya-land and Sokhman-land so the Ishqern and Beni Mguild refugees could sow grain and feed themselves. This was readily allowed in the name of Muslim solidarity.

Also, there was some good news—a new *sharif* had appeared in the region: a certain Ben 'Aomar, a preacher from Ayt Sgougou who had left his home after the French occupation. Initially supported by Sidi Mohand ou-Lhajj, he claimed his *baraka* was strong enough to evict the French from the area. The illusion lasted barely a month. Entertained in style wherever he went, he would haughtily preside over the company as men came forward to touch the hem of his garment. They would drink his every word, such was their faith in their forthcoming deliverance from the *irumin*. However, as the nights grew colder, he was urged to act. The moment of truth came on November 15, 1922, when his attempt to goad the tribesmen into assaulting Alemsid failed dismally in the face of machine-gun fire.[23] Yet again, a bard was on hand to comment on this disappointing event:

> Now consider the man Ben 'Aomar with his forty tents,
> Was compelled to shave the hair he'd allowed to grow![24]
> Methinks, says I, a lamb to Alemsid is come this day;
> Yet another one who's strong in words, weak in deeds!"[25]

Famine was rife in the mountains throughout that terrible winter of 1922–3. Obliged to remain on the heights, entire herds were decimated by insufficient grazing and snowstorms, while the cost of grain soared.[26] As they shivered beneath their tents, the Berbers had to make do with boiled grass or ersatz flour made of acorns![27]

Before we move to another sector of the Atlas front we must describe a nasty little reverse suffered by the pro-French Zaïan element. As the dissidents regularly patrolled the strip of land at the Moulouya source between Tagouzalt and Bou Wattas to intercept the faint-hearted trying to reach the French lines, Moha ou Hammou's swashbuckling son, Bou'azza, set out with his hundred horsemen to intercept them. In the afternoon of March 27, 1923, he charged boldly after the dissidents, who skillfully enticed him south into their territory. They then counter-attacked, seriously wounding Bou'azza as he attempted to rally his men. Finally, he was brought back to Alemsid where he gave up the ghost shortly afterwards, not before having exclaimed, "I am glad to be laid low

Fig. 25: The snow-covered Middle Atlas massif of Jbel Tishshoukt seen from the southeast.

Fig. 26: Marmousha plateau on a fine winter's morning, Bou Nasser in the background.

by an enemy bullet. For a man there's no better death!"[28] Bou'azza's demise, a well-deserved fate for this traitor in the eyes of the *imjuhad*, also caused much grief and concern among his own kith and kin.[29] This event temporarily restored Imhiwash prestige. However, their ceaseless squabbles, their scandalous conduct vis-à-vis their womenfolk, and their overall failure against the French could no longer be concealed.

Increasingly seen as false prophets, the sands were running out for the *igwerramn*. Some hundred miles to the northeast, a conspicuous hill, Jbel Tishshoukt, was developing a fearsome reputation among the locals as an inviolable bastion of the resistance.

Bitter Battles Around Jbel Tishshoukt

The Berber tribes that occupied the northeast corner of the Middle Atlas had so far escaped the invader's attention. Not for much longer, though. Unknown to them, their very presence on the heights, their military strength and innate fighting spirit unimpaired, constituted a permanent threat to "useful Morocco" and all-important communications with Algeria, especially along the vulnerable Taza corridor. This was the nightmare that had long been haunting Marshal Lyautey and his staff in Rabat.

The chunk of rebel territory known in French military parlance of those days as *la Tache de Taza* lies within the Sefrou–Boulman–Gerssif triangle, boasting peaks of over 3,000 m and drained by numerous rivers including the mighty Sebou's upstream tributaries. For all its beauty, it is a harsh, ungrateful land, featuring rugged hills, a maze of ravines and gorges full of boxwood bushes, with forests of cedar, juniper, oak, and pine higher up. In winter, snow covers vast areas above 1,800 m, unwary shepherds freeze to death in blizzards, and travel becomes arduous. In summer, eastward-facing valleys can become unpleasantly hot and dry. All of which makes for ideal guerrilla country. No wonder its three main peaks became natural fortresses for the tribes: Jbel Bou Iblan (3,190 m), its immaculate white ridge visible in clear weather from Fez for six months a year; stocky, bull-shouldered Bou Nasser (3,340 m) and its satellites overlooking the Moulouya and eastern plains; and finally, the distinctive triangular peak of Jbel Tishshoukt (2,796 m), dominating the former *triq es-sseltan* and destined to become a tribal stronghold of almost mythical fame for upwards of ten years.

Four warlike tribes

Four major tribes shared this particular piece of country, their men proudly independent and well versed in derring-do. Never had a sultan really violated their innermost sanctuaries, although in May 1984 I saw the cairn erected at the point, southwest of Tamjilt village, in Souf Ifeltasen ravine, where the 'Alawid sultan reportedly turned back.[1] As Lyautey himself acknowledged in December 1920 in a speech to his officers, "This, the main military problem that remains for us to solve in Morocco, is of course compounded by the very nature of the terrain, among the most rugged in the Middle Atlas, not to mention the warlike qualities of tribes that have never bowed down to any invader."[2] The French had hopes of quickly neutralizing the Ayt Youssi as they had been fairly consistent servants of the *makhzan*. Actually, one of their northern clans[3] threw in their lot with the invaders at an early stage in the fighting. However, the remainder of the tribe closed ranks behind Sidi Raho's chief supporters—the Ayt Fringo clan, and especially their Ayt Halli neighbors, who could muster 1,000 warriors.

Sidi Raho's prestige was even greater among the Ayt Seghroushen of Sidi 'Ali, a tribe "whose territory was only limited by their neighbours' ability to resist."[4] After 1870 they had begun expanding north and south from their home base around Jbel Tishshoukt. At the time of our story, their war chief was Moulay Mohammed Seghroushni, backed by 2,000 foot-soldiers and 100 horsemen. They had two main centres: Skoura "the red," nestling at the foot of Tishshoukt's northern slopes, with fertile springs to water olive groves and wheat fields; and tree-encircled El-Mers on the upper Serghina, south of Tishshoukt, and sacred resting place of Sidi 'Ali ou Yahya.[5]

East of the Seghrina, amid the desolate, windswept uplands that ascend towards the great shining mass of Bou Iblan, lived a tribe renowned for its uncompromising hostility to the *makhzan*—the Marmousha.[6] Owning few kasbahs, they were predominantly nomadic sheepherders, one of their clans migrating towards the Moulouya[7] while others would resort to pastures on the upper Sebou.[8] These were just the kind of people who would take a dim view of any attempt at outside domination, as the Native Affairs officer of the Sefrou garrison observed in 1918: "The Marmousha fear any further advance in their direction as this would restrain their freedom of movement. That is why they band together against us with their tribal neighbours."[9] Nor had these attempts at concerted action been unavailing as, in addition to their own 2,500 foot and 200 horse warriors equipped with breech-loaders and plentiful supplies of ammunition, they could probably count on the support of 3,000 similarly-armed fighters from valleys to the east at the foot of Bou Nasser.[10] The present operation now had them bottled up in their rocky fastness. Last but not least were the powerful Beni Ouaraïn confederation[11] that held considerable tracts of territory on both sides of Jbel Bou Iblan and enjoyed some measure of strategic depth.

The Beni Ouaraïn tribe were rated by their opponents as arguably the best fighters in the area; "they behave like lions on the battle-field"[12] were the most frequently heard words of praise. In fact, long afterwards, when French *Tache de Taza* veterans gathered together, the Beni Ouaraïn's military prowess would inevitably be referred to. So long as the Great War lasted it was a case of "all quiet on the Taza front." There were good reasons for this: in view of the limited manpower available to him, Lyautey was understandably reluctant to stir up the hornets' nest. In fact Lyautey was constantly restraining the hawks in his entourage, as he explained in a letter to a friend:

> I always refrain from attacking areas which are inactive—"asleep," as it were—and biding their time. To go in would result in high loss of life and cause great distress, whereas these people, faced with gradual encirclement, will surrender of their own accord once their neighbours have thrown up the sponge.[13]

Saving Skoura from the French (1917)

This was the basis of Lyautey's later much-maligned policy of peaceful penetration.[14] The occupying forces had been inactive, maintaining their chain of outposts along the Fez–Taza–Gerssif corridor and consolidating their positions to the south. In the spring of 1917 this had entailed setting up a front-line post at Tazouta, within easy striking distance of Tishshoukt. From here work started on a *piste* to project French power further south.

Not slow to perceive the threat, the Ayt Seghroushen hardly needed prompting from Sidi Raho to carry out a surprise dawn attack on May 28 against a detachment protecting road workers at Tizi n-Tagnanaït. Galvanized by the presence of several resistance chiefs,[15] the 1,500 warriors involved soon forced the enemy to retire, harrying them a mite too closely for comfort. In the end, a platoon of *laliju* had to fix bayonets and charge to extricate the French detachment, but not without losing some twenty men. As Berber scouts watching from the hills could not fail to observe, work subsequently resumed on the track via Tizi n-Tagnanaït. This was obviously in preparation for the expected summer attack on Skoura "the red," the Ayt Seghroushen capital. The marabouts accordingly continued to maintain fighting spirit at boiling point, promising to give the invader a hot welcome. Early in July 1917, two French columns converged on Skoura, whereupon, egged on by Sidi Raho, the "wild boars of Tishshoukt"[16] came out from behind boxwood bush or cedar trunk to do battle.

They did so to such good purpose that both enemy detachments were brought to a halt. Such was the pressure that on July 8, handicapped by heat haze and a scorching sirocco wind, both enemy columns of thirsty, exhausted men were forced into a fighting retreat towards Tazouta. As usual, the Moroccan combatants were not slow to seize their opportunity; for seven hours they kept outflanking the enemy, creeping close enough through rocks and sparse vegetation to attack at point-blank range. Ceaselessly harassed, almost cut off at times from the main body, by the time it reached the safety of Tazouta fort the French rearguard had paid a stiff price, suffering some 150 casualties.[17] Despite the losses they had taken, Sidi Raho and the Ayt Seghroushen were delighted at the drubbing they had given the invader; numerous rifles had been recovered from the enemy dead.

Up among the tents on Tishshoukt, grandmothers and grandchildren had listened all day to distant gunfire. At the foot of the slope, bedecked in all their finery, the womenfolk were making ready to welcome home dust-covered, war-weary husbands and sons, victors of a hard-fought battle.[18]

In 1918, while El-Shinguetti was still busy stirring up the tribes against the occupant, the Marmousha descended from their bleak plateau to trade shots with the garrison of the newly-founded outpost at Outat El-Haj, on the Moulouya.[19] Otherwise the area enjoyed a brief reprieve, being left to its own devices till 1921. In June of that year, as the Middle Atlas front was quietly reactivated, the Beni Ouaraïn had at last to face concerted action by the French: one column came in from the northeast up the Melloulou Valley and pushed on beyond Kasba El-Farah; and a second followed the Zloul past Ahermoumou and eventually joined up with the other column on June 9 at Souk El-'Arba, though not without a fierce firefight which cost the French sixty soldiers.[20] By this move the French imagined they had pacified the western Beni Ouaraïn; actually, large groups of diehards had retired south towards the Bou Iblan bastion to fight another day. Meanwhile, Souk el-'Arba was a mere stone's throw away from the reputedly impregnable Shiker massif, just southwest of Taza, inhabited by yet another Ouaraïni clan, the Beni Bou Zert—peaceful enough people if left undisturbed, but redoubtable fighters when provoked.

"Under the high peak of Tishshoukt"

On February 25, 1922, the Beni Bou Zert proved their mettle as they faced off a first attempt by a scratch force of Goums and partisans,[21] winning themselves a further year of independence. French plans that year for the *Tache de Taza*, however, chiefly concerned its readily approachable southwest corner; so, back we must go to Jbel Tishshoukt for yet another scenario involving converging columns. The French columns would take the field to bring to book these unruly mountain tribes. Marshal Lyautey was adamant that the operation should be successfully concluded by the end of 1922, as Aubert, one of his generals, confidently told a British writer then visiting his Rabat HQ:

> Now [in 1922] I shall advance from Missour, in April ... and so tighten the cord on
> the neck of the Seghroushen under the high peak of Tishshoukt. In May and June I
> shall finish with them. The Marshall's policy is always: first, to occupy their pasture-
> lands, and then, to compel their submission in the mountains, leaving those who
> are irreconcilable to stew in their own juice on the unprofitable summits.[22]

Thus by a pincer movement did they hope to seal off Tishshoukt. Then would it fall like a ripe plum within a year or so, once the politicals (Native Affairs officers) had completed their "softening-up" process. No doubt all nice and easy when planned on a map at HQ, though little allowance was made for difficult terrain, the vagaries of the weather, or determined opposition by a skillful, valiant foe. General Aubert was in for a rough ride.

For a start, the defending team were in no mood to stand idly by. When they learnt that Aubert's southeast force had occupied Taniat Msamir, a mere eight miles west of Missour, they staged repeated counter-attacks, effectively blocking his advance for three weeks. Not till the end of March did they abandon the heights overlooking the Shouf esh-Sherg Valley from the south. Early in April they refrained from interfering when he at last moved on Douirat and established an outpost further up the valley at Azinous, nor did they seriously dispute his subsequent advance to Almis-Marmousha. So far, in the face of superior firepower, the mountaineers had given a good account of themselves with locally available forces. Considerable reinforcements, however, were expected once the Marmousha shepherds got back from their winter grazing grounds on the Moulouya steppe.[23]

By early May the Marmousha were poised for a counter-thrust. The obvious place to strike was near Azinous, as the French were busy building a dirt road from there, up and round the north slopes of Jbel Tafgourt, to link Missour with Almis-Marmousha. On May 6, several thousand fighters suddenly materialized from the barren hillsides and fell upon the labor gang and covering force, obliging them to fall back in disorder on the Azinous outpost with over 150 casualties.[24] The Battle of Azinous proved one of the severest setbacks suffered by the French during the *Tache de Taza* operations. After their victory the Berbers consolidated their gains, holding the environs of Azinous in some strength with strong detachments in reserve further northeast on the hills leading to Immouzzer-Marmousha.

When, six days later, they saw the French returning to the ambush site in an attempt to recover their dead, they again gave them a hot welcome, driving them back with sixty casualties. Such was the impression made on Aubert that it forced him to rethink his strategy. The general was now far less upbeat as to a possible link-up with the northern force. Obviously, further attempts to revive his stalled offensive without reliable maps were out of the question, given the Marmousha ability to defend impossible terrain; better, by far, to make an outflanking move into the Seghrina Valley, whose wide-open spaces should lend themselves perfectly to unimpeded troop movement. Accordingly, on May 23, in the face of light resistance, his men secured the village of Tignamas on the Seghrina river, and built a new post there. They were now only twelve miles southeast of "fortress Tishshoukt," on which Seghrouschen campfires could be seen twinkling at night. Yet further progress that summer was unlikely, given the trouble the northern force had run into.[25] A soon-to-be-famous French subaltern had been immensely impressed by the Berbers' fighting prowess. In a letter home, young Bournazel had nothing but praise for Sidi Raho and his men: "The Ayt Seghroushen are conspicuously brave; nothing will stop them . . . one of the rare tribes that have enough guts to stand up to us in a fight." Nor was he too sanguine as to the outcome of the expedition: "We probably won't reach Skoura this time around."[26] How right he was. And yet, things had gone fairly well, at first.

From Taghzout the troops had pushed their way southwest over the Nador plateau on April 27, meeting only token resistance, while another column came in from the northeast. Supported by artillery, they had advanced on Skoura the next day until the Ayt Seghroushen stopped them four kilometers short of their goal. For several days the sharp crack of the Gras rifle, expertly handled by determined mountaineers, echoed back from the hillsides as they thwarted French attempts to outflank their positions east of Skoura, finally beating off a battalion of *laliju* with heavy losses at Tizi Adni on May 6.[27] From both sides of Tishshoukt the troops were ordered back to base to count their losses: 240 dead all told. Sidi Raho had done more than well: on May 6, his perfectly coordinated defensive strategy had resulted in two decisive operations at Azinous and at Tizi Adni; El-Mers and Skoura remained inviolate.

Further campaigning in *Tache de Taza*: 1923 season

Naturally, in the Lyautey camp there were long faces. Losses had been unacceptably high for meager territorial gains. The shortcomings of a dual command thus exposed, an overall commander-in-chief would be appointed for 1923; he would also be provided with enough troops to settle the business once and for all. Still recovering from a hideous face wound, the ever cheerful Poeymirau was the one selected for the job. First, Lyautey planned to clear marauding bands from the approaches to the two great cols over the Middle Atlas—the Taghzeft pass and Enjil gap southwest of Tishshoukt—at which point he would establish his base camp.[28] As if in contempt of these preparations, bold raiders made off one March morning with some 250 sheep belonging to the Timhadit garrison![29]

Then, before a fresh offensive could get under way, on Easter Sunday (1923), heavy rain and snow started falling, especially south of Taza, where the Ayt Jellidasen were coming under attack from a column under Colonel Freydenberg. The Ayt Jellidasen, under their saintly leader, Sidi Mohand Belqasm Azeroual from the Berkin zaouia, had hitherto maintained somewhat ambiguous relations with the French authorities. In winter they went through the motions of being a loyal tribe, just like any other, to avoid being deprived of the all-important Moulouya grazing grounds; in summer, from their mountain fastnesses they would harass French outposts or plunder recently submitted clans, faithfully following Sidi Mohand who had concluded an alliance with the Marmousha.[30] On April 12, despite the mud, a 700-strong force of mountaineers bravely attacked Freydenberg's force on the Mismental plateau east of Berkin, only to be mown down by machine-gun fire.

Attempts to regroup having been foiled by artillery fire, the warriors dispersed, while Sidi Mohand Azeroual escaped towards the heights where he would hold out for another three years. However, to hedge the family's bets in typical Berber fashion, the marabout's son surrendered to the French.[31]

Meanwhile a formidable threat was developing southwest of Tishshoukt. In his muddy, rain-soaked camp at Enjil, Poeymirau had gathered a formidable fighting force[32] to finish off Saïd ou Mohand's 6,000 well-armed Ayt Seghroushen warriors defending Tishshoukt. At the beginning of May, as the rains eased off, Berber lookouts on the rugged heights watched the ponderous column slowly move north and establish a bivouac at Oum Jeniba, just south of the mountain. On May 20, 1923, began one of the hardest-fought battles of the entire Atlas campaign. Rather than defend the vulnerable hollow of Boulman, the Berbers had concentrated their men opposite the Bou 'Arfa ridge, a line of low cliffs with a tangle of rocks, boxwood bushes, juniper and oak trees at their feet, of which Bournazel had observed, "Unless you're on a knoll, it's difficult to see beyond three yards in the undergrowth!"[33]

Early-morning French attacks, supported by mortar fire and involving swarms of *lbertiza*, were beaten back: the partisans under the *qayd* of Timhadit ran away, some of the Enjil *qayd*'s levies actually changing sides![34] Well into the afternoon the battle raged on the Bou 'Arfa ridge.[35] At 3 pm, however, a thunderstorm, followed by thick mist, dramatically reduced visibility and allowed the Imazighen to infiltrate French positions and demonstrate their talent at knife-work. Some wielded the standard issue curved dagger; others preferred using bayonets, either separately as a short thrusting sword or lashed to stout staves. Whichever the combination, all proved devastating at close quarters. None the less, for all their skill and bravery, after desperate hand-to-hand fighting they were eventually forced to withdraw after having inflicted 127 casualties on the column. Sergeant Klose, a German in charge of a *minenwerfer* battery with the

Foreign legion, noted after the battle that many of the Berbers who had been on the receiving end of his bombs were equipped with "mostly Spanish rifles of a modern pattern, although there were a few old French ones among them."[36] Tragically, among the dead lay an obscure Berber heroine:

> Before me, lying on his face, was the body of a very young warrior, with a shock of pitch-black hair, but when I turned it over, I found it to be the corpse of a girl of about sixteen years of age. Her handsome features were set in a look of grim determination, mingled, as it … appeared to me, with an expression of intense cruelty that was heightened by the aspect of the long, light, slender, sharp dagger in its embossed copper sheath attached to her waist by a red leather strap.[37]

Undaunted by the losses they had suffered, the hill men were back on subsequent nights to harass the hastily-prepared French outpost. In one nocturnal scrimmage, they narrowly failed to storm Poeymirau's main bivouac at Oum Jeniba, two companies of Moroccan *Tirailleurs* deserting to the Seghroushen. So well coordinated was the mountaineers' attack that it was commonly held that somebody with military expertise was advising them. To quote one eyewitness, "The whole mountain was alive with fanatical tribesmen, well equipped with machine-guns and mountain artillery which they had learnt to use ably under the tutelage of deserters from the Legion."[38] The Berbers on Tishshoukt now enjoyed a momentary respite as Poeymirau's force moved about 40 kilometers east to establish camp at Ifkern[39] before attempting to capture some commanding heights close to Immouzzer-Marmousha.

The Bou Khamouj plateau, key to Immouzzer, was strongly held by a joint Seghroushen–Marmousha force, many of whom had dug in. They again repulsed initial attacks on June 9, including one by the Moroccan *Tirailleurs* that had performed so poorly at Bou 'Arfa the previous month.[40] The Imazighen finally gave way in the face of assault by *laliju* and vigorous outflanking moves, though even then they came roaring back before end of play in several savage counter-attacks. At the close of the day the French flag flew over Bou Khamouj, yet seventy-one killed and 159 wounded was the toll the Berbers exacted.[41] Given the unwelcome attention their Marmousha neighbors had come in for, the Ayt Seghroushen had little doubt as to where the enemy's next blow would fall: El-Mers—their religious capital and key to "fortress Tishshoukt." Before dawn on June 24, 1923, Saïd ou Mohand el-Seghroushni mustered his men as the French were moving in on El-Mers over undulating terrain. With the start of a hot summer's day, the proceedings developed into the archetypal stand-up firefight. The Berbers defended their holy village unflinchingly, their sharpshooters pouring a withering fire into the assailants, others lurking in tall stands of wheat the better to ambush their assailants at knife-point.

As the artillery joined in the fray, they would give way, only to regroup further back, ready to counter-attack, encouraged all the while by the fierce, ululating cries of their womenfolk, whose very honor they were defending so dearly. The few fighters that were captured and interrogated defiantly answered that both Sidi Raho and Saïd ou Mohand were present, and would only allow the *irumin* to occupy their holy places over their dead bodies.[42] Their resistance finally caved in around nightfall, when the

French occupied El-Mers.[43] To quote young Bournazel, "El-Mers was ours. We could see it there, at our feet, with its cubic houses, its gardens, its kasbah and finely-turreted saints' tombs. Of course, victory had come at a price; over 200 killed and wounded on our side."[44]

While the events just described had been taking place, a bare 20 kilometers to the north other Ayt Seghroushen contingents were hotly engaged. Six enemy battalions under Freydenberg were attempting to capture Skoura, circumvent it via Tizi Adni, and link up with Poeymirau's force attacking El-Mers from the south. On June 22, a short, sharp fight took place among the tangled ravines near Tizi Adni, but this time the *laliju* came out on top, as the gods stepped in to help.[45] Indeed, Mauser rifles at the ready, Berber defenders were horrified to see *laliju* with their white *képis* charge out of the small cemetery where their 1922 comrades had been buried. Thinking the ghosts of the dead were returning to the fray, many Berbers lost heart and withdrew. Four days later, Skoura, together with the fertile Tadout plateau, was occupied by the French at the cost of 111 casualties.[46]

For three hot weeks in July, the Berbers bravely contested the French advance from Bou Khamouj towards Immouzzer-Marmousha. No sooner had they lost one hill than they would attempt to retake it by day, then laying down harassing fire at night to keep the *laliju* awake. Even after Immouzzer had fallen on the 23rd, they massed their forces on two nearby hills—Issouka and Idlan—from which it took the enemy another two weeks to dislodge them. Unshakable in their defiance, however, on August 31 they ambushed a party of mounted legionnaires as they were watering their mules not far north of Immouzzer, which place again came under attack a few days later. But by mid-September the French offensive had run out of steam: apart from the 120 killed and 360 wounded in the past forty days, the troops were exhausted by the excessively dry heat.[47] Plans for a thrust northeast from Immouzzer to occupy Talzemt and the lush Meskeddal pastures were put on hold.[48] Bournazel, due to be posted back to France for a short stay, shrewdly observed, "I don't believe we'll keep on hammering away at this very difficult region; at any rate not this year—due to lack of funds."[49]

Sure enough, Lyautey's frantic efforts to conquer as much of "useful Morocco" in as short time as possible had been dictated partly by the need to create the impression that *pacification* of the Atlas was practically over, partly by drastic budgetary restrictions that would shortly lead to cutbacks in manpower.[50] In the meantime, although a wedge had been driven between Marmousha and Seghroushen, the Imazighen had prevented the French from achieving the crossing to Skoura via Tizi Tigoulmamin, and with it the capture of "fortress Tishshoukt." Resolute and defiant as ever, home to Saïd ou Mohand and his plucky Ayt Sehgroushen, Tishshoukt was nevertheless surrounded. Indeed, the broad Seghina–Mdez corridor separated it from the Bou Iblan–Bou Nasser massif where the Marmousha, Beni Ouaraïn, and other warriors were continuing to hold out. Reduced to a small green circle on French military HQ maps, the latter area was all that remained of the main *Tache de Taza*.

The fighting had achieved a scale and an intensity hitherto unknown in Morocco. However, Lyautey's forward policy, aimed initially at erasing the *Tache de Taza* from the map, had resulted in only partial success, not to mention the highest casualty figures so far. Yet in the north the Ayt Bou Slama pocket, held by a small force of doughty tribesmen, had finally been eliminated in May 1923 after a week's fierce fighting in difficult, wooded terrain at a cost of 100 casualties on the French side. Interestingly, at the moment of surrender, it transpired that the sixty stalwarts involved in the showdown at Waoumchach had been outnumbered roughly ten to one. Some warriors, those Ayt Bou Slama![51]

Thus, to resistance fighters in this part of the Atlas it was obvious that operations were entering a fresh, decisive phase. Forced back into the innermost recesses of the range, obliged to suffer the hardships of winter at altitude with families, flocks, and herds, their resistance was taking on a nobler, more tragic dimension. Some, however, were entertaining doubts as to the ultimate triumph of their cause. After El-Mers, another sacred spot nearby, Tilmirat, had fallen. Had not an old Seghroushen prophesy claimed that the "Master of the Hour" would emerge from the sacred tree at Tilmirat to succor his people in their hour of need?[52] In the event, nothing had happened, further undermining what little faith some *imjuhad* still had in their saintly leaders. Yet the vast majority remained steadfast in their determination to see things through to the finish.[53]

We must now leave the Middle Atlas to its own devices and cast a glance northwards to the Mediterranean coast where Rif tribesmen were successfully pitting their forces against the armed might of Spain, the other colonial power eager to have its share of the Moroccan pie, even if they were mere pickings.

The Rif War (1921–7)[1]

The Rif had always been a world apart from Morocco proper. A long, rocky Mediterranean coastline with relatively well-watered valleys reaching southward to a rugged, wooded crestline, snow-covered in winter, it was Morocco's natural northern frontier facing the Iberian Peninsula with which it shared a common history going back over a thousand years. Its population of hardy, independent-minded Berber mountaineers, specialists of the feud and vendetta, had usually paid but lip service to the *makhzan*. Contemporary with the Berghaouata, the Banu Salih emirate of Nekkour had even thrived and prospered, becoming the commercial and maritime hub of northern Morocco in the ninth and tenth centuries, before being sacked by the Norwegians, after which it underwent attacks from other quarters and went into decline.[2]

Throughout the Middle Ages the Rif remained something of a backwater, only recovering its importance subsequent to the eviction of the Moors from Spain. In this context, one figure does emerge: that of a flamboyant Joan of Arc of northern Morocco,

Map 5: General map of northern Morocco and the Rif (Cartes CARIMA).

Sayyida El-Hourra, a refugee from Andalucia after the fall of Granada, who resisted Christian encroachments from bases in Shefshawn and Tetouan. It is difficult to unravel myth from history, though she does come across as a warrior-princess and consort of Sultan Ahmed El-Ouattasi.[3] Shortly afterwards crusader-minded intruders from the Iberian Peninsula captured Badis and Melilla. Much later, Ceuta (Sebta) and Tetouan were also captured by Spain, these tiny enclaves becoming the source of countless border conflicts, unresolved to this day. It was as part of a national reaction to foreign encroachment that an influential marabout, El-'Ayyashi, established himself as "amir of the Gharb," his influence extending all over northern Morocco, until his elimination by the Dila'yin in 1541.[4] The Rif none the less remained Morocco's front line in the long-running, undeclared war against the Spanish neighbor.

Opening skirmishes

Towards the close of the nineteenth century, after Morocco's humiliation in the "War of Tetouan" (1860), and bitter fighting near Melilla (1893), Rifian hostility vis-à-vis Iberian intrusion became a way of life. Thus, once the pretender Jilali Zerhouni (aka Bouhmara) had set himself up in Selwan (within sight of Melilla), his supporters among the local population turned against him when it was discovered that he was in cahoots with the Spaniards and had granted them mining rights![5] That he was actually forced to abandon his Rifian base proved instrumental in causing his downfall. However, as the Spanish did not abandon their iron mining activities at Jbel Ouiksen, the tribesmen made repeated attacks on the Melilla enclave.

Early in the twentieth century these attacks were led by a charismatic figure, *sharif* Mohand Amezian from Nador, who inflicted several defeats on Spanish forces, the most famous at Barranco del Lobo on July 25, 1909, even claiming the life of a general.[6] This disaster foreshadowed further Spanish reverses in the Rif, even though, tragically, Amezian himself was killed in action near Melilla on May 15, 1912.[7]

By then the Spanish were attempting to come to grips with their reluctant North African protectorate. This was no easy task. Due to geographical constraints, the Spanish hold on north Morocco was as multifaceted as it was tenuous. It consisted of three distinct entities: 1) an Atlantic coastal strip from Larache to near Tangier; 2) the Ceuta-Tetouan area; and 3) the Melilla enclave. Between Larache and Tetouan were hills bordering on territory held by the powerful and unruly Jbala tribe, more or less under the control of mercurial warlord Moulay Ahmed Raissouni, part bandit, part resistance fighter, part *makhzan* official and lifetime schemer, operating from bases at Azila and Tazarout.[8]

The Jbala are part of a large bilingual Arab-Berber population who have drifted towards Arabic for two centuries, but retain to this day about 20 percent of Amazigh-derived words in their *patois*; several local place names are also unmistakenly of Berber origin. However, these troublesome tribesmen, who rejected *makhzan* authority, were proving uncomfortable neighbors for the Spanish-held coastal towns. Headstrong General Silvestre attempted to pacify and/or appease them, failing signally to do so after falling foul of Raissouni, who rather fancied himself as leader of the anti-colonial

Fig. 27: Town of Shefshawn: evening view, looking west (Rif).

jihad in northern Morocco. Silvestre's successor Berenguer was slightly more successful, managing to win over Raissouni, and eventually occupying the strategic hillside town of Shefshawn (Xauen) in 1920.

But the most inaccessible tract of country, well beyond Spanish control, lay between Oued Laou and Melilla: the heart of the Rif, containing the Berber-speaking Ayt Waryaghar, Temsaman, Ayt Touzin, Iboqqoyen, Gelaya, and other warlike tribes. Understandably, after the 1914–18 war this was the strip of territory that Spain wished to subdue, and this was where it came to grief. Spanish strategists toyed endlessly with plans for an amphibious landing in Alhoceima Bay to link up with land forces that would have pushed westward from the Melilla enclave, building outposts along the way. From 1918 onward, this was the game plan, repeatedly hatched, indefinitely postponed.[9] After 1920, with Silvestre in command at Melilla, a line of Spanish outposts crept south to Monte Arruit, then west to to Anoual; even beyond to Igherriben and Dar Oubarran. The Rifians cunningly allowed the Spaniards to become committed deeper and deeper into their heartland, all the while biding their time, knowing that their enemy was encircled; patiently awaiting the hour of reckoning, this resilience one of their greatest strengths.

All they needed was to find an appropriate leader to guide them to victory. And one was shortly to come forward. Like his father, Mohamed 'Abdelkrim El-Khattabi (*pajarito*, 'little bird') was one of the "Friends of Spain" on whom the colonial power was counting to legitimize its hold on the Rif. He had learned their language and worked as a religious judge for them at Melilla. However, as Spanish encroachments drew closer to Ayt Waryaghar territory, he had become increasingly disenchanted with the invaders—to the point of switching his allegiance to the forces of resistance.[10]

Spectacular victory of Anoual

'Abdelkrim had at his command arguably the most expert Berber fighters in Morocco, some of them crack shots into the bargain, with an intimate knowledge of the terrain. Above all, they were driven by a burning desire to evict the invader. As the summer of 1921 approached, they found ample scope for their fighting abilities. In July of that year, Silvestre was reinstated as commander of the forces in the Melilla area. He moved to Anoual, furthest west of a string of weakly garrisoned forts, planning to resume the advance towards Ajdir and Alhoceima Bay. He never got the chance. With the whole country up in arms around him, foolish Silvestre found himself cooped up in Anoual, totally surrounded by hostile forces.

Even more foolishly, instead of attempting to hold out pending the arrival of reinforcements, he decided to abandon his position and attempt a fighting retreat back to Melilla. This was a gift to the Rifians who, like other Berbers, were champions in the noble art of harrying a retreating enemy. Harassed and forlorn, the Spaniards, most of them poorly-trained conscripts, began their withdrawal, Silvestre being killed at the very outset. Everything was against the Spaniards: the heat, the lack of water, the terrain, the withering fire from Rifian marksmen. From one little fort to the next they withdrew, taking casualties all the way. At Monte Arruit a last heroic stand was made, but nothing came of it, the demoralized defenders finally surrendering to the victorious Rifians, only to be slaughtered pitilessly. Spanish losses amounted to some 20,000 killed in all; 20,000 rifles, 400 machine guns, and over 120 artillery pieces fell into Rifian hands.[11]

'Abdelkrim was surprised at the extent of the disaster inflicted on Spain, undoubtedly the most severe in any colonial war. However, he failed to capture Melilla which lay at his mercy, possibly fearing collateral losses among other Europeans residing there. And yet, whereas at first he had sought mere recognition by the colonial power of Rifian independence, now fresh possibilities were emerging.[12] Meanwhile, he declared a republic and consolidated his hold on the Rif, bringing to book certain refractory tribes that questioned his authority.

Simultaneously, he put an end to the age-old practice of vendetta that had always weakened Rifian society, instituting Koranic law (*sharia'*) where hitherto customary law had held sway, resorting to Arabic, introducing the locals to the notion of imprisonment, where before punishment had been graduated according to a system of fines. There is even a suggestion of an attempt at a jihadist state cast in Salafi terms, that Abdelkrim may have been mildly fundamentalist in his approach.[13] To further buttress his authority, a pseudo-*makhzan* was set up: his brother M'hammed becoming Minister for War, and governmental responsibilities being shared out between other relatives, while his personal bodyguard was recruited from fellow Ayt Waryaghar tribesmen. An effort was made to improve communications: a network of dirt roads was developed and a crude telephone link was set up between his Ajdir HQ and nearby villages.[14] From the vast captured arsenal, artillery units were formed, some 5,000 former Spanish *regulares* electing to serve in his forces; there were even a few German mercenaries and deserters from the French Foreign Legion who came forwards as advisers. His expanding forces, also drawing on manpower from local tribes, were ready for greater things. From a purely local rebellion his movement was rapidly acquiring a more ambitious dimension: dreams of expansion beyond his southern borders materialized, taking in Morocco as a whole. As *de facto* amir of the Rif, and head of its recently proclaimed republic, he now severed all ties with the sultan of Morocco, allegedly declaring, "Moulay Youssef is a mere puppet. The real sultan in Moroco is Lyautey!"[15] 'Abdelkrim also took comfort from the knowledge that not only was the Rif War unpopular in France, but that his struggle enjoyed the support of Communist MPs in the French *Assemblée*.

The Rifian offensive: The battles for Fez and Taza

At the end of November 1924, Hamed Kheriro the Jebli, one of 'Abdelkrim's best lieutenants, took Shefshawn from the Spanish, forcing them into a retreat to Tetouan in which they lost over 10,000 men.[16] This development brought pressure to bear on the Jbala. Shortly afterwards, Raissouni, by now old and ailing, was neutralized and sent to Ajdir where he died a little later; the Jbala warriors were absorbed into the Rifian forces.

Lyauytey had seen the writing on the wall; it was obvious that sooner or later the Rifs would launch an attack on his thin cordon of outposts north of the River Ouergha. For 'Abdelkrim the news was good. After his overwhelming victory over the Spaniards at Anoual (July 1921), practically the entire Rif lay in his hands. Now, encouraged by the local population to further exploit a favorable military situation, his legions were poised for action. Once they were unleashed there was no telling how far south they would reach, especially as they would bring to bear field guns captured from the Spaniards; and French border outposts like Beni Derkoul had not been designed to withstand artillery shells.

As the gunrunners diligently plied the dusty paths between Rif and Atlas, the French redeployed some of their forces to head off this northern threat. But it was a thankless task. Having for several months anticipated the coming attack, Lyautey had sent Paris an urgent request for reinforcements. However, this was the transition period between the outgoing Herriot government and the incoming Painlevé administration, strongly left-wing in outlook. As a result, the French dithered, reinforcements were sent in dribs and drabs, and then much too late.[17]

Throughout April 1925 the north of Morocco was in turmoil; the Rifian forces started building trenches close to the French outposts along Oued Ouergha, also contaminating "loyal" tribes so they would declare for 'Abdelkrim. On April 14, some 4,000 Rifians invested Beni Zeroual country, forcing *sharif* 'Abderahman Derqawi to flee for his life as the entire tribe went over to 'Abdelkrim.[18] The Rifs were extremely well organized: recently rallied tribesmen constituting highly mobile little units, with a leavening of uniformed regulars, backed by machine-gun and artillery units whose action proved decisive when it came to breaching the walls of French outposts. Most of these were thus easily overwhelmed, so that despite air support and artillery bombardment, Lyautey's overworked *groupes mobiles* had difficulty relieving the outposts, doing so with heavy loss of life and, in cases such as Biban, ultimately ordering the garrisons to blow up their forts and withdraw south.[19]

From mid-April to early July the battle raged as the Rifs applied pressure at different points north of a notional Ouezzan–Fez–Taza defense line. Without going into detail, suffice to say that this was the scene of the most intense fighting anywhere, at any time throughout the Moroccan mountain campaigns. So far, in the Middle Atlas, resistance fighters had only had rifles to oppose the French, precluding the need for heavily fortified outposts. Here, thanks to captured weapons, the Rifians and Jbala (some of the best infantry in the world) could use machine guns, artillery, and hand grenades, giving them a decisive edge. Mere rifle-slits could be subjected to volleys of machine-gun fire, artillery shells could blow apart flimsily-constructed walls, placing outpost defenders at a distinct disadvantage. In countless cases the scenario varied little. Whether at Aoulay, Biban in June, or above Taounat in early July, outworks designed to ease the pressure on the main outpost, sometimes equipped with a 75 mm gun, were early casualties, usually succumbing to a mass assault. Without let-up or hindrance, the main outpost then came under continual artillery and machine-gun fire, especially when thick mists blanketed the hills, preventing the French air force from lending a hand. To make matters worse, the onset of summer brought heat and thirst in its train, access to water being problematical as most outposts were hilltop constructions sited far from springs. Once such outposts were closely besieged, they could at best survive a few days, after which the defenders were at their last gasp.

Costly counter-attacks then had to be mounted to relieve them, as often as not resulting in an order to blow up and evacuate the fort anyway, as with Aoulay and Biban. One fort in Jbala country—Beni Derkoul—held by a handful of Senegalese *Tirailleurs*, was blown up at the eleventh hour (July 14) by the young officer in command. For the defenders, death was indeed better than capture, because the Rifs were well known for showing little mercy, often emasculating and killing their prisoners.[20] The situation was getting out of hand; the supposed superiority of colonial troops was being openly challenged.

In the meantime, many of the Rifs had become experienced fighters, quite the equal of the Moroccan and Algerian *Tirailleurs* units that generally opposed them. What's more, in the fighting near Taounat, at least four Europeans were identified in their ranks—probably Foreign Legion deserters.[21] By the end of June, with a gradually disintegrating front and Rifian forces making spectacular gains, 'Abdelkrim boastfully announced that his forces, numbering some 100,000 men in all, would capture Fez in time for the great *ayd lkbir* feast (July 3), and even sent the Fez *ulama*s letters to this effect. This drew a fitting response from his liege lord—Sultan Moulay Youssef of Morocco. Not only did the latter announce that he himself would be in Fez on that day (and he kept his word), but he advised all his *qayd*s to have no truck with the Rifian upstart; he eventually raised a *harka* of some 6,000 fighters to defend the sacred city.[22]

However, the French were still far from recovering the initiative. North of Taza, fate hung in the balance. In the meantime, *groupes mobiles* under General Colombat and Colonels Freidenberg, Noguès, and Cambay were doing yeoman service, incessantly marching and counter-marching, plugging gaps in the front. While his colleagues fought on undismayed, Cambay's resolve was weakening in the face of adversity. He was so disheartened after losing all his Tsoul and Brans partisans, when those tribes went over to 'Abdelkrim in the first week of July, that he even suggested abandoning

Taza and retreating east to the Moulouya Valley. This, however, was too serious a move to countenance: the loss of Taza would have allowed the Rifians to join the Beni Ouaraïn and other dissident tribal groups in the Middle Atlas, sparking an unforeseeable chain reaction. Lyautey therefore ordered that all units were to stand firm and that under no circumstance should Taza be evacuated.[23]

Turning point of the war?

This may be seen as the turning point of the Rif War, 'Abdelkrim's offensive having reached its high-water mark. Although suffering from ill health and overwork, though not necessarily from senility, Lyautey marked what was to be the end of his tenure with decisions that undoubtedly saved the Protectorate from 'Abdelkrim.

On July 6, things appeared to be looking up: north of Taza, Lieutenant-Colonel Giraud achieved some measure of success, likewise General Billotte northeast of Fez on the same day.[24] Furthermore, reinforcements were at last arriving from Algeria, some 32,000 men by the end of July.[25] Simultaneously, a chain of events was set in train on both sides of the Mediterranean with a view to bringing the conflict to an end. At home, Painlevé was consulting his advisers about appointing an *el supremo* for the Rif front who would achieve decisive results. Weygand was briefly contemplated but dismissed as too right-wing. Eventually quiet, efficient Naulin was nominated. However, he saw too eye-to-eye with Lyautey, which made the Paris politicians suspicious, their choice finally falling on Marshall Philippe Pétain, victor of Verdun and Inspector-General of the French Army. He flew to Morocco on July 17 for a week's visit to the *Résidence* in Rabat and the Rif front. On the whole, he got on relatively well with Lyautey, albeit somewhat stiffly during meals, there being very little common ground between them.[26] Convinced that the French forces in Morocco were suffering

Fig. 28: French 155 mm howitzers in action north of Fez (*L'Illustration*, summer 1925).

from a lack of *troupes blanches* to oppose the Rifs, Pétain returned after a week with a shopping list of quality reinforcements.

At the same time, the French had been putting out feelers to 'Abdelkrim in an attempt to bring him to the negotiating table. The linchpin on the French side, a civil servant called Gabrielli, had access to the amir of the Rif through a certain *qayd* Haddou. Gabrielli made a couple of trips to Ajdir only to come away empty handed, his attempts foiled partly by 'Abdelkrim's insistence on the non-negotiable independence of the Rif, partly by incompatibility between French and Spanish designs.

Although the main Rifian offensive had been slowed to a standstill, the situation remained serious until early August. In mid-July, at the western end of the front, the important town of Ouazzan was threatened, small parties of Rifs going even further to attack settlers' farms in the Gharb.[27] In a bold night raid (July 29–30), the Fez–Taza railway line was occupied and telephone lines cut.[28] As of August, however, 'Abdelkrim began to suffer significant losses of territory. Strengthened—thanks to Pétain—by incoming reinforcements, General Naulin was able to muster twenty-five battalions in the pre-Rif to subjugate the Tsoul tribe on August 16. But bringing the Brans tribe back into the fold was to prove more arduous, due to the difficult terrain: sixteen battalions had their work cut out subduing those recalcitrant tribesmen (August 26).[29]

Come September, the tide was definitely beginning to turn. In Rabat, Lyautey and Naulin were busy preparing a limited offensive aimed at repossessing the Beni Zeroual country north of Oued Ouergha, thus driving a wedge between the Jbala and Rif proper. This was now feasible due to the arrival of massive reinforcements.[30] Marshall Pétain, soon to take over from Lyautey as commander-in-chief, had other ideas: far better, he argued, to launch an offensive due north and east from Taza, to encircle the main Rif backbone and link up with the Spaniards near Melilla. It was also agreed that a French offensive would be met halfway by Spanish forces on Oued Kert. That was the plan. We shall see to what extent it materialized.

War on two fronts

In contrast to Lyautey, who distrusted them, Pétain saw the Spaniards as useful allies, and had made short stopovers in Madrid on each of his trips to and from Morocco, hobnobbing with moderate dictator Primo de Rivera in whom he found a kindred spirit. In Madrid, a thirst for vengeance in the wake of Spain's recent disasters, backed by the Catholic Church dreaming of a fresh *reconquista*, not to mention staunch *africanista* elements, urged a resumption of hostilities.[31] Their pet plan for a naval landing near Alhoceima was reinstated, Pétain promising that a French squadron from Mers-el-Kebir would be at hand to support the Spanish navy.

In fact the long-expected landings finally took place on September 9 after a bombardment by the combined Franco-Spanish fleet. The northern front, which had lain dormant for several months since the Spanish had retreated from Oued Laou to Tetouan, was reactivated in a spectacular manner. Confronted with war on two fronts, a situation he had sought to avoid, 'Abdelkrim was thus hoist with his own petard.[32] The Spanish expeditionary force, including elements of the Spanish Foreign Legion, or

Tercio, under Francesco Franco, advanced slowly over rugged terrain, the Rifs contesting every inch of their advance.

After desperate Rifian counter-attacks, there were cases where no prisoners were taken, the tribesmen being, in Franco's words, "put to the sword."[33] By October 3, after overcoming bitter resistance, Spanish forces had captured Ajdir, capital of the Rif republic, and burnt 'Abdelkrim's house. Yet this had little strategic significance and next to no immediate impact on the course of the war; the Rifs simply retreated into the hills, their ability to further wage war relatively unimpaired. 'Abdelkrim, wounded in a chemical attack, went with them, undaunted, his prestige unimpaired.[34]

Meanwhile, we must return to early September and relate 'Abdelkrim's last attempt to create a diversion on the Tetouan front. To tie down forces around Tetouan and prevent them from embarking on board ship for the Alhoceima landings, he instructed the able Kheriro with 3,000 men to attack and capture the prominent hilltop fort of Kudia Tahar, which was held by 170 Spaniards with four artillery pieces. Possession of this commanding position would enable the Rifs to bombard Tetouan and even invest the capital. After six days of furious Rifian assaults had killed more than three-quarters of the garrison, a handful of survivors were hanging on grimly. The situation called for drastic action. As there was a serious risk of this strategic position falling into Rifian hands, Spanish reinforcements under Franco were rushed to the scene from Alhoceima. It took another desperate two-day battle, "from rock to rock" in the words of one participant, to finally force the Rifs to relinquish their hold on the position (September 11–12).[35] 'Abdelkrim's gamble had failed, though not for want of trying.

On the Ouergha front a limited French offensive was under way. Starting from Tafrant and Taounat on September 11, some forty battalions pushed north above Oued Ouergha into Beni Zeroual country, symbolically reoccupying the strategic hill of Biban, while the Rifian regulars withdrew northwards. As for the Deraqawi *sharif* who had been ousted in April, he was restored to his zaouia at Amjot.[36] Shortly afterwards, on September 25, Pétain's would-be decisive offensive got under way from Kiffan with some fifty battalions in three columns. It was a mixed brood: there were Moroccan regulars and Algerian *goumiers* and *Tirailleurs* allegedly inured to the exigencies of North African campaigning, but also tanks, armored cars, and artillery with contingents of those *troupes blanches* Pétain had insisted on, little used to confronting hill tribes in their own back yard. To Pétain's way of thinking, the very fact that they came from Metropolitan France endowed them with a built-in superiority which would overcome any resistance. This attitude underscored the prickly relationship between troops drawn from the spit and polish of French home garrisons and their counterparts used to roughing it in the ranks of the *Armée d'Afrique*. As French staff officer Catroux pointed out:

> It proved difficult to convince Pétain that the Rif War had little in common with military operations in Europe, that the enemy failed to abide by the rules obtaining in conflicts between regular armies, and that to overcome them you needed to adapt your tactics to theirs, based on the element of surprise and guerilla operations.[37]

Meanwhile, Pétain's offensive north of Taza was running into trouble. Typically, Pétain had chosen to ignore warnings from old Morocco hands that if he waited until October the onset of the rainy season could jeopardize his plans. After a while, this is precisely what happened: the sluice-gates of heaven opened wide and for several days a continuous downpour turned dirt roads into a giant quagmire. Impatient with these unforeseen delays, Pétain moved his HQ to Taza, the better to supervise operations. The offensive, which had begun well, advance units reaching Si'Ali Bou Rokba on Oued Kert as planned on October 9, was now literally bogged down. Even worse, the planned link-up with Spanish forces went awry, only a token force of their native cavalry reaching the rendezvous, while the French advance guard of *Spahis* under Durand found itself in a highly exposed position.[38] Annoyed that the Spanish had welshed on their side of the bargain, Pétain ordered Durand to carry out a "partial withdrawal of the eastern part of the front."[39] As ever in Morocco, this kind of movement was fraught with danger. During the ensuing counter-attacks by Berber tribesmen, Durand lost some thirty men and horses; mules transporting 75 mm guns slithered down slimy banks and were lost; a detachment of tanks embedded in the mud was knocked out by Rifian tribesmen who fired through slits, killing the crews; and as for the Algerian *goumiers*, they cut a sorry figure in the face of accurate rifle fire.

A general retreat brought all these forces back to their start lines, and on October 27 Pétain explained away the recent washout by declaring, "Morocco is at peace, 'Abdelkrim is no longer a threat, and now is the time for politics," and also that adverse weather conditions precluded further fighting, thus bringing the 1925 campaign to a close.[40] For all his bluster, Pétain had visibly achieved only partial success, a point several French press articles hastened to point out, including one by Robert Poulaine in the *Temps*. Correspondingly, the stock of Lyautey—who had meanwhile resigned as Resident-General and returned to France—went up as he was absolved from blame for his handling of the Rifian emergency. Conversely, Pétain's unfinished offensive had left 'Abdelkrim in a relatively strong position, the more so as the tribes that had submitted to France during the advance had relapsed into dissidence.[41]

Winter of 1925–6

Actually, the Rif republic was not yet done for; 'Abdelkrim was far from inactive during the winter months. Able politician that he was, he had detected weaknesses in the uneasy Franco–Spanish military alliance and was determined to exploit them to the best of his ability.[42] Nor was he lacking in foreign support. The French Communist Party (PCF) was as active as ever. An anti-war strike organized on October 12 by the PCF had little success, but there was much agitation and even rioting in Paris, where police fired on demonstrators. Throughout the winter, the French were busy placating and ultimately winning over Rifian border tribes such as the Igzennayn, their *Affaires Indigènes* ("Native Affairs") officers playing a prominent role in what was very much a hearts and minds operation.

A young cavalry lieutenant, Henri de Bournazel, was to achieve excellent results at the head of a group of Brans partisans, also foiling attacks on French outposts by Rifian *harka*s.[43] As the spring of 1926 drew near, the sands were running out for 'Abdelkrim. The Spanish landings in the heart of Ayt Waryaghar country meant that his secular enemy had gained an unassailable foothold on the Mediterranean coast. Other losses of terrain in the south had dented his prestige, foodstuffs were beginning to dwindle, while ceaseless aerial bombardment by the French air force and Spanish chemical attacks were sapping the morale of even the staunchest fighters. The only way out appeared to be through a negotiated settlement. However, he was now wary of approaches by the Franco–Spanish pair, Gabrielli–Marin, to the point of refusing to receive them. Walter Harris, the famous Tangier-based journalist, after expressing early support for the Rifian cause, had proved a disappointment. Now, a high-minded Englishman by the name of Gordon Canning appeared to be a possible last resort. Authorized by Painlevé to visit the Rif, Canning made a month-long trip and emerged with a blueprint for a negotiated peace guaranteeing Rifian independence.

End of the Rif republic

However, Canning had antagonized Paris through his anti-French stance, being denounced by Aristide Briand in the most withering terms, and fared even worse with Madrid. By the end of 1925 his mission had proved a complete flop.[44] A final attempt was to be made on April 16, 1926, at a conference in Oujda, the Rifian delegation being led by their Foreign Secretary, Azerkan. Again, various scenarios were discussed. Steeg, the French Resident-General, who was angling for a separate peace with the Rifs, had incurred distrust from the Spaniards, also being at loggerheads with Pétain, who was against any sign of weakness vis-à-vis the enemy, and insisting that as a military leader, 'Abdelkrim should accept the fortunes of war: that is, the terms imposed upon him.[45] Finally, on May 5, when negotiations were broken off, the warlike Azerkan declared that he was delighted at the prospect of a resumption of hostilities![46]

Before the main campaign got under way in May, there had been various skirmishes with the as yet defiant Rifs; wherever possible they had harassed the invaders. One typical affray was the capture of Jbel Bou Zeitoun by Colonel Millán Astray of the *Tercio* on March 4, 1926. This was important because a gun the Rifians had sited up there had been subjecting Tetouan to random bombardment.[47] On May 7, 1926, the final offensive was launched. While Spanish forces thrust south, anxious to avenge earlier defeats, the French captured Jbel Hammam and its outliers, and within a few days had met their allies between Targuist and Melilla.

The Rifs resisted with their customary bravery but their hearts were no longer in it; several months of hardship, and aerial bombardment sometimes with chemical weapons, had taken their toll.[48] Previously loyal tribes caved in almost immediately and, after two weeks of desperate fighting, 'Abdelkrim at last sued for peace. Wary of the Spaniards, he preferred to surrender to the French on May 22. He was treated with respect and eventually sent into exile to Reunion in the Indian Ocean. But for all that, there were still some diehards up in the hills and—in typical Berber fashion—they held out for another year, Kheriro the irrepressible Jebli continuing the fight, finally being killed by the Spaniards north of Ouazzan on November 3, 1926. In July 1927 French forces finally forced the Beni Mestara to surrender—and thus did the episode of the Rif republic and the 1921–7 war pass into history.[49] However, it had been an exceedingly serious affair and restored hope to many nationalists:

> Although his ['Abdelkrim's] anti-colonial political field was ultimately eliminated by the overwhelming military onslaught of two industrialized European powers, the legacy of the Rif republic and collective experience of autonomy, state formation, and military resistance reinforced a firm sense of separate Rif identity for subsequent generations.[50]

In fact, the whole episode, especially the setting up of a republic, left a strong imprint on local minds and later inspired the ideology of the 2017 *hiraq* leaders in the Nador area.

Fig. 29: Spanish troops west of Melilla (1921 photo, Archive Vidal).

Phoney War on the Atlas Front (1926–9)

We must now return to the Middle Atlas. The *irumin*'s columns had cut their way through the cedar forests of Fazaz towards the Sahara; their line of outposts had been pushed sufficiently forward to neutralize any threat to the Meknes–Boudenib road, or to that vital Fez–Taza–Guercif axis leading eastwards to Algeria.[1] By this time, most of the recalcitrant Ouaraïni and Zaïan tribesmen had been brought to book; it was but a matter of months before their beleaguered brethren on Tishshoukt and Bou Iblan suffered a similar fate. Once their strongholds fell, the *imjuhad* would have to regroup in the Great Atlas if the fight were to go on. Down there the overall picture was slightly more encouraging: the expansionist tendencies of El-Glaoui had been checked in Ayt Bouguemmez, while the Tafilalt oasis remained uncompromisingly hostile. More significantly, in their reputedly impregnable citadels of the Great Atlas, the major warlike tribes, their fighting potential unimpaired, remained confident that they could see off the foe. However, it would be unfortunate if a potentially critical French home opinion became unduly alarmed by a catalog of unpleasant facts and figures. Rarely has there been such a masterly cover-up. As a British journalist observed:

> Never was a campaign of conquest more discreetly carried on.... The skeleton of Berber "dissidence" was ... concealed with the same skill that a Parisian restaurant manager would show in withholding from his guests the fact that a homicidal affray was going on below-stairs among his kitchen staff.[2]

Yet of late there had been little scope for warlike prowess. Once the Rif war had broken out, the entire Atlas front had subsided into lethargy; a "phoney war" atmosphere pervaded. Apart from the final *Tache de Taza* operations in 1926–7, which were to benefit from a short-lived manpower bonanza subsequent to the Rif war, this situation prevailed well after 'Abdelkrim's surrender, only ending in 1929 with the Ayt Ya'qoub campaign. Given this prolonged period of masterly inactivity on the part of the French, small *imjuhad* groups girded their loins for battle and soon made their presence felt. In their aptitude for combat these combatants were definitely "cutting edge." Skilled in the arts of ambush and raid, their admirable use of terrain combined with great mobility and accurate firepower, they would more than once make fools of French patrols sent out after them. Such were the Ayt Hammou who, through countless feats of arms, would become living legends as they ranged from the alfa steppe of Talsinnt and cedar groves of Tounfit to the great dunes of the southern sand-sea and the hills of Jbel Bani

(1927–34). To a great extent their fate was linked to that of bogus sultan Belqasm Ngadi, who had evicted the French from the Tafilalt palm grove in 1918. Cruel and unscrupulous as he was, this self-proclaimed defender of Islam and champion of Moroccan independence was regularly sending out his war bands to harass enemy outposts.[3]

For the French, Tafilalt was a den of thieves and robbers that would have to be cleaned up; it was also a constant reminder of past failure. However, the penultimate episode of Amazigh resistance needs to be considered in a totally different light. As a curtain-raiser, the early-1933 Jbel Saghro episode set the tone. The unprecedented expenditure of men and ammunition necessary to reduce those stoutly defended citadels of unhewn rock is the stuff of legend. Under charismatic leader Hassou ou Ba Slam, for forty days did a thousand Ayt 'Atta warriors oppose with unerring fire several attempts to storm the heights by an 80,000-strong enemy force; an inspired resistance of such magnitude that it enabled them to surrender more or less on their own terms. Protagonists on both sides had displayed a hardening of resolve, a grim, no-nonsense approach to combat: a foretaste of equally bitter battles to come amid the barren summits of the Great Atlas.[4] Finally, from among the stocky, cliff-dwelling Ayt 'Abdi, or feud-ridden Ayt Merghad and Ayt Hadiddou, it was no easy task to pick out the toughest Great Atlas fighters. All had distinguished track records; all had figured prominently in anti-French resistance; all would be among the last diehards to surrender at the close of the 1933 campaign. From Ayt Ya'qoub to Tazizaout and Kousser, from Tarda to Msedrid, Hamdoun, Kerdous, and Baddou, each and every one of them would achieve undying glory in scores of firefights. The following chapters will highlight the closing phases of this *gesta barbarorum*.

The politicals at work

During this phoney war period, officers of the *Affaires Indigènes* (AI, Native Affairs) became the sole active agents of French military penetration, as Berbers soon found out. These were the strangely courteous, often idealistic young men with whom they now came into contact. What was their goal? The method differed so radically from that of previous representatives of authority that the Imazighen were genuinely puzzled:

> Wherefore does the Christian oppress us?
> The entire country does dominate, his roads are
> Kept clear; heavily does his hand lie upon us![5]

Given the important role that Native Affairs officers were to play, given the intimate relationship that often developed between them and Imazighen, some space must be devoted to this interesting, much maligned band of brothers. After being exposed to the rudiments of Arabic and Berber, together with a crash course in Moroccan history at the Rabat Institute for Higher Moroccan Studies, each of these young officers, imbued with apostolic zeal, was unleashed upon the tribe that had been allotted to them, whether it had submitted or not. It would be perceived as their own personal property. Pending the end of spring and the resumption of the campaigning season, there would be ample time to milk informers of all they knew.

The officer would attempt to win over any unsubdued tribesmen who might venture into the local market or hospital; spy out the nakedness of the land by poring over inadequate maps and aerial photographs; jot down information gleaned on the local socio-political scene; unravel complex cases of intra-tribal litigation. It usually proved very much a hearts and minds operation and, in terms of sociology and human geography in the raw, a heady, rewarding task for the youngster fresh from military college—one designed to alleviate life in a lonely outpost, with its emergencies, its expectations, its night alarms, and its vigils.

It was a task fit for men, for born leaders, one tailor made for the likes of Ernest Psichari, an early twentieth-century empire-builder turned mystic, killed by Ma el-Aïnin's men in southeast Morocco, and source of inspiration for many a young French AI officer, who unambiguously announced, "Let the waverers, the faint of heart, or those who fear honest home truths, stay away from Africa and her rough medicine. Here, one's outlook on life must be pure, unflinching. The outlook of a young man, frank and clear,"[6] one such as the young officer a journalist met one day in a remote Atlas Valley, whom he described as "yet another of those who behave like some latter-day apostle. Who are Native Affairs officers to their very finger-tips!"[7] Similar to others met by French *académicien* Henri Bordeaux in 1933, who "perpetuate the tradition of Rome and her legions; city-builders, for sure, but ready on the morrow to resume military operations interrupted the day before."[8] Some twenty years later, the message had not changed, the inspiration was identical. Captain Ithier, one of France's most dedicated politicals, would describe the "thrillingly hallowed task" he had undertaken with Atlas Berbers as "definitely not for those whose enthusiasm was lukewarm."[9]

Thus emerges the identikit picture of the typical *Affaires Indigènes* officer embarking upon his challenging career. Basically, we have an honest, horsy extrovert, a mite naïve and unashamedly confident in what he sees as his civilizing mission; also something of an enlightened feudal lord, steeped in the classics, and convinced he belongs to an elite, though without the dragoon mentality that characterizes most regular combat officers. Not so much a fighter (though fight he does at times—and then well) as a charmer, a tamer of men. Thus would he appear to the bemused tribesmen, as he walked towards them, complete with swagger stick, blue pillbox cap, and cloak, a smile on his face and, on his lips, words of greeting in patiently rehearsed Tamazight. Much would depend on that initial meeting; on the figure he cut, on the impression he made. Whether he genuinely had their well-being at heart, or whether he was merely there to exploit them, to plunder their poultry yard, in which case the relationship would be one based on expediency, servility, and guile. In the words of one official, "Tribesmen need to admire their *hakim*. They want him to be prestigious, generous, self-confident, and jovial. At the shooting-range, on horseback, at work, in battle, whether in sorrow or in sadness, at all times must he impose respect."[10]

Should he fail to pass muster on these accounts, all kinds of unpleasantness might result, especially if appointed to some Atlas flashpoint, as with the unfortunate Lieutenant Despax, killed in the marketplace at Talsinnt (December 16, 1925) by a posse of disgruntled Ayt Hammou.[11]

Some of the Berbers who came to the fort, often out of sheer curiosity, would take service in the officer's personal guard of *mokhaznis*, conspicuous in their immaculate white turbans and blue cloaks, under the orders of an NCO, the *chaouch*, who was his right-hand man. Sometimes, this individual got too big for his boots, lording it over visiting tribesmen, and rapidly becoming the most hated man in the place. Contemporary Amazigh poetry echoes this kind of situation: "Am now loath to visit *Ibiru*: before this unworthy / Individual am forced to kow tow; I have to call him *sidi!*"[12]

Then there would be a detachment of some 150 or so Goums, irregular infantry and cavalry from previously tamed tribes, speaking a dialect not unlike that of the locals. These were athletic-looking, bearded men with black turbans, brown cloaks, and sandals, commanded by two similarly attired French NCOs. The outpost itself would consist of a rectangular outer wall about 1m 50 cm high, with an enhanced breastwork, or casemate, at each corner equipped with a swivel-mounted Hotchkiss machine gun, backed up by one or two centrally sited 65 mm mountain guns served by Foreign Legion gunners. Beyond the wall lay a first line of defense: barbed-wire entanglements festooned with empty sardine cans! As many a would-be Berber infiltrator discovered to his cost, the midnight jangle of these crude detection devices, calculated to arouse sleepy, trigger-happy sentries, could prove counterproductive.[13] The nerve centre would be the central redoubt, or *bordj*, with a wireless shack, an heliograph, and the officer's quarters—"something of a monk's cell with its white-washed walls, at once study and sleeping-chamber, spartanly furnished with a few mats, carpets and book-cases."[14] This perhaps in the Tounfit area, reflecting a fluctuating situation when, during the closing stages of the campaign, officers were ceaselessly on the move and living out of their suitcases. Not so with one of his more comfortably housed counterparts visited by a British writer at an earlier, more stable period on the Atlas front, and described as having:

> . . . a bed-sitting room with a divan in a corner over-laid with Berber rugs; and a bookcase full of French paper-covered volumes . . . next to it his office with a table and a chair, an array of *dossiers*, his sword and revolver. Facing these across an open space, there is a dining-room decorated with pictures from *La Vie parisienne*, the solace in hard times of many a lonely soldier . . .
>
> Upon the threshold of his door sits a clansman but recently retrieved from the insurgent sections of his tribe; a tall Berber in a blue military cloak . . .[15]

To which bed-sitting room might come the officer's Berber concubine, helping him improve his knowledge of the vernacular. Whatever the contribution to the Atlas gene pool, this kind of hobnobbing with the natives was officially frowned upon in high places, though it could prove useful for the officer's mission—when spring came and the snow had melted and the young *hakim* could start off again on the war trail with his Goums.[16] On the vital day he might even have the honor of heading the main force that would bludgeon wayward elements of *his* tribe into submission. On most occasions, milder counsels would prevail and the dissident element would fall like a ripe plum, merely presenting token resistance—the *baroud d'honneur*. Then, once the sacrificial bull was slaughtered during the *ta'argiba* ceremony, once the top brass and their hangers-on had departed for Rabat, the young political could bask in the pleasure of a job well done, at the same time anticipating further stages in the taming process he had to undertake if he were to achieve 100 percent success.[17]

Native Affairs officers: positive and negative angles

From perusing period material, whatever reservations one may have about colonial times, one comes away with the impression that AI Officers formed an élite. It was an opinion shared by many of their successors—post-independence *qayd*s, most of them trained in Kenitra. In fact, the hard work, the scrupulous fairness and professionalism displayed by 90 percent of the AI officers is remembered to this day in tribal areas.[18] Whatever criticism may since have been leveled at them, they always attempted to discharge their duties with intelligence (*bel ma'aqul*), a fact driven home by Commandant Ayard—an old Atlas hand—in his courses for incoming trainees.[19] In the words of another observer:

> Their mission was enacted in France's name, for sure, but for the benefit of Sharifian authority, and in an attempt to guarantee social equity for the Moroccan people. No doubt results were not always up to expectation, yet it was not for want of trying, dedication, enthusiasm and personal commitment characterizing their action.[20]

Fig. 30: French AI officer on patrol with his bodyguards in the Middle Atlas (*L'Illustration*, winter 1923–4).

Furthermore, there is little doubt that they often took up the cudgels on behalf of the poorer elements from among their parishioners, an insistence on fairness which was part of the education they received. This a point substantiated by the well-known story of the Native Affairs officer who, just after "his" tribe has submitted, strives might and main to get it exonerated from tax payments before the Inland Revenue vultures can home in on their prey.[21] Thus were they real empire-builders, who in the mid-1930s still fitted snugly into an overall imperialist vision of the world with its comfortable, unassailable certitudes, such as that:

> Arabic can never act as the vehicle of civilization in Berber territory, just as the instrument of progress will never be the cordially detested, rapacious representative of the *makhzan*; even less the great *qayd*. These roles will be played by the French language and the Native Affairs officer.[22]

The latter must under no circumstances forget that he was there to "conquer hearts."[23] To quote another Lyautey cliché, "to begin thinking of the welfare of the country and its people the morning after they had beaten them in action."[24]

Thus, once the guns had fallen silent, he would be the first to exhort tribesmen to come out and plough their fields, probably providing the seed to be sown, as did Captain Parlange (*qebtan burlanj*) with the Ayt Yahya of Tounfit.[25] The wounded were sent to the infirmary for treatment, the toddlers to newly created schools for enlightenment. Gradually, an entire infrastructure was put in place: dirt roads were hacked out of the rock by Foreign Legion sappers; rushing rivers were bridged to access markets deep in the High Atlas; footbaths for sheep were provided, also cemented irrigation ditches, more efficient than old ones, like those built in the Tounfit area by Parlange.[26] Some fifty years down the road, dedicated men like his colleagues Paulin (*bulan*) of Tinghir, De Latour (*muha w latur*), or Ithier (*iti*) of Zaouit Ahansal, are still remembered for their unflagging efforts to improve the everyday life of the folk committed to their care.

So much for the positive side of the political officer's activities; naturally, modern detractors, many of whom have never visited the Atlas, will be quick to find fault. Whereas the Legionaries had built the *pistes*, their maintenance was up to the local Berbers, who were expected to provide unpaid labor—the unpopular *corvées*.[27]

While tracks improved communications, they were of strategic importance enabling reinforcements to be rushed to the spot should disturbances break out. Yet others would take the new schools to task for the absence from their programs of Arabic and Islamic teaching, though this may have been attributable to concern over possible attempts to thwart "Ottoman-inspired Pan-Islamism, or Arab-Muslim reform."[28] Taking their cue from French writers Berque, Julien, and Monteil, other critics will be swift to point out that the Native Affairs officer's performance was based on bluff—that he and his colleagues arrogantly posed as the sole experts on things Arab and Berber.[29] That the AI officer was little more than a paternalistic Robinson Crusoe catering to the needs of an "unlikely Man Friday" and ensuring that with their institutions Berber areas be "put on ice," the better to retain their supposed pristine purity as national parks, or as "the last reservations in the Mediterranean still inhabited by white barbarians."[30] After General Mangin's pre-1914 theory on black soldiers to fight France's wars, are we to believe that the French were aiming to set up a fresh manpower reservoir to cover her future military and industrial needs? Or that she intended to transform all Berbers into Frenchmen, possibly making pious Catholics of them into the bargain?[31] Whatever the answers to those questions, the debate on this much-vexed topic is still ongoing. For a more balanced look at AI officers, the reader should turn to the works of Robin Bidwell and Rom Landau.[32]

But what of the fighters still lurking in the hills? What did they think of attempts to cajole them into submission? Were they sensitive to this iron fist in a velvet glove? Were they favorably disposed towards the man riding a white horse who would become their *hakim*? Probably not, despite what some Protectorate period novellas would have us believe.[33] For centuries the Imazighen had been their own masters, suspicious of any measure that might curtail that freedom. How could they bow down overnight to a conqueror, to an administration whose ulterior motives they failed to understand? Why should they abandon a noble, timeless lifestyle which allowed a man to raid his neighbors on horseback whenever he felt like it and confront his foe with cold steel? Period poetry is redolent with allusions to these heart-searchings, as in this tirade attributed to a recently-tamed tribesman:

> O horses, today gone is bravery; should one of
> Our young men mount his steed, he rides unarmed;
> Truthfully, now has the spice of life departed!
> Our guns have been taken away, O Berbers,
> The sound of steel is silent, gone is honour,
> You react at present to an alien form of logic!
> The Roumi now oppresses us, over us
> Does keep watch; O Islam, fate is unkind to you.
> Should you raise a little finger into prison you go!
> Over us the *qebtan* does hold sway . . .[34]

A conquest of hearts and minds?

However proficient the Native Affairs *qebtan* might be at psychological warfare, his work could be easily undone by whichever local saint was urging the diehards to resist Islam's traditional enemies—the accursed *irumin*, with their disgusting habits: urinating standing up, eating pork, drinking wine, trampling finely-woven carpets with their leather riding boots, or indulging in their favorite pastime: womanizing. This last was the most potent argument: the marabout could play on the Berber fighter's exacerbated sense of honor, ultimately embodied in his wife, visualized as an undefilable sanctuary (*hurma*); under no circumstances must she fall prey to the infidel. However, the better to keep an eye on the enemy, to sound him out on his intentions, sending an elderly female to the nearest outpost was all part of the game.[35]

She would come to the infirmary complaining of some ailment, pass on harmless tidbits of information to the *qebtan*, question the *mokhaznis* as to goings-on in the fort, possibly branding them as traitors if she was too old to seduce them, and finally make her way back to camp.

Through a mix of trickery, patience, and prudence, the tribe put off as long as possible the actual moment of submission. Right up to the last minute it was in danger of being raided and plundered by recalcitrant neighbors.[36] Possibilities for double-dealing were unlimited, as in the case of the Imtchimen clan of the Ayt Yahya throughout the period 1922–31. Whenever they descended from the hills on market day to sell their surplus sheep, men and women would attend surgeries at the Midelt infirmary like any other chastened tribal folk; at night, however, their war parties would set off to harass French front-line outposts or raid villages belonging to recently submitted tribes.[37] On another occasion, the only means of winning over some notable was to promise him the future *qayd*ship of the tribe if he could bring about its surrender. Thus, as we have seen, bringing recalcitrant tribesmen back into the fold could be a long-drawn-out process, alternating between a labor of love and barely disguised attempts at intimidation. On the part of the politicals it required dedication, determination, infinite patience, and unflagging energy. Even then there was no guaranteeing that a handful of hotheads would not stage a face-saving last stand, or perhaps make a fighting retreat further into the Atlas:

> Thus speaks Terwillal hill: "A wild boar have I wed;
>   Go, live with mountaineers, O Hammou ou 'Amr, head
> Into the hills beyond, better becomes you bitter cold
>   Than cowardly knuckling under to Christian dogs!"[38]

Terror on Tishshoukt: Prelude to surrender

During these quiet years on the Atlas front, nowhere was this more obvious than among the Ayt Seghroushen. Though cut off from neighboring clans since the 1923 campaign, Saïd ou Mohand's faithful war band, some 400-strong, had retreated with womenfolk and children to the inner fastnesses of Jbel Tishshoukt for a final stand. Despite the hardships of life at altitude—hiding in caverns or miserable, dung-insulated hovels, squatting over small fires and shivering till dawn—they managed to hold out up there for three winters.

Better still, they kept hunger at bay by sowing and harvesting barley at well above 2000 m in the valleys of Ikkis, Ljoua, and Bessam—something of an agricultural record for the area.[39] On certain nights, having kept their powder dry, small groups would steal softly down the slopes and wake up the French garrison at Skoura, or rustle cattle from villages that had gone over to the French.

Meanwhile, a new *hakim* had taken over the Skoura outpost: Laffitte. This was bad news for the Ayt Seghroushen. Something of a rough diamond, this controversial individual was quite different from the usual polished, St. Cyr-trained officer. A somewhat loutish, latter-day *condottiere* and a firm believer in brute force, he had served in South America, with the Foreign Legion, with the Turks, and in the Great War. According to one observer, a saber-cut across the nose "gave him a most formidable

Fig. 31: Jbel Tishshoukt, Middle Atlas citadel of the Ayt Seghroushen (1923–6).

appearance, and he added to its effect by an aggressive and overbearing manner which sometimes aroused the resentment of his seniors."[40] A fellow officer, however, claims that his ugly features were occasionally redeemed by a "charmingly friendly smile."[41] With a name equal to his reputation, that could be interpreted locally either as *la'afit*, "fire," or *la'afrit*, "demon," it was obvious that the Seghroushen were in for a rough time. They soon discovered that his anti-raider operations, conducted with a personal guard of Berber partisans, were as ruthlessly effective as their own raids. After one of their bands had found shelter in a friendly village, Laffitte punished its inhabitants by forcing all the men to strip, then sending them up the slope in their birthday suits to join the dissidents.[42] The resultant loss of face proved as damaging as it was hard to live down. Even worse, hard on the heels of a serious attack on a settled village, which had allegedly broken a truce engineered by Laffitte, many of the participants were later killed by a crude explosive device he had planted along one of the paths they were wont to use. Worse still, he concealed a hand grenade in a sugarloaf and had it surreptitiously dispatched to the *amghar* whom he suspected of having instigated the attack, with fatal results the next time tea was served in that notable's tent.

For this ungentlemanly deed the top brass, who were not at all amused, sent him to the rear for fifteen months in total disgrace. Afterwards, on many an *ahidus* dance evening, this wild lament might have been heard:

Up into the hills did *la'afrit* go,
Unceasingly were explosions heard,
la'afrit shook the hills' very foundations,
Our women their slain husbands do mourn.[43]

Came the day, however, when this fire-eater's services were again needed, and Laffitte was reinstated. Although his brother officers had, during his absence, continued tightening the net around Tishshoukt—one of them (Durosoy) even making a bold night crossing of the range via Tizi Tigoulmamin disguised as a Berber—Saïd ou Mohand and his merry men remained obdurately defiant. Laffitte accordingly resumed his anti-raider operations with renewed vigor. Hours in the saddle would he spend, quartering the boxwood and oak scrub of Tishshoukt on the trail of some war band.

On the morning of June 12, 1924, as he was "riding herd" on a convoy of mules that was resupplying an outpost, a small *jish* attacked his rear and made off with some pack animals. Wheeling about, Laffitte dashed off in pursuit and soon closed in on the raiders, only to be ambushed by a small party. A bullet from a model '74 rifle shattered his thigh bone and the "prince of terror" died from loss of blood before he could be evacuated to Skoura.[44] Thus did *la'afrit* pass away, highly regarded for his swashbuckling habits by many of his contemporary officers, regretted only by his Berber concubine Raba', reviled by the families of resistance fighters who had lost loved ones at his hands.[45]

Subsequent events in the Tishshoukt epic were something of an anticlimax. Two years were to elapse before, taking advantage of the presence of back-up troops[46] who had just taken part in the successful Rif campaign, the French command brought overwhelming force to bear on that defiant hill. Two days of *baroud d'honneur* were all it took in June 1926 to force Saïd ou Mohand to submit with most Ayt Seghroushen of the area.[47] Fittingly, the French lieutenant who accepted his surrender was the selfsame Durosoy whose earlier nocturnal traverse of Tizi Tigoulmamin had earned him a reputation for daring. The surrender proved a courteous affair between brave combatants with mutual respect for each other; there were no reprisals, and many a Seghroushen fighter was soon to enroll in the Goums and participate in subsequent campaigns in the Great Atlas.[48] The larger part of the *Tache de Taza* had yet to be subjugated.

If the French military thought they were going to walk this one they were in for a surprise.

Sidi Raho's last stand on Bou Iblan

Already, on September 7, 1925, there had been serious fighting north of Immouzer-Marmousha—emboldened by news of 'Abdelkrim's victories in the Rif, Sidi Raho's men had dislodged the French from Ras Ashkourn. Three days later they launched several lethal counter-attacks on a mixed force of Goums, partisans, and Foreign Legion who were trying to establish another forward position on Jbel 'Ayyad, inflicting heavy losses on them.[49]

Tactically speaking, the Berbers had several aces in their pack: diabolically difficult terrain ideal for waging defensive warfare; convenient interior lines of communication; at least 3,000 fighters armed for the most part with breech-loaders and plentiful supplies of ammunition,[50] and who were prepared to sell their lives dearly. On the debit side, no unified command, no artillery, no automatic weapons, although sizeable stocks of hand grenades had trickled south from the Rif. While concepts of overall strategy

Fig. 32: Village assembly, Qsar Arrwadi, deep in former "*Tache de Taza*."

may have been embryonic, the irreconcilables of the *Tache de Taza* cannot have failed to observe the enemy build-up.

Sidi Raho and his close companions, their backs to the wall after a fifteen-year fighting retreat with few parallels in military history, could count on local Beni Ouaraïn clans, including a tried war band under Mohand ou Hammou, together with numerous displaced bellicose elements from Ayt Seghroushen and Marmousha, all of them full of fight. These were concentrated in a nightmarish, triangular tangle of precipitous escarpments and forested gullies—*miyat khandaq u khandaq* ("the hundred and one ravines")—its base running from the peak of Ish n-Tili to Tizi Ouidal along the cedar-covered backbone of Bou Iblan.

Sidi Raho, who was ready to fight to the bitter end, knew this was the final bastion of resistance in the area. Defend it he must; otherwise the game was up. As to support from the east and south, the situation was more doubtful. Most of the Ayt Jellidasen around Berkin, he knew, would listen to rival marabout Mohand ou Belqasm and surrender when the first rumble of artillery was heard. The Bou Illoul clan, however, protected by the Soufoulud gorge, its back to the crags and corries of Bou Nasser and Adrar n-Siwan, could be relied upon to give a good account of itself. The same applied to the southerly Beni Hassan and Oulad 'Ali clans, whose fine, terraced villages occupied the fertile, steep-sided Shegg El-'Ard valley. Their fighting strength intact, they would distinguish themselves against a numerically and technologically superior enemy.

By now, in every village and war camp, blacksmiths, armorers, and combatants would have been working overtime sharpening knives, cleaning and readying rifles, indulging in last-minute target practice With memories of the drubbings they had taken in 1922–3, the French were taking no chances. Three divisions, five brigade groups, with cavalry, Foreign Legion mounted companies, and five Goums backed by some 6,500 *mokhaznis* and partisans, were to join hands in the Taffert cedar forest and on the Meskeddal plateau in the heart of the massif. Some fourteen squadrons of biplanes and thirty field batteries, not to mention Ahermoumou-based, rail-mounted 340 mm naval guns would provide supporting fire.[51]

Lastly, where occasional flat ground proved more congenial, crude armored cars and toy-like Renault tanks of Great War fame would enter the fray.[52] From July 8 to 13 forward deployment was implemented, start lines were reached and consolidated, with D-Day scheduled for July 14, by which time the various units would be converging on their final objectives. It should be all over in a week.

Well might French staff officers at General Vernois's Field Headquarters at Immouzzer-Marmousha twirl their moustaches in gleeful anticipation as they pored over the barely adequate 1/200,000 maps. Later on, in their mess tent, over glasses of *pastis*, bets would no doubt be taken as to the duration of the campaign.

As with all battle plans, things went somewhat awry and operations eventually lasted a fortnight. Debouching northeast from Tilmirat, General Freydenberg's detachment met with heavy resistance on the first day. Meanwhile, attacking from due north, and after winning a precarious foothold on Aoujja hill and on the steep slopes of Jbal Gra', Colonel Cauvin's forces were hurled back by the Ighezran clan after two days of exceptionally fierce fighting. Predictably, though, Mohand ou Belqasm hedged his bets by throwing in the sponge, laying the eastern approaches of the massif wide open. Into this breach stormed Commandant Denis and his partisans, straddling the Tizi n-Tantatart before treading gingerly westward along ledge trails that bypass Tanchraramt, then on to Bou Iblan's northern slopes, by which time his colleague Matterne traversed Jbel Ajjou from the southeast to threaten Bou Illoul territory. By July 14 the French had managed to isolate Sidi Raho and his hard core of fighters around Taffert from a still defiant southern pocket, thanks to the speed with which the eastern front of the Bou Iblan pocket caved in.[53] So far so good. Last-ditch Berber resistance now kicked in.

Throughout the day, the balance of Sidi Raho's men battled with Freydenberg's Goums for every inch of Ich n-Tili's rugged, wooded ridge, while his main force heroically defended cedar-girt Tizi Ouidal, actually repelling with grenade and dagger a bloody assault by two battalions of regulars[54] and killing their commanding officers for good measure. The worst was yet to come. To neutralize the southern pocket the French had detached two forces, consisting mostly of Algerian *Spahis*, backed by Goums and partisans. Now, if the cavalry's mobility proved an asset on open ground, once it came to the nitty-gritty of combat over broken terrain, these horse soldiers on foot were at a disadvantage, their *mousquetons* ("cavalry carbines") outranged by the Berbers' longer-barrelled '83–'84 Lebel rifles. Furthermore, being Algerian army, they were unfamiliar with the finer aspects of Moroccan mountain warfare, sometimes mistaking dissidents for their own partisans, with fatal results.[55] Each detachment in turn ran into serious trouble.

Commandant Burnol's *Spahis* lumbered east from Immouzzer to occupy the heights at the head of the Shegg El-'Ard valley. Early on the morning of Bastille Day the detachment was pinned down by lethal fire from determined contingents of Beni Hassan. Heavy casualties were taken; one *Spahi* machine gun jammed, another was knocked out. By evening, however they had extricated themselves from the trap, repatriated their dead and wounded to Immouzzer, and then retired to Tizi Hamri; from whence, two days later, they were able to resume their advance southeast towards Beni Hassan territory. The other detachment under Colonel Prioux, with which they should by now have joined forces, fared far worse. Soon after occupying a position 2 km south of Oulad 'Ali to block attempts by hostiles to flee towards the Moulouya Valley, they came under attack. Ill protected as they were by makeshift stone parapets, they suffered heavy losses.

By July 18, after several of their officers had been killed by Berber marksmen, the remainder of the detachment commenced a desperate fighting retreat, abandoning their camp, which was immediately ransacked by victorious Amazigh fighters.

This was an unexpected success for the resistance, and a rare case of a French outpost being overrun, but one that French communiqués usually gloss over,[56] coming as it did after the successful conclusion of operations around Taffert, to which we must now turn. July 15 had seen further desperate hand-to-hand fighting among tall cedars on the main ridge of Bou Iblan. Sidi Raho and his last-ditch fighters were more than holding their own. The next day, however, gradually caught in a pincer movement in Taffert forest between the Freydenberg column to the west and the Denis group coming in from the east, the tempo of their resistance slackened visibly. On the morning of July 17, however, realizing the enemy had penetrated his inner ring of defense, knowing there was no hope of outside help, Sidi Raho finally surrendered.[57] And so came the moment of truth for the unassuming, black-bearded marabout as he stood before French officers curious to meet the man who had defied them so long. As the sacrificial *ta'argiba* bull was slaughtered in a sign of surrender, according to one eyewitness account, Sidi Raho told General Freydenberg:

> The influence I had on my people was solely religious. I merely reminded true believers that the obligation to wage *jihad* against infidels is written in the *qur'an*. Each time your forces were attacked, I was there—that I acknowledge; however, I never organised anything; I never actually held a rifle.[58]

Fig. 33: Tea-drinking Berbers, Qsar Arrwadi, near Oulad 'Ali.

The writer goes on to describe a somewhat grimy, cheerful, convivial individual with a flashing, white-toothed smile. This was surprising from a formerly rich person, now ruined, after giving up his kasbah at Annosser back in 1911–12, losing two brothers, five horses, sixty mules and numerous herds of sheep in the process. Sidi Raho appears to have been placed under house arrest,[59] though he cannot have been very harshly treated.[60] After his surrender, the Beni Zeggout held out for another couple of days, briefly defying two Moroccan *Tirailleur* regiments, while mopping-up operations went on till July 30. Most of the irreconcilables from Bou Illoul, Beni Hassan, and Oulad 'Ali were rounded up, though a courageous handful managed to break out, cross the Moulouya Valley and link up with resistance fighters still holding out in the Eastern High Atlas.

Thus had Sidi Raho made good on his promise to fight to the bitter end. Sinking like a man-o'-war of old, her colors firmly nailed to the mast, the Bou Iblan redoubt had certainly not disappointed the armchair strategists. Meanwhile, as a fitting postscript to their desperate resistance of July 1926, a few surviving war bands continued to harry the enemy. The most formidable was the *jish* under Mohand ou Hammou, later to become a national hero, which was wiped out on the night of January 19–20, 1927, near Ahermoumou.

Summoned to surrender, Mohand ou Hammou resolved to sell his life dearly, for he knew the French bore him a serious grudge for the numerous successful ambushes he had mounted against them in his time, killing seven of their officers. At best, prison awaited him; at worst the firing squad. "I have several rounds of ammunition in this rifle," he apparently called out, at the beginning of the encounter—"and I'm keeping the last bullet for myself." He proved as good as his word; he and all of his men perished in the subsequent firefight.[61]

Other pockets of resistance enjoyed but a short reprieve. After their footprints had been spotted in the snow leading to a cave in the Meskeddal gorges on February 9, another band was destroyed by a detachment from Immouzzer;[62] yet another suffered a similar fate northeast of Taffert on February 16, 1927.[63] And so the *Tache de Taza* passed into history. In his landmark work, Jean Saulay confesses that "thus through sheer force did we impose social change upon the region, destroying in the process an authentic—albeit archaic—society living curled up on itself. We replaced it with another form of society owing allegiance to a hitherto rejected central government."[64] This is a reminder that *Pacification* was conducted in the sultan's name. Whichever way one cares to consider the outcome, there is no denying that a combination of unflinching Berber bravery and French panache had just completed one of the most gripping chapters in Atlas history.

Rarely in their Moroccan campaigns had the French encountered such desperate resistance; rarely had they suffered such heavy losses. Their casualties for two weeks fighting were as follows: seventy-nine killed and 117 wounded from among the auxiliaries (Goums and partisans); 222 killed and 417 wounded in the ranks of the regular army— the Foreign Legion and *Spahis* having paid the highest toll.[65] For the French, it had certainly been no picnic on Jbel Bou Iblan. Celebrations among the *pastis* drinkers at Field HQ must have been correspondingly muted.

As French staff officers knew perfectly well, losses of that kind were only acceptable to public opinion at home in so far as they could be offset against substantial territorial gain, application of the "oil stain" policy as in the *Tache de Taza*, or the defeat of some famous leader, as with 'Abdelkrim in the Rif.

Over the period 1926–9, now that "useful Morocco" had been occupied, any talk of further military operations became politically incorrect. Otherwise it would spoil the atmosphere of peaceful harmony that supposedly prevailed as the *colons* and urban entrepreneurial elements made hay while the sun shone. It was as good an excuse as any for imposing masterly inactivity.

Berber attempts at containing the "oil stain policy"

Greater emphasis would accordingly be placed on the role of Native Affairs officers in command of Moroccan irregulars, both Goums and Partisans sometimes organized into *fezzas* or *groupes francs*, the philosophy being to "set a Berber to catch a Berber."[66] These small, would-be mobile detachments were designed to pursue and destroy war bands of the *jish* kind which periodically erupted from dissident areas to cause havoc among recently subdued clans. In a worst case scenario, the deaths of a few tribal levies would go down better at the *Ministère de la Guerre* in Paris, than if regulars were involved. In these early post-Lyautey years, the French military command and the *Résidence* in Rabat were performing a delicate balancing act.

Two years later, with the Rif war over and 'Abdelkrim packed off to exile, contemporary official-speak was anxious to represent Morocco—at any rate that part known as "useful Morocco"—as totally *pacifiée*. The remaining pockets (*taches*) of resistance would be either contained by the military or chloroformed by the politicals. Should force ever become necessary, punitive expeditions known as *opérations de police* would be sufficient to crush the last irreconcilables, enabling career-minded young French officers either to win their spurs or end up in an unmarked grave on some barren Atlas hillside.

Almost imperceptible advances were planned on the periphery of the dissident areas, gradually whittling away at their territory with a minimum amount of fuss and publicity. Under no circumstances must French journalists and MPs be alerted as to the real nature of these operations. Thus was implemented the *politique de la tache d'huile* ("oil stain policy").[67]

Chiefly affected by this policy were the Oued L'abid Valley and upper Moulouya. It was not good, so ran the contemporary rationale, to give the dissidents too much leeway. In the words of Guillaume, "a strictly passive attitude, far from leading to a hoped-for neutralization of the front, would undoubtedly have been interpreted by our adversaries as a sign of weakness on our part."[68] True enough; the resistance fighters observed this lack of activity and came to the conclusion that the invader's reluctance to be drawn into battle could prove but one thing—that he was afraid!

The French left the dissident tribesmen but a short respite. They soon found themselves confronted by an amiable, ambitious, white-moustached colonel. De Loustal by name, he became the chief "oil stain" exponent. In a series of boldly executed raids he caught them out by his somewhat unorthodox tactics. Instead of a spectacular advance after softening up by the artillery, swarms of partisans would occupy a hill in the small hours, followed shortly afterwards by a regular detachment which would dig in and/or erect stone parapets in time for the inevitable reaction from the resistance. Between January and May 1926, De Loustal carried out three such incursions near the Moulouya sources. In September of the same year, the heights of Midrassen overlooking

Bou Wattas were occupied. When the Amazigh fighters counter-attacked they were checked by well-aimed volleys from Legionaries and eventually forced to disperse as the Zaïan cavalry thundered down on them with a vengeance.

Some 200 of their number were left dead on the field. Sidi Lmekki retreated to nearby Ta'adlount on Asif Ouirin. Ten days later, Aghbala, which had for long been Sidi 'Ali Amhaoush's fief, was occupied by the French.[69] Undismayed by these setbacks, the *imjuhad* remained defiant and resolute.

Life in the mountains, an area of Morocco known in Berber as *tamazirt n isatten* ("land of heroes"), still had its rewards, especially towards the end of a long summer, in these ultimate years of Berber independence. After all, these purely local reverses had in no way depleted the resources of the principal fighting clans of the Atlas, whether Ayt Yahya, Ayt Sokhman, or Ayt Hadiddou—the last-named seen by all as the outright champions of Berber resistance. And what if the *irumin* did fight their way through the pine- and oak-studded Atlas foothills which constituted their outer line of defense? Such a prospect barely dampened the enthusiasm of the veterans from the *jbel*, who, when the time came to oppose the French advance, would put their trust as much in their own warlike ability as in the chaotic terrain.

Dignity and honor were not empty words. A man could hold his head high as he walked, confident in the accuracy of his aim when he squinted down the sights of his rifle. He retained a priceless virtue: that of being a free man, an Amazigh, duly respected by his womenfolk. No matter if he ate his fill less frequently than before. A frugal diner at the best of times, he preferred to eat grass gruel and acorn paste rather than be humbled by submission to the French.[70] The Berber fighters holding this last, vast dissident tract of the High Atlas and southeast Morocco must have had an inkling that the time to confront the *irumin* would eventually come.

Despite the feeling of inevitability they may have felt vis-à-vis their impending fate, warlike preparations went forward. Now that the *Tache de Taza* and Rif could no longer provide weapons, an alternative source had to be tapped; fresh consignments of guns were expected via the Rio de Oro and Anti-Atlas—outstanding shipments of Mausers, but mostly Spanish rifles, in plentiful supply at that time. These proved a welcome addition to the Lebels and *mousquetons* wrested from the French, through desertions and/or nocturnal infiltrations. Arms shipments, however, had to be paid for in cash. To raise ready money a simple expedient was adopted—kidnapping *colons*, who had recently settled in the Tadla in some numbers; then holding them to ransom. Beginning in 1927, local farms were raided and a few settlers hijacked. In October of that year one such raid yielded a rich prize: two young men from Resident-General Steeg's entourage, dating two ladies in the Dar Ould Zidouh olive groves,[71] were grabbed by a *jish* and whisked away into the mountains.

Not before two months had elapsed were they freed, and then only after a ransom of 1,300,000 hassani pesetas had been paid.[72] It is easy to imagine the number of rifles, grenades, and bullets that subsequently found their way into the resistance armory!

They were to be put to good use. One night in March 1929, the Waouizaght outpost, between Beni Mellal and Azilal, was subjected to a serious attack by Ayt Iseha warriors, highlighting the excellent morale of these Atlas fighters, and prompting Guillaume to observe, "The rebels are now taking the initiative. The time is ripe for some new 'Abdelkrim to unite the Atlas tribes against us."[73]

Now must we return to the wastes of the Eastern High Atlas and southeast Morocco to see how battle-hardened Ayt Hammou and Ayt Khebbash raiders were ruthlessly harrying French columns throughout 1931–2. Epic battles would ensue in the Tadighoust gorge, near Tounfit, and in the Ifegh palm grove, witnessing the rise to fame of a certain war leader of the Ayt Merghad—Ou-Skounti was his name—masterful tacitican that he was. The resistance fighters, their morale apparently intact, were doing their best to retard the inevitable capture of the by now encircled Tafilalt oasis. The fall of Tafilalt would lead to the discomfiture of Belqasm Ngadi, the bogus sultan, and his unending, fighting retreat to Rio de Oro. With this increase in momentum, however, *Pacification* would enter a final, ungentlemanly phase, a far cry from Lyautey's initial concept of *pénétration pacifique*.

Fig. 34: Ploughing fields below a lone *tighremt*, Azilal area.

Reckless Raiders Rule the Roost (1927–34)

Raiders extraordinary to a man, those hardened fighters chiefly came from the clans of Ayt Hammou, Ayt Khebbash, and Ayt 'Isa Izem. Forming a small, unstoppable band (*jish*) or group (*tarbi'at*) of dedicated combatants, under some charismatic figure, they would stage raids deep into reputedly pacified territory, causing death, destruction, and dismay. The French had their work cut out devising ways and means of intercepting those whom they variously defined as *pillards* ("plunderers"), *rôdeurs* ("prowlers"), *magiciens du crime*, or *bandits sympathiques*. Most of these definitions were unsatisfactory oversimplifications. They failed to perceive that the frequent attacks were a way of keeping alive the resistance, guaranteeing its very survival as when herds of livestock were rustled; that the protection these robber chiefs granted in certain cases to their own settled, castle-dwelling folk—in exchange for tribute in cash or in kind—was part of an age-old social balance. As Captain Spillman, a well-known Native Affairs expert, explained: "The nomad, hardened by desert life is brave, frugal and enduring, but lazy once it comes to satisfying his modest requirements. He's a lord, who considers the sedentary oasis dweller his vassal."[1] Practices of this kind were institutionalized by the nomadic elements of the Ayt Merghad and Ayt 'Atta, who used to take turns at inviting themselves among the Tafilalt *qsur* dwellers after harvest time.[2]

That said, among the *djicheurs*, there was a hard core of professional highwaymen. As another contemporary observer points out, "It is a fallacy to consider these nomadic plunderers as people who are attached to their freedom and fighting to defend it. The war they are waging is first and foremost a business undertaking of which they are anxious to diminish the risks."[3] This was true, in some well-known cases, as with Zaïd ou Hmad from the Ayt Merghad. These bandits were, however, operating alongside genuine resistance fighters, irreconcilables who had been evicted from their tribal territory and refused to submit to the French. People to whom notions of raid and counter-raid were second nature; who loved the rough and ready life in tented encampments, amid windy plateaus of esparto grass or stone-covered escarpments. Who were prepared to fight to the finish to preserve their way of life, to defend their womenfolk's honor. They had been particularly active during the French withdrawal from the Tafilalt palm-grove. Then, following the failure of the 1918–19 general revolt, the area had been abandoned while the *irumin* ("Christians") had their hands full elsewhere. Masterly inactivity on the part of the occupation forces linked to rumors of French reverses in the Rif had fueled underlying unrest and dissatisfaction, especially in the Talsinnt area, fief of the Ayt Hammou. During the period 1924–7 no fewer than four French officers had been killed in the course of various ambushes.[4]

The year 1927 was to prove an eventful one. First, the Ayt Hammou welcomed Ayt Seghroushen fugitives from Jbel Tishshoukt whose grit and determination to continue the fight proved contagious. After the pretender Belqasm Ngadi, operating from Tafilalt, had captured a French post at Bou Hadi on the Lower Ziz, in March, he urged the nomadic war bands to greater efforts, many a clan seizing the opportunity to take to the hills in open defiance of the invader. Meanwhile, French action was limited to construction of the road south from Midelt and down the Ziz Valley (May–October 1927), together with strict road discipline for convoys to limit the effects of ambush and harassment. Despite which, local commander General Freydenberg confessed that "neither our tribal levies, nor the Saharan Company of the Ziz can do much to thwart the Ayt Hammou."[5]

As of January 1928, several bands, "some of them real *harka*-s of between 100 to 300 fighters,"[6] were formed for the specific purpose of long-range harassment behind the French lines. All were under tried leaders, *bandits d'honneur*, already inured to a life of frugality and mobility, experts in the art of waylaying caravans. It was part of traditional Berber culture to respect open robbery, especially where an element of skill and risk was involved. The fact that they were now pitting their hard-won experience against the infidel automatically conferred *imjuhad* status upon them. Four action-packed years awaited them.

On May 16, 1928, an Ayt Hammou *jish* surprised a group of tribal levies by the spring of Aïn El-Ouirra, some twenty-five miles northwest of Aïn Shaïr, and dropped fifteen of them dead in their tracks before retiring unpursued into the surrounding hills. A month later they won an even greater success against one of the newly-formed *groupes francs* at the outpost of Anoual. This time they were up against a purpose-trained anti-raider unit. No matter. No sooner had the garrison emerged from behind its walls than it was locked in a bitter firefight from sunup till sundown. By the time the Ayt Hammou slipped away into the distance, they had accounted for twenty-five of the enemy. As if this was not good enough, on July 16, they totally defeated the Saharan Company of the Guir near the Bou Bernous wells.[7] The score was almost evened in the enemy's favor before the year was out in a surprisingly chivalrous way.

On October 28, as Lieutenant Tournemire, a young veteran of the Tishshoukt campaign, was entertaining a brother officer in his post at Aoufous, he heard that a band of Ayt Hammou raiders had gone to ground in the cliffs just across Oued Ziz. Interestingly, the *jish* leader was challenging him to come out and fight. Battle royal was accordingly joined and good sport was had by all. The French detachment forded the river, stormed the Ayt Hammou position and repelled two vicious counter-attacks. Honors in this unusual, medieval-style tournament, however, were even, as a force of partisans sent to cut off the retreating Ayt Hammou was ambushed and took some casualties.[8]

It is debatable whether Ayt Hammou prestige suffered from this reverse. The next year they were back on the warpath with undiminished vigor. At the end of May, they participated in the annihilation of a battalion of *Tirailleurs* near Ayt Y'aqoub, as will be described in a subsequent chapter. On September 8, we learn they had returned to their usual hunting grounds of the upper Guir where, for some time, they had been observing the Atchana outpost. The garrison had fallen into a life of routine, sending out a detachment every morning to cut esparto grass. That day they came under fire from an Ayt Hammou *jish*, the noise of the fusillade perfectly calculated to make the garrison, a *groupe franc* spoiling for battle, come out into the open. Come out they did—only to be ambushed with devastating results: twenty-six dead and fifteen wounded. It required a frantic SOS by radio to Boudenib, to call in a squadron of armored cars and save the remainder of the detachment.[9] A month later, at Jihani in the same area, a 150-strong Ayt Hammou *jish* came across a Mounted Company of the Foreign Legion, killed fifty of them and wounded twenty-one more.[10]

This spate of successful attacks understandably bolstered the raiders' morale, just as it caused disarray and frustration in the enemy camp. Nothing, it seemed, could stop Ayt Hammou and Ayt Khebbash raiders; worse still, they could retire with impunity to the safe haven of Tafilalt, whence pretender Belqasm Ngadi continued to defy the French from his palace in Rissani, surrounded by chosen bodyguards and advised by Foreign Legion deserters.[11] In an effort to hamper the raiders' efficiency, as of March 1930 a new Algero–Moroccan Border Command was set up, under General Giraud, its HQ in Boudenib. Ceaseless anti-raider patrols by Goums, *Spahis*, camel corps, and armored cars (some equipped with machine guns, others with cannon)[12] became the order of the day. Eventually, aeroplanes would contribute to surveillance activities, but the new measures took time to take effect.

Undaunted, the Ayt Hammou and their allies meanwhile stepped up the tempo of their raids. In mid-April 1930, a 120-strong Ayt Hammou detachment moved like a will-o'-the-wisp throughout the desolate hills between Beni Tadjit and Atchana. En route they were brought to action three times, on each occasion inflicting heavy casualties on their pursuers (thirty-nine killed and nineteen wounded), and finally showing them a clean pair of heels.[13] On July 12, at Kemkemia, southeast of Erfoud, a force of 500 Ayt Hammou and Ayt Khebbash ran into the Saharan Company of the Ziz, later reinforced by its sister company from the Guir. This time, the raiders were forced to retreat on Tafilalt—their first serious setback.[14] Simultaneously another group of between 250 and 500 Ayt Hammou and Ayt 'Isa Izem were operating in the upper Ziz Valley.

Ou-Skounti: Charismatic diehard chief

Their leader, a certain Zaïd ou-Skounti, was a prominent member of the Ayt 'Isa Izem (Ayt Merghad), a nomadic clan who, while wandering with tents and flocks from the snows of 'Ayyashi to the *qsur* of Oued Ghriss, were not averse to plundering the occasional caravan. Although in 1929 Ou-Skounti went on to lead Ayt Merghad contingents in the fighting around Ayt Ya'qoub, in 1927 Parlange (*burlanj*), then a portly Native Affairs lieutenant, had made this disparaging comment:

> Among the Ayt Merghad, another person whose name often comes up is Ou-Skounti, a worthless puppet masquerading as a great chief. He is always on the

lookout for a quarrel, in which he will involve himself if he feels he stands to gain some advantage, however trifling, through doing so. An unimportant character, though wielding some influence.[15]

Rarely has there been such an error of judgment. Ou-Skounti was a daring, up-and-coming leader among the Ayt Merghad, a skilled tactician with a reputation for bravery and ruthlessness, not to mention some talent for organization and inter-clan cohesion; before the Atlas campaigns were over the French would learn to know him for what he was worth. The rare pictures we have of him show a straggly-bearded resolute-looking individual. His *tarbi'at* ("combat group") were from the same mold: a hand-picked selection of fighters—dedicated, white-turbaned, black-cloaked men from the Ayt 'Isa Izem clan.[16]

Early on the morning of July 13, they descended from the stony hills to attack the *qsar* of Tiydrin. The crackle of musketry triggered a swift French response: a Goum emerged from Mzizel, while other forces set off in pursuit from nearby Ammougger. Acting like genuine professionals, Ou-Skounti's raiders simulated a retreat to the southeast.[17] In the ensuing engagement, a *groupe franc* from Tagendoust attempted to cut them off but were decimated, after which Ou-Skounti made for Tizi n-Timezjalin, where he lay in wait for the Goum from Mzizel which was on his tracks. Out in front rode Lieutenant De Hautecloque (*laqluq* to the Berbers, later Marshall Leclerc), a cool gentleman from Picardy in charge of the Goum's cavalry. A mile or so from the col, his command was greeted by accurate fire. The horsemen dismounted and fired back as best they could, clinging to a small hill until forced to make for another ridge to avoid being outflanked. The future Marshall of France was deeply impressed by the speed of the raiders' movements: "In front and slightly to our left, between 400 and 500 men suddenly emerged at a run from the esparto grass, making rapidly forward to head us off ... although we lost several horses, and some of my *goumiers* were wounded, all managed to remount and withdraw."[18]

A general mêlée now ensued, with the Goum's infantry taking some pressure off the horsemen, who charged twice when the raiders drew too near. Luckily too, a group of friendly partisans had occupied neighboring Tizi n-Timezdarin in some strength, denying access to the raiders. Eventually the *jish* effected a textbook retreat, keeping its pursuers at bay by a succession of counter-charges carried out by a rearguard that was "skilled at manoeuvring in open order, keeping out of sight in deep ravines, and shooting in such a way as would become unpleasantly accurate whenever our cavalry closed the range."[19]

All in all, it proved an unqualified success for the raiders. Their total mark-up for the day was twenty-nine killed and twenty-three wounded. Ou-Skounti had inflicted another lesson on the French: never indulge in headlong pursuit of a *jish* retreating through broken terrain where it can rapidly adopt a horseshoe formation and turn on its pursuers. Yet again, a raiding party had appeared where it was least expected, then vanished after inflicting as much damage as possible. French prestige suffered correspondingly. Small wonder General Giraud was anxious to achieve a morale-boosting success.

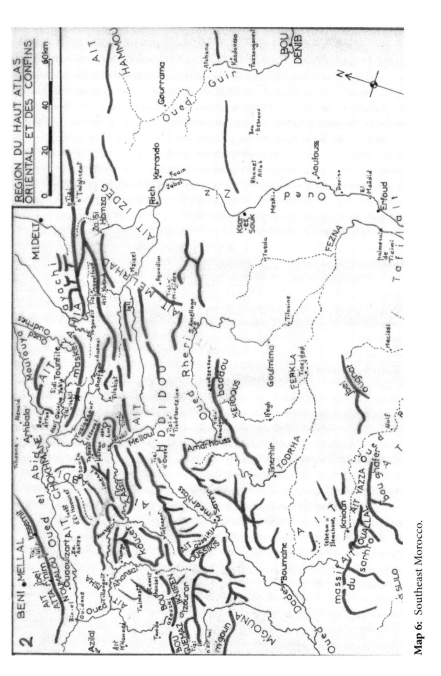

Map 6: Southeast Morocco.

wi n-iwaliwn: A fresh Berber victory[20]

The French thought a perfect opportunity had come their way when scouts reported an Ayt Hammou encampment at a spot named Bou Leggou, by a palm grove near the Tadighoust gorge, some forty miles west of Tarda outpost. As soon as the report was confirmed a surprise attack was planned. At 9.30 pm on August 30, 1930, a small task force accordingly left Tarda. It comprised a Goum under Lieutenant Boulet-Desbareau,[21] a mounted company of the Foreign Legion, and the usual assortment of partisans and *mokhaznis*. Unfortunately for them, the element of surprise was lost as bright fires lit up the night to the north, proving that the Berbers were on the alert.

This was indeed the case. Abandoning internecine feuding, the Ayt Merghad clans—fully aware what the French were up to—had concluded *tada*-type alliances between themselves and sent delegations to local saint Sidi 'Abdallah to confirm these arrangements. Against the common enemy a joint battle plan was hatched whereby the *imjuhad* were divided into three groups: the first, by way of a diversion, was to attack the van of the French column; the second group would act against the enemy's main body; the third would be charged with loot and plunder.[22] Once the French had marched about twenty miles, Boulet-Desbareau left his infantry and the Legionaires as a backstop, then surged forward with his cavalry. Reaching the encampment at 05.30, he found it deserted, apart from eight dromedaries and 400 goats, which were immediately seized and led off. Then all hell broke loose; it was almost a rerun of El-Herri.

An impressive number of Ayt Hammou, Ayt Hadiddou, and Ayt Merghad—with Ou-Skounti co-ordinating the attack—bore down on the French detachment from all points of the compass. Withdrawing in gradual stages, the French narrowly avoided total disaster. Once they had joined up with the Foreign Legion, the cavalry were able to better organize their retreat and became involved in serious hand-to-hand fighting, even recapturing a machine gun that had fallen into Berber hands; yet they paid a stiff price: some sixty of their number had to be left behind.[23] Young Boulet-Desbareau afterwards commented on the battle in these terms:

> It is unthinkable that fire from a full machine-gun group and half-company of the Foreign Legion should have been incapable of stopping an enemy charging over open ground. Not one machine-gun jammed. Failing to anticipate the inefficiency of their fire, the gunners allowed themselves to be over-run instead of breaking off the engagement. Each one continued to press the trigger till the last moment. Several officers who had experienced the Great War were reluctant to believe such a thing possible.[24]

Thanks to the joint intervention of armored cars and aircraft, they finally extricated themselves from the jaws of the trap—some consolation for an unmitigated defeat! For the French, the only positive element stemming from this Battle of *wi n-iwaliwn*, or Tarda, was an even healthier respect for the fighting ability of the nomadic Berber tribesmen, though the evaluation of the total number who had participated was variously put at between 1,500 and 6,000 men.[25] Two weeks later, a large force returned along the Tadighoust trail for the grisly task of repatriating the dead bodies. In the words of Lieutenant Boulet-Desbareau, "When we came back to pick up our dead, the corpses were in an advanced state of decomposition because of the heat; the Berber women had also been at them … Why wreak vengeance this way on dead bodies?"[26]

No doubt Tafilalt leader Belqasm Ngadi and his people were privy to the plan, several corpses being recovered on September 14 minus their heads. These, as in the good old days, later found their way to the ramparts of the dissident leader's palace in Rissani, as tangible evidence of yet another *arumi* defeat.[27] Faced with a deteriorating situation, Belqasm certainly needed to boost the morale of the Tafilalt inhabitants living under his oppressive rule. On February 28, 1931, the *qsar* of Taouz was captured by the French, following which General Giraud rode right round the Tafilalt palm grove on horseback.[28]

Belqasm's people reacted resolutely on two occasions that spring, inflicting serious losses on armored car patrols, one rifleman even killing the observer of a photo-reconnaissance biplane with a lucky shot through the heart.[29] In the meantime, raiding had resumed: on May 15, a *jish* of 200 Ayt Hammou ambushed a road-construction gang near Merzouga; ten days later, Ou-Skounti himself, with his usual mix of Ayt Hammou and Ayt 'Isa Izem, harassed the *qsar* of Igli for the second year running.[30] No doubt about it, Tafilalt was surrounded: the sands were running out for Belqasm and the raiders. The pretender's only hope lay in the possible prevarications of Paris-based politicians who might yet object to potentially costly, large-scale operations against a hard target such as the Tafilalt.

Little did he know, however, that the winter of 1928–9 had been a watershed. Alphonse Steeg, artisan of masterly inactivity, was no longer Resident-General in Morocco. His place had been taken by Lucien Saint who, co-ordinating with old Lyautey hands such as General Noguès and Lieutenant-Colonel Juin, now "tried his utmost to convince the French government to modify its Moroccan policy and abandon the military passivity adopted by Monsieur Steeg. He insisted on a resumption of activity on all fronts to finish off the remaining dissident areas."[31]

Events in southeast Morocco contributed to Lucien Saint getting his way. Chief among these were the assassination of General Clavery and his escort, by a *jish* from Tafilalt in December 1928, not to mention the disastrous May 1929 Ayt Ya'qoub episode, of which more shortly. Since then, the recent run of raiders' successes had strengthened the hand of the French military. More men, money, and equipment were provided for prosecution of a resolute forward policy. The noose was tightening around Saharan raiders and Atlas tribesmen, who could expect help from nobody, as a Berber bard complained: "Numerous and unending are the enemy columns [*lkunur*], / Yet today nobody will raise a hand to help us!"[32]

Serious events on the north side of the Eastern High Atlas now attracted Ou-Skounti's attention. By July of 1931 it was clear the French intended to occupy Tounfit. This relatively well-to-do Ayt Yahya Berber heartland settlement had for some forty years been in a state of turmoil. Attempts to bring it into line had proved ineffectual, the few government appointed *qayd*s eventually losing their grip on the tribesmen and being ousted from office. At the close of the nineteenth century the resultant power vacuum had been filled by Sidi 'Ali Amhaoush, whose influence had become preponderant in the area.[33] This had not prevented Ayt Yahya clans occupying the valleys on both sides of Jbel Ma'asker[34] from living in a state of almost permanent feud and tension right up to the arrival of the French on the upper Moulouya.[35]

Tounfit, as a commercial center, and gateway to Asif Melloul, the Upper Ziz, and Ghriss, thrived on the caravan trade. Goods and money regularly changed hands at its weekly market, for sure, but protection rackets if not outright banditry aimed at passing merchants also proved highly lucrative. The Ayt Yahya, especially its southern clans, thus acquired an unenviable reputation for lawlessness.[36] The situation was further complicated by the fact that since Sidi 'Ali's death in 1918, his former *ttalb* ("religious preacher"), Sidi Mohand ou-Lhajj, exercised control over the Tounfit area from his nearby Zaouia Sidi Yahya ou Youssef, while Sidi 'Ali's eldest son, Sidi Lmekki, became his chief rival. Furthermore, the turbulent Imtchimen clan of the Ayt Yahya had, since 1922, been exposed to the propaganda of the Midelt political officer. Some Imtchimen notables were apparently making ready to welcome the Christians, but were at loggerheads with the irreconcilable element of the clan who remained confident in their fighting ability and had arranged for the Ayt Hammou to come to their assistance early in July. In fact, the Imtchimen entertained visions of glorious forays north into the Meknes area with their fellow Ayt Yahya clans, spearheaded by the southern raiders![37] The inclination was certainly there; here is how an Ou-Yahya clansman felt:

Shall we have a final chance on our chargers to advance,
To tighten the reins and at full gallop ride across the plain,
To our heart's content, unto each a rifle and 200 rounds?
On that day in the field our foemen can but yield![38]

Ou-Skounti in Yahya-land

Thus it was with high hopes that a *harka* of approximately 600 Ayt 'Isa Izem, Ayt Hadiddou, and Ayt Hammou warriors under Ou-Skounti traversed the high, cedar-girt cols, came out on the shaded slopes of the Atlas, crossed the Anzegmir gorge, and set up camp at Tizi n-Meshfrawn, east of Tounfit. Visiting the various Imtchimen villages in person, Ou-Skounti attempted to dissuade their leaders from dishonorable surrender to the enemy. They should turn a deaf ear, he told them, to the siren calls of the *akhenzir* ("swine") with their talk of security, schools, hospitals, and civilization. Otherwise, no longer would they be free to defend their land, their herds, their families; they would no longer dare look their wives in the face. Heated verbal exchanges ensued between the diehards and those in favor of surrender.[39] Preparations were accordingly made to resist the French.

On July 15, 1931, at break of day, the sky was already a deep blue, while mist lingered on the distant Moulouya plain. Crouching, rifle in hand, at the foot of gaunt cedar and evergreen oak, or behind boxwood bushes, Ou-Skounti's warriors awaited the inevitable onslaught. Nearby would have been circles of charred stones and smoking embers where they had heated their morning tea.

Fig. 35: Jbel 'Ayyashi main ridge seen from Imtchimen.

Behind and to their right rose the 3,700-meter main ridge of 'Ayyashi where snow still lingered. To the north, whence the main threat would come, they could hear confused sounds of military preparation. Overhead, the enemy's war birds were on the prowl: flimsy yet lethal contraptions of wood, metal, and canvas. Soon, armed men attired in a fashion similar to theirs could be seen advancing stealthily on the opposite slope. These were *lbertiza* ("partisans"), recently submitted tribesmen now operating against their dissident Berber brethren, with a Goum unit in close support. The opposing parties proceeded to trade shots with gusto, opponents swearing at each other in Tamazight during lulls in the fighting. Thus for three hours, till the whistle of incoming artillery rounds and stutter of machine guns from overflying planes turned the tide of battle in the attackers' favor. Powerless in the face of such a barrage, Ou-Skounti ordered his men to regroup south on Assatour hill.[40]

He held out there for another two days. In this he was taking advantage of General Nieger's reluctance to move forward so long as the political intentions of the Imtchimen clan—constituting a potential threat on his left flank—remained unclear; so long as his troops had not recovered from the stress of battle and the early summer heat.[41]

On July 18, however, as the French advanced to capture Tounfit, Ou-Skounti decided discretion was the better part of valor and retreated up the Anzegmir gorge, then back over the passes to the Ghriss Valley.[42] Three days fighting had cost the dissidents some 100 killed; the morale of the Ayt Yahya had taken a battering with the discomfiture of the hitherto invincible Ayt Hammou.

In many ways, this was the turning-point in the final phase of Morocco's "Thirty Years' War" on the northern Atlas front. Any illusions the resistance may have harbored as to holding off the foe were now shattered. Given the overwhelming military strength the enemy was concentrating along the outer rim of the Atlas, Ou-Skounti must have realized that events were entering a new, desperate phase that would surely spell the end of the *imjuhad* epic within the foreseeable future. One or two local successes notwithstanding, such as the assassination by one of his bands of a French officer near Tounfit the following winter,[43] developments early in 1932 were full of foreboding for resistance stalwarts.

Far to the south of Tounfit, on the night of January 14–15, 1932, troops of the Algero–Moroccan Border Command under General Giraud had moved to encircle Tafilalt. Whereas some Filala may secretly have heaved a sigh of relief on learning that Belqasm Ngadi's tyranny would soon be over, others, determined to resist to the end, requested they be given weapons to resist the Unbelievers, while their religious leaders harangued the crowds, preaching *jihad*. Meanwhile oasis women had been out collecting branches of oleander which, suitably burnt down to form charcoal, later mixed with sulphur and saltpetre, eventually produced gunpowder, or *barud*.

Tafilalt takeover

This mixture was used in vintage *bushfer* muskets, or by local gunsmiths skilled at recharging empty cartridge cases.[44] Re-equipped with lead shot, the makeshift rounds would then be fired from single-shot breech-loaders with varying accuracy, coupled with telltale emissions of smoke. As the women ground the charcoal into fine powder, they chanted thus:

> Warriors, O warriors!
> 'Tis for you that we now prepare *barud*,
> Home, hearth and country to defend!
> Go you shall, with firm step, the Christians
> to confront!
> Go you shall, ever bold as in days of old,
> Ever forward, perhaps ne'er to return!
> Warriors, O warriors!
> Should you fall on strife's fatal field,
> Who will for burial prepare your bodies?
> Who will to Mother Earth commit you?
> Who will read the *sura* of Eternal Grace?
> 'Tis for you we now prepare *barud*,
> Fit for powder-play or for reckoning day.
> Fight for the Faith, with honour and bravery![45]

Proud, poignant words summing up wives' eternal obsessions, oscillating between horror at countenancing their spouses' possible death, and dishonor should they return safe but defeated from the fray. Prophetic utterances, too, for many a Filali defender was destined to bite the dust in the coming battle.

On the morning of January 15, 1932, the defenders on the north side of the vast palm grove came under attack from Bournazel and his partisans. Baulked a while by a broad trench and unexpectedly fierce resistance by Belqasm's regulars, the French finally overran the position after calling in the Goums, backed by some armor. The way was now clear for the capture of Belqasm's palace, which fell by mid-afternoon. Anticipating disaster, however, the pretender had gathered some goods and chattels, his wives, and a hard core of followers with whom he broke out of Tafilalt before the net could be drawn tight. As he headed for the Regg plateau he was ambushed by moonlight at Tagerroumt castle by a troop of French-officered irregulars, losing his brother, Moulay Tahar. Further on, as he approached the Regg, his men detected another French unit already in position; so the fugitives veered southeast and finally escaped towards Oued Dra'a, eventually to link up with Merebbi Rebbo in Rio de Oro.[46]

Once the Filala heard of his ignominious flight they lost no time surrendering and sacrificing the *ta'argiba* bulls in the presence of General Huré, the new commander-in-chief for Morocco. For the French, this event wiped the slate clean after thirteen frustrating years following upon their 1919 eviction from Tighmart. The sultan of Morocco himself, satisfied that the shrine of his ancestor Moulay 'Ali Sharif should be once again within the *makhzan* fold, awarded General Giraud the Sharifian Military Merit. At Rissani, the junketing continued for a week, with Resident-General Lucien Saint in full-dress regalia making his official entry on a white charger and receiving the traditional offering of milk and dates from one of the locals, while Bournazel, impeccably attired with gloves, medals, *képi*, and all, looked on.[47] Bluff, confident Bournazel, the swashbuckler turned administrator, had reached the pinnacle of his career. Recently promoted to captain, the self-styled "governor" of Tafilalt had at once set about repairing the ravages of war, reopening markets, setting up schools, repairing water channels, and eradicating *bayud*, a disease that was decimating the Tafilalt date palms. As a sensible precaution he had also handed their guns back to the recently-surrendered Filala, so they could give a good account of themselves should the raiders return. Although deprived of their main base, Tafilalt, the professional waylayers of caravans were still out there, somewhere, biding their time;[48] a fact of which the French top brass, for all their apparent complacency, were well aware.

Although most of the Ayt Hammou and Ayt Khebbash had followed Belqasm into the wastes of southwest Morocco, others had simply moved about seventy kilometers west to the Ayt Merghad-controlled Ferkla oasis, whose *qsur* provided them with a suitable base of operations. Evicting them from this stronghold would need a full-scale operation.[49] Left with a short respite, the raiders holed up in the Ferkla oasis and watched the two approaching French *groupes mobiles* undismayed. Once the local *qsur* dwellers had surrendered to the Marrakesh troops on February 11, 1932, some Ayt Merghad and their Ayt Hammou "guests"—400-strong all told[50]—wisely concentrated their defense on the small *qsar* of Ifegh, its nearby gorge and palm grove backed by rugged hills.

Fierce firefight at Ifegh

Now, General Giraud's initial intention had been to capture Ifegh and establish an outpost there to monitor potential sorties from the hills by hostiles. Yet the way his troops went about the operation was another classic example of how not to fight a battle in a palm grove.[51] On ground of this sort and in a tactically sound situation, fighters from southeast Morocco were second to none, as had been proved on many an occasion. Given their by now considerable experience in this operational theater, it is strange that the French should have failed to allow for this. Their recent success in Tafilalt, together with the impressive force they were bringing to bear, possibly encouraged a return to gung-ho tactics.

In the morning, a Goum with armored cars in attendance occupied Bou Tarrisen hill despite stiff resistance, while another reached a point opposite the Ifegh gorge; a third Goum cleared the heights beyond the village. When, around midday, a mixed force of partisans, Goums, *Tirailleurs*, and *mokhazni* from Tinghir under Captain Paulin (*bula*) attempted to invest the palm grove with artillery and air support, they received a hot reception. A withering fire was directed at them from the gorge and surrounding ridges and heavy losses were taken. This was followed by a ferocious rough and tumble of the kind in which the Ayt Merghad excel. The striped *jellabas* most combatants were wearing—whether *imjuhad*, *lbertiza*, or *mokhazni*—made it impossible to distinguish friend from foe, even at close range.

Confronted with determined adversaries, their chief shot dead, the native auxiliaries lost heart. As the afternoon drew to a close, Lieutenant-Colonel Chardon (*shardu*), a leading Native Affairs expert, rapidly reappraised the situation, after which the palm grove was evacuated under protection from Foreign Legion machine guns.[52] The Berbers had artfully blocked the irrigation ditches upstream from Ifegh, cutting off water to the troops who were planning on camping there. Deprived of drinking water, the entire French force was now obliged to forsake what meager territorial gains it had made and retire to a waterhole about five kilometers to the southwest.

At dawn the next day jubilant resistance fighters reoccupied Ifegh and its gardens.[53] More to the point, rallying to the sound of gunfire, and emboldened by reports of the previous evening's apparent French retreat, large contingents of Ayt Merghad and Ayt Hadiddou had converged on the spot to support the fighters at Ifegh. If fighters from Aghbalou n-Kerdous were involved, one can surmise that Ayt Yahya elements living there were also drawn into the Ifegh battle.[54] The following day, obviously having second thoughts as to occupying Ifegh itself—now judged too close to the hills for comfort—the French started redeploying towards Azgin, considered a more suitable site for an outpost.

To cover completion of the redeployment, on February 13, orders were given for a reoccupation *en masse* of the Ifegh palm grove. This went ahead successfully, so that by noon the Berbers had been driven back into the gorge and hills. However, the French then disengaged. As usual, the ever watchful dissidents saw their opportunity: two Goum units, withdrawing over broken terrain, were at a considerable distance from the main body. They were immediately set upon, taking heavy casualties. Such was the desperate nature of the fighting that, while the French wounded were evacuated, the dead had to be abandoned. They were then harried by the mountain warriors all the way down into the plain, where some dissidents, refusing to be thwarted of their prey, took on almost bare-handed the Renault tanks and armored cars that intervened to save the retreating Goums! The three days' fighting had cost the French thirty-two killed and twenty-six wounded.[55] This amounted to another tactical success for the resistance, though offset by the French having achieved their strategic objectives: depriving the raiders of their Ferkla safe haven and, more significantly, isolating Jbel Saghro.[56]

Raid and counter-raid: The southern sector

The raiders were far from done for. In fact, 1932 proved to be a bumper year. Their activities actually covered two distinct regions: a southern, pre-Saharan sector between the Regg plateau and palm groves of Oued Dra'a; and a northern one focused on the Ayt Merghad region. The southern sector was activated during the night of February 20–21 when 250 Ayt 'Atta raiders from Jbel Saghro failed in an attempted assault on a French camp at Mecissi, killing an officer, but losing some thirty killed and wounded all told.[57] In a separate nocturnal raid on March 5–6, an Ayt Khebbash *jish*, under Mohammed ou Bani, harassed a French bivouac at Askjour on Oued Dra'a, southeast of Zagora. This action, closely linked to Belqasm Ngadi's presence in the area, demonstrated that the Ayt Khebbash remained masters of long-range desert warfare.[58] To appreciate the significance of this development we need to go back to early 1931. With an eye to the immediate future, Belqasm had sent one of his henchmen, a certain Ahmed Zerban, to reconnoiter the bend of the Dra'a, specifically the rich agricultural district of Ktaoua, and to set up house there with the Ayt Khebbash.

Such a glowing report did he receive that Belqasm immediately dispatched 250 well-armed Ayt 'Atta warriors to the area to proclaim *jihad* ("Holy War") and upset as best they could the local inter-clan balance of power. The power game lasted throughout the summer with mixed results, Belqasm's propaganda being ably countered by two very active Native Affairs specialists: Lieutenant-Colonel Chardon (*shardu*), whom we last met on Oued Ifegh, and his brilliant young aide, Captain Spillman (*sliman*), appointed to command, as of January 1932, the freshly established Zagora outpost with three Goum units under his orders. Through efficient political action they managed to win over most of a local Ayt 'Atta clan, a distribution of 5,000 cartridges proving a clincher. For this reason, when Belqasm Ngadi turned away from the Regg and made straight for the Dra'a south of Zagora, he initially received a lukewarm welcome from the local *qsur* dwellers. Nevertheless, appealing to a large group of Ayt Hammou and Ayt Khebbash, Belqasm soon had the area back under control. With some 600 seasoned warriors and stores of grain at his disposal, Belqasm had regained a significant power base from which to resume where he had left off in Tafilalt.

Obviously, the French could not stand idly by. Work on a *piste* southeast from Zagora accordingly went forward at a brisk pace. By March 5, the road gang, covered by a Foreign Legion motorized unit and two Goums, had bivouacked next door to the palm grove at Askjour, when they were subjected to all-night harassment, plus two furious frontal assaults, by Mohammed ou Bani's warriors. As at Ifegh, proximity to a palm grove had proved anything but an asset; so the French wisely moved their bivouac the next day to a nearby hill, where an outpost was eventually built.[59] The French advance resumed shortly after. By the end of March, Belqasm abandoned the Ktaoua, retiring with his escort along the Jbel Bani escarpment and, after turning for a brief clash with his pursuers at the Hassi El-Kerma wells, pitched camp on the *hammada* southeast of Tata.[60]

In June, the Ayt Khebbash staged a comeback in the Ktaoua, reoccupying several *qsur* and urging their inhabitants not to submit so tamely to the French. Captain Spillman at once sent in his auxiliaries to retrieve the situation, also building two watchtowers overlooking the strategic Foum Anagam gorge and reinforcing the Askjour outpost. Nothing daunted, from their encampments on the Dra'a *hammada*, the Ayt Khebbash maintained secret links throughout the summer of 1932 with one of the local Ayt 'Atta clans, exacting tribute and hoping to regain a foothold.[61] Though this action proved inconsequential, the Ktaoua being finally occupied in November by the energetic Spillman, it deserves to be mentioned as demonstrative of the unflagging efforts of the local resistance, also proving that the vestigial prestige of the tenacious Ayt Khebbash, as anti-French standard-bearers, still commanded respect throughout the pre-Sahara.[62]

Raid and counter-raid: The Atlas front

At the end of May 1932, the Ayt 'Isa Izem won a brilliant success. Earlier on, General Giraud had dispatched a force of Goums under Captain Guyetand (*qebtan jida*), together with some *lbartiza* under *qayd* 'Addi ou-Bihi, south from Ammougger to occupy Amellago in the Ghriss Valley, while two other Goums advanced north from Tadighoust to meet them. After occupying Agouddim Ikhf n-Ouaman without firing a shot, followed by a brisk encounter at Imelouan, an outpost was established, together with a Native Affairs *bureau*, under Guyetand, with Lieutenant Weygand (*biga*) as his second-in-command. Meanwhile, work went ahead on a dirt road to provide a link with the Ziz Valley. It so happened that on the morning of May 26, a battalion of *Tirailleurs* had moved north from Amellago to reconnoiter a feasible site for an outpost to cover the future *piste*.

Now a unit of this size takes up plenty of space on the ground and is likely to attract notice and invite attack, especially if its flank-guards are not doing their job properly. As the battalion approached Tizi n-Midjider it ran into an ambush. Several *Tirailleurs* were killed, while the others fired back and retired in good order to the main body, rescuing some of their wounded. However, they remained powerless to make any impression on the Ayt 'Isa Izem, who continued to rain bullets on them from well protected positions on the rocky hillside. Finally, the *Tirailleurs* were forced to retire to Amellago leaving behind thirty dead.[63]

That year Zaïd ou-Skounti and his raiders were to show the stuff they were made of. On July 25, 1932, a tiny *jish* of only four fighters was reported on Oued Idmouma, within the French pacified area east of the Ghriss Valley, some fifteen to twenty kilometers northeast of Amellago. Captain Guyetand at once repaired to the spot with the cavalry of his Goum and made contact at the *qsar* of Idmouma. Heavily outnumbered, the raiders none the less displayed characteristic mobility and skill in the surrounding gardens—killing a French officer, an NCO, and three of his men in the process—before performing their usual vanishing act.[64] That such a small force should have evaded capture also speaks volumes as to the support they could command from the locals.

Indeed, the Ayt Merghad were incensed at the French occupation, the more so as the *shurafa* of the nearby Taghia district, in particular those of Ayt Sidi Mha and Sidi Bou Ya'qoub, let alone Ou-Skounti himself, were strongly supportive of this defiant attitude. In fact, many *qsur* upstream from Imelouan were empty, their inhabitants—together with numerous resistance diehards—being concentrated around Assoul. Captain Guyetand spent the rest of the summer vainly attempting to placate the irreconcilable elements.[65] Psychological warfare cut little ice with the Ayt 'Isa Izem. Such was their intransigence that none contemplated contact with the French otherwise than down a gun barrel. Actually, the situation on the upper Ghriss boiled down to a personal confrontation between Ou-Skounti and Captain Guyetand, an episode fittingly fictionalized by Lieutenant Weygand in his novel, *Goumier de l'Atlas*.

On October 25 came the *dénouement* to this duel. The Ayt 'Isa Izem had cut the telephone wire between Amellago and Agouddim, prompting Captain Guyetand to head for the spot with all the cavalry and infantry of his Goum.[66] Lying in wait were Ou-Skounti and sixty of his best fighters. Unluckily for them, Guyetand detected them in the nick of time and, using the high ground, successfully engaged them: twenty-two of the raiders were killed; whereupon Ou-Skounti, who had been wounded in the exchange, disengaged in style in the direction of Taghia, with the Goums in hot pursuit.

Fig. 36: Camels graze on esparto grass east of Amellago, with a fresh dusting of snow on the tops.

In Aqqa Bou Tafersit, however, thanks to intimate knowledge of the terrain, the *jish* turned the tables on its pursuers, Guyetand receiving a bullet in the head from a wounded raider, to whom, in a Victor Hugo-style gesture, he was about to give a drink.

Apart from the fact that his own devoted *goumiers* erected a pile of stones in his honor, Guyetand appears to have been a charismatic figure; as *qebtan jida*, he has since found a niche in local oral tradition.[67] A childless Ayt Merghad woman, so the story goes, who happened to be passing by, saw the cairn and, believing it was dedicated to Sidi Serdrar, a local saint, uttered a prayer that she might be blessed with child.

Subsequently her wish came true and she had a baby, only to become the laughing stock of her peers at the very idea that her offspring's father by proxy might be *qebtan jida*![68] Later that winter, possibly to avoid further misunderstanding, the Ayt 'Isa Izem destroyed the cairn; so, in 1933, the French erected a more substantial monument to the captain and his unit, the battle-tried 38th Goum.[69]

While the days of the resistance were numbered, the exploits of its courageous fighters on the Atlas front proved that their morale remained intact. No wonder the reputation of their leader, Ou-Skounti, increased at each successful coup. Operating on their native heath, masters of hit-and-run tactics, they knew how to make full use of the terrain: jagged ridges; sparse vegetation of esparto grass and gnarled junipers; eroded escarpments with side-ravines full of dead ground; and gorges lined by *gruyère*-holed cliffs—all ideal for ambush and concealment.

According to a contemporary journalist, no sane European would dream of wandering single-handed through there at sunset after butterflies or rock samples—not if he valued his life![70] That being said, there was a touch of inevitability in the air at the close of the 1932 campaign. After twenty years of unrelenting warfare, the tribes of the Eastern High Atlas and southeast Morocco now had their backs to the wall as the territory under their rule gradually shrank before the merciless blows of the French war machine. Their raiding activities increasingly restricted, whether Ayt Hammou/Khebbash on the Oued Dra'a *hammada*, or Ayt 'Isa Izem of the Atlas, now was the time for a switch to a defensive strategy, to think in terms of conserving the few chunks of land they still possessed.

We will see how in the Tounfit area the sons of Sidi Ali Amhaoush were regrouping around the citadel of Tazigzaout, where the Christians would hopefully be defeated. Simultaneously, Zaïd Ou-Skounti was toying with the idea of a last stand on Jbel Baddou, a conspicuous peak rising almost to the 3,000-meter mark between the entrenched meanders of Oued Ghriss and Oued Todgha. There, according to local prophesies, the *imjuhad* would crush the invaders.[71] How could it be otherwise, Ou-Skounti assured his Ayt 'Isa Izem followers, "sanctified as it had been by the passage of Mahomet's mule"?[72] The Baddou episode was yet to come, however, and will be described in due course.

Fig. 37: Berber family, Oul Ghazi, Asif Melloul, Ayt Sokhman.

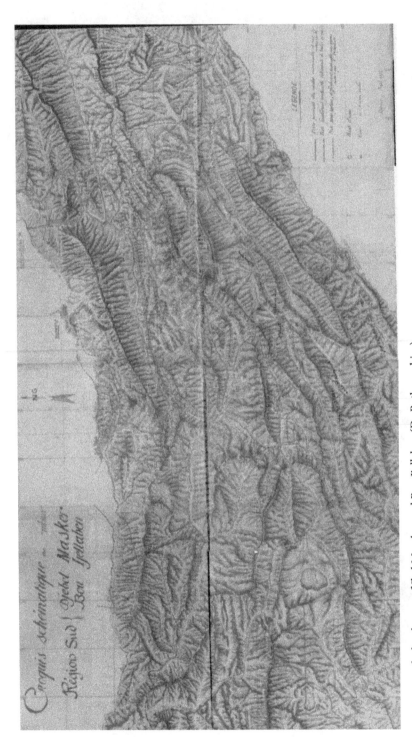

Map 7: Rough sketch map of Jbel Maasker and Bou Ijellaben (De Butler archive).

The Opening Rounds of the Atlas Endgame: Ayt Ya'qoub to Tazizaout (1929–32)

Into the uncharted Berber borderlands

We must now return to the Atlas front at the close of the "phoney war" period. What of the resistance? Its prestige strengthened by successful raids in the Tadla region, its ammunition supply replenished, it still held the southwest spur of the Middle Atlas lying between Jbel Tasemmit and the Oued L'abid–Moulouya watershed. This acted as an outlying line of defense for the Grand Atlas, a portion of the Atlas front known to French HQ staff as *la courtine de l'Oued el Abid* ("the Oued L'abid salient").[1] Further east, the virtually intact Ayt Yahya mountain redoubt, defended by 1,500 well-armed warriors, promised some famous fighting should the *irumin* choose to tangle with them. Indeed, readiness for battle was second nature to them, as amply demonstrated in the following lines:

> Just two things, O Lord, from you I do implore:
> First, a rifle fit for a first-class combatant;
> Second, a steed well-trained, itching for battle![2]

Overlooking Ayt Yahya country lay the impressive barrier of Jbel 'Ayyashi, one of Morocco's main water towers, snowbound some six or seven months a year, a regional hub of pastoralism and natural regulator of human activity.[3] A popular saying from the Midelt area similarly echoes the mountain's vital role: "Sell not your grain till 'Ayyashi has received snow and rain!" Unsurprisingly its deep, sheltered valleys, studded with irrigated fields and fortified hamlets, were home to highly civilized, industrious, and peaceful Ayt 'Ayyash *qsur* dwellers—not to mention the long-established, Sufi-inspired saints of Zaouit Si Hamza. More to the point, in view of the coming operations, 'Ayyashi and its outliers were also inhabited by mountaineers with a deep, nostalgic attachment to their inhospitable hills, even when they wander afar, as expressed through the famous lines:

> Who knows, O native land, whether on you shall ever set eyes again;
> Or whether, far from home, some unknown pass shall mark my grave?![4]

These Berbers were well practiced in the arts of vendetta and guerrilla warfare, with plundering caravans as an extra skill.[5] No wonder strikingly conspicuous 'Ayyashi symbolized a well-defined frontier between the settled and the unsettled, pacified and unsubdued territory. Beyond its ridge lay the little-known, unmapped highlands of the Ayt Hadiddou and Ayt Yaflman, so far penetrated by a mere handful of intrepid, turn-of-the-twentieth-century European travelers in disguise,[6] and/or Berber informants in French pay. From their surprisingly detailed reports, cartographers attempted to piece together the lie of the land.

Given the then dearth of hard information, the resultant maps are surprisingly accurate, yet basically flawed, as is immediately obvious to any knowledgeable observer. Take Lieutenant Naudin's late-1920s sketch map of the High Atlas between 'Ayyashi and Azourki. While tribal names are accurately rendered, place names are often garbled, and the relief is schematically presented with such scant regard for scale or accuracy as to prove a nightmare for any officer contemplating successful ground operations.[7] By contrast, pioneering photo-reconnaissance missions, carried out during the same period by planes of the Tadla squadron of the *Armée de l'Air*, yield more promising data. Typical of these is a survey of the Asif Melloul region by Captain Kauffman of the 6th squadron of the 37th Air Regiment, based on oblique (rather than vertical) aerial photographs. Whereas no attempt is made to sketch in the relief, the principal mountains are named and the main watercourses accurately portrayed, together with most of the villages that line their banks.[8] More significantly, it is drawn to scale and probably acted as a basis for the full-fledged ordnance survey 1/100,000 coverage of the area issued in 1933, possibly in time for the final operations. No wonder French military planners had a complex, confused idea of what really awaited them up there. This partial accuracy also applied, to a lesser degree, to their written sources of documentation. These were the sum total of annual Native Officers' intelligence reports on the area regularly sent to the Résidence in Rabat, the chief contributors being officers like Bouverot, Tarrit, and Guennoun.[9]

While there is a wealth of information on the ethnography, hydrology, climate, agriculture, vegetation, resources, and communications network of the region, it is occasionally marred by inconsistency and inaccuracy. For example, on the Naudin map, *taida*, "pine tree," is glossed as "European fir"; likewise *tawalt* (a variety of juniper) is translated as "cedar," whereas the latter is usually rendered *idyil* or *itgel*. Place names are misleadingly translated or misplaced, as in the case of Asif Temga mistaken for Asif Melloul. Some are garbled: Ambrouz for Amdghous; likewise wrongly spelled Ighoudlen (for *igudlan*), meaning "pastures," erroneously presented as a toponym.[10]

Mountain diehards: Ayt Hadiddou and Ayt Sokhman

Meanwhile, oblivious to this flurry of activity, apart from the occasional low-flying biplane which would provide them with target practice, or the summary execution of any turncoat Berber spy caught red-handed, highland tribesmen went about their lawful business. Well aware that the French were attempting to blockade them into submission, they were beginning to feel the pinch, as the cost of grain soared and livestock prices and availability of other staples dwindled. Yet they remained resolutely defiant.[11] At the expense of frittering away their strength, they continued to hone their fighting skills. For example, until the early-1930s, the *igwerramn* of Ayt Taddart (Ayt Hadiddou) from the Upper Ziz regularly indulged in more than realistic war games with their southerly Irbiben (Ayt Merghad) neighbors of Tana.[12] This penchant for gratuitous hostilities was such that, as one observer shrewdly pointed out:

> Had it not been for the fact that these Berbers of the Atlas are incorrigible cattle-thieves, it is likely that the French authorities of the Protectorate would have been glad enough to leave the Grand Atlas as a sort of Hagenbeck's Zoo, where the wild clansmen might have been allowed to carry on their intertribal warfare undisturbed.[13]

So much for tactical preparation; as regards overall cohesion and strategy, there were a few attempts at co-ordination. That said, while all and sundry protested undying commitment to the cause of anti-Christian resistance in the name of *jihad*, actual defensive operations tended to be conducted in piecemeal fashion.

Running true to form, the heirs of Sidi 'Ali Amhaoush carried on their Byzantine feuding in the Tounfit area,[14] despite Sidi Lmekki's persistent prophecies that the key to Amazigh destiny lay in the not-too-distant future on a nearby mountain named Tazizaout. The Ayt Hadiddou, for their part, remained apparently unperturbed and aloof, confident in the protection afforded both by an outer ring of as yet unsubdued tribes and by their inner redoubt of barren hills. An additional asset lay in the leadership qualities of charismatic Sidi ben-Hmad of Tilmi, part-saint and part-warrior, better known as Ou-Sidi. Unsurprisingly, observers on both sides visualized Hadiddou-land as the supreme sanctuary of the resistance, as the place where the diehards would make their last stand.[15] The Ayt Hadiddou were indeed highly rated as fighters, eventually prepared to operate "out of area" when the *irumin* threatened the sanctity of the hills. Nor was their fame as pastoralists any less great—their wool, ideal for weaving homespun cloaks, being reputedly second to none. No wonder they were seen as incarnating the finest example of Berber *timuzgha* ("Berberhood"), especially the Ayt Y'azza and Ayt Brahim clans inhabiting the Asif Melloul and Isellaten districts. Though possibly blurred by a romantic, Orientalist-inspired, postcolonial reconstruction of Berber identity, this was how I saw the Ayt Hadiddou as I tramped through their valleys in the 1970s.

Nowhere else in the Atlas were traditions of customary law, rotating chieftainship, language purity, honor, and the spoken word so strictly adhered to, a notion popularized by the Ayt Hadiddou of Ayt Hani (Amdghous),[16] a truly noble tribe of mountain Imazighen.[17]

Away from their grotty administrative center, Imilshil, with its modicum of civilization, poor plumbing, and irksome officialdom, Hadiddou life retained an untainted timelessness. Short-scale seasonal migration was practiced between summer encampments on upland *igudlan* ("pastures") and elegant, mud-turreted *igherman* ("castles") surrounded by poplar trees and potato patches. The men, often fine, distinguished-looking individuals, would wear spotless white turbans and woollen

Fig. 38: Tighremt n Ayt Saïd, downstream from Imillshil, Asif Melloul (Ayt Hadiddou).

cloaks; their attractive, strong-minded womenfolk similarly resplendent in conical headdresses and striped gowns. Through dire necessity the latter also headed daily into the hills, foraging ever further afield for firewood, contributing to erosion and a land strangely devoid of vegetation, apart from the scrub-willow (*tassemlilt*) that grows along the banks of Asif Melloul.[18]

Equally entrenched in their Atlas fastnesses were the various Ayt Sokhman clans.[19] Chief among these were the Ayt Hemama, Ayt Daoud ou 'Ali, and Ayt 'Abdi, their spirit of resistance kept at boiling point by various *igwerramn*, not all of them skilled warriors. Among the most genuine tribal groups of the Atlas, they had fought long and hard to retain a toehold on the fertile slopes near Anergui and its surrounding pastures. They had also preserved intact many of their age-old traditions, no doubt inherited from the ancient Berghaouata, such as sheep-shoulder divination, an ancient practice enabling them to predict the weather; or charting forthcoming events by scanning constellations in the night sky.[20] These tribesmen did not, however, impart the same impression of nonchalant ease and grace as their Ayt Hadiddou neighbors. Rather did they appear as poor relatives, leading an arduous, uncomfortable existence: in winter hiding in smoky,[21] cliff-side caves precariously perched above the Asif Melloul gorge; in summer huddling halfway up mountain slopes in *iskifen* ("sheep-enclosures") and small *igherman*—massive, stunted affairs of undressed stone and stout juniper.

Apart from those near Anergui, rare were the buildings with fine, tapering, corner-turrets. Reflecting the severe winter climate, emphasized by snow-dusted forests of pine and oak, not to mention sub-zero temperatures, some of the hovel-like Sokhman dwellings appeared to hug the ground. Here again, there was no escaping a pastorally-oriented existence: each year flocks and herds would nibble their way upwards, over and above the vast El-Houant forest with its improbable, gnarled junipers, wild boars, elusive jackals, and lurking panthers; their ultimate goal the rich Isrouta plateau, the verdant pastures of Tingerft, the undulating highlands of Mouriq or Kousser at over 3,000 m.[22]

Finally, the Asif n-Ouhansal Valley delineated dissident territory to the west. On staff maps, near the point where that river joins the Asif Melloul, could be seen a small salient where a thousand fighters equipped with breech-loaders were still holding out.[23] This land of pine forests and small brown castles nestling at the feet of towering slab-sided escarpments like Aghembou n-Masko, over which many a veteran had sworn to jump with his family rather than surrender to the *irumin*, was firmly under the spiritual sway of the Ahansala marabouts. For sure, Sidi Mah El-Hansali had surrendered to the French in 1922 as part of a bet-hedging operation; his cousins, however, keeping their options open, still reigned at Zaouit Ahansal, which remained a focal point of uncompromising mountain resistance.

Here then, did the Atlas frontier come to an end. A few hours' walk to the southwest, beyond Azourki's lofty, snow-streaked whaleback, along the mountain trails that crisscrossed above Lake Izoughar—perilous, raider-infested territory—went the mule caravans, hurrying for the safety of Ayt M'Hammed and its Native Affairs outpost.[24]

These, then, were the inhospitable, imperfectly mapped mountains in which some of the best fighters in the Atlas had gone to ground.[25] To flush them out of their hiding places in impressive gorges, or from wooded hillsides, would require a painstaking approach. Such was the residual impact of the "prestige of the hills," even as the Atlas endgame was about to get under way, that the French would only commence operations once they were confident they could muster overwhelmingly superior forces. Even then, the *imjuhad* were determined not to give in without a fight. In the difficult, broken country that was their home, they would no doubt inflict severe casualties on their assailants, whatever the odds.

Capua of the borderlands

Let us return to the founding of Midelt, a garrison-town that was to play an important role in the final phase of the Atlas campaigns. In pre-Protectorate Morocco, it was known as Aoutat n-Ayt Izdeg, a cluster of mud-grey *qsur* and a staging-post on the Fez–Tafilalt caravan track. The local sedentary Berbers had made the most of the fertile soil along the banks of the snow-fed Aoutat stream and organized their lifestyle along coherent and harmonious lines. A few miles to the northeast rises a steep-sided, flat-topped hill resembling a dish-cover (*timidelt*), thus providing an ideal site where a regular souk was held, naturally protected from the predatory gangs that worked the old trade route. When the French arrived in 1917 and set up an outpost at Aoutat, they took the name of the hill and corrupted it into "Midelt."[26]

Poised between the Middle and Great Atlas, from Poeymirau's 1922 thrust to the Moulouya source in 1922 till the 1931–3 campaigns in Ayt Yaflman country, Midelt was to become indispensable as an advanced base. There would the *Groupes Mobiles* muster in the spring; there, come autumn, they would return. Relatively snow-free in winter, when the passes over the Middle Atlas would be snowbound, it was ideally sited. Access in any season was guaranteed by an 0.60 m narrow-gauge branch line from Gerssif that followed the Moulouya down to Bouasidi—a Wild West-style terminus in the middle of nowhere; from there a lorry shuttle linked the station to Midelt, by then promoted to the status of "Capua of the borderlands."

It was all that and much more: part military depot, part recreation center, its fleshpots afforded the local military some relief from the tedium of garrison duty, from life in the *bled*. Around the hilltop outpost a new village had sprung up almost miraculously, where Greek and Jewish traders, tired of following the columns into the dusty hills, had set up shop, confident that the returning troops would have money to spend on tepid beer and rotgut liquor. Their more ambitious colleagues had opened up restaurants, bars, small hotels. The Roi de la Bière, with its famous piano—visible today, though out of action—used to serve as a mess for non-commissioned officers,[27] some of whom were in the habit of firing their revolvers at the ceiling when drunk.

Inevitably, a few madames, making the most of the available, despondent manhood, had set up bordellos to provide them with badly needed *belles de nuit*. These establishments operated on a roster system whereby specific evenings were assigned to each unit, great care being taken not to have soldiers from rival outfits on the premises at the same time; otherwise, it was a sure recipe for disaster. In spite of these elaborate precautions, former Midelt residents tell harrowing tales of revelry by night; of prostitute-related fisticuffs, knife fights, and even pitched battles between the Foreign Legion and *Tirailleurs*.[28] Contributing to the nocturnal din would be marauding jackals confronting packs of local curs around trash heaps, making for a decidedly tourist-unfriendly environment, not that many foreign travelers would have followed the Edith Wharton trail this far south at the time. What the Berbers made of this unbridled debauchery hardly bears thinking about.

As for their brethren in the mountains above Midelt, they were enjoying a comparative lull in the fighting, interrupted by the usual raids deep into pacified territory and the occasional skirmish whenever a Foreign Legion party, foraging for firewood, ventured too deeply into the foothills.[29] In 1927, Lieutenant Parlange had written a promising report advocating a further nibble at the Atlas front, a mere jaunt from Zaouit Sidi Hamza to occupy Ayt Ya'qoub, El-Bordj, and the Igli region along Oued Ziz. Such an operation, so he argued, could be effected with minimal risk, and would most likely not provoke a reaction by the Ayt Hadiddou of Asif Melloul.[30] Events were soon to show what a grave miscalculation that was.

Desperate battle at Ayt Ya'qoub

The planned operation accordingly went ahead at the end of April 1929, and, after a brief fracas at Tanneghrift, various high altitude village-oases beneath the strategically important Tizi n-Maoutfoud were occupied. Lucien Saint, the new Resident-General, was delighted. Here was the perfect example of a low-cost operation with maximum results.[31] For an entire week, hardly anything happened. On the resistance side, however, faced with this threat to the integrity of the Berber heartland, there was dialogue between two prominent religious leaders—Ou-Sidi from Tilmi and Sidi Mohand Ou-Lhajj—with a co-ordination meeting at the latter's zaouia of Sidi Yahya ou Youssef, near Tounfit.[32] Plans as to appropriate tactics of stealth and guile seem to have been made, together with a promise of joint action between Ayt Hadiddou, Ayt Yahya, Ayt Merghad, and Ayt Hammou.

On May 9 some Yahya warriors on a left-bank Oued Ziz tributary drove back a reconnaissance party of *lbertiza*, while the next day a force of some 300 dissidents attempted to take over the newly established outpost at El-Bordj through a *ruse de guerre*. Advancing under a white flag as if to effect their submission they approached to less than a mile before opening fire on the garrison.

A three-hour firefight followed; at the end of the day strafing runs by low-flying biplanes from Boudenib proved decisive in dispersing the assailants.[33] Though not immediately apparent, this was but the prelude to more lethal action. Meanwhile, throughout the month of May, the energetic Ou-Sidi was busy on Asif Melloul mustering a large *harka* of 1,500 Ayt Hadiddou and Ayt Merghad, information as to this build-up filtering through to the Ayt Ya'qoub outpost.[34] Another account suggests that, counting Ayt Yahya elements, the *harka* amounted to 2,500 combatants, many of whom were equipped with repeating rifles and a machine gun or two.[35] Yet another source puts their strength at some 1,000 warriors—a mix of Ayt Hadiddou and Yahya.[36]

Whatever the exact composition of the *harka* it was ably commanded. Ou-Sidi decided to lure the French garrison away from its outpost towards an ideal killing-ground: the narrow Tahiant Valley leading southwest from Ayt Ya'qoub. What better way than resort to the old raiders' ruse of cutting the telegraph wire? A group of about forty men was accordingly despatched to do the deed on the evening of June 7.

Sure enough, a small detachment of Goums and Foreign Legion was sent out early the following morning to repair the line. Naturally, the wire-cutters ambushed them. On hearing the gunfire, Commandant Emmanuel marched out of Ayt Ya'qoub outpost at the head of two companies of his 7th Moroccan *Tirailleurs*, a platoon of machine-gunners with another of Legionaires, roughly 400 men in all, amounting to two-thirds of the total garrison strength. The Berber raiders traded fire with the approaching column, before falling back towards the southwest, luring Emmanuel and his command as far away as possible from the outpost. Meanwhile, beyond the surrounding ridges, Ou-Sidi's main body was closing in. When the French about-turned it was already too late, their line of retreat cut off; in the narrow valley close to the village of Tahiant they came under devastating fire, losing some eighty killed including all their officers. The remainder retired as best they could to Ayt Ya'qoub. Though on a smaller scale than El-Herri, this was one of the worst defeats inflicted by Moroccan Berbers on French forces during the entire Atlas war.[37]

Worse was to follow. For ten days, the victorious *harka*, reinforced by numerous Ayt Hammou and Ayt Yahya warriors, closely invested the fort, the Foreign Legion encampment, and the *qsar* of Ayt Ya'qoub held by the Goums. Several attempted assaults came within an ace of success, though the attackers were hampered by the Boudenib fliers' incessant air raids. By June 18, with the death of the garrison's surviving officers, Ayt Ya'qoub fort was about to fall. Yet Ou-Sidi hesitated. Intelligence had reached him that General Nieger's relief column was on its way from Midelt. He was

Fig. 39: Ruined French outpost, Ayt Ya'qoub; Foreign Legion camp above *qsar* in right background.

undecided as to whether to await the enemy on favorable terrain near Tanneghrift, or to stake all on a desperate attempt to storm Ayt Ya'qoub outpost.

Choosing the latter course of action, he mounted a vigorous attack that night on the *qsar*, torched it, dislodged the Goums and forced them to fall back on the fort and Foreign Legion camp, which continued to hold out. On June 19, the relief column arrived on the scene and, in the subsequent stand-up firefight, though the Berbers ultimately came off second best, eventually retreating with heavy casualties, they inflicted further losses on the enemy.[38]

Fallout from the nine-day battle was disastrous. Significantly, it had witnessed an almost unprecedented alliance between four tribes, while the unexpectedly high number of French casualties caused a ministerial crisis and put a temporary damper on over-hasty Gallic ambitions, also delaying conquest of the Atlas by four years. The French should not have been caught napping. "So long as you have un-subdued tribesmen out there," warned General Nieger, fresh from rescuing Ayt Ya'qoub oupost, "and whatever precautions are taken, you can expect a surprise!"[39] At Rabat HQ, Commander-in-Chief General Jean Vidalon,[40] anxious to find a scapegoat, clamored for the scalp of Meknes Divisonal commander Freydenberg. He eventually got it.

Henri Freydenberg, a soldier's soldier and seasoned Atlas campaigner, was kicked upstairs to major-general and posted back to France. Meanwhile the French government had to field a barrage of awkward questions in parliament, while Vidalon urged caution on the Atlas front for the rest of the year.[41] A contemporary observer thus comments on the psychological impact of the battle: "Our dead at Ayt Ya'qoub were a sorry sight.

Fig. 40: Tounfit and Jbel Ma'asker (3,277 m), seen from due north.

Those who hadn't been killed outright had been tortured and stabbed to death. The French officers had had their stomachs ripped open and stuffed with stones."[42]

In an oral society where news travels fast, word went out across the Great Atlas that the Christian invader had been defeated; by the Ayt Hadiddou according to some, by the Ayt Hammou according to others. Whoever was responsible, the blow to French prestige was undoubtedly damaging. Despite numerous casualties among the Berbers there occurred a noticeable hardening of resolve, a willingness to fight to the finish.

Interestingly, on June 18, at the height of the battle, Freydenberg had ordered a mixed force of Goums and partisans to raid Tounfit from the Moulouya side, in an attempt to relieve the pressure on Ayt Ya'qoub and deter the bulk of the Ayt Yahya from joining in the fighting. Though several houses were torched, some merchants killed, and a few rifles seized, this hit-and-run affair actually achieved little.[43] Although the anxious Tounfit inhabitants manned observation posts overlooking the Moulouya on the days that followed to forestall further French incursions, "with time, the memory of the lesson received passed away as the Ayt Yahya resumed their usual raids, ambushes and attacks."[44]

Neutralizing the Oued L'abid salient

Meanwhile, above the Tadla area at the other end of the Atlas front, goaded into action by a dramatic, unexpected attack on their Waouizaght outpost, the French had taken another nibble at dissident territory. A short advance had enabled them, on August 29, 1929, to occupy some wooded heights north of Azaghar Fal despite an attempt by Sidi Mohammed Taïbi to recapture the French position on Bou Adian, a failure which gravely tarnished the marabout's reputation.[45] The 1930 campaign, however, got off to a good start for Ayt Sokhman resistance fighters. On January 3, near Outrouzou, they ambushed a group of pro-French partisans and inflicted heavy casualties on them, although the survivors managed to return to base after nightfall.[46]

In April 1930, the French nevertheless managed to gain a foothold on the flat-topped Sgatt hill overlooking the Oued La'abid gorge upstream from Waouizaght. This brought within range of their artillery Zaouia Asker, a noteworthy resistance center in the area, where Sidi Housseyn ou Temga, one of the Ahansal marabouts, died about this time of old age.[47] Further operations in 1930 were concentrated on the Oued L'abid area and aimed at establishing a continuous line of outposts between Ksiba and Aghbala.

They were all of a low-key nature with the exception of a gallant attempt by another local saint—El-Ouali—to recapture Maokayn hill, occupied in July by Goums and Foreign Legion. Against a solidly entrenched position defended by barbed wire entanglements and well-sighted machine guns, it was a forlorn hope. None the less, on August 1, 1930, anxious to demonstrate his *baraka*, El-Ouali rode unarmed at the head of a 700-strong force of Ayt Ouirra and Ayt Mohand combatants in a desperate bid to storm the Maokayn heights. Predictably, he and about twenty of his faithful followers were mown down as the attack failed gloriously.[48] This forlorn hope proved the only serious reaction to the French advance, an event thus commented on by a contemporary observer: "our occupation of this Oued La'abid salient will protect the plains from incursions by un-subdued tribes."[49]

Though the tribes in question were not immediately aware of this development, an important change in French strategic thinking was actually just round the corner. In October 1931 there was a meeting in Kasba Tadla between local military chiefs and visiting top brass from Paris, followed by an excursion to a vantage-point above Oued La'abid whence the unsubdued Central High Atlas was clearly visible. In answer to War Minister Maginot's plea for a speeded-up calendar of mopping-up operations, the sooner to free army units to face a perceived German threat in Europe after 1934, Colonel De Loustal, a portly, white-haired campaigner with handlebar moustaches, outlined the series of immediate nibbles he proposed to take at the Atlas front.[50]

This cut far more ice with the visitors than Vidalon's timorous strategy of "only cautious advances," and explains why the mantle of commander-in-chief, Morocco, was shortly removed from his shoulders to those of the more dynamic general Huré.[51] One of the first directives the latter issued in May 1931 prioritized:

> ... advances conducted in the most humane manner possible after steady build-ups to avoid being caught off-guard, together with an accelerated operational rhythm dictated by imperative exigencies of national defence, and designed to subdue the last dissident areas by 1934.[52]

At the end of spring 1931, De Loustal's Tadla region troops dislodged dissident elements from the Sgatt area, across Oued L'abid and established outposts at Tigleft and Tiffert n-Ayt Hamza.[53] The Oued La'abid salient existed no more.

In defense of Yahya-land

The time had come for the Ayt Yahya to defend their homeland. Confident in the inviolability of their wooded hills, they continued to turn a deaf ear to attempts by

Fig. 41: Woman from Ayt Yahya, Ayt Bou Arbi clan, Tounfit region.

French political officers urging them to surrender. Their men patronized the Sunday *ssuq* at Tounfit to barter lean cattle for handfuls of barley or dates (*tiyni*), to get skillful Saharan craftsmen to refurbish their cartridges, or to lend an ear to impassioned, anti-French homilies by Sidi Mohand ou-Lhajj. The latter remained engrossed in internecine quarrels with Sidi Lmekki and his brothers, thus weakening the cause of the resistance.[54]

A two-pronged attack was being mounted: from the west under De Loustal, now a brigadier-general; from the north by General Nieger at the head of the Meknes region troops. As we have seen in an earlier chapter, this offensive went forward successfully on July 15, Tounfit being occupied fairly easily as Ou-Skounti retired southwards.

The main Ayt Yahya forces, however, were regrouped around Zaouia Sidi Yahya ou Youssef, stronghold of Sidi Mohand ou-Lhajj. This marabout was a colorful figure, and very much a ladies' man, every day getting a different woman to comb his long hair.

More practically, he had drawn a line on the ground alleging that the French would never cross it. He also claimed that Sidi Yahya ou Youssef in person had appeared to him in a dream and announced that he would ride to the rescue on the fateful day of confrontation with the *irumin*![55] His zaouia eventually came under attack on the morning of July 26, 1931. A large village nestling in the entrenched meanders of Asif Ouirin, its position was patently unsuitable for defensive purposes. However, desperate house-to-house fighting lasted till midday, when Sidi Mohand and some 200 of his disciples surrendered. The remaining stalwarts stole off southwards into the hills.[56]

That same day, Ayt Hnini and Ichqern contingents had been driven from their encampments beneath Jbel Toujjit by De Loustal's forces and had fallen back across Asif Ouirin, where they made a brief stand at Talat n-Ou'arab before being dispersed by Zaïan cavalry under *qayd*s Amharoq and Hassan.[57] Further west, Sidi Lmekki and his brothers left Ta'adlount and sought refuge in the rugged terrain around Jbel Tazizaout, the site ordained by fate for their last stand against the Christians. After the battle at Zaouia Sidi Yahya ou Youssef, many were the local Berbers who, mourning their dead, simultaneously reviled Mohand ou-Lhajj for having let them down with his false prophecies that the *irumin*'s planes would be changed into storks and their bombs become melons![58] Unsurprisingly, local bards waxed eloquent over his discomfiture. Some of them, too, were astonished at the restraint displayed by their conquerors. General Goudot, for one, ordered that fifty sheep his partisans had just captured be returned to their lawful owner; he also sent a truck full of fruit trees to Tounfit, there to be planted.[59]

Also near Tounfit, some tribesmen returning to their village were amazed to find their fields had been ploughed and sown by the occupying forces.[60] By August, however,

Fig. 42: Sheep grazing at hamlet of Mshitt, behind Jbel Ma'asker, Tounfit region.

having overcome their initial disarray, the Ayt Yahya were preparing to retaliate. Of the 1,300 combatants they could count on at the beginning of the campaign, only 600 remained. These had regrouped in a *tazemmalt* (war camp) at Mshitt hamlet, south of Jbel Ma'asker, and during the night of August 5–6, 1931, hurled themselves at the barbed wire and machine guns of a French outpost on Amalou n-Tmezra ridge. Several gallant attempts were pushed home; the fighting lasted till dawn, all to no avail. As usual, the lack of grenades and automatic weapons proved an insurmountable handicap to the Berbers in confrontations of this kind.[61]

Towards Ayt Hadiddou country

However, once the *irumin* were out in the open, they lost their tactical edge and remained vulnerable, as in the little-known skirmish on Ifou hill. This rocky, wooded promontory overlooks the confluence of Asif Ouirin and Asif n-Ougheddou above Ta'adlount village, which the 31st Goum had occupied at the end of July. To command the southern approaches from Ayt Hadiddou country, the main threat axis, a 75 mm field gun was hauled up there and a small outpost built around it, manned by some *Tirailleurs*.

Every morning, a patrol on horseback would be sent up from Ta'adlount to establish contact with the outpost. Early on August 25, about 200 Ayt Hadiddou and Ayt Sokhman came and opened fire on the patrol just as it was reaching the ridge. The Goum commander, a certain Lieutenant Debray, was in bed with his Berber girl friend, a famous Ishqern courtesan by the name of Itto Ben Zouggat,[62] when he was awoken by the sound of gunfire.

Dressing hastily, he jumped onto his horse, still in shirtsleeves, and headed rapidly up the cedar-covered slopes with the rest of his Goum. Arriving on the scene a little ahead of his men, he charged impetuously, revolver in hand, only to be shot down by the raiders.

It took all of his men's courage to counter-attack and retrieve his body. Once again, Amazigh resistance had shown it remained lethal.[63] Actions such as these, however, were mere flashes in the pan, as, blockaded within their inhospitable hills, the diehards could feel the noose gradually tightening. There was, as yet, no talk of surrender, the prospect of foreign domination being impossible to countenance.

Beyond Jbel Ma'asker lay the southern Ayt Yahya, able to field some 700 riflemen. First, they had to be softened up, for which reason they now became exposed to intense propaganda from Captain Parlange (*burlanj*), the Native Affairs officer in charge of the Tounfit outpost. Their time came in the summer of 1932 when their area was occupied with relative ease, the only reaction coming from Ou-Sidi's Ayt Hadiddou who launched two separate attacks on Foreign Legion positions near Tizi n-Ighil.[64] By the end of June, the remaining Ayt Yahya had thus submitted and the Ayt Hadiddou were next on the list. They were to prove a tougher nut to crack. First in line were the Ayt 'Amr clan whose two main *qsur*, Anefgou and Tirghist, lay on either side of Jbel Fazaz's rugged escarpments. A brisk, two-day battle in mid-July put an end to their hopes: while one column outflanked Tirghist from the south, another force, with partisans out in front

Fig. 43: Woman from Ayt Yahya, Ayt Sliman clan, Tounfit region.

as cannon fodder, headed straight for Anefgou, only to encounter determined resistance. In the subsequent battle, fought out over exceedingly rugged, bushy terrain, the partisans suffered some 120 casualties all told, but were saved by the Foreign Legion's automatic weapons. The Ayt ʿAmr finally fled the field. Many of the dead never received a decent burial—their corpses were devoured by jackals.[65] As commented upon by a contemporary poet:

On those corpses gorge your fill while the shepherd is absent,
O ravenous jackal; our warriors lie dead on Anefgou's fatal field![66]

A month later, the *irumin* advance guards debouched on the Lakes Plateau and Imilshil, the Ayt Hadiddou "capital," was occupied. The unthinkable had occurred. That September the annual gathering of the clans, the Ayt Hadiddou trade fair, was cancelled.

Meanwhile, above Beni Mellal, various groups south of Oued L'abid indulged in desultory skirmishes with the advancing Tadla region troops. Badly let down by *igwerramn* such as Sidi ou Hsseyn of Temga, outperformed by a technically superior foe, they felt resigned to their fate. Thus was Tillouggit n-Ayt Iseha occupied on May 12, 1932, by partisans from Waouizaght under a famous soldier, a certain Captain Boyer de Latour (*muha w latur*), who later married a Berber woman and was France's last Resident-General in Morocco. Simultaneously, another detachment traversed El-Hwant forest, occupied the vital well of Tanout n-Bouwourgh, and drove the Ayt Daoud ou 'Ali back towards Jbel Mouriq.[67]

The local resistance chief was Sidi 'Ali ou Hsseyn who, from his zaouia at Anergui, was urging his tribe, the Ayt Daoud ou 'Ali, never to come to terms with the *irumin*. However, concomitantly with the latest enemy advances from the north, Marrakesh area troops had been pushing northeast along the flank of Jbel Azourki, and Zaouit Ahansal had fallen almost without a fight. Now, French artillery could reach Zaouia Temga, Anergui, and the slopes of Jbel Mouriq. Such a rapid, undisputed advance was nothing short of amazing, given the strength of the Ayt Iseha and their allies, credited (on paper) with 1,000 repeating rifles. Here again, as in Yahya land, the very nature of

Fig. 44: The Imilshil *mawsim*, trade fair of the Ayt Hadiddou, on Asif Melloul.

the terrain gave the locals an exaggerated confidence in their ability to resist encroachment from outsiders. Even when Moulay Hassan I had sent in troops some fifty years earlier, they had made but little impression on the Sokhman heartland. Now, so the local Berbers believed, it would be no different: the rugged, wooded slopes of Jbel Kousser, not to mention the cliff-side fortresses of the area's numerous canyons, would provide a sure refuge for the *imjuhad*; would enable them to defy the infidel indefinitely. About forty miles northeast, like-minded resistance fighters were preparing to defend an almost impregnable mountain redoubt.

23

Heroic Defense of Tazizaout

"A silver bullet my father left me"

Sure enough, Sidi Lmekki was about to write the last page in the protracted epic of the Amhaoush lineage.[1] South of the Agheddou river, in the wild, remote borderlands of the Ayt Sokhman, Ayt Yahya, and Ayt Hadiddou tribes, the long, cedar-clad ridge of Tazizaout rises to above 9,000 feet, high enough to catch winter snows, clearly visible on a fine day from Azaghar Fal. It was at its western end that, on a journey in the late nineteenth century, Sidi 'Ali Amhaoush briefly stayed in a small hamlet named Tafza, close to where a left-bank tributary—Aqqa n-Zebzbat—joins the parent stream. A few apple trees, blackberry bushes, and wild vine are to be found along the banks of Aqqa n-Zebzbat. Left and right, steep ridges rise towards thickly wooded heights. The sheer loneliness of the place no doubt caught his fancy as ideal for a mountain retreat. In the event of war with the *irumin*, mused Sidi 'Ali, he could utter one of his doomsday prophecies to the effect that invading hordes, like ocean waves, would break against the inviolable citadel of Tazizaout.

Sidi Lmekki must have known of this place, must have heard his father foretelling that at Tazizaout would be fought the battle of destiny. After Sidi 'Ali's death in 1918, on retelling the prophecy, he would add as a rider, "a silver-bullet my father left me."[2] Thus would Sidi Lmekki speak to his followers, assuring them that when he fired that fateful shot on the great day, the Christians would be defeated; the Tazizaout prophecy became part of his stock-in-trade.

As the days of spring 1932 lengthened into summer, it even became the central item of his strategy. Local clans were to plan their movements to fit in with the marabout's predictions. Sidi Lmekki and his brothers had already moved to Tafza. The various eastern Ayt Sokhman components, gathering tents and flocks, bag and baggage, gradually converged on Tazizaout. Interestingly, despite the gravity of the situation, the laws governing *lhujjat* ("vendetta-avoiding exile") remained in force. Thus, any Ayt 'Abdi who had murdered one of his fellows did not rejoin his home encampment, but stayed with his Ayt Hemama hosts. Even when you were digging in at a time of general emergency such as this, when the group as a whole was united against an external threat, you did not sink your differences. Amazingly, the murderer was still not safe from knife or bullet at the hands of his victim's next of kin![3]

Sidi Lmekki had managed to gather an impressive force of some 1,000 warriors, all armed with breech-loaders, not to mention their dependents and livestock. Here were malcontents who had been withdrawing before the French advance for more than ten years: Beni Mguild, Ishqern, and others from the Middle Atlas; not to mention local Ayt Sokhman, Ayt Yahya, Ayt Hadiddou, together with highwaymen and deserters from the French ranks. Skillful use had been made of the terrain, with strong-points half-buried beneath old oak trees, buttressed by cedar logs and, in certain sectors, an interconnecting system of trenches and caves. The most elaborate entrenchments were to be found in Aqqa n-Tefza, between Tizi n-Tkoushtamt and Tizi n-Mesfergh, all on the left bank of Aqqa n-Zebzbat, also at the westernmost point of Tazizaout, in Aqqa n-Oushlou. The livestock, on the whole, were left to roam at will, hence the large numbers subsequently killed or maimed by artillery shells.[4]

In August 1932 the French, who had advanced to the Lakes Plateau, became somewhat anxious at reports about this vast tribal gathering along the Agheddou. Most disquietingly, groups of warriors appeared to be avoiding contact with the French and merely withdrawing towards the western end of Tazizaout. Any envoys sent to establish contact with the dissidents, however, would be killed out of hand. It was also impossible to evaluate the number of dissidents; some reports spoke of 700 tents, but this was obviously below the mark.[5] Informants agreed that these diehards were keeping well out of the way—but for what purpose? The solution of bypassing this pocket of resistance and letting it wither on the vine contained one big disadvantage: leaving a large, undefeated force of hill men on the army's flank could jeopardize further operations along upper Asif Melloul. Also, such tame behavior on the part of the French military could convey the wrong psychological message, to the effect that they were afraid of taking on Sidi Lmekki.[6] The Tazizaout campaign may conveniently be sub-divided into four phases:

1. Initial build-up and opening attacks, August 16–24;
2. Lull allowing of a fresh reappraisal of the situation, August 25–September 4;
3. Decisive assault on Sidi Lmekki's encampments, September 5–13;
4. Break-out and mopping-up operations, September 13–22.

The appropriate forces for the Tazizaout operation were drawn from Meknes and Tadla region troops. The former, under General Dubuisson, included four battalions (with *Tirailleurs* and Legion units), one artillery battery, three Goums, and various auxiliaries; the latter, under General De Loustal, who retained overall command, comprised two battalions, two batteries of mountain guns, three Goums, and 1,000 Zaïan partisans. On August 21, the Meknes region troops, with their rear base at Tamalout, prepared to advance from east to west along Asif n-Ougheddou and the main ridge of Tazizaout.

The Tadla region troops had set up a rear base at Tassent, some five miles northwest of Imilshil, from which advance units near the Alegmou heights and on the Lakes Plateau were kept supplied with food and ammunition by mule train. The main artillery position, once its 75 mm guns had been literally manhandled uphill, was established on Jbel Bou Genfou, between the Ikassen and Agheddou valleys, with a scant 100 partisans

Fig. 45: Ruined Foreign Legion fort, Tizi n-Ighil, Tazizaout left background.

for close protection. This battery was ideally sited to pound Aqqa n-Oushlou ravine, where numerous Berber encampments were concentrated. In all, four mountain batteries, equipped with the 1906 model 65 mm pack howitzer, were set up on the Tasaount n-Ouidammen ridge north of the Lakes Plateau. The Meknes region troops moved their one mountain battery, using 75 mm Schneider pack howitzers, up through the cedars and onto the Tizi n-Ighil ridge to a position named Agerd n-Oulghoum, overlooking Asif n-Ougheddou.

'Hold on steadfastly!"

In Sidi Lmekki's encampments, Amazigh hillmen were making ready for battle. Sheep were sacrificed as their leaders exhorted them thus:

> Hold on steadfastly to the land between Tazra stream and Aqqa n-Zebzbat! Let there be no rift in your ranks during the battle that you shall witness this day! Sidi Lmekki himself uttered a short *fatha*: "May God grant you strength such as you never did know! May God grant you courage such as only He can give! The time for *jihad* has come, make good use of your weapons, that you may be blessed by the Lord; may God's grace be with you!"

Not to be outdone, his brother Sidi Mohand Lmehdi, actually more of a fire-eater than a man of words, could barely hide his contempt, and answered in more practical vein:

> Hark, O tribesmen! May God's blessing be upon you! Listen not to *bakki*'s lies! Strive might and main, may God strengthen the blows you strike; if death comes, it shall be God's will! He who perishes shall know God's mercy; if he escapes with his life, it shall be God's will! Let us prepare for the supreme sacrifice and respect our sacred *shahada* ["prayer"], and for the sake of our children and womenfolk! Now go and dig trenches! Dig trenches to protect your children and womenfolk! As to death in God's service, this is ordained by the Almighty, none must feel abandoned by him; as for the word *fear*, we know it not![7]

After Jbel Saghro this was undoubtedly the toughest siege in the whole Atlas campaign; once the area was sealed off, it took from August 21 to September 22 for the Tazizaout defenders finally to lay down their arms.[8] All was ready for a swift strike on August 22. A *Tirailleur* battalion and a Goum (*lqum*) detachment from the Meknes region were to sweep the right bank of Asif n-Ougheddou as far as the cliff of Tazra n-Ismekh, to overlook dissident elements at Ashlou and Tazra.

Simultaneously, 1,000 Zaïan partisans from the Tadla region were to move north from Tasaount n-Ouidammen and storm the Taoujja'aoutt heights, whence they could dominate Sidi Lmekki's encampments on the other slope, in Aqqa n-Tefza. Caught between two fires, the dissidents were bound to cave in rapidly.[9] The Meknes group, its artillery battery established on Agerd n-Oulghoum, advanced easily along the Tazizaout ridge. Down below, their Agheddou Valley detachment, however, was considerably delayed by resistance met along the way, although by 3 pm they were atop the Tazra n-Ismekh cliff. In a textbook exercise of tactical redeployment, the Berbers that had been opposing them now moved up Aqqa n-Zebzbat, arriving just in time to help head off the Zaïan threat from the south.

On the morning of August 22, a large force of Zaïan partisans moved north from Tasaount n-Ouidammen over ground still drenched by the previous night's thunderstorm, and set foot on the southern slopes of Taoujja'aoutt, prosaically known to the French as *Crête no 1*. Once they reached the top of this large, wooded hill, they barely had time to put up the usual low, stone parapet before they were vigorously counter-attacked by swarms of tribesmen. After several hours of savage hand-to-hand fighting, stalemate ensued; the Zaïans stood firm, as Guillaume is at pains to point out in his book,[10] but there was no escaping the fact that the French advance was firmly checked. De Loustal's potentially brilliant cut-and-thrust operation had stalled.

The partisans were in a semi-demoralized state after losing eighteen men killed and thirty wounded. What chiefly affected them was the recklessness of the resistance fighters, reciting the *fatha* and encouraged by shouts from nearby encampments; the sound of collective prayer chanted in unison by hundreds of voices greatly impressed the partisans.[11]

The next morning, August 23, the Zaïan underwent further harassment. In the afternoon, after a brief softening-up by artillery, they charged further north as far as the Takoushtamt ridge, at the cost of extra casualties: four dead and six wounded.

They had, however, shot their bolt. The following day they were relieved by a battalion of Moroccan *Tirailleurs*, who immediately had to stave off further desperate counter-attacks.[12] The fight for the Taoujja'aoutt ridge is well remembered in the area:

> Thus spoke Taoujja'aoutt hill: had it not been for the Zaïan partisans,
> Never would those dogs in hob-nailed boots have scaled my heights![13]

On August 23, *Tirailleurs* advancing west along the main Tazizaout ridge were also stopped by a combination of determined frontal resistance and well-organized outflanking moves, as a result of which they took some casualties.[14] The weariness of his Zaïan partisans, together with fresh intelligence that came in regarding the actual number of resistance fighters, prompted General De Loustal to do a rethink.

Leaving the scene of operations, he traveled to Rabat for a conference with the *Résident-Général* and the Commander-in-Chief, General Huré. The Zaïan partisans would be reinforced by 900 fresh recruits from Khenifra. Tactically speaking, to reduce the number of casualties, laborious attempts to assault successive ridges from south to north would be abandoned and the emphasis placed on west-to-east advances along valley floors so as to subject the defenders to enfilading fire. Operations would resume on September 5.

Meanwhile, the besieging forces tightened their grip on Tazizaout. All day long, droning biplanes dropped bombs where it hurt most, while big guns thundered from the surrounding heights. Resistance fighters also began to feel the pinch of hunger. Meat there was aplenty, for sure, as each day brought its toll of slaughtered livestock; flour, however, was in short supply leading to a dearth of bread as the Berbers had had no time to harvest their fields. People often ate grass or locusts.[15] Even at night there was no let-up. Under cover of darkness, women bearing goatskins would bravely head down the Ashlou ravine towards Asif n-Ougheddou to fetch water. But this was fraught with danger as, on the opposite bank, the French had set up machine-gun emplacements specially sited to deal with such nocturnal activities.[16] In the dark they would open fire at random. On one occasion the mother of one of this writer's informants was thus wounded.[17] Next morning, in the stream, "there would be blood mingled with water," as some veterans recall.[18]

On September 4, finally heeding Sidi Lmekki's calls for help, a large Ayt Hadiddou force had attempted to storm French positions on the Lakes Plateau, only to be dispersed by Amharoq's Zaïan cavalry. One group of ten resistance fighters, holed up in a cave, was exterminated with hand grenades.[19] On September 6 a similar attack mounted by the Ayt Sokhmane on Jbel Imghal also came to nothing.

Meanwhile, on September 5, the decisive phase had got under way. Tadla region troops that had gathered under cover of darkness attacked from the west and occupied both the heights of Alegmou and the western end of the Takoushtamt ridge with minimal losses. Meanwhile, the Meknes region forces encountered gradually stiffening resistance on the Tazizaout ridge and took a dozen casualties. There ensued a twenty-four-hour lull, during which two notables were sent by Sidi Lmekki to negotiate a truce. The French refused to comply but specified that any tent or group that raised the white flag would not be fired upon. On the Tadla region front, operations resumed with a vengeance early in the morning of September 7. A large force of partisans, Goums, and a *groupe franc* from a *Tirailleur* regiment occupied the ridge southeast of Tazra hamlet, Amalou n-Tezra (*crête no 2* to the French). This placed them in a commanding position in relation to the main dissident encampments on the left bank of Aqqa n-Zebzbat. The French position is thus summed up by Guillaume:

> We had hitherto entertained hopes that a peaceful solution would be found allowing us to spare both the lives and belongings of our adversaries. Given their attitude, however, we now felt compelled to pursue operations with the utmost energy.[20]

Battle for "Cedar Pinnacle"

Level with Tazizaout's final peak to the west, from which it is separated by a shallow saddle, lies one of a succession of northerly outliers covered in a tangle of green oak and cedar. This *Piton des cèdres* ("Cedar Pinnacle") was seen as having some tactical importance, for which reason, on September 6–7, around midnight, it was occupied by about 200 *Ibertiza* backed by a company of Moroccan *Tirailleurs*. Almost at once the resistance fighters, past masters at nocturnal infiltration, mounted a successful counter-thrust and threw the enemy back on his starting line, capturing two FM 24 light machine guns and some ammunition in the process.[21]

Emboldened by their success, the dissidents launched a series of counter-attacks on Legion positions along the main ridge. A young lieutenant serving with the Moroccan *Tirailleurs* has left us a vivid description of this desperate scrimmage:

> Up there, tragic events were unfolding. For more than three hours, the Foreign Legion had been battling it out on the ridges of Jbel Tazizaout . . . Totally fanaticized, four times in three hours, die-hard Berbers had made desperate charges dagger in hand. Squalidly dishevelled, almost naked under their jellabas, wielding wicked-looking knives fit for slaughtering sheep, they had savagely assaulted the Legionaires and *Tirailleurs*. Behind them, from precarious shelters on "Cedar Pinnacle", elderly men and women urged them on with barbaric songs, at once religious and warlike, obscene and frightful. Small wonder that, around one in the morning, the partisans had lost their nerve, as if cursed by Allah himself.[22]

By the end of the morning the French put words into deeds and descended on those of Sidi Lmekki's encampments that were situated near Tizi n-Mesfergh. One after another, each strong-point was invested and cleaned out with hand grenades. In the words of one resistance veteran, "They plied us with grenades as if they were throwing cedar cones at us!"[23] The Tazizaout fighters now suffered their worst losses so far: several hundred dead, 300 captured, not to mention 5,000 head of cattle lost. Meanwhile, the Meknes region troops operating along the backbone of Tazizaout were slowing down. The further west they advanced, the more desperate the fighting. No wonder: by approaching the main resistance strong-point under Sidi Lmortada and Sidi Mohand Lmehdi, the knife was getting too close to the bone. During the night of September 6–7 occurred the dramatic episode at *Piton des cèdres*.

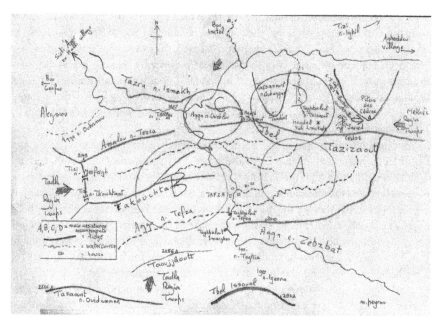

Map 8: Rough sketch map showing Berber encampments at the western end of Tazizaout ridge.

Fig. 46: Sidi Lmortada's grave on the left; Cedar Pinnacle, Tazizaout.

It is difficult to establish what use the resistance made of the captured automatic weapons. Guillaume specifies that the LMGs were handed back on September 13 when the main body of Sidi Lmekki's men surrendered. However, one resistance fighter, Hmad ou-Haqqar by name, won considerable renown by making expert use of a machine gun (*lemteryuz*) until the final surrender.[24] At any rate, this heroic individual (hailing, so it seems, from the Ishqern tribe) is described as having joined the Tazizaout defenders because his livestock in the Moulouya Valley had twice been confiscated by French-backed partisans.[25]

Throughout September 7, the Berbers continued counter-attacking Legion and Goum units. Naturally, biplanes flew close support missions, dropping bombs, and it is doubtless at this time that the Tazizaout resistance lost its two most able leaders, both of them brothers to Sidi Lmekki. Sidi Lmortada, whose decorated, cedar-wood coffin is visible today to pilgrims on the northwest flank of Cedar Pinnacle, is said to have been killed by a bomb, together with his wife and children. His brother, Sidi Mohand Lmehdi, enjoyed an unparalleled reputation for bravery; all oral accounts agree on this point. In fact, it was said of him that he would fire his rifle till it was too hot to hold, then ask for a replacement to be handed to him so that he could continue the fight.[26] At this time, he had established his command-post at the foot of a prominent, stately cedar on the Tazizaout ridge, a few hundred yards west of the final peak. His kith and kin remonstrated with him, saying:

> "Do not pitch your tent here. You are visible to the enemy on the south side and could catch a machine-gun bullet; this is a dangerous spot!" To which he replied: "I shall face up to the roumis till I die!" Despite his objections they finally persuaded him to descend, slightly to the north, to a safer place. And that was where he was hit by shrapnel from a bomb! [27]

The inevitability of fate! Another account tells of how a friend dragged him home by the heels. Actually, the wound was fatal and Sidi Mohand passed away a few days later.[28] This period of aerial and artillery bombardment has left a terrible trauma on some veterans' minds, that has still not gone away. One individual, Abraray, became literally demented after his mother was blown to pieces before his eyes and her head left stuck high up a tree. He knew no peace till he had painstakingly gathered all parts of her body and given them a decent burial. He then went on to perform the same functions each time one of his companions was killed. One grimly humorous little fantasy throws strange light on the memory patterns of some of these veterans: an individual was decapitated by a shell fired from Bou Genfou; whereupon the headless corpse ran after the head, shouting, "Give back my head at once!"[29]

On the morning of September 8, negotiations were opened in a fresh effort to encourage the Ayt Sokhman encampments on the left bank of Aqqa n-Zebzbat to surrender. Sidi Lmekki, however, took advantage of this lull to retire to Tafza, a large group of dissidents following suite. *Tirailleurs*, Goums and partisans followed, cleaning up further strong-points, at the cost of thirteen killed and thirty-three wounded, and eventually reaching Aqqa n-Zebzbat.[30] Later in the day, so it appears from oral sources, Sidi Lmekki made good his escape from Tafza to a secure hideout in Aqqa n-Oushlou.[31]

"The enemy came and dislodged us from our fox-holes"

Up on the main Tazizaout ridge, the Foreign Legion and *Tirailleurs* had to drive back further counter-attacks throughout the day. Fully aware that they had their backs to the wall, Sidi Lmekki's supporters were fighting heroically against ten-to-one odds. If their ammunition gave out they would roll boulders on their assailants; if captured, they would refuse to have their wounds seen to. Such behavior created an unfavorable impression on Moroccans serving as Goums and partisans, recruited from the Zaïan, Beni-Mguild, and Seghroushen. "All the *azaghar* ["plain"] tribes had ganged up on us!"[32] Thus spoke an eyewitness: "Never would your people have won—had it not been for your artillery, machine-guns and planes!"[33] A two-day lull now ensued, while 150 partisans under Captain Parlange from Tounfit prepared to participate in the final clean-up of the encampments situated on the southwest side of Tazizaout.

Operations got under way early on September 11 with an artillery bombardment, after which the Foreign Legion occupied the western end of Tazizaout. By 08:00 they had achieved their objectives, while a large detachment of Zaïan horsemen under Amharoq followed Aqqa n-Zebzbat north to Tazra, thus cutting off dissident elements in Aqqa n-Oushlou from their water supply. This cavalry charge left a lasting impression on resistance fighters watching from their foxholes, veterans still recalling horsemen in such numbers that *da tsentall tafuyt* ("they obscured the sun").[34] Starving, surrounded, and outgunned, resistance fighters had little stomach left to fight on into the afternoon, when emissaries were sent to the French to negotiate a ceasefire. It was arranged that Sidi Lmekki would meet *qayd* Amharoq of the Zaïan on September 12, pending his official surrender the following day. One veteran stated:

> Forty days did we resist on Tazizaout. On the fortieth day, after heavy artillery bombardment, the enemy came and dislodged us from our *ixba* ["fox-holes"]. We had to surrender and give up our arms. But before that we had given a good account of ourselves. We had captured some machine-guns, munitions and mortars from the enemy. The dead lay everywhere—we even had to step over their corpses. During the last twenty nights we never dared show a light.[35]

In the words of an Ayt Sokhman bard:

> Tazizaout was the place by our saintly leaders appointed.
> Hiding in caves the *mujahidin*'s undoing did prove,
> Hunger more lethal than bullets vanquished famished fighters!
> In holes you did hide, O defenders of Tazizaout!
> O Lord! Those caves ultimately became your graves;
> Perished so many good men, carrion for ravenous jackals![36]

Tazizaout: The morning after

Finally, on September 13, Sidi Lmekki surrendered with most of his followers.[37] It would appear, however, that Sidi Lmekki's official surrender did not spell a total termination of hostilities. Even the act of capitulation itself did not reflect a consensus. During one heated debate a few days earlier, an Ayt Hadiddou chief had openly threatened Sidi Lmekki, saying, "If you give in, Bakki, I shall disembowel you!"[38] Actually, that chief was a diehard to his fingertips. Anxious to continue the fight, he later managed to break out with some fellow trisbesmen through the encircling French forces towards Ayt Hadiddou country, "because the people there were still God-fearing Muslims."[39]

Most of these irreconcilables eventually made their way south to Hamdoun, a mountain northeast of Tinghir where the resistance later made a resolute stand. There is also evidence pointing to continued mopping-up operations around Tazizaout itself, lasting for something like a week. One account specifies that troops had "to flush those savage Berber fighters and their families from their holes. For an entire week, protected by nearby outposts of regular troops, our partisans searched one position after another and did great execution among the defenders."[40] This is confirmed by a resistance veteran who claims that "we held out another week till they forced their way in and captured us."[41] Sergeant Major Marcireau of the Goums also claims that operations lasted until September 22.[42]

About this time, in the fields near Tazra hamlet, opposite Aqqa n-Oushlou, Berber wives and widows lined up for an *ahidus n-wiyyah* ("mourning dance"), scratching their cheeks and chanting, "O men-folk! Why did you have to surrender?"[43] Thus yet another saint's *baraka* had proved ineffectual. Fittingly, many were the sarcastic songs coined at his expense, the more so as the French appointed Sidi Lmekki *qayd* over the Ayt Sokhman. This was adding insult to injury as far as his former parishioners were concerned. Here are some snatches of song typical of the time:

> Thus spoke Sidi Lmekki: "By God's grace, let us feast and rejoice,
> Did dream that they had appointed me *qayd* of the *ayt bujur*!"

> Could I but shove Sidi Lmekki's head into a boxwood thicket
> Would make him smell camel carcasses, to remind him of all
> Those wretches who with him vainly camped in the hills!

> All that the Ayt Sidi 'Ali said turned out to be pure lies,
> Henceforth can only trust in the French officer's word![44]

The Tazizaout defenders, however, have not been forgotten. The slopes of this mountain have become hallowed ground. Every year Sidi Lmekki's grandson, Sidi Hmad, accompanied by the faithful, journeys to the sacred Tazizaout cedar to commemorate the sacrifice of their illustrious forbears. A full corpus of oral literature, ranging from little snatches of verse to full, ballad-length efforts (*timdyazin*), exists to this day, thus enshrining the exploits of yesteryear. Typical of these poems is the following:

> In my mind will you long remain, O Tazizaout, as a war
> In which with rifle-fire the Roumi destroyed the Prophet.
> Brothers Lmehdi and Lmortada were like unto little

Lambs that die from a surfeit of thyme in the enclosure.
Forgive He who ploughed land, differentiates from fallow,
Who created the suns and stars; the whole world grieves,
O you who forgiveness promised if the oath we swore!
To Tazra did make my way and reached it feeling footsore,
A cave I there did dig, entered it and slept for evermore![45]

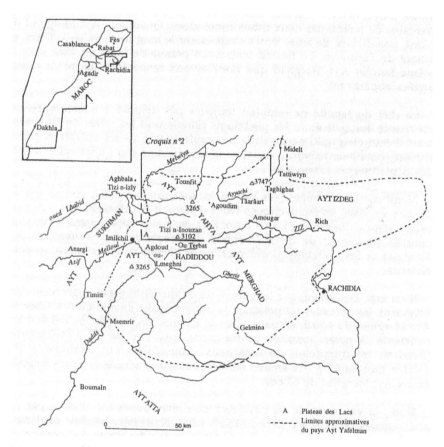

Map 9: Ayt Yafelman country, Eastern High Atlas, corresponding to the area still holding out (1933).

Atlas Endgame: The Closing Stages (1933–4)

Ayt 'Atta win immortal fame in Saghro battle

Among all the areas of southeast Morocco, Jbel Saghro was ideally suited for a showdown of this kind. Waterless pre-Saharan valleys climb gradually to the 2,700 m cliffs of Amalou n-Mansour overlooking the *qsur* of Iknioun. Wherever the eye can see, stretches broken, snake- and scorpion-infested terrain, scree slides and slopes studded with tufts of esparto grass and stunted juniper. The shimmering, furnace-like heat of summer alternates with freezing cold winter mornings when ice gleams in northward-facing gullies. This, with a vengeance, is a land of thirst, an environment fit for the camel and the nomad, these the ungrateful wastes the Ayt 'Atta called home.

In the very heart of this hostile habitat, in the Imsaden hollow at the foot of the precipitous Bougafer rock spires (*Aiguilles*), some 2,000 tried and trusted warriors had gathered, determined to sell their lives dearly.[1] They comprised the dregs and the flower of the resistance: besides the usual hotchpotch of professional bandits, cut-throats, and deserters, stood genuine patriots from Ayt Hammou and Ayt Khebbash who had been fighting the French for years: some of their Ayt Hadiddou neighbors, together with the Ayt Y'azza from the nearby Regg Valley, not to mention a famous 'Atta clan, the Ilemshan, who were to provide this warlike gathering with a worthy chief. 'Assou ou Ba Slam was a seasoned fifty-year-old, "a man with a handsome, serious face, a lithe and muscular body, impassive and apparently indifferent, but whose proud dignity inspired confidence."[2] A British observer who met him about this time concurs, up to a point: "A person of much dignity, but with something crafty about him, amounting to a warning that he must be watched …"[3] This was the man who had managed to mould a heterogeneous rabble into a coherent fighting force. He remained at daggers drawn with his colleague, Mouhadash, chiefly because the latter had tamely submitted to the French at an early stage of *Pacification*.

In a typical episode, the French bombed an Ilemshan *qsar* after some raiders had made nuisances of themselves. Later, the authorities wrote in explanation, very pedagogically, that the bombardment had merely been a form of punishment, causing the proud Berber to exclaim, "Let the person who wrote this letter come here and fetch the reply!"[4]

Throughout the winter of 1932–3 the raiders made periodic sorties from their inviolable sanctuaries to work the trade routes in the Ferkla and Tafilalt areas. Their prey would be lightly-escorted convoys or small military detachments that failed to detect their presence in time. Whenever an anti-raider patrol set off in pursuit, the raiders' trail would invariably head towards the inhospitable fastnesses of the Saghro. No wonder the French decided the time had come to eradicate this "nest of pirates."

Around mid-January 1933, preparations got underway as Marrakesh and Algero–Morocco Border troops invested the massif. At this point, however, French staff officers at HQ made a grave miscalculation. Going on the scanty information contained in imperfect 1/200,000 and 1/100,000 maps, they anticipated a carefully executed, methodical campaign that failed to allow for the arduous nature of the terrain. By unleashing swarms of partisans, buttressed by a few companies of the Foreign Legion, they confidently expected to conquer the Saghro with minimum casualties, just as they had done at Tazizaout.[5]

An initial series of onslaughts launched by El-Glaoui's partisans on February 12, on the western periphery of the massif, were easily repulsed. Although General Huré came to Boumaln to take personal command of the operations, the closer the French got to the Imsaden hollow, the tougher the resistance. Well protected behind their low, stone parapets, the Ayt 'Atta were in a tactically sound defensive posture; to counter incoming bombs or artillery rounds they would hide in adjacent caves. Meanwhile, their womenfolk were constantly at hand to reload their rifles or, come nightfall, to fetch water from the closest spring. They knew there was nowhere to retreat to. Their *qsur* bombed and gutted, the people from the Regg Valley, from Nkob, and Ayt Flilou crouched behind the rocks like cornered wild beasts. Feeling the pangs of hunger, shivering in their woollen cloaks, they gathered round smoky fires made from prickly hassocks, and kept thirst at bay with glasses of herb tea.

For a whole week, Bournazel attempted in vain to urge his partisans up those steep slopes, ceaselessly raked by murderously accurate fire. On February 28, in cold, windy, and sleety weather, he made a final, tragic attempt to storm the heights. Mortally wounded almost at once, he lived long enough to see his Brans partisans in full retreat around him. Bitter was his death, though the episode was subsequently glorified for the purpose of colonial-period mythology.

Anxious to avoid further losses, the French settled down to starve the Ayt 'Atta into submission. No more attempted assaults; instead, a regular pounding by artillery and planes, rendered even more intolerable by cold, thirst, and hunger. Thus, three weeks after Bournazel's death, despite their wives' scornful attitude at the mere mention of surrender, the resistance fighters finally agreed to bring the forty-two-day siege to a close. Such had been their valor, however, not to mention the losses inflicted on the enemy, that 'Assou ou Ba Slam was able to obtain fairly favorable terms: firm undertakings that the Ayt 'Atta would not be submitted to Glaoui rule; guarantees that their women would not be forced to dance in the presence of Christian visitors; that their customs would be respected; that their rifles would eventually be handed back to them.[6]

Closing moves of the Atlas campaign

As the campaigning season opened in the early spring of 1933, the frontiers of the last dissident area of the Great Atlas were clearly defined: the Asif Melloul Valley to the north, Jbel Kousser and the Ayt 'Abdi plateau to the west, the heights opposite Tirghist to the northeast, the Amdghous Valley, Jbel Baddou, Jbel Hamdoun, and Aghbalou n-Kerdous to the southeast. Through their informants, the French political officers knew there were some 1,000 breech-loaders available among the Ayt Iseha, Ayt 'Abdi, Ayt Wanergui, and Ayt Sokhman refugees, with another 2,500 still serviceable weapons among the Ayt Merghad and Ayt Hadiddou. The last-named had displayed a somewhat ambiguous attitude up till now. After opposing token resistance to the French occupation of Imilshil, they appeared chiefly concerned with concealing family, goods, and chattels in some forgotten, hilltop refuge. Staunch believers in the *baraka* of the Tilmi *sharif*, Ou-Sidi, they were also confident that the rugged nature of their mountainous homeland was defense enough.[7]

Ayt Hadiddou tribesmen were destined to start the final round of fighting with a signal victory—only a local one, for sure—but a sensational reminder of their fighting potential all the same. As regards the May Day 1933 Mesdrid battle, which took place on the eastern edge of the Lakes Plateau, I was fortunate to get the inside story from an eyewitness, a former NCO in the Goums.[8] The previous August a fresh outpost had been set up on Jbel Issoual, above Tirghist. In the words of Guillaume:

> To guarantee the security of the road gangs working on the *piste* between Anefgou and Tikhedouin, it was necessary to occupy Tizi n-Issoual and Jbel Msedrid. This was done on May 1st, but, recovering from their surprise, the dissidents took advantage of the mist to counter-attack the troops and throw them back in disorder.[9]

This laconic communiqué obviously conceals some unpleasant truths; Voinot's ten-line account is more forthcoming and admits that the Foreign Legion were involved.[10] Everything becomes clear if one recalls the date, May 1—the day after Camerone Day (April 30)—when every Legionnaire worth his salt is blind drunk to commemorate a past heroic deed in the Mexican War of the 1860s. Thus did a detachment of men still very much in their cups have to leave Tirghist fort and haul themselves 500 m up uncompromisingly barren slopes towards cloud-capped ridges, there to establish a couple of defensive outworks. Informed by his scouts that the enemy was operating in poor visibility up on Msedrid, Ou-Sidi realized the tactical advantage that this gave him and ascended from Tilmi with about 450 warriors.

These were all experienced fighters, the same ones who, on August 12, 1932, had successfully confronted Captain Parlange's Goum at Tikhedouin. Taking advantage of the mist, they easily invested the Msedrid outpost. In the words of an onlooker:

> The Ayt Hadiddou stormed the position. Each time the Legionaries threw a hand-grenade the Berbers would throw it back at them, finally putting the entire detachment out of action. Once the Legionaries were defeated Tirhgist outpost came under heavy fire and this lasted till nightfall.[11]

Hand-to-hand fighting ensued, one grenade, hurled back by a resistance fighter named Zerban, causing numerous casualties among the defenders, who fled downhill.

Eventually, and despite support from some Goum units, the Tizi n-Issoual outposts had to be abandoned, as numerous Berbers rallied to the sound of gunfire from all points of the compass. It was a nasty little setback, proving yet again that Berber mountaineers were valiant foemen, quick to exploit any weakness.[12] However, it was to prove to be their last success. "Afterwards," explained the former *goumier* NCO, "we crushed them. And I can tell you, we did it good and proper. We used overwhelming force [*On a mis lepaquet*]!"[13]

Indeed, elsewhere on the Atlas front that spring, preliminary operations had gone favorably for the French. By May 17, the residual Ayt Iseha salient in the southwest had been absorbed during a daring nocturnal raid by Goums that had witnessed the capture of a huge sheer-sided hill, Aghembo n-Mestfran, called *la Grande Cathédrale* by the French, where a select band of resistance fighters had chosen to take a stand.[14]

Msedrid paved the way for the last battles of the Atlas campaign. Holed up in their final pocket on the map, 120 kilometers long and 80 kilometers broad, galvanized by leaders such as Sidi 'Ali ou Hsseyn, Zaïd ou-Skounti, Ou-Sidi, and 'Ali Ou-Termoun, the hillmen confidently awaited the denouement of their long-drawn-out campaign with the *irumin*.

Chief among these were the Ayt Hadiddou. Access to their high country was never really simple. From the north, after arriving at Tassent beneath Bab n-Ouayyad escarpment, you could follow the stream south through the Aqqa n-Tassent gorge, dominated in the west by the lofty hill of Ijberten. This was excessively rugged terrain, like the jagged Tintorfa ridge; each one of the few cols was held by a small group of watchful, trigger-happy warriors. And yet the French had taken Ijberten by surprise in a midnight assault, exploiting their advantage by advancing to the edge of the Asif Melloul Valley where they had set up two outposts. The Ayt Hadiddou had withdrawn to Tissekt n-Temda and the heights opposite, while the Asif n-Tilmi Valley, with its expert fighters under Ou-Sidi, was still theirs. Meanwhile, French troops from four different military regions were converging on the *dernière tache* ("final stain") on the Great Atlas map, which they were planning to cut up into smaller zones, the better to stifle final acts of resistance.

The resultant 1933 High Atlas campaign was, in many ways, different from its predecessors. Where conditions were suitable, light tanks and armored cars were deployed. Overhead, biplanes buzzed ceaselessly. Artillery and heavy machine guns bombarded mud-brick castles and miserable mule trains bearing Berber belongings to remote points of refuge. Up till then, the confrontation had been a relatively chivalrous one, with the Atlas fighter retaining a sporting chance of success. Not so any more. France was up against the last square of diehards, the last pockets of resistance, and there was a noticeable change of mood. Many of these mountain stalwarts had shortly before inflicted some ignominious reverses on the French, introducing an element of revenge into the process. Accordingly, there was actually little humanitarian action during these final operations, for all General Huré has to say on the issue.[15] Whenever the Berbers turned on their tormentors, the resultant firefights would be desperate and unforgiving. But before the 1933 campaign got under way, the Ayt Hadiddou suffered a grievous body blow.

As he was reconnoitering the French positions before Tizi n-Inouzan on the morning of July 8, Ou-Sidi himself was killed by an enemy patrol. Although Sidi Taïb

Fig. 47: Ou Terbat and other Ayt Hadiddou villages east-southeast of Imilshil, aerial photo, *c.* 1932 (Ralph De Butler archive).

Fig. 48: Jbel Hamdoun dominates the hamlet of Itto Fezzou.

immediately took over, he lacked his brother's forceful leadership qualities and the Ayt Hadiddou commenced the final operations under a grave handicap. That same day they launched countless counter-attacks on Tizi n-Oughroum and Tissekt n–Temda, all to no avail. Within a few days they had been dislodged from the Azaghar Irs plateau, Tilmi, and Agoudal by use of superior force, including armor, and obliged to go to ground in a jumble of arid canyons between the Imdghas Valley and Jbel Hamdoun.

Later in the month large contingents of partisans, including many under Ayt Izdeg leader 'Addi ou-Bihi, sent to flush them out, suffered heavily in the upper Imedghas sector.[16] Having managed to escape southeast, most of the Ayt Hadiddou had found refuge in the hilly Kerdous–Hamdoun–Baddou triangle. Their capacity for resistance in no way diminished, they staged a brilliant counter-attack on August 5 at Tizi n-Hamdoun, inflicting heavy losses on the Foreign Legion.

A veteran *goumier* recalls how, in this battle above Itto Fezzou, his platoon faced off a determined assault by resistance fighters, attacking in a thunderstorm, and how the fighting continued till nightfall, after which they bivouacked on the spot, Lebel rifles at the ready.

After an uneasy night came daybreak and the revelation that their adversaries had withdrawn.[17] The same day, in further fierce fighting, another French detachment lost forty-four men as it completed an encircling movement from the Ghriss Valley.[18] The next day witnessed a desperate battle at Talat n-Irshi that left another thirty dead in the French ranks.[19] Aghbalou n-Kerdous and its strategic source was the site of the penultimate battle in the area. This was a remarkable fight (August 9–11), in the course of which about 8,000 people including Ayt Hadiddou, Ayt Merghad, refugees from

Fig. 49: North side of Jbel Baddou, seen from the stone parapets of the former *Tirailleurs'* camp.

Tazizaout, the Middle Atlas, and Tadla regions, under Sidi Taïbi and ʿAli ou Termoun, resisted desperately for two days from a network of caves and *qsur*, using hand grenades and light machine guns. They managed to kill fifty of their assailants and wound 170, until they had spent all their ammunition. Their efforts eventually proved vain in the face of overflying aircraft and Goums supported by Renault tanks boulder-hopping along the dry riverbed.[20]

Afterwards, events moved swiftly for the handful of diehards still holding out in the hills. By August 14, Jbel Baddou had finally been surrounded and cut off. That vaunted citadel, towering above Asoul, so impressed the onlooker that few partisans were bold enough to approach what they perceived as the last stronghold of the independent *amghar* Ou-Skounti.

Baddou battle

In fact, Ou-Skounti's own legend was growing. He had become head of the resistance since Ou-Sidi's death. Now, with about 100 families and some 250 Ayt ʿIsa Izem warriors, he was hunkering down for the final battle.[21] His ceaseless campaigning, the fact that he had been wounded on two occasions, not to mention the tactical results he had achieved in firefights with the French, had enhanced his aura as a ruthlessly successful war leader.[22] A British journalist, working for the *Daily Mail*, accompanied French forces laying siege to Baddou, and describes thus the battle scene:

> I looked down a precipice into a deep gorge, the other side of which was formed by the main northern face of Mount Baddou, 700 yards away, falling almost sheer for 2000 feet from the summit. Though the mountain was dotted with the smoke of bursting shells, the only sign of life upon it was a flock of about 600 sheep or goats, accompanied by four tribesmen . . . In a few moments shells were bursting among them, the range presumably being regulated by an aeroplane that was already cruising overhead, and very quickly the flock and its shepherds had disappeared into some invisible ravine . . . Only when I flew over Mount Baddou in an aeroplane some days later did I realise that, though its sides were precipitous, its summit consisted of a tableland a mile long and several hundred yards broad.[23]

Although Baddou was subjected to daily bombardment, resistance stalwarts were still full of fight. A few days before the end they actually stormed down the mountainside to ambush a supply convoy. On two other occasions, planes making strafing runs at flocks of sheep met heavy ground fire and had to make crash landings. By the morning of August 26, however, the sands were running out. Tazibout, a talented and influential lady, had finally rallied the French, while Ou-Skounti launched a last vain attack on unconventional swashbuckler Lieutenant Pillafort who, with his partisans, had just scaled Ouksersou, the crowning peak of Baddou.[24] Ward Price had interviewed this young officer:

> I asked young Lieutenant Pïllafort, of the *Chasseurs d'Afrique*: "But how do you give them orders if you can't speak their language?" . . . "Well, I begin by patting

them on the back and laughing. Then I point to a ridge I want them to occupy, and generally they smile too, and go off just to oblige me. If they don't, then I give them a good welt with my stick and that does the trick."[25]

That same afternoon, Ou-Skounti, after a final, vain attempt to escape through the encircling French forces, surrendered to General Giraud.[26] Here is a Berber version:

> Baddou is a mountain in the region of Aghbalou n-Kerdous near Sidi Bou Ya'qoub. The French army was superior militarily and the tribes had old weapons like *buhaba, bushfer, sassbu, lklata*, and *al 'asharia*. The French army was led by captain *gita* and lieutenant *badi*. Who came from Goulmima. Their armies came up together and made up approximately one battalion whereas the tribal fighters were all volunteers. Their leaders were Ou-Skounti from the tribe of 'Isa Izem, Ou-Brouz and Ou-Khnouch from the tribe of Ayt Merghad, Hrou Ou-Hana, the leader of Imlilshil and Outerbat, and the leader Tamnousht. The battle lasted nearly a month or a month and a half, day and night. In the end the French army won, but captain *gita* was killed in battle. Afterwards, the French imposed their authority.[27]

This account makes nonsense of chronology and telescopes various events into one, which is typical of oral tradition, mistakenly granting *jida/gita* (Guyetand) prominence in the Baddou battle, whereas he had been killed several months earlier. As for *badi* (Badie), he was chiefly concerned in fighting along Oued Ifegh and is not mentioned as having figured prominently in the Baddou battle. The account also gives a fairly detailed picture of the contemporary Berber armory. During the subsequent official surrender ceremony the resistance fighters must have been puzzled not to have been shot out of hand as they handed in their weapons and returned to their villages. What did the French authorities expect of the Berbers? Why were they lenient after such merciless battles? Eventually, some of them would actually retrieve their rifles if they joined the Goums.

Some of the tribesmen seemed reluctant at the last moment to part with the weapons upon which their self-defense and social prestige depended. They fumbled with them reluctantly, but the blue-coated mokhazenis snatched them from their hands and threw them on to the ever-growing pile. No war reparations or cession of territory ever hurt a defeated nation more than this surrender of their rifles distressed and humiliated the Berbers, but their natural dignity restrained them from allowing their resentment to appear.[28]

The fight for Baddou (*ti n-baddu*), marking as it did the end of warfare in southeast Morocco, has left almost as traumatic an impression on the local inhabitants as Tazizaout. Here are some couplets that convey the sufferings endured by the combatants:

> Baddou was reluctant with water to supply us,
> To see us go thirsty the very stones laughed!

Let us eat the grind-stone, let us eat grass if we must,
Or lick the earth rather than bow down to the roumi!
Had I known what lay in store for me, / Never would
Have accepted to be dragged into the Baddou affair![29]

The Baddou defenders who flouted authority were forced to submit.
Likewise do I feel humiliated when before your husband I grovel![30]

However, the fact that things were organized, the markets regularly supplied, the needy provided for, and the wounded tended for must have aroused some confidence in the newcomers' intentions. Especially those who experienced Captain Paulin's (*bula*) firm but just rule in the Tinghir area. Even if it was no longer feasible to raid the gardens of the Ferkla *qsur* dwellers, or to avenge one's honor by murdering one's neighbor, the general peace and quiet that prevailed was hardly a negative thing. Operations in the area were brought to a close on August 26–27, when, after a brief skirmish, Goums and partisans rounded up a small band of irreconcilables in the Jbel Youb area, north of Baddou.[31]

Last stand on Jbel Kousser

At the end of July 1933, demoralized by news from Ayt Hadiddou country, the Ayt 'Abdi n-Kousser were seriously contemplating surrender. Feelers were put out in the direction of the Azilal outpost by the Zaouit Ahansal saints, Sidi Mah el-Hansali fulfilling the role of honest broker. Whereas half of the Ayt Wanergui tribe were under his direct influence, the other half remained faithful to Sidi 'Ali ou Hsseyn. Early in August various Ayt 'Abdi and Ayt Haddiddou groups were caught in a pincer movement by the enemy on the Ayt 'Abdi plateau and forced to capitulate. By the middle of the month most of the surviving refractory individuals had made for the rugged fastnesses of Jbel Kousser. From the northern side the Goums were also closing in under Captain Boyer de Latour (*muha w latur*), as the dissidents, some equipped with hand grenades, grappled with them among cliff-side oaks and pines overlooking Asif n-Oukhashan.

On the last day of August the Ayt Bindeq and Ayt Wanergui threw in the sponge, while Sidi 'Ali ou Hsseyn, followed by about a hundred families, clambered up onto Jbel Kousser to make his last stand. Five hundred tribesmen armed with breech-loaders, concealed in caverns, or hiding behind thick boxwood bushes in exceedingly broken terrain surrounding Asif Temga, amply supplied with water, were a daunting proposition. By rights, they should have put up a long, determined resistance.

The all-encircling dragnet, however, was closing in. On September 3, 1933, the last Ayt Iseha diehards holding Jbel Lqroun were rudely dislodged from their lofty eyrie by *muha w latur* and his Goums, while a full battalion invested Aghembo n-Shinzer. The seizure of these twin 3,000-meter peaks overlooking their final refuge and symbolically representing the "gates of heaven" (*imawn n igenwan*),[32] against which the *irumin* assault should have failed dismally, threw the dissidents' defensive strategy into total disarray.

Their frantic attempts to retrieve those strategic heights all failed in the face of remorseless machine-gun fire, and in doing so provided a fitting conclusion to a thirty-year epic. Surrender, however, now remained the only option; on September 5, the last marabouts from the Temga zaouia negotiated their return into the *makhzan* fold.[33]

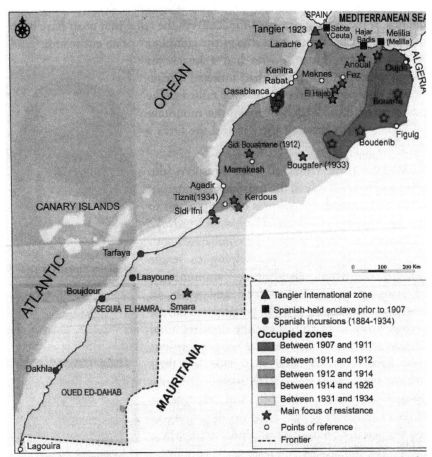

Adapted from - *Au Maroc, la paix française, Renseignements Coloniaux*, Publication du Comité de
l'Afrique française et Comité du Maroc, Paris, 1936.
- *La résistance marocaine contre la colonisation (1904-1955)*, (in Arabic), Conferenc
proceedings, published by the Faculty of Letters, Agadir, 1997.

Map 10: Stage-by-stage conquest and main resistance areas, 1907–34 (M. Kably, *History of Morocco*, 2015; RIRHM, Rabat).

Pacification Aftermath

Last shots in "Morocco's Thirty Years' War"

After that, peace and quiet gradually returned to southeast Morocco, with one exception: the solitary *jihad* waged by Zaïd ou-Hmad, an obdurate Ou-Merghad from the Todgha area. After the final surrenders, this lone wolf, who had previously earned himself a reputation for raiding and gunrunning, was ruined, his property confiscated, his wife killed. Descending to the role of mere highwayman and murderer, he took to waylaying French officers in the expectation that they might be carrying cash. At times single-handed, at times with one or two companions, he carried out several attacks between Tinjdad and Imilshil; on another occasion he performed a night-time harassment of a camp occupied by Paulin and his partisans. His greatest exploit: a raid into Tinghir on New Year's Eve, 1935, when four Legionaries, celebrating in a café, were downed in a hail of bullets.

Time was against Zaïd ou-Hmad, however. The land was now criss-crossed by telegraph wires, patrols were out after him, his closest associates captured, and his secrets betrayed under interrogation. It was only a matter of time before they captured him. Finally, came a tip-off. The *qsar* of Tadafelt on the Todgha was where the trail led one morning in March 1936. Zaïd ou-Hmad and his small band were gunned down mercilessly by a Foreign Legion detachment. Thus disappeared an individual with a controversial reputation; bandit to some, last-ditch resistance fighter and *amazigh iburz* ("true Berber") to others.[1]

Down in the southwest corner of Morocco, however, one final campaign remained to be fought. Since the 1914–18 war the Anti-Atlas front had been relatively calm. At first, El-Hiba, the "Blue Sultan," in whose name prayers continued to be said in local mosques, had continued the fight from Kerdous, with his brother Merebbi Rebbo taking over after his death. At the time, help from the Kaiser's Germany had served to buttress resistance against a French-imposed *makhzan*. In 1917 the Ayt Ba 'Amran had successfully lured a well-armed *harka* under Haïda ou Mouiz, pasha of Taroudannt, into an ambush and killed him.[2]

After which, apart from a limited punitive expedition under General Lamothe, a minimal French presence had been maintained in Tiznit around Captain Justinard (locally known as *qebtan shluh*, and a famous Berberist in his own right), backed by the tribal levies of his friend *qayd* Si Taïb El-Goundafi. Throughout the 1920s the Anti-Atlas tribes had been neutralized through political means, every effort being made to allow Berbers from that area to find jobs in France and send home their pay in the shape of money orders—an arrangement that survives down to the present day. By 1933, resistance in the area centered on a still defiant Merebbi Rebbo in Kerdous, the Ayt Ba ʿAmran of the nearby Spanish Ifni enclave, and a few scattered encampments of surviving Ayt Khebbash and Ayt Hammou nomads, recent arrivals from Tafilalt.

There was still plenty of fight left in the latter as was proved on September 17, 1933, when Ayt Hammou raiders attacked a French convoy at Foum Taouerda, near Jbel Bani, and inflicted stiff casualties on a defending force of Goums.[3] Final operations were launched in February/March of 1934. It took a week's fighting, including a short, sharp firefight at Tizi, to break the Ayt Ba ʿAmran.[4] Then, near the mouth of Oued Draʿa, a rapid advance by motorized forces obtained the neutralization of some guerrilla bands that had been in the field for twenty years or more. Among those that surrendered were Belqasm Ngadi, the former pretender of Tafilalt, and Miʾami oul-Tfassiyt, one of Moha ou Hammou's sons who had fled from the Middle Atlas rather than face justice after murdering a French political officer. Defiant to the last, Miʾami managed to escape custody and found refuge in Rio de Oro with Merebbi Rebbo.[5]

First years of peace

As one of the last colonial conflicts, "Morocco's Thirty Years' War" was generally carried out in a gentlemanly manner. Although actual chivalry was rarely present, there was little of the gratuitous violence and abuse that usually accompanies such campaigns. With few exceptions, systematic torture of suspects and summary executions were unknown. On the whole, the French officer felt grudging respect for these dour Berber fighters, themselves admirers of bravery. Once the battle was over, generally decent treatment by the conqueror reaped dividends among those who had recently surrendered.[5]

Many Native Affairs officers were highly appreciated by the tribesmen committed to their care. In retrospect this conflict clearly appears as the high-water mark of French expansion. A bevy of idealistic young French officers were prepared, for the last time, to sacrifice their lives for classic colonial period clichés; some did so with panache.[6] Few, such as De Hautecloque, entertained any heart-searching as to the justice of their mission. These, however, were easy laurels, obtained in asymmetrical warfare against a weakly organized, low-tech adversary, and proved but poor preparation for the challenge of June 1940 that lay just six years down the road.

Considered from the combatant angle, there is little doubt that the average Moroccan Berber fighter easily outperformed his French opponent.[7] Once battle was joined, Berber tactics and mobility were usually unimpeachable, their sense of terrain admirable. Harassing a retreating enemy was undoubtedly their forte, characterized by an innate ability to bring force to bear on a particular point of the firing line.

Notions of overall strategy usually went overboard as soon as concerted action was contemplated. There being no unified command structure among the Atlas Berbers, more often than not their contingents were engaged in piecemeal fashion with detrimental effects on cohesion. Worse still, they were limited to their own resources, apart from the weapons obtained through contraband with the Rif and the Spaniards, and suffered from an ultimately crippling lack of strategic depth. With the possible exception of Rio de Oro, a strip of desert affording precious little in the way of resources, there was no safe haven for them to fall back on; nowhere to retire and recuperate.

Ultimately, the day was decided by blockade, air and artillery bombardment, combined with superior military strength. God has always been on the side of the big battalions, and this conflict proved no exception. Success was guaranteed through massive recourse to the Foreign Legion, to Algerian *Tirailleurs* and *Spahis*, not to mention countless Moroccans fighting as *Chasseurs d'Afrique*, *Tirailleurs*, Goums, and partisans, making this, ultimately, something of a civil war.[8] Seen through Amazigh eyes, it had undoubtedly been a national war against a common enemy, their contribution total and spontaneous. Unfortunately, it was to be willfully downplayed and ignored by the post-independence nationalist discourse—an injustice for which this book purports to make amends.

Set against the broader backcloth of Moroccan history, even if representing *Pacification* as having been conducted nominally on behalf of the *makhzan* and the reigning sultan was visualized as a blatant fiction,[9] France had effectively achieved the reunification of the country, though minus the Spanish zone.[10] Another coincidence lay in the date: 1934. Interestingly, the very year that saw the Ayt Ba 'Amran lay down their arms, concluding the era of classic rural dissidence, witnessed as an almost natural corollary the upsurge of urban nationalist unrest. Not even a dyed-in-the-wool colonialist like Alphonse Juin could help noticing this fact.[11] True, according to official-speak, that was when the nationalist movement kicked in. Developments in the Atlas and southeast Morocco prior to that are conveniently ignored, amounting to a textbook example of historical denial. The role of the Istiqlal and its Fassi supporters alone is lionized in Moroccan historiography, as if there had previously been no resistance worth speaking of.[12]

As for the Atlas campaigns, they were to have incalculable consequences on existing social structures. First, they destroyed a traditional lifestyle that had hitherto successfully stood the test of time. Areas whose inhabitants had been living in seclusion since time immemorial were brutally exposed to outside influences. A network of *pistes* built by Foreign Legion labor gangs reached the innermost recesses of the hills. Trucks arrived, soon followed by traders riding mules and donkeys. Inevitably, in their wake, came preachers, or *ttelba*, from other regions of Morocco, long Islamicized, bringing with them the orthodox faith and Arabic language.

Thus did the state religion impose itself in the Berber heartland where a peculiarly Moroccan Sufi form of Islam had long survived. History abounds with such paradoxes; fifty years after Moulay Hassan I's death, his dream of bringing the Berber tribes into the *makhzan* fold was realized by an alien administration, itself blissfully unaware that it was thus sowing the seeds of its own eviction from Morocco. Even though many Berber warriors would embark on a lengthy honeymoon with their new masters,[13] their feelings of respect, admiration, even friendship, somewhat impaired by France's 1940 defeat, finally disintegrated in the face of Nationalist propaganda of the early 1950s.

There had always been malcontents in former dissident areas. It should not be imagined that all resistance fighters tamely submitted to France in the aftermath of

Pacification. Many of them had deep scars, such as the memory of lost loved ones, that would not go away. Furthermore, despite reassurances by Native Affairs officers that their traditions would be respected, they had difficulty stomaching the loss of liberty that was inflicted upon them. Others, who had taken to the hills after their villages had fallen, discovered on returning that they had been purely and simply despoiled. Their time-serving neighbors, quick to curry favor through rapid surrender, had been authorized by the colonial authorities to take over their property.[14] Likewise, even though law and order was now guaranteed, with regularly functioning weekly markets, schools, and infirmaries, certain constraints, difficult to stomach for semi-nomadic pastoralists long accustomed to a freewheeling way of life, must have been intolerable to some.

Regarding access to natural resources, chiefly woodland, pastureland, and spring, it was no longer a case of first come first served, with eventual arbitration by marabouts. "Right is Might" henceforth played second fiddle to an orderly, regulated way of life. No more inter-clan warfare; any martially inclined Berber could enlist in the Goums or *Tirailleurs.* No more dues to collect from trading caravans crossing their territory; no more cattle-rustling. Distribution of water rights, access to pastures, regulations concerning firewood collection, all was overseen by the Native Affairs officer, or the local forester. It has been established that the Marmousha revolt, on the eve of independence, was sparked by constraints imposed on their seasonal migration to pastures northwest of Bou Iblan.[15] Hence disenchantment that Nationalist (Istiqlal) agents lost no time in exploiting. The same applied to forests, long considered as a communal resource benefiting from total and permanent access. After 1934, Berbers failed to appreciate by what right a foreign administration had suddenly decreed that any unplanted tree was state property.

This created a situation that placed them at loggerheads with the Forestry service, and which has lasted down to the present day. Thus, although appearing obedient and submissive, there were causes aplenty for Berber dissatisfaction and frustration, leading to forms of secondary resistance. No wonder Native Affairs officers were surprised when in the 1950s their faithful parishioners, whom they prided themselves on knowing so well, inexplicably sided with the Nationalists. Some of them were vulnerable to propaganda warning them that the French were planning to separate them from the Moroccan community at large.

The "Berber dahir"

This move was dismissed as divide and rule by the Nationalist bourgeois element, in connection with what eventually became known as the "Berber dahir" of 1930. Actually, this was the last of several decrees brought in to officialize, in a very French and Cartesian manner, supposed social differences between the "Arab" and "Berber" components of the Moroccan population. Basically, the former would continue to answer to Koranic law, or *sharia,* while the Imazighen would be subject to *izerf* ("customary law"). When word reached the glitterati of Fez and other cities they protested at being separated from their Berber brothers, whereas it is common knowledge that they had little common ground with people whom they traditionally regard as backward and uncouth. That Islamic solidarity appeared at stake merely proved a heaven-sent propaganda ploy that the Istiqlal were quick to exploit.[16]

Subsequent scholarship, much of it of the bandwagon-jumping variety, strove hard to establish the fact that in those days Berbers were suffering from the isolation which they suffered under the Protectorate, severing links to the Islamic community, *dar al-islam*.[17] In fact, the *dahir* aimed at respecting both their social framework and their customs. Had not resistance leaders insisted on the retention of customary law before surrendering? At any rate, certain period texts convey the impression that the *dahir* went down fairly well in the mountains, guaranteeing some permanence as far as their institutions were concerned.[18] The Arabic-speaking, often corrupt, town-bred *qadhi* ("judge"), with whom they had little in common, would not lord it over them. Justice would be done. Such was the reputation of Native Affairs officers for fairness that the poor bastard would get a fair hearing. Justice would no longer be bought or sold as in the bad days of old!

Unfortunately, at the time, certain French Catholic bishops had been advocating that the Berbers return to the Christian fold. This set of measures appeared to confirm the suspicions of many urban intellectuals that the occupying power was aiming at reducing Islam in tribal areas, the better to divide the Moroccan community. This was a mere knee-jerk reaction, for there was not the slightest chance of a secular France—with the separation between church and state firmly established since 1905—allowing its clergy to dictate policy, but it fitted in beautifully with the indignation aroused by the *dahir*. The perceived French favoritism vis-à-vis the Berbers was destined to poison the political atmosphere in Morocco for generations to come, as the urban glitterati effectively sidelined the Amazigh element, accusing it of being a neo-colonialist fifth column. Their history and cultural identity in post-independence Morocco was effectively played down—"confiscated," as many Amazigh observers subsequently contended. Such was the capital that the Istiqlal made out of this that today some even speak of an "Istiqlal *dahir*" as opposed to a "Berber *dahir*."[19]

Transition to Modernity: Protectorate and Independence

Thus had the *gesta barbarorum* passed into history. Now began for the Imazighen the painful process of adapting to a radically changed social set of rules, to modern ways of doing things imposed by an intrusive Christian administration. This entailed putting firmly behind them the "Heroic Age" rationale based on notions of honor (*l'azz*), vendetta, and kinship ties. That it was a relatively painful process there is little doubt. We have already quoted instances from poetry as to how Berbers reacted to the Protectorate, in the shape of customary law tribunals presided over by the ever watchful *qebtan*; how they perceived peace and prosperity, coupled with a ban on feuding, as a genuine calamity.

What of their status under the Protectorate? On the face of things, it appeared relatively favorable. A plentiful literature, skillfully mingling fact with fiction, romance with real-life events, was to appear throughout the colonial period,[1] glorifying the "good" Berber, seen as honest, trustworthy, and pro-French, as opposed to the "bad" Arab, visualized as deceitful, devious, seditious, and unreliable. This was part and parcel of a comfortable ideology: the "Protectorate Vulgate."[2] A built-in French certitude, namely that they possessed a unique gift for understanding other races and cultures, prompted simplistic value judgments when discussing the relative merits of Moroccans, seen either as Arabs or Berbers.

The convenient Arab–Berber dichotomy was actually erroneous and unfair, contributing as it did to creating a distorted picture of Morocco in the eyes of European residents, whether civil servant, settler, small white (small-time settler), or soldier. Worse still, it has survived to the present day. The more so as, in actual fact, an *Amazigh* origin could easily be found for many Moroccans blithely described as "Arabs"! Possibly the greatest error was to claim that Berbers were lukewarm Muslims. That French authorities wished to protect them as much as possible from Islam, there is little doubt. This was the whole strategy behind the *Collège berbère d'Azrou*, an institution founded in a Middle Atlas foothill town to educate the sons of Berber notables along French lines, in order to set up a body of cadres grateful to the colonial nation and likely to buttress her rule in Morocco. Hence, Arabic and Islam figured understandably low on the syllabus, a situation that eventually aroused dissatisfaction among some students who felt deprived of a portion of their cultural heritage. And yet, all in all, there had been some cosmetic improvements in Tamazight-speaking areas: the introduction of law courts, hospitals, schools, markets, and access roads. *Pax Gallica* now reigned, the souks were regularly supplied, and people ate their fill.[3]

Added to this, there were job opportunities for unskilled labor in the Gharb or Atlantic plains; even the French job market had become a popular destination for voluntarily exiled *Tashelhit*-speakers from southwest Morocco. Not to mention the army and auxiliary forces, for which Berber-speaking areas, and the Middle Atlas in particular, were perceived as a natural recruiting ground, pretty much as they are today.

In spite of this, however, there was no escaping the fact that, basically, most mountain areas, declared *zones d'insécurité* and with travel regulated by the military, retained a distinctly medieval flavor—very much a case of modernity denied. To these areas did dedicated travelers, alpinists, and journalists come to climb and walk amidst a quaintly archaic, exotic people, whose institutions had been "put on ice."[4] That French Native Affairs officers were there to preserve the purity of their Berber charges from perceived "Ottoman-inspired, Pan-Islamist, or Arab-Muslim" influences, there is little doubt.[5] That they wished to create Berber "national parks," as contended by Berque, is questionable.[6]

Whatever its purpose, this perceived pro-Berber policy actually did little to develop creature comforts in their rural areas. In step with the Protectorate rationale, far more effort went into developing the "useful Morocco" of the cities, including Fez, whose good citizens were fully aware of their debt to Lyautey. So much so that, when, on one occasion, the marshal fell gravely ill, prayers for his recovery were said in Fez mosques; an oft-forgotten fact when assessing France's contribution to specific segments of the Moroccan population.[7]

Until the outbreak of the Second World War, the Berber element and their administrators enjoyed a honeymoon period. This was further cemented, in 1940, by Sultan Ben Youssef's undertaking to remain faithful to France for the duration of hostilities. The loyalty of the Berber rank and file, especially in the Goums, was further proved when the latter agreed to participate in secret maneuvers with their French officers in defiance of Axis armistice regulations officially disbanding such units.[8]

This commitment went one stage further, with their unstinting participation in the North African campaign, never mind their contribution to the fighting in Italy, or to liberating the French motherland. The blood debt in the shape of Moroccan casualties thus incurred aroused hopes that a grateful France would, in exchange for all the *goumiers* and *Tirailleurs* who had given their lives, grant some improvements in social status, possibly going as far as national autonomy.[9] It is a fact that expectations of this kind were disappointed. Rather the reverse occurred: the French were convinced that there could be no limits to Moroccan loyalty; a case of political short-sightedness that would cost them dear.

On the surface, however, an occasional ripple would indicate that all was not well. In 1938, in Khemisset, "capital" of the Zemmour tribe, street demonstrations were staged in favor of a reinstatement of *sharia*.[10] In the big cities, in the wake of the 1943 Casablanca conference, the Salafist vociferations of Shakib Arsalan coupled with the exiling of nationalist stalwart Allal el-Fassi to Aghbalou n-Kerdous were the first ominous signs; however, the rural areas, by and large, remained quiescent. This was as it should be, in keeping with the comfortable, above-mentioned Vulgate. Overweening

French confidence in the righteousness of their colonial mission led them to pay scant attention to such danger signals. Surely the rural Berber masses would understand what was good for them and realize that the French administration, in spite of its paternalistic attitude, had their well-being at heart? Basically, while urbanites might cause trouble, the countryside was deemed secure.

Postwar problems

The postwar period, especially under Eric Labonne's tenure, was marked by timid attempts at reform. Unfortunately, due to a number of factors, partly resentment at the extension of the *Istiqlal* movement, partly opposition from the settler lobby, partly the sultan's reluctance to grant greater powers to Middle Atlas *jemmas*,[11] the Protectorate authorities failed to deliver. Rather the reverse, in fact; with a hardening of resolve marked by a succession of military Resident-Generals. First was Marshal Juin, an Algerian-born *pied-noir*; second, General Guillaume, who had won his spurs with the Goums in the Atlas and in the Italian campaign; finally, on the eve of independence, General Boyer de Latour (*muha w latur*), also an old Atlas hand, though possibly the most pro-Moroccan, the most humane of the lot, whose Berber wife had borne him a son. All three believed firmly in traditional Morocco, implying the Berbers, as a force for bolstering French rule in the country. Early in the 1950s, an axis of intrigue developed between the *Résidence* and the Pasha of Marrakesh.

This was our old acquaintance Thami El-Glaoui, an uncompromisingly feudal Berber overlord from the High Atlas, and the surviving member of a trio of "great *qayds*" who had sided with the French in 1912. Thanks to his undisputed rule over southwest Morocco, however, that part of the country had remained quiet, thus avoiding campaigns that would otherwise have been costly in French lives and money. As a result, El-Glaoui, seen by the Rabat *Résidence* as France's faithful and indispensable ally, became all-powerful in the country. A controversial figure, he was an all-star attraction, playing golf with Winston Churchill and the quality of Europe, who had nothing but praise for this urbane, courteous man, after tasting lavish hospitality in his Marrakesh palace or castle at Telouet, a hair's breadth from the Atlas snows. Few, however, caught a glimpse of his less reputable side: prisoners languishing in dank dungeons, speculations in a mining consortium, or the fact that this brave Berber warrior was also the greatest brothel-owner in the country.[12] Indeed, to thousands of Berbers in an empire stretching from Sraghna to the Dra'a valley, he was little more than an unpopular tyrant, and the focus of a peculiar form of passive resistance.

Meanwhile, in the early 1950s, dissatisfaction set in. There were riots and bombing outrages in Casablanca, followed by a police crackdown on Nationalist elements. Matters came to a head after El-Glaoui took Sultan Ben Youssef to task for his supposed links to the Nationalists, and got himself thrown out of the palace. Convinced that the former was now the "sultan of the *Istiqlal*" (actually less than accurate at the time), El-Glaoui plotted with the *Résidence* to have him removed. An opportunity occurred in August 1953, Berber horsemen being brought down from the Middle Atlas to camp around Rabat in an attempt to intimidate the sultan. Requested in no uncertain terms by Resident-General Guillaume to disown the Nationalists, the sultan refused and was immediately exiled: first to Corsica, ultimately to Madagascar.[13] Thus had El-Glaoui apparently won the power struggle.

One of the sultan's uncles, Moulay Ben 'Arafa, was hauled out of retirement to become a most reluctant figurehead monarch, with the Pasha of Marrakesh as the power behind the throne. The whole exercise, however, proved an unmitigated error. Although there is little evidence that Sultan Ben Youssef had been overly popular prior to this episode, almost overnight his forced exile conferred upon him the aura of a martyr. Nationalist activity continued unabated, while extraordinary tales circulated among Moroccans, some claiming to have seen his profile up in the Moon, others telling of Ben Youssef sitting in an African forest with leopards lying at his feet, as if he were some Atlas *agwerram*.

The road to independence

Worse still, the unthinkable was happening: thanks to Nationalist agitation, disenchantment with French rule was spreading to Berber tribal areas. This is hardly surprising. While a form of pro-Berber favoritism still colored French colonial thinking, the idealized picture of the happy, obedient Berber, as conveyed through works of fiction such as *La Légende du Goumier Saïd*, had little to do with reality in the field. There is no denying that, in actual fact, Berber areas had been largely neglected. Basically, although some devoted Native Affairs officers spared no efforts on behalf of their tribal charges, developing traditional irrigation systems or foot baths for sheep, for example, Berber institutions remained as they had been. In the final analysis, Berbers had very little indeed to show for this supposed French preference in their favor. Furthermore, shilly-shallying by successive governments of the make-believe Fourth Republic, its Paris-based politicians totally ignorant as to real conditions in Morocco and ready to lend an ear to articulate, pro-*Istiqlal* agents, gave a sorry demonstration of French weakness. That dissatisfaction finally set in should come as no surprise. This was the period that Jacques Berque has caricatured with his allegations that Berber tribal areas were little more than "national parks for white barbarians," fascinating enclaves where high-minded, Quixotic young French Native Affairs officers, raised on James Fenimore Cooper and Jean-Jacques Rousseau,[14] played at being Robinson Crusoe and lorded it over "noble savages."[15]

This is perhaps a rather unkind picture, given the undoubted dedication of these officers to the Berbers committed to their care, but possibly not without a germ of truth. Be that as it may, to the Imazighen, the sultan was *amir al-muminin*; this was what really mattered. That he had been sent into exile was, for many of them, unacceptable.

About this time, the Moroccan Liberation Army (MLA), drawing heavily on the Berber element, was set up in the Rif, Middle Atlas and Anti-Atlas. First to distinguish themselves were two men from the Marmousha—Mimoun ou Aqqa and Ahmed Ou Lahssen—who, having found refuge and British-supplied armaments in the Spanish zone, had infiltrated the Middle Atlas in September with a rebel group. They soon made their presence felt. During the night of October 1–2, 1955, Native Affairs outposts at

Berkin and Immouzzer-Marmousha close to Jbel Bou Iblan were attacked. The former resisted stoutly; the latter was taken by surprise, together with most of its weapons, because of a ridiculous directive whereby rifles were to be kept chained in the armory![16] A vigorous search and destroy operation by Goums and Foreign Legion rounded up the majority of the culprits and most of the captured weapons within a fornight.[17]

On visiting Immouzzer-Marmousha shortly afterwards, Boyer de Latour was surprised at the cordiality with which he was received. As they danced *ahidus* for his benefit, however, the Berbers warned the Resident-General, whom they admired, of difficulties to come:

> Beware! Two threads on the loom have become entangled,
> Pull not too strongly while weaving lest they snap![18]

Throughout the winter of 1955–6 the French fought the MLA along the border with the Rif. But the sands were running out for the Protectorate; the threads were indeed ready to snap. Brought back from Madagascar to France by a French government in total disarray and prepared for a sell-out at any terms, Sultan Ben Youssef agreed to pardon El-Glaoui, who at last "went to Canossa" and groveled at his lawful sovereign's feet. Betrayed without the slightest compunction by the French, this was the end for El-Glaoui. On November 12, some 3,000 people, both Moroccan and French, turned out at Rabat-Salé airport to say goodbye to a disappointed Boyer de Latour who had finally agreed, against his better judgment, to resign and fly home. A few months later, in the spring of 1956, Morocco secured its independence, and Berber–*makhzan* relations entered a new and delicate phase.[19] In post-Protectorate Morocco, Mohammed V used the Berber element in government to counterbalance *Istiqlal* influence.[20] In keeping with nation-building logic, a fresh Vulgate concentrated on Pan-Arabism and Oriental culture, militant sympathy and support for the Palestinian cause, together with the spiritual legacy of Islam, possibly as a reaction to long exposure to French culture and a supposed attempt to Christianize the Berbers.

Descent into oblivion

As they did not fit in with the Nationalist concept, the Berber language and culture were sidelined; basically, for those Imazighen unprepared to play the Arabization game, this resulted in relegation to second-class citizenship. The more so as the Protectorate's perceived fascination with the Berber community, highlighted by the episode of the so-called "Berber Dahir," now rendered the Amazigh element highly suspect, even potentially dangerous vis-à-vis national unity, according to the new conventional wisdom—a kind of "Post-Independence Moroccan Vulgate" based on Islam, the Arabic language, and links to the Middle East. This clearly depicted the Berber highlands, and especially Amazigh country, as a hotbed of revolt, separatism, irredentism, debauchery, and dissent.

The impression was, in fact, not entirely groundless, as a spate of rebellions now rocked the country: the abortive 'Addi ou-Bihi uprising (1957) in southwest Morocco, not to mention a revolt in the Rif that somehow harked back to 'Abdelkrim epic of the 1920s, both due to disenchantment with *Istiqlal* officials, both put down by Crown Prince Moulay Hassan in 1959.[21] Later in the same year, a *qayd* of the Tadla region led the Ayt 'Abdi n-Kousser into short-lived dissidence. By this time, too, most of the MLA detachments had been rounded up, disarmed, or otherwise neutralized in circumstances that have yet to be fully elucidated. As a result of these various flare-ups and general dissatisfaction, more Marxist or populist than avowedly "Berberist" in inspiration, all things Amazigh became officially ostracized. The Amazigh contribution to Moroccan history, especially resistance to *Pacification*, was henceforth systematically downplayed. Worse still, the actual notion of Berberism (*timuzgha*) was diligently swept under the carpet. As censorship and official-speak clamped down, the very adjective "Berber" became a dirty word. What remained of Berber opposition now became cultural in nature, featuring *muqawama lughawiyya* ("linguistic resistance").

The French euphemisms *ruraux*, or *populaires*, or *montagnards* alone enjoyed full Ministry of Information approval in describing the Berber population or culture. Only carpets and folklore were still referred to as Berber.[22] Even the avowedly Berber political party, founded by militant Mahjoubi Aherdan, had to call itself the *Mouvement Populaire*. It is hardly surprising that for a couple of decades, many Moroccans, fearing the sting of social ostracism, were reluctant actually to admit to being Berber. As the *Istiqlal* cast its net far and wide, most members of the Moroccan Civil Service became members of this party, while some Berbers, especially in southwest Morocco, harbored doubts as to whether independence had actually occurred!

There was certainly little difference between the outgoing colonial administration and the new authorities, with their non-Berber-speaking *qayds* appointed by Rabat. This state of affairs lasted well into the 1970s. I clearly remember how, in 1974, a student at the Rabat Faculty of Letters showed me an official memo explicitly forbidding students from doing research on the Ahansal and Imhiwash *igweramn*, probably because members of these orders had defied *makhzan* authority on several occasions between the seventeenth and nineteenth centuries in the Tadla and Fazaz areas. These topics had become an academic no-go area![23]

Again, recent events understandably fueled government suspicion vis-à-vis anything that smacked of Amazigh specificity. The abortive 1971 Skhirat coup, followed by a similar, ill-fated effort the following year, both of them heavily implicating the Berber element in the armed forces, hardly improved the official view on the Imazighen. True, those involved in these failed rebellions, officers like Medboh, Ab'abou, Shelouati, Bougrin, Ameqran, or Hammou, hailed mostly from the Rif and Middle Atlas. As a result, the Moroccan general staff was purged of its Berber elements, unwarlike Fassi officers being appointed in their stead.

Then, in the spring of 1973, came the failed Tanzim revolt, involving outside attempts at infiltrating the Eastern High Atlas from the Figuig area, mostly affecting the Ayt Merghad and Ayt Hadiddou country. Thanks to the rapid deployment of helicopter-borne troops, however, not to mention *le loyalisme des populations*,[24] these intruders were rapidly neutralized. There were short, sharp skirmishes above Sountat, near Imilshil,[25] while Ayt Merghad in some numbers were involved near Goulmima. Those insurgents who were not gunned down in the hills faced trial in Rabat during the autumn of 1973: some were executed, some sent into solitary confinement, many to the Tazmamart hellhole.[26] In the Imilshil area, suspected sympathizers were ruthlessly punished, a Middle Atlas bard summarizing these events in a well-known *tamdyazt* that was censored for over thirty years.[27]

For Moroccan Berbers this marked the nadir of their fortunes as Imazighen, their language and culture being placed under maximum surveillance. The object of intense suspicion following the recent disturbances, never before had these elements of Moroccan society felt so ostracized. To make matters worse, any claim they might have to cultural specificity was now dismissed. They were Moroccans, part of the Arab world, and that was that. In similar vein, official history books, while acknowledging that they were the original inhabitants of the Maghrib, trotted out the old Himyarite theory of a southern Arabian origin of the Berbers, thus converting them at a stroke of the pen into Arabs.[28]

Start of Berber revival

Luckily, however, they recovered. King Hassan II's *tawada tazizawt* ("Green March"), by giving many Berbers an opportunity to participate in this exercise in national unity, went part of the way to restoring their dignity and respectability.[29] It was no secret that the army was still made up, for the most part, of Rifs and Middle Atlas Berbers, and their sacrifice on the Saharan front during the coming years, as they bore the brunt of the fighting against Polisario guerrillas, was to earn them some measure of fame. Even better, this event was shortly to usher in a gradual cultural renaissance that ultimately proved a genuine Amazigh reawakening destined to last into the following century.

This was sparked by the 1980 *tafsut n imazighen* ("Berber spring") in Kabylia[30] and one or two measures taken in Morocco in order to keep pace with events next door. One was the timely recognition by Moroccan press magnate Moulay Ahmed 'Alaoui of the *berbéritude* phenomenon as being part and parcel of Moroccan culture, a move inspired by Lépold Senghor's similar *négritude* theory. The other, merely an administrative decision, henceforth allowed the study of Tamazight in universities from a linguistic and cultural angle. Better still, though, Mahjoubi Aherdan's son, Ouzzin, founded a journal, *Amazigh*, that enjoyed a considerable run of success.

Simultaneously, restrictions on the import of books on Amazigh culture were raised. Morocco's Berbers, after those difficult years since the battles at Tazizaout and Baddou, had clearly come a long way. That these carefully calculated measures contributed to clearing the air there is little no doubt. They also enabled Amazigh culture to make a slow climb back from the brink of oblivion. Though the way ahead was still fraught with obstacles, hesitations, and perils, for the Imazighen, hope had returned.[31]

Now is the time to examine the manner in which, largely due to their own efforts, and in spite of not inconsiderable opposition, Morocco's Berbers finally managed to assert their identity at the turn of the twentieth and twenty-first centuries.

From Oblivion to Recognition

In the 1980s Morocco witnessed an unexpected upsurge of interest in things Berber. Associations were founded; the *Amazigh* journal, with Ouzzin Aherdan as chief editor, enjoyed a brief run of success, until a critical article by 'Ali Sedki Azaykou questioning Morocco's historic claim to the Western Sahara triggered a backlash by the authorities, the offender being jailed for two years, the editor and 'Abd el-Malek Ou-Sadden getting away with shorter prison terms, after which the journal was closed down.[1] Despite this setback, however, the Amazigh renaissance remained on course. Heedful of official touchiness as soon as political affairs were broached, however, militants tended to avoid dangerous ground and concentrate on cultural matters. None the less, during 1986, two papers on Berber poetry were read at a colloquium in Meknes.[2]

In 1987 and 1988, thanks to funding by the Konrad Adenauer federation, the Rabat Faculty of Letters witnessed an international conference in which Amazigh-related topics occupied pride of place, with the participation of eminent guest speakers such as Lionel Galand and Paulette Galand-Pernet. This was a major breakthrough. Berber studies had recovered a well-deserved niche in Morocco-based scholarship. Other conferences in Rabat followed, each one succeeded by a scholarly publication of its proceedings, as at the 1992 oral tradition colloquium in which Tasadit Yassin, a well-known Kabyle researcher, played a leading role.[3] Of equal importance was the Agadir charter of August 1991, in which six associations claimed official recognition for Tamazight, and its inclusion in the realms of education and mass media.[4]

The watershed year was 1994. A May Day celebration in the Ayt Merghad "capital," Goulmima, provoked a clampdown. Several militants of the *Tilelli* association, including groundbreaking author 'Ali Iken, waved banners written in Tifinagh demanding official recognition; they were subsequently arrested.[5] This immediately became a *cause célèbre*, as scores of Berber lawyers converged on Goulmima to defend their own. Such was the outcry at this blatant disregard for cultural rights that King Hassan II himself intervened and the offenders were released shortly afterwards.

In August of the same year, the monarch announced that Tamazight would be taught in schools and that, for starters, brief news bulletins on national television in the three main dialects would be introduced. Unfortunately much of this was not set in place quickly enough, causing the usual griping among militants, but it was a step in the right direction. More significantly, however, viewers sitting through the entire broadcast noticed the similarities, rather than the differences, between dialects.

Even more significantly, Pan-Berberism emerged as a force to be reckoned with. Militants floated the idea of an *Agraw Amadlan Amazigh* ("World Amazigh Congress") to uphold and protect Berber interests and identity worldwide. This assembly met for the first time at Saint-Rome de Dolan, a small town in the south of France. The 2nd WAC conference was held in the Canary Islands in August 1997, the 3rd Congress in Roubaix at the close of August 2002. It was encouraging that members of such a body should have been able to meet and air their views on issues pending.

Thus, throughout the 1990s, the Amazigh cultural movement had gained momentum, both in the Maghrib and among members of the Berber *diaspora*, the latter mostly residing in France. International academia, however, was still proving reluctant to fully take on board the phenomenon of an Amazigh cultural renaissance. If one adds feet-dragging on the part of the international research intelligentsia, prompted to some extent by sympathy with Pan-Arabist elements in Morocco, not to mention the slanted vision vis-à-vis Berber affairs characteristic of many Arabic scholars worldwide, one will understand why Amazigh studies were slow in acquiring full recognition on the world scene. It was a shortcoming that famously prompted an up-and-coming American researcher to pen an article on "Morocco's invisible Imazighen"![6]

Berber studies, however, were not totally absent from the academic scene. A yearly jamboree organized in France by the AFEMAM provided a small niche for researchers interested in Berber studies, chiefly thanks to a workshop set up by the *LOAB* team,[7] to which I contributed on a number of occasions. There were also articles by scholars inspired by Jacques Berque. Rather than segmentation, they argued, Atlas Berber societies are based on notions of self-help and contract-fulfillment.[8]

Likewise, an Austrian anthropologist, who has done exhaustive fieldwork in the Eastern High Atlas, observed little more than residual segmentation in Ayt Hadiddou.[9] It should also be noted that Claude Brenier-Estrine, at the Arsène Roux Research center in Aix-en-Provence, produced a yearly catalog on Berber-related publications and co-operated with Dutch Berberists Harry Stroomer and Nico van den Boogert (and also with myself) on various research projects. Another development: by the end of the twentieth century, American fieldworkers focusing on Berber studies and actually doing fieldwork were fewer in number than in the 1960s, with the exception of David Crawford, Katherine Hoffman, and Helene Hagan.[10]

During the final years of Hassan II's reign, Al-Akhawayn University was founded by the king and his Saudi colleague, King Fahd, in the forested heart of the Middle Atlas, at Ifran. Here, for the first time since the Protectorate, were conducted experiments aimed at reinstating Berber studies; all in all, quite a breakthrough. That was where, for a five-week period in the spring of 1999, I taught a course entitled "Introduction to Amazigh poetry." The extent to which the Amazigh cultural movement is visualized by the *makhzan* as a counter to the ongoing Islamist revival should be emphasized. Since the Iranian Revolution, the ripple effects of which have been felt far into the Maghrib, in Morocco the powers that be have had the jitters. The number of bearded youths and scarf-wearing girls has been increasing by leaps and bounds, as a result of which the formerly active left-wing element has been evinced by infiltration and intimidation from Moroccan university campuses. As a former lecturer at the Faculty of Letters, Mohammed V University in Rabat, I have kept careful pictorial records of my classes. The first *hijab*-wearing girl appeared in 1979–80, concurrently with the Shah's downfall. By 1988, the year I left Rabat, there was an average of two to three of them per class.[11] Nowadays, they are to be seen all over: in the streets of the big towns; far out into the Berber countryside, in places like Azrou and Beni Mellal.[12]

Since the closing years of Hassan II's reign, visiting Saudi Imams have been active in the propagation of pure Wahhabism, actually paying fathers to get their daughters to wear the *hijab*, as if without this totally unMoroccan headgear (and badge of feminine subservience) a girl's modesty would be imperilled! Suffice to say that at least two Islamic parties, one of them judged "moderate"—the Party for Justice and Democracy (PJD)—have seen the light of day. Shanty towns and rural slums, even in the High and Middle Atlas, have provided them with an ideal recruiting ground. Accordingly, the central government may well have seen fit to play off the Berbers against the bearded youths.[13]

Traditional Islam as practiced by the relatively democratic and tolerant Imazighen no doubt qualifies them as ideal agents to combat religious obscurantism. That, however, will not suffice. The evil needs to be rooted out at the core. Only by removing the grinding poverty prevalent in the *bidon-villes* ("shanty towns") and other depressed areas—creating moderately priced housing estates, providing education, jobs, and health care—can the government deprive religious agitators of a fertile breeding ground for both locally active and export-oriented terrorists. Thus, in this context, the Amazigh identity movement and the Sufi revival of the big brotherhoods such as the Boutchichiya have been visualized by the *makhzan* as a counter to Islamist activity by the *Al-Salafiyya Al-Jihadiyya*, which has a strong clandestine following in Morocco, much of it encouraged by PJD-affiliated NGOs.[14]

Founding of IRCAM

In the meantime, Mohammed VI had taken over from his deceased father. His arrival on the throne was warmly welcomed by most Berbers as, on his mother's side, he was descended from the great resistance leader Moha ou Hammou of Khenifra fame, and he was expected to give the Amazigh element of the Moroccan population a fair hearing.

This was soon forthcoming in the shape of a Berber academy, the Royal Institute for Amazigh Culture (IRCAM) in Rabat, which has done admirable work since 2003–4, its foundation a timely achievement for Moroccan Berbers. Getting IRCAM off the ground, however, has proved a time-consuming task. Eventually, Mohamed Chafik, the erudite author of a bilingual Arab–Berber dictionary, and a former professor at the Royal College, proved a suitable choice as the first Rector. However, weakened by ill-health, Chafik agreed to take the post on condition that he was allowed to stand down once he had got the Institute on the rails. This accordingly took place during 2003, Chafik gallantly doing his opening stint before being succeeded by Ahmed Boukous, a leading academic and authority on Amazigh matters.

The opening years witnessed a flurry of activity. Priority was given to choosing an official alphabet; Tifinagh and Arabic script were favored by a few, the majority coming out in favor of Latin diacritic characters. However, to forestall a possible outcry by the Islamists, Latin characters were sidelined, as was Arabic script, Tifinagh being finally chosen as a middle-of-the-road solution. It was, after all, the original script of the Saharan-dwelling Amazigh ancestors, thus giving Berber greater historic depth. It did prove, however, a somewhat questionable choice, chiefly among the associations and academia, Salem Chaker (a Paris-based researcher of Kabyle origin) dismissing the decision as impractical and counterproductive.[15]

Some Berber cultural extremists in Morocco argue that founding IRCAM merely put the whole problem of Amazigh culture under wraps; that is to say, under *makhzan* tutelage. This, of course, is rather unfair, being partly attributable to sour grapes, as I have fairly close links to IRCAM, many of whose members are friends and colleagues going back to my Rabat Faculty of Letters days of the 1980s. I can assert that they are dedicated professionals, fully determined to succeed in the delicate task with which they have been saddled: refining the Tifinagh alphabet (streamlined from thirty-six characters to thirty-one);[16] putting in place beginners' classes in Tamazight; preparing illustrated, user-friendly manuals incorporating Tifinagh script;[17] revisiting Moroccan history from a more Berber-oriented perspective;[18] organizing conferences on Berber oral literature and journalism; translating Tamazight into other languages; and other topics.[19]

Unfortunately, during the run-up to the September elections of 2007, with the prospect of a PJD landslide and the lack of an adequate Amazigh presence among the candidates, there was widespread discontent and calls for a boycott. At the end of 2006 there had also been the disgraceful Anefgou episode, when two mothers and some

Fig. 50: Grafitti promoting Amazigh identity on rocks above Asif Melloul (2008).

twenty-six or so infants had perished, "of the cold" according to the authorities (conveniently forgetting that it freezes in Anefgou every winter!), but more likely because of some "mysterious" illness, sounding suspiciously like pneumonia. The event received coverage from Al-Jazeera TV, guaranteeing maximum publicity, simultaneously exposing cases of gross dereliction of duty on the part of local health authorities, and also the fact that the cedar forest, the only resource of the Eastern High Atlas, was being wantonly squandered by local profiteers. It also drew the king's attention and he repaired to the area and set in train changes to improve the situation.

There was also trouble on university campuses at Marrakesh, Meknes, Taza, and Agadir in the spring of 2007 between "Arabist," Sahraoui, and Amazigh students from the MCA (*Mouvement Culturel Amazigh*). When more than a dozen Amazigh activists were jailed, demonstrations occurred at the end of August.[20] For the first time, however, massive, well-orchestrated pro-Amazigh protests, complete with the red, green, and blue Amazigh flag, and participants making the triple V-sign with their fingers, were held in rural areas, in and outside Msemrir, even on Taswiqt Square in Tounfit in the Eastern High Atlas.

Apart from demanding the students' release, these demonstrations also released long pent-up complaints over the underdeveloped nature of the boondock areas: bad roads, insufficient schooling and health care, and generally being "left out in the cold," a situation encapsulated in the term *hogra*.

This was an ominous, hitherto unheard of development, the more so as the issue was widely publicized by videos on the web. In the event, the September 2007 elections were bad news for Morocco's Imazighen. The much-expected PJD breakthrough never happened. Instead, after an election marked by an almost total absence of vote rigging, though stymied by mass abstention, the old warhorses of the Istiqlal Party were returned to power under Abbas El-Fassi, who could by no means be described as a supporter of the Amazigh movement. Thus was the Amazigh cultural movement subjected to a slowdown, until such a time as a balanced, fair policy vis-à-vis Moroccan Imazighen could be defined by king and government.

However, it should be emphasized that a little later the PJD government swept into power, also setting up countless NGOs that play a major role in "Salafization" of the Moroccan population in depressed urban and rural areas. Foreign financial aid to the ANLCA (*Agence Nationale de Lutte contre l'Analphabétisme*) allows that organization, ostensibly set up to combat illiteracy, to in fact dispense Salafist ideology aimed at criticizing unbelievers, "who shall be eternally committed to hell's fires," and at the same time undermining Moroccan society and ultimately constituting a threat to Morocco's monarchy.[21] This grave aspect of the contemporary Moroccan scene should be borne in mind.

28

Conclusion

During the last twenty years, Tamazight, together with Amazigh culture, has moved center stage on the Moroccan social scene. It has not been an easy task; in fact it has often had to fight to assert itself. The pro-Arabic element in Moroccan society has opposed potential gains by the Amazigh identity movement every inch of the way. Whereas its following was chiefly among the country's educated Berbers, an awareness that *timuzgha* ("Berberdom") is somehow equated with *hogra* ("neglect") has recently spread to the Berber outback, fanning flames of discontent. Thus has Amazigh resistance survived, not in primary form, but as a secondary kind of opposition entailing *muqawama lughawiyya* ("linguistic resistance").

While there have been victories, there have also been setbacks. One of these was the decision by the *Istiqlal* government on April 17, 2008, to dissolve Ahmed Adgherni's *Parti Démocratique Amazigh* (PDA), on the assumption that no political party in Morocco could be ethnically oriented.[1] Another setback was an announcement in 2016 by Benkiran's PJD government that put implementation of official use of Tamazight firmly on the back-burner.[2] Among the victories, though, was a decision in 2011 to grant Tamazight official status as the country's second language. Yet here again, whereas this could be seen as the coming of age of the Berber language in Morocco, in practice it remains sidelined, despite the way Tifinagh letters have been sprouting on government buildings and road signs.

Thus has the wheel turned full cycle; now has the time come to take stock. The outlook is far from promising, given the widespread radicalization of the Rif, social disenchantment, together with the present *hiraq* unrest and the imprisonment of its leader, a young Rifi activist called Nasser Zafzafi, as well as the *hogra*-related lack of development.

What have we learned of Morocco's inconspicuous rural Berbers in their struggle for identity down the centuries? They come from a very ancient stock, and have flourished under various forms of lifestyle, presenting different physical types and skin color, for which reason the notion of a pure Berber race remains hazy in the extreme. Rather should linguistic similarities between groups be highlighted. As country folk rather than town dwellers, they have understandably forged close links with nature, from which has sprung a deep attachment to their motherland—of which they have proved the staunchest defenders. Many a time have they been called upon to prove this, for, throughout their checkered history, numerous are the threats and encroachments they have had to counter, whether from outside foes or from the enemy within.

Whenever they have confronted an invader, tactically speaking the Imazighen have displayed an uncanny "eye for country," allied with high mobility and mastery in the art of guerilla warfare. Sadly, they have often proved incapable of concerted action, of presenting a united front to the adversary. Their purely defensive action has rarely exceeded the local or regional context. True, from Abou Ghoufair El-Berghaouati to Belqasm Ngadi, cases of short-lived alliances have been noted, but they have proved the exception rather than the rule.

This probably stems from the fragmented nature of Berber society, divided as it used to be into a galaxy of tribes, clans, and subgroups of various denominations, submitted to the rule of temporal chiefs elected through rotation and complementarity,[3] with saintly leaders acting as arbiters for the common good (barring a handful of cunning charlatans), thereby introducing an element of balance and stability. Now split by feud, now achieving harmony under the aegis of the local *agwerram*, as with Bou Bekr Amhaoush, they seemingly paid lip service to some unspoken rule such as, "Divide that ye need not be ruled."[4] Ever present in the psyche of these basically democratic people was a dread that some village bully would nurse ambitions to take over the tribe, and develop into that recurrent character in Amazigh history—the regional warlord—requiring another form of resistance.[5]

Despite apparent *al fitna al barbariyya* ("Berber anarchy"), this society was reasonably happy until well-meaning Westerners intruded upon its age-old structure. However, these apparently strife-prone communities have been characterized by a degree of flexibility perfectly adapted to the exigencies of the moment; a state of mind where one alternates between audacity, perspicacity, and caution. With survivability the supreme watchword, one was constantly hedging one's bets with an eye to the future; giving away a little here, making up for it there through some slight, yet significant gain. Thanks to this adaptability alone has Amazigh society managed to survive the passage of time.

The Berbers' potential for evolution is debatably their major asset. The way this rural society was brusquely confronted by the twentieth century, shifting without transition from a pre-industrial pastoral economy to the age of airplanes, telephones, information technology, and nuclear energy, has amply demonstrated their ability to face fresh challenges. Their common sense, however, has demonstrably guaranteed that such change has not been too reckless in its application. While accepting the so-called benefits of modern civilization, care has been taken not to throw overboard all of the old. Wise counsels such as these have often prevailed.

Will it always be thus? Unfortunately, there are indications to the contrary, given the impatience of youth, driven by a thirst for modern gadgetry and/or attracted by publicity and the bright city lights. This most aptly sums up the "Berber problem" today. A thorny one, indeed, of a socio-economic nature: how to stop the rural exodus? How to deter droves of rural emigrants from leaving Berber areas and making for Europe, even if the money remittances they regularly send home contribute handsomely to the Moroccan balance of payments? Is it a positive factor for a country to boast of such a brain drain? Better, by far, for them to stay at home, for, as a local proverb reminds them, "Better be poor in your home country, than wealthy in a foreign land!" Only thus can the countryside, the villages, be prevented from emptying out. When they reach the hoped-for El Dorado, the welcome carpets won't necessarily be laid out for them; in the words of a modern Amazigh poet:

I salute, you people of a cold, inhospitable land,
For today were we destined to meet![6]

Unimpeded rural exodus merely creates more shanty towns and further scope for Salafi-inspired *id bu tmart* ("bearded ones") to achieve their sinister ends. Providing incentives for young people not to desert their Atlas valleys, as part of an overall strategy to achieve an urban–rural balance and defeat *hogra*, should become a Moroccan governmental priority. Here, eco-tourism is undoubtedly a potential niche in terms of job creation.[7]

What of the Berbers' role within the Moroccan state? There is no reason why they should get the leftovers. The more so as its Tamazight-speaking inhabitants are the very bedrock of Morocco's society, a yardstick by which its special identity may be measured among Arab nations. Berbers belong firmly to *dar al-islam*, even if, when saints and zaouias were predominant, their faith was occasionally tainted by unorthodoxy. Whether they are Jebli, Rifi, Soussi, or Amazigh from the Middle Atlas, their bravery, industry, and basic honesty are an asset to the country's development.

In the 1970s many Moroccans were reluctant to make much of their Amazigh identity. That shameful period is now past. Apart from a handful of extremists, none entertain separatist dreams. They merely insist on having a place in the sun; that their culture, their traditions, poetry, and music, be respected, and especially their language. The true badge of an individual's *timuzgha* ("Berberhood") is undoubtedly Tamazight, as taught by one's mother. Tamazight obviously loses out to Moroccan Arabic and French in the course of lengthy stays in an urban context, especially if the wife does not speak Berber, for it is through the womenfolk that the language is perpetuated. And yet Tamazight has revealed remarkable resilience. Despite attempts at the "Arabization" of education, coupled with media coverage in a form of Arabic often incomprehensible to the majority of Moroccans, some 50 percent of the population still speaks, or at least understands, Tamazight. Actual daily use, together with negative attitudes towards the language, resulting in some areas in "language loss," varies according to context, circumstance, gender, and/or upbringing.[8] Most men are bilingual; village women tend to be monolingual. Over recent years, the number of Moroccans anxious to recover their mother tongue has risen; declaring that one is Berber, displaying a mysterious affinity for an age-old culture, has actually become a source of pride to some individuals.

Meanwhile, thanks to the existence of IRCAM (though there is a dubious plan to melt it down into the CNLCM),[9] and despite in-fighting and the fact that the government is, at times, seen to be dragging its heels, Tamazight teaching has got under way in over 250 Moroccan state schools and is soon to be extended to higher education. Whatever perils lie ahead, this is no mean achievement. Where there is a will there is a way; it is up to the Imazighen to cease bickering, remain vigilant and patient, get their act together, and guarantee the place they richly deserve in the Moroccan community (*tamughrabiyt*).

Notes

Preface

1 Arsène Roux, a French Arabist, collected a goldmine of material on the Berber language in the Middle Atlas area as of 1914.
2 For general discussion of primary and secondary resistance, see Ranger 1968: 437–53; Talton 2011; K. van Walraven and J. Abbink n.d.; https://openaccess.leidenuniv.nl/bitstream/handle/1887/9605/ASC_1267345_085.pdf?sequence=1 http://exhibitions.nypl.org/africanaage/essay-resistance.html.
3 Among others, Burke III 1976: xiii; Bourqia and Miller 1999: 3–4.
4 I express a debt of heartfelt gratitude to David Crawford and Michael Willis for their constructive, insightful reading of an earlier version of the present work; also to Rory Gormley, G. Thomson, Ronnie Hanna, Merv Honeywood and Yasmin Garcha for help with the MS and illustrations.

Introduction

1 Maxwell 1966. A highly readable volume, in 2002 it ran to a new luxury, coffee-table edition.
2 Sitwell 1940 : 128.
3 Noyce 1962: 65.
4 There are descriptions of the Atlas ranges in my *Great Atlas Traverse* (1989/1990), and Brown 2012.
5 Bertrand 1977, one of the less obnoxious coffee-table efforts.
6 Brett and Fentress 1997, which provides the best general account to date in English.

Chapter 1

1 Ward Price 1934: 48; also Gautier 1927: 24.
2 Ibn Khaldoun 1925/1999: 1/168. "What is that *berbera* ["mixture of unintelligible cries"] you use in lieu of speech!" one of the newcomers is quoted as saying.
3 Sing. *amazigh* "free man," "son of Mazigh," their semi-mythical ancestor Mazigh. Arab genealogists often attribute descent from Goliath (*jalut*), this being also seen as a title, "king" (Ber. *ajellid/agellid*); Norris 1982: 67.
4 Brett and Fentress 1997: 13.
5 Scott O'Connor 1923/1929: 139.
6 Camps 1980: 49.
7 Mazel 1971 suggests an Atlantean origin.
8 Rinn 1887: 402. Rinn's theories were recently described as possibly not far removed from the truth by several writers in the Berber journal *Tifinagh*.

9   Ibn Khaldoun 1925/1999: 2/4. Amply discussed Naciri 1925: 155; Slouschz 1908: 315; Norris 1975: 30; Shatzmiller 1983: 149.
10 Norris 1982: 69; Shatzmiller 2000: ch.2.
11 Ibn Khaldoun 1925/1999: 1/182–4. For more on *jalut*, whose name in Hebrew means "exile," see Camps 1980: 23; Peyron 1995a: 2375; Hart 2000: 37.
12 Bounfour 1994: 56.
13 Cf. L. Rinn's theory above (n. 8).
14 Norris 1975: 102.
15 Except for those who search for a Basque linguistic affiliation. Otherwise, cf. G. Camps 1980: 55; Chafik 1996/2000: 29. In the nineteenth century, Renan had classified Berber among the Chamitic languages; Mercier 1871, 420–3. A. Allati (2002), however, pushes for an earlier, pre-Semitic origin of Berber.
16 Hachid 2000: 27. This is an authoritative, well-researched, survey; also Arnaiz-Villena 2002.
17 Camps 1980: 41.
18 Hachid 2000: 27–9, 37.
19 Wellard 1967: 39; H. Lhote, *Encyclopédie Berbère* 6 (1989): 925–9.
20 Simoneau 1967: 67.
21 Simoneau 1967: 73; Mazel 1971: 30. They disagree dramatically, however, on the actual date, the former suggesting 1600 BC, the latter an earlier date, viz. 5000 BC. The first independent Berber kingdoms are generally thought to have appeared some thirty-three centuries ago, *c.* 1300 BC; cf. M. Chafik 1996/2000.
22 Lawless 1973: 229–37.
23 Morsy 1984: 11–12; for Berber origins, see also Ibn Khaldoun 1925/1999: 1/182–4; Simoneau 1967: 75; de Planhol 1962: 113–30; Norris 1982: 33–43; Brett and Fentress 1997: 14–24. The suggestion that they "migrated through Arabia" gives credence to those who argue in favor of an Arab origin for the Berbers (my translation from the French, as with other quotes in this book).

Chapter 2

1   Brett and Fentress 1997: 27. Massinissa is claimed to be derived from Ber. *yemma (a) sen izza*, "their mother (was) Izza"; reasonable, given early Berber matrilineal traditions and Izza being a fairly well-documented woman's name.
2   Terrasse 1952: 42.
3   Naciri 1925: 38.
4   Yugurten, Ber. *iuger ten*, "he surpasses them."
5   Last 1932: 125–30. This betrayal by Bocchus parallels that of a nineteenth-century Moroccan sultan who delivered Algerian resistance leader 'Abd el-Kader to the French.
6   Gautier 1927: 149; also Barbour 1965 for details of the AD 41 rising. Recent scholarship suggests that Suetonius Paulinus may have reached Tafilalt from the northeast (conversation with M. Lebbar, at the "Le Maroc des resistances conference", IRCAM, 2005).
7   Terrasse 1952: 48. The villagers of Asaka, southwest of Tounfit (Ayt Yahya), claim that a wooded knoll west of the village was originally a Roman fortress equipped with a cistern.
8   Pl. of *qsar*, more commonly written *ksar*, pl. *ksour*, in French.

9 For an interesting comparison between Yemeni and southern Moroccan vernacular achitecture, cf. Swanson 2000: 158–64.

10 Terrasse 1938: 70.

11 Sitwell 1940: 152–3.

12 Slouschz 1908: 320. Laroui (1975: 1/66) suggests that the camel may have been in the Sahara all along. Among Moroccan revisionist historians, Laroui tends to debunk the writings of Protectorate period writers.

13 Mazel 1971: 111.

14 Mazel 1971: 132; also Gautier 1927: 202.

15 Norris 1975: 13; Laroui (1975: 55) expresses similar misgivings.

16 Mtouggui *c.* 1935: 56; Camps 1980: 169.

17 Norris 1975: 44. He attributes this to the recruitment of Berbers into the army soon to conquer Spain, intermarriage between Arabs and Berbers, and the latter's fascination with the oriental religion.

18 Watt 1965/1967: 9; Barbour 1965: 44; Terrasse 1952: 51.

19 Kharijism, the name given to a Berber-inspired, heretical form of Islam, derived from *kharaj,* "land tax," which Berbers resented having to pay to Arabs, this being one of the reasons for their discontent.

20 Isolated Christian communities are thought to have survived in the Fazaz area well into the thirteenth century, and a sixteenth-century traveler in the area reported that memories of a previous Christian presence remained strong. See Dufourcq 1968: 315, drawing on accounts by Ibn Abu Zar' (1918/1999) and D. de Torres (1650).

21 Weygand 1954: 214.

22 Personal observation over the past ten years in the Atlas Mts.

Chapter 3

1 Ibn Khaldoun 1925/1999: 1/203; Lugan 2012: 52–4; Barbour 1965: 45; Laroui 1975: 1/87;Brett 1999: 1/63.

2 The two last-named, Senhaja (or Zenaga) and Zenata, having allegedly arrived from further east, were among the major Berber tribal groups in Morocco, descendants of whom are to be found to this day in various parts of the Middle and Eastern High Atlas. On first- and third-race Senhaja, cf. Ibn Khaldoun 1925/1999: 2/4, 121–4.

3 Ibn Abu Zar' 1918/1999: 164. Idris was *imam al-muminin,* "leader of the faithful," a title that subsequent sultans of Morocco automatically acquired; cf. also Ibn Khaldoun 1925/1999: 1/560.

4 Also Barghawata; *iburghwaten* in Ber. Origin of the term is apparently *barghwati balghwati* (a case of r < l, a typical trait of Berber pronunciation). Confirmed by note in Tadili 1995: 357, which explains that *ilghwaten* = "those that have deviated." Cf. √RGHWT = "to sulk, to be angry," Taifi 1991: 574. Other possibility: Barghawati < Barbati, i.e. a native of Berbat, near Xeres in *al-andalus* (Ibn Khaldoun 1925/1999: 2/133; Lagardère 1998: 31).

5 Ibn Abu Zar' 1918/1999; also Arnaud 1916. In the eleventh century, ram-worship survived among some Atlas Berbers; Brignon et al. 1967: 81.

6 *Le Matin du Sahara,* January 9, 2003, 8.

7 Ennahid 2001: 45. Tinghir may have paid mere lip-service to the Idrissids.

8 According to M. Kably, as proof of his legitimacy, Ibn Toumert, the Almohad *mahdi* "presented himself as a direct descendent of Idriss" (*In the Shadow of the Sultan*: 21).

9   Ibn Khaldoun 1925/1999: 2/125–33. G. Marçais 1947: 126–7; Ferhat and Triki 1988–9:
     7–9; Norris 1982: 98–104; Lagardère 1998: 32.

10   Barbour 1965: 48. The influence of Judaism no doubt contributed to the elaboration of
     the Berghaouata creed. Saleh's father was possibly Simon al-Ya'qoubi (Ibn Khaldoun
     1925/1999: 2/132).

11   Ibn Khaldoun 1925/1999: 2/129; Lagardère 1998: 27. There were Senhaja, Beni Ifran
     and mountain Zenata contingents from Jbel Fazaz, including the Beni Idjfashi
     defenders of Qala'at el-Mehdi.

12   Lagardère 1998: 27. Contrary to Norris (1982: 100), Lagardère argues that the
     Berghaouata were of Masmouda stock; cf. Ibn Khaldoun (1925/1999: 2/133).

13   Probably Oued Beht in central Morocco, the northeast boundary of the Berghaouata
     state, and a location associated in later years with some of Sidi 'Ali Amhaoush's
     apocalyptic verse (Roux and Peyron 2002: 191) referring to horrendous losses in men
     and horses at this battle. For an analysis of Berghaouata strategy, see my article in *Le
     Maroc des resistances* (Rabat: IRCAM, 2005).

14   Such practices still survive in Berber villages: the cock referred to as *fqih*, or *ttaleb*, the
     person who calls the faithful to prayer, while *lfjer*, "dawn prayer," is sometimes referred
     to as *tazalit n ufulus*, the "cockerel's prayer." El-Bekri 1913: 265; Marçais 1947: 127;
     A. Laroui 1975: 1/98; Ferhat and Triki 1988–9: 13.

15   El-Bekri 1913: 263; Agnouche 2002: 1.

16   Ibn Khaldoun 1925/1999: 1/260–2; G. Marçais 1947: 144; Cambon 1952: 25;
     Abun-Nasr 1971: 50.

17   Ibn Khaldoun 1925/1999: 1/265; Naciri 1925: 68; Ibn Abu Zar' 1918/1999: 118.

18   Naciri 1925: 106; Ibn Abu Zar' 1918/1999: 138.

19   Ibn Khaldoun 1925/1999: 1/265; Naciri 1925: 68; Ibn Abu Zar' 1918/1999: 118.

20   Lagardère 1998: 70.

21   El-Bekri 1913: 1068. Various spellings occur: Yhafash, Idjeshi, Djeyfeshi; also Idjfesh
     (Ibn Khaldoun 1925/1999: 2/73; *Kitab al-Istibçar*), or Bejfash (*Kitab al-Juman*). For
     further references, cf. file 79.1 'Fazaz' in Arsène Roux Archive, Aix-en-Provence.
     There are other references to Qala'at El-Mehdi in Colin n.d.: 894–5.

22   Cf. Roux archive, file 79.1; quotes Massignon 1906/2018: 257.

23   Africanus 1897: 365.

24   Ibn Abu Zar' 1918/1999: 104.

25   Ibn Khaldoun 1925/1999: 2/72–3; Naciri 1925: 148; Ibn Abu Zar' 1918/1999: 198.

26   Lagardère 1998: 185–6, 193–4.

27   Al-Idrissi 1836–40: 87. Cf. Lagardère (1998: 73) for a different account.

28   Tisigdelt is a fairly widespread place name in Morocco, always associated with a
     location of difficult access, protected by natural obstacles (< Ber. √GDL = "to
     protect").

29   Questioned about this wall on April 21, 2002, by my Al-Akhawayn students, local
     villagers claimed it had been built by the Portuguese, who had inhabited the plateau in
     the distant past. A former Jewish presence was also referred to, seemingly tallying with
     details on Qala'at El-Mehdi.

30   *Istibçar*, 135–6. For further details on Qala'at El-Mehdi, including other possible sites
     in the area, cf. my extensive coverage of the topic in *JNAS*, summer 2003: 115–23.

31   For a comprehensive survey of the southeast–northwest Senhaja push, cf. Hart 1993:
     21–55.

32   Terrasse 1952: 69.

33   Ibn Khaldoun 1925/1999: 2/70; Ibn Abu Zar' 1918/1999: 175; A. Naciri 1925: 113.

34 Ibn Khaldoun 1925/1999: 2/67. *mrabtin* (sing. *mrabet*) = "marabout." "Lemtouna"
    < *litham*, "veil, face-muffler" > *al-mulaththamun*, "veiled men"; also Barbour 1965: 50;
    Lagardère (1998: 59), drawing on the *hulal al-mawshiyya*, claims *ribat* = "tie, link,"
    because their attachment to the Faith made the *al-murabitun* brave in battle, plus the
    notion of fixed *ribat*, contrary to nomadic lifestyle.

35 Norris (1982: 106–7, 124–5) draws heavily on medieval sources including Ibn Hawqal,
    al-Bakri, and anonymous *hulal al-mawshiyya*. Cf. also Brett and Fentress 1997: 101–2;
    Marçais 1947: 241.

36 Ibn Khaldoun 1925/1999: 2/70; Bovill 1958/1999: 73.

37 Ibn Khaldoun 1925/1999: 2/71; Lagardère 1998: 70.

38 Ibn Yassin's shrine is visible to this day, on a wooded hill above the left bank of Oued
    Khorifla.

39 Lagardère 1998: 71.

40 Among *tashelhit*-speaking Berbers, although situated slightly to the southeast, Aghmat
    tends to remain the old name for Marrakesh. Marrakesh also has another, long-
    standing etymology of questionable authenticity: Merrakush < *amur a yakush*, which
    takes us back to the Berghaouata, for whom Yakush was a kind of Jehovah (= "We
    crave your protection, O God").

41 Ibn Khaldoun 1925/1999: 2/71; Lagardère 1998: 72; Marçais 1947: 244–5; H. Cambon
    1952: 31; Barbour 1965: 51.

42 Ibn Khaldoun 1925/1999: 2/71; Naciri 1925: 147; also Daoud 2004.

43 Ibn Khaldoun 1925/1999: 2/75.

44 Lugan 2012: 71.

45 Ibn Khaldoun 1925/1999: 2/75; Watt 1965/1967: 98–9; H. Terrasse 1952: 75. Today,
    however, by a quirk of fate, El-Mou'atamid is hailed by the Spanish as an early
    Andalucian hero.

46 Al-Merrakushi 1951: 4/273.

Chapter 4

1   Montagne 1930/1989: 18.

2   For a similar episode, though situated in the twentieth century, cf. Euloge 1952: 64.

3   Epton 1958: 107.

4   Also spelled Abu I'azza Yilanur, "the man of light." Cf. Tadili 1995: 158.

5   There is a shrine dedicated to Moulay Bou'azza at the summit of Jbel Ouirzan (3396
    m), in Guedmioua country, whence springs a fountain whose waters are so cold that it
    is impossible to extract more than seven pebbles in succession without catching frozen
    fingers. He was known locally as *bab n-gurza* ("master of Jbel Gourza"), as he often
    pastured his flocks on that mountain and they were safe from attack by jackals
    (Stroomer 2001: 147). Moulay Bou'azza eventually settled among the hills of Iyroujan
    in central Morocco. He died in 1176 (Ibn Abi Zar' 1918/1999: 221).

6   Ibn Khaldoun 1925/1999: 2/73; Montagne 1930/1989: 80; Barbour 1965: 69.

7   Terrasse 1952: 81.

8   Ibn Khaldoun 1925/1999: 2/163. The term signifies "spark, live wire," although *tumert*
    means "joy" in *tashelhit* (Van den Boogert 1997: 110).

9   Cambon 1952: 32.

10 Ibn Abi Zar' 1918/1999: 147; Ibn Kaldoun 1925/1999: 2/163

11 Ibn Kaldoun 1925/1999: 2/166; for a readable account in English of this episode cf. Barbour 1965: 70–1.

12 Ibn Abi Zar' 1918/1999: 148; Barbour 1965: 72; Fletcher 2006.

13 Ibn Khaldoun 1925/1999: 2/166–7

14 Ibn Khaldoun 1925/1999: 2/169; N. Barbour 1965: 73; Marçais 1947: 256.

15 Tinmel (Tinmal) < *tin mellel*, "the white one," an allusion to nearby slopes regularly whitened by winter snows (Ibn Khaldoun 1925/1999: 2/171, note 2).

16 Ferhat and Triki 1988–9: 12.

17 Barbour 1965: 74. Cf. other versions of how Ibn Toumert declared himself *mahdi*: Ibn Khaldoun 1925/1999: 2/170, Ibn Abi Zar' 1918/1999: 151; Watt 1965/1967: 104.

18 Absent from the line-up were the Hazmira, the original Tinmel inhabitants of doubtful loyalty, 15,000 of whom Ibn Toumert had massacred wholesale at a prayer gathering. Cf. de Gogorza Fletcher 1988–9: 32–3 (quoting from Ibn Qattan, *Nazm al-Juman*, 93–4, 97).

19 Ibn Khaldoun 1925/1999: 2/170; Montagne 1930/1989: 63; Laroui 1975: 1/163.

20 De Gogorza Fletcher 1988–9: 33, 35.

21 Barbour 1965: 60.

22 Brett and Fentress 1997: 108 (quoting from Al-Merrakushi, *History of the Almohads*, 122, 127–8); Barbour 1965: 57–8 (quoting from Ibn Rashiq, *Kitab al-Mujaib fi Talkhis Akhbar al-Maghrib*, 47); Lugan 2012: 86.

23 Ibn Abi Zar' 1918/1999: 152. Interestingly, during this tour he discovered some pagan tribesmen on the Tishka plateau and persuaded them henceforth to follow the straight and narrow path (Lhajj Brahim Ez-Zarhuni, 25).

24 Ibn Khaldoun 1925/1999: 2/171.

25 Ibn Khaldoun 1925/1999: 2/172–3; Arnaud 1916: 73; Barbour 1965: 74.

26 Ibn Khaldoun 1925/1999: 2/174.

27 Lesur 1920: 141–7; Peyron 1984: 119.

28 Peyron 1984: 175; Ibn Abi Zar' 1918/1999: 159.

29 Cf. El-Baidaq 1928: 143–6. The governorship in Almoravid fortresses appears to have been hereditary. Naciri (1925: 151) states that in 1074 a certain Sir Ibn Abou Bekr was made governor of Jbel Fazaz; this was presumably Yahya Ibn Sir's father.

30 J. Brignon et al. 1967: 107.

31 Guillaume 1946: 38.

32 Cf. El-Baidaq 1928: 146.

33 El-Baidaq 1928: 14.

34 Ibn Abi Zar' 1918/1999: 159; Naciri 1927: 39–41.

35 Laroui 1975: 1/165.

36 Ibn Khaldoun 1925/1999: 2/178; Ibn Abi Zar' 1918/1999: 159.

37 Ibn Khaldoun 1925/1999: 2/181–2; Ibn Abi Zar' 1918/1999: 161–3; Terrasse 1952: 84; Barbour 1965: 75.

38 Brett and E. Fentress 1997: 109–11; Marçais 1947: 269–75.

39 Van den Boogert 1998: 11.

40 Their language was *al-lisan al-gharbi*, a medieval form of Berber closely resembling *tashelhit*, spoken in the Gharb from the Oum Rbia' to the Bou Regreg. Two centuries later, however, as a result of the Beni Hilal and Ma'qil invasions, it had retreated towards the higher ground.

41 Barbour 1965: 77.

42 Van den Boogert 1998.

Chapter 5

1 Marçais 1947: 268.
2 Marçais 1947: 268.
3 Ibn Abi Zar' 1918/1999: 175.
4 Guillaume 1946: 39.
5 Laroui 1975: 1/138. Die-hard revisionists consider de Slane's Ibn Khaldoun translation as a "colonial text"; cf. Hannoum 2003: 137. Both sides of the argument have received ample treatment: cf. the doctoral thesis by Idris 1962; Poncet 1967 and correspondence thereon in other issues of the same journal; de Planhol's theory on the *Bédouinization* of the pre-Sahara (1962); also Brett 1999.
6 Barbour 1965: 78. This is a mid-1960s opinion that would probably be considered by a revisionist historian to be out of step with the post-colonial Moroccan Vulgate.
7 Ibn Abi Zar' 1918/1999: 191.
8 Mtouggui *c.* 1935: 94–5, drawing on Ibn Khaldoun: "No cataclysm can be compared to the intrusion of these invaders, whose sole concern is violence and devastation . . . A tragic silence pervaded all villages: the cock-crow was heard no more . . . Thus ended the promising Berber Senhaja Empire: the beautiful bird was struck down by the Arab predator just as it was flying away towards the light." Cf. also Moukhlis 1999: "The Hilalian invasion was, in every way, a catastrophe for North Africa; Imazighen today continue to feel the consequences. These nomads had but one aim: to conquer new lands, to plunder, to enslave men and women, the latter destined for the harems of Arabo-Muslim monarchs in the East."
9 Marçais 1947: 201–6; Camps 1980: 137, 187–8.
10 Laroui 1975: 1/178–9.
11 The Oulad Khaoua and Sabbah.
12 Laroui 1975: 1/172, 176. Watt elucidates further causes of decline (1965/1967: 108–9), as do Marçais 1947: 265 and Terrasse 1952: 90, 92–3.
13 El-Baidaq 1928: 209.
14 Ibn Abi Zar' 1918/1999: 238; Naciri 1927: 25.
15 Terrasse 1952: 97.
16 Ibn Abi Zar' 1918/1999: 210; cf. also Ibn Khaldoun 1925/1999: 2/235–6; Marçais 1947: 266; Cambon 1952: 34; Barbour 1965: 80; Laroui 1975: 2/177–88.
17 Ibn Abi Zar' 1918/1999: 212.
18 Ibn Abi Zar' 1918/1999: 212.
19 Ibn Abi Zar' 1918/1999: 239; Ibn Khaldoun 1925/1999: 4/33.
20 Ibn Khaldoun 1925/1999: 2/244–5.
21 Ibn Khaldoun 1925/1999: 2/252. More on Yaghmourasn available on http://perso. ksurf.net/sidi_said/Tlemcen.htm. As for Yaghmourasn, the name appears to have a Berber etymology < *yugh amur nsen* = "he purchased/their/share." See also a biography by de La Véronne 2002.
22 Ibn Khaldoun 1925/1999: 3/349–51.
23 Ibn Khaldoun 1925/1999: 2/241. The silver mines are situated in the Middle Atlas, a few miles west of the town of Mrirt.
24 Ibn Khaldoun 1925/1999: 2/215.
25 Ibn Khaldoun 1925/1999: 2/250.
26 Ibn Khaldoun 1925/1999: 2/252.
27 Ibn Khaldoun 1925/1999: 2/255. Ibn Abi Zar' 1918/1999: 248. Note that Ya'qoub Ibn 'Abd el-Haqq is usually called Abu Youssef Ya'qoub in history books.

28 Ibn Abi Zar' 1918/1999: 217, 249.
29 Ibn Abi Zar' 1918/1999: 250.
30 Ibn Abi Zar' 1918/1999: 251; Ibn Khaldoun 1925/1999: 2/257.
31 Terrasse 1952: 90; cf. also Brett and Fentress 1997: 111.
32 Ibn Khaldoun 1925/1999: 3/411–12. Cf. also Lugan 2012: 127. There was, of course, a brief 'Abdelouadid revival in Tlemcen (1348–58) until Merinid amir Abou Inan finally shattered their power (Ibn Khaldoun 1925/1999: 3/422–36).
33 Terrasse 1952: 109–10.
34 Lugan 2012: 134–7.
35 Cook Jr. 1993.
36 Conversation with Harry Stroomer, Leiden University, author of *Tashelhiyt Berber Folktales* (2001).

Chapter 6

1   Ibn Khaldoun 1925/1999: 2/257; Terrasse 1952: 91; Montagne 1930/1989: 89; Lugan 2012: 116. However, Laroui (1975: 1/182) specifies that this event occurred in 1275.
2   Guillaume 1946: 39.
3   Hart 1993: 23.
4   De la Chapelle 1931; G. Couvreur, *RGM*, 13/1968, 14.
5   Hart 1984a : 138; de la Chapelle 1931: 48. When staying with the *muqqadam* of Boutferda, Beni Mellal province (March 1980), I learnt that his clan—the Ayt 'Abdi n Oughbala—originally came from Jbel Kousser in the Anergui region.
6   Hart 1993: 21.
7   Ibn Khaldoun 1925/1999: 2/269.
8   Ibn Khaldoun 1925/1999: 2/270; Montagne 1930/1989: 67.
9   Berque 1955: 43. The Almoravid affiliation would have been impossible by about a century. The importance attached in the Atlas hills to a tradition of convenient assumption and oversimplification concerning the past is typical of the problems confronting the historian.
10 Ibn Khaldoun 1925/1999: 2/270; Montagne 1930/1989: 67; *agellid* (pl. *igeldan*) = "king" in Ber.
11 Ibn Khaldoun 1925/1999: 2/271; Montagne 1930/1989: 96–7.
12 Berque 1955: 299 states that it remains a site of pilgrimage to this very day.
13 Berque 1955: 71.
14 Montagne 1930/1989: 75.
15 Montagne 1930/1989: 77. This was to become standard *makhzan* policy, cf. Azaykou 2001: 62–3.
16 Berque 1955: 43 (my translation).
17 Montagne 1930/1989: 78.
18 Montagne 1930/1989: 291.
19 Montagne 1930/1989: 79
20 Berque 1955: 298.
21 Terrasse 1952: 103.
22 Terrasse 1952: 111. Also Kably 2015: 336.
23 French term "marabout" < *mrabet*, or *murabit*, pl. *mrabtin* (ar.); *agwerram*, pl. *igwerramn*, in Berber. For their historical role cf. Kably 2015: 353–9.

24 *zawiya* in Arabic, *zawit* in Berber. Variously defined as a "non-celibate monastery" (Barbour 1965: 115); a "lodge", or "holy settlement" (Gellner 1969: 317); cf. also Cornell 1998.

25 Arberry 1950/1969: 27; based on "direct experience of God" (J. Trimingham 1971: 1).

26 Justinard 1954: 30.

27 From the local tribal name, Ida ou Semlal; Justinard 1954: 18.

28 Justinard 1954: 30.

29 Terrasse 1952: 119; Montagne 1930/1989: 88–9.

30 Montagne 1930/1989: 90.

31 Montagne 1930/1989: 92. In some ways the forerunner of a pro-Makhzan *amazigh sserbis*, our Ayt Waouzgit *qayd* is an example of a "tame" Berber, who has little reason to claim for supposed ethnic or cultural recognition, as opposed to his "untamed" brethren of the mountain/desert periphery.

32 Montagne 1930/1989: 93, quoting de la Chapelle 1931.

33 Amusingly referred to as "Bum Hully" by early English commentators; Barbour 1965: 115.

34 Berque 1958/2001: 87; Mezzine 1987: 286–9; Kilito 1999: 30–3. The "ball of rags" in question is used in a kind of Berber hand-ball, called *takkwurt* in some areas.

35 Julien 1969: 588.

36 Montagne 1930/1989: 96; Arnaud 1916: 76; Brignon et al. 1967: 226. The marabout's intervention had been dependent on certain conditions, on which he now insisted: governmental reform, banishing royal favorites, including a Jew, Ben Wash, and certain youths guilty "of that villainous practice of sodomy" (Justinard 1954: 49, quoting unpublished consular sources of Moroccan history: John Harrison, who was Consul-General in Morocco in the early seventeenth century).

37 These debatable definitions, source of subsequent academic warfare, will be re-examined elsewhere.

Chapter 7

1 De la Chapelle 1931: 49; Couvreur 1968: 13.

2 J. Tharaud and J. Tharaud 1929: 198.

3 Morsy (1986: 307) suggests that Dadda Saïd came from a small zaouia between the Dadds and Todgha in the thirteenth century; see *Les Ahansala* (8–10) by same author. Gellner (1969: xxi) specifies 1397/1398 as the date of Dadda Saïd's probable arrival, with Dadda 'Atta joining him seven years later to help oust the Ayt Ouassar (Waster).

4 De la Chapelle 1931: 46; Henry 1937: 2.

5 Cf. Peyron 1990: 95; interview with Bassou ou 'Addi, from the Irbiben clan of Tana, Ayt Merghad. Near-cousins living in *mésentente cordiale*, the Ayt Hadiddou jokingly refer to the Ayt Merghad as the Ayt Melghad, the latter calling the Ayt Hadiddou the Ayt Haliddou!

6 Henry 1937: 2; Hart 1981: 12–13 and 1984: 55.

7 Laoust 1932/1934: 190, quoting Lieut. Lecomte of the AI ("Native Affairs").

8 The choice would be made by a tribal council of elders according to the *amghar n-tuga* principle, the chosen one having grass placed in his turban. Personal interview with Moha Y., a truck driver, at Agoudim, Ayt Yahya, October 1978.

9 A well-known Ayt Hadiddou proverb states, "Crooked are the words of men; ours alone are as straight and true as the shuttle of the loom!" Cf. Peyron 1992: 81.

10 Lesur 1920: 141–7; J. Chiapuris 1979: 25–6.

11 One of the most famous rural intellectuals of his day, fluent in Berber and proficient in Arabic, Bou Salim is famous for his *Rihla*, based on travels to the Near East, not to mention his fine poetry, and figures in many Atlas legends (Laoust 1939: 245; Roux 1942: 20).

12 The massif, named after the famous marabout, may have been previously known as Jbel Anaghrif, a poem by Bou Salim containing a reference to such a mountain "as overlooking his home." This is possible, as a nearby *qsar* bears the name Tannghrift; cf. Lakhdar 1971: 75.

13 Couvreur 1968: 14; the land deed was signed in 1598, according to E. Gellner 1969: xxi, 176–7. The Ayt Ouassar (Waster) vanished from the map some time in the seventeenth century (M. Morsy 1972: 28), though some survivors were absorbed by the Ayt Bou Guemmez (Hart 1993: 23) and others by the Ayt Attab (cf. Peyron 2020: 341).

14 Spillman 1936: 32.

15 Hart 1981: 11.

16 Dunn 1972: 85–107.

17 In Morocco, the notion of "Saharan" is vague. It may serve to designate a true desert dweller, or merely somebody living on the south slopes of the High Atlas.

18 Spillman 1936: 36.

19 The chief exponents in the Ayt 'Atta drive were the Ayt Ouanir and Ayt Ouallal, the Ayt Bou Iknifen, the Ayt Ousikis and Ilemshan. The Ayt 'Atta avoided the upper Dadds, as their vassals, the Ayt Hadiddou, were in occupancy, but that changed after 1645 with the Ayt Yaflman alliance.

20 Peyron 1984: 125.

21 Marcy 1929: 79–142.

22 Berque 1958/2001: 46–8, 69–70.

23 Brignon et al. 1967: 225; Julien 1969: 220–1. This appears to have coincided with what one observer styles as "a growing Berber hatred of the Arabs, and a corresponding desire to take over the good agricultural land in the plains" (Hart 1993: 39).

24 Mezzine 1987: 302.

25 Mezzine 1987: 96–8, 306–7, 319. Mezzine makes out a case for 1630 as being the date of the foundation of the Ayt Yaflman alliance, arranged by the Dila'yin marabouts to counter Tazeroualt and/or 'Alaouite designs. This contradicts another version whereby the Yaflman confederation "though probably ante-dating the 'Alaouite dynasty . . . was founded under the aegis of an ancestor of the present sultan" (de la Chapelle 1931: 27) and was probably directed against the Ayt 'Atta.

26 Laroui makes no bones over defining zaouias like Dila' as "expressive of Berber nationalism, a movement to rejuvenate the Senhaja race" (1977: 146). Mezzine (1987: 305) concurs: "this zaouia . . . crystallised a feeling of local nationalism."

27 For an account of these events in English, cf. Blunt 1951.

28 Jacques-Meunié 1951: 206; Julien 1969: 224.

29 Justinard 1954: 47.

30 Arnaud 1916: 76; Julien 1969: 226; Jacques-Meunié 1951: 207, all of whom draw on Naciri 1906–7: 21.

31 Naciri 1906–7: 22.

32 Naciri 1906–7: 24. The reader will no doubt appreciate the devastatingly dubious logic underlying some of the above niceties.

Chapter 8

1 Jacques-Meunié 1951: 207.
2 Naciri 1906–7: 39. At the Zaouia of Dila' he probably studied under al-Youssi (Berque 1958/2001: 14), whom he was to invite to the Qarawiyin after the sack of the zaouia.
3 Blunt 1951: n.p.ref.
4 Berque 1958/2001: 85; Drouin 1975: 30.
5 Drouin (1975: 33) publishes a photo showing the ruins of the zaouia. When I visited Ma'ammar in December 1992, on joining conversation with some locals, I was informed that it was the site of the *zawiya n igwerramn n dila'*. In June 2004 one of my American students from AUI, Alaina Joyce Cates, secured some interesting pictures of a ruined *madrassa*; see the cover of my *Amazigh Studies Reader* (2008).
6 De la Chapelle 1931: 23.
7 Naciri 1906–7: 40.
8 Montagne 1930/1989: 99; Justinard 1954: 58.
9 Montagne 1930/1989: 100; Jacques-Meunié 1951: 208. Tazeroualt power was crippled for nearly a century, while the local population regretted Sidi 'Ali's reign as a golden age.
10 Seeking revenge, 'Ali Ben Haïdar gathered a large force of blacks with which he swept north to the Sous in 1672. Hearing of Moulay Rashi'd's death in Marrakesh, however, and considering himself sufficiently avenged, he disbanded his large African contingent, who later formed a "Black Guard," the nucleus of Moulay Ismaïl's army (Justinard 1954: 60–1; Morsy 1967: 102).
11 Byrne 2009: 126–33 for an interesting parallel between the "hammer of the Scots" and the "scourge of the Berbers," both of them experts in the noble art of unchivalrous medieval warfare.
12 Byrne 2009: 108; Morsy 1967: 109.
13 Arnaud 1916: 77.
14 Terrasse 1952: 136.
15 Terrasse 1952: 78.
16 Cf. popular poetic couplet (*izli*) of the Ayt Myill: "The hen thus implores her owner: 'Protect me and keep away the egg-collector'"! Roux Archive, IREMAM, Aix-en-Provence, file 56.2.1.
17 Blunt 1951: n.p.ref.
18 Guillaume 1946: 44; plus old Moroccan saying ("Rebellious Arabs are punished by fines, rebellious Berbers by death!"), which goes some way to disproving remarks in subsequent revisionist claims that the supposed Arabo–Berber dichotomy was a creation of colonial propaganda.
19 Strangely enough, the Dila'i pretender who had sparked the rebellion remained in the area till 1680, when he suddenly vanished (Chiapuris 1979: 22).
20 For a somewhat romanticized account of this affray, cf. Boutet *c.* 1935: 95–7. There is some evidence that early firearms, mostly matchlocks, had been available on the south side of the Atlas since Ouattasid times; Cook Jr. 1993.
21 Cf. Ayt Khebbach: "There are 99 ruses, and war is the 100th!" Weygand 1954: 20.
22 Hart 1984: 58.
23 Naciri 1906–7: 79.
24 Blunt 1951: n.p.ref.
25 R. Boutet *c.* 1935: 98–9.
26 Arnaud 1916: 78.

27 Michel 1994: 83.
28 Naciri 1906–7: 88.
29 Chiapuris 1979: 22.
30 Chiapuris 1979: 92. "The tribes fled to Jbel 'Ayyashi, scattered and sought refuge among the mountain's ravines."
31 Naciri 1906–7: 92.
32 Lqsabi is a shortened form of Qasbaht al-Makhzan, the original name.
33 Bouverot 1920: 78.
34 Bouverot 1920: 79. The alliance between *qayd* 'Ali ben Ishou Aqebli, the prominent feudal leader of a *jaysh* ("loyalist") tribe, and the sultan was apparently a purely tactical, commonsensical move dictated by expediency (Morsy 1967: 100, 115).
35 Guillaume (1946: 44) provides different figures: 2,500 Doukkali horsemen at Adekhsan, 2,500 of their colleagues from the Shaouia. This probably applies to the post-1693 situation.
36 Bouverot 1920: 79; Naciri 1906–7: 107.
37 Naciri 1906–7: 108.
38 Chiapuris 1979: 23.
39 Naciri 1906–7: 108–9.
40 Naciri 1906–7: 109.

Chapter 9

1   Berque 1955: 268–9.
2   Montagne 1930/1989: 308.
3   Montagne's *leff* theory, which may well have been valid when he undertook his research, comes in for criticism from E. Gellner, who observes that J. Berque (on the strength of a mid-twentieth-century survey) concludes that "the Seksawa, did not fit into the *leff* system" (1969: 66). See also p. xxix of D. Seddon's introduction to an English translation of R. Montagne's classic, *The Berbers* (1973), where he unfairly criticizes the Frenchman for having "failed to analyse in detail [the] inter-relationship between economic and political factors," not all of which were then available. Seddon's arguments rest on *a posteriori* reinterpretation, with post-colonial hindsight giving him an added advantage.
4   Berque 1955: 41.
5   His first name was 'Abdallah, not Mohammed, according to Sadki 1988–9: 67.
6   Justinard 1940: 15 (my translation for all subsequent quotations in this chapter).
7   Justinard 1940: 34.
8   Justinard 1940: 18.
9   Justinard 1940: 33.
10 Justinard 1940: 39.
11 Justinard 1940: 49.
12 Justinard 1940: 55.
13 Justinard 1940: 60.
14 Justinard 1940: 79.
15 Justinard 1940: 83.
16 Justinard 1940: 91–2.
17 Justinard 1940: 114.
18 Sadki 1988–9: 89. "All Moroccan dynasties since the Almohads have been suspicious of this part of the range, haunted as they are by the ghosts of the Almohads."

19 Justinard 1940: 154.
20 Pellow 1890: 135.
21 De la Chapelle 1931: 47. Drouin 1975: 37–52 contains the best account of the saga of the Ayt Yoummour and *qayd* Ou-Barka (or Ou-Barsha). The latter, Arabicized as 'Ali ben Barakat in the *Istiqça* chronicle (Naciri 1906–7), appears to have been a local man, probably an Ayt Idrassen; for further info., cf. Peyron 1991: 1435–6.
22 De la Chapelle 1931: 49; a ruined "Ksiret ou Berka" lies southeast of Tounfit on a strategic knoll overlooking the Ayt Bou 'Arbi gorges; cf. Midelt folio of the old 1/200.000 ordnance survey map; also Peyron 1984: 122.
23 As frequently happened; cf. Lahlimi 1978: 25.
24 Drouin 1975: 46.
25 Drouin 1975: 47.
26 Drouin 1975: 39, n. 21; Roux Archive, IREMAM, Aix-en-Provence, file 56.5.
27 A volume I was unable to consult, having to make do with the 1890 edition (Pellow 1890: 379), featuring an excellent introduction together with notes by Dr. Robert Brown. Cf. also Morsy-Patchett 1963: 289–311.
28 Gellner 1969: xxi.
29 Pellow 1890: 203.
30 The numbers quoted by Pellow are probably grossly exaggerated.
31 Pellow 1890: 203.
32 Morsy 1972: 23–4.
33 Pellow 1890: 203.

Chapter 10

1 Arnaud 1916: 80; Cambon 1952: 62. His mother was a Ma'qil Arab from the Sous. The first time he was deposed (1735) it was for having had 10,000 soldiers of the Black Guard massacred; cf. Brignon et al. 1967: 259.
2 Terrasse 1952: 140.
3 Arnaud 1916: 80.
4 Arnaud 1916: 80.
5 Berque 1955: 81. Seksawa oral tradition cites a similar episode after a village *agadir* had been stormed by a rival group: "those among the besieged whose lives were spared, had their muskets and daggers confiscated and were stripped of their clothing. They escaped stark naked."
6 Arnaud 1916: 80; Brignon et al. 1967: 259.
7 Arnaud 1916: 80. The sultan's payment of these services is interpreted by Arnaud as a form of tribute.
8 Arnaud 1916: 80.
9 Barbour 1965: 122, quoting Terrasse 1952: 140, and both drawing on the *Istiqça* chronicle.
10 Arnaud 1916: 80; this is the first appearance of the B. Mtir in the Meknès *azaghar*.
11 Barbour 1965: 122; described as "a promising individual, conspicuously lacking in self-control," Julien 1969: n.p.ref.
12 Arnaud 1916: 81. Actually spelled "Aït Shtouka," a garbled version of Zaouit Ayt Ishaq, on the site of the first zaouia of Dila', Naciri 1906–7: 366. For a comprehensive survey of the Imhiwach, cf. Drouin 1975: 54–134; also Peyron 2001: 3694–703.
13 Also known as Ben Nasser ou 'Ali, especially in oral tradition; Drouin 1975: 55.

14 Arnaud 1916: 81.

15 Early in the eighteenth century, the Ishqern were summoned by an Amhaoush marabout to occupy former Ayt Yoummour territory; Peyron 2000a: 3614.

16 Michel 1994: 82.

17 Terrasse 1952: 142. A biased post-Protectorate interpretation takes to task Terrasse and other colonial writers over this issue. Admittedly, presenting the *blad as-siba/blad makhzan* dichotomy as a cast-iron absolute is a somewhat restrictive, unimaginative view, though it would be dishonest not to accept a plain fact: sultans who failed to venture beyond their palace walls certainly had trouble ensuring regular payment of taxes! As regards the actual rebellions, they were, in the words of N. Michel, "frequent though limited in scope" (1994: 82).

18 Actually the Ayt Sri; Naciri 1906–7: 335; Arnaud 1916: 81.

19 Terrasse 1952: 143. Terrasse's insistence on these severed lines of communications as supporting his *blad as-siba/blad makhzan* dichotomy is frowned upon by post-colonial historians.

20 'Ali ben Hamida Ezzirari; Naciri 1906–7: 338; with the necessary caveat that claims by the official Vulgate historian need to be taken with a pinch of salt.

21 Arnaud 1916: 81; Michel 1994: 101, quoting M. ad-Du'ayyif, *Tarikh ad-dawla as-sa'ida*, ed. Ahmed el-'Omari, Rabat, 1986.

22 Four times was his father obliged to send him off on the *hajj* (Terrasse 1952: 145). One occasion was in 1778, after he had been proclaimed sultan by the *'abid* (Michel 1994: 85, n. 12).

23 Naciri 1906–7: 370.

24 The 'Alawid *shurafa* usually dismissed the Fazaz Berbers as living in a state of pre-Islamic barbarity (*jahiliyya*) and ungodliness, worshipping springs, rocks, and mountains. After 1812, under strong Wahhabi influence from Arabia, Moulay Sliman made a point of fighting such forms of deviousness and heresy among the mountain folk (Chiapuris 1979: 32; Brignon et al. 1967: 267).

25 Hart 1993: 37. His description of the northwest Berber push is excellent.

26 As an another American researcher has rightly commented, "If the Yaflman tribes had been less successful in blockading them, it is likely the 'Atta would have infiltrated the high country in much greater numbers or even migrated out of the pre-Sahara altogether" (Dunn 1972: 89).

27 Brignon et al. 1967: 260. On Ayt 'Atta stalemate in Atlas, cf. Couvreur 1968: 5.

28 Brignon et al. 1967: 267. This occurred coincidentally with a renewal by Moulay Sliman of *makhzan* ties with Touat between 1800 and 1802 (El Mansour 1990: 104).

29 Dunn 1972: 90.

30 Bouverot 1920: 44, based on oral tradition.

31 Couvreur 1968: 15.

32 Or *'ari w 'ayyash* to give it its Berber name.

33 *asif n-melwiyt* in *tamazight*.

34 Laoust 1932/1934: 137–8; Terrasse 1938; Despois 1949; Peyron 1975: 81–4.

35 Bouverot 1920, according to M. El Mansour (1990: 101): "The Ayt Idrassen were, by the end of the century, the most important military force of central Morocco."

36 Terrasse 1952: 145.

37 For an excellent analysis of these campaigns, see Michel 1994: 85–6.

38 Refers to his last disastrous expedition leading up to the Battle of Lenda (1818).

39 Bouverot 1920: 45. Actually, the Azrou affair was an indecisive victory for Moulay Sliman, and Lenda a total defeat. His other campaigns were moderately successful.

40 For a vivid, if romanticized, account of such a visitation, cf. Boutet *c.* 1935: 39–50.

41 For a discussion of the implications of *dar al-mulk,* cf. Hammoudi 1999: 133–40.

42 El Mansour 1990: 102.

43 El Mansour 1990: 102.

44 Bouverot 1920: 45. (The event apparently occurred in June 1800, the sultan himself being involved with a large army, according to Michel 1994: 106.)

45 Chiapuris 1979: 29; El Mansour 1990: 103. With Mohammed Oua'ziz falling out of favor, his brother Bou'azza Oua'ziz had taken over, an appointment little to the liking of the Beni Mtir.

46 Raynal 1960: 295; Chiapuris 1979: 29; both drawing on the *Istiqça* chronicle.

47 Raynal 1960: 296.

48 Raynal 1960: 296. When, almost a century later, the French explorer de Segonzac (1910: 103) visited the Ayt 'Ayyash, he heard the Beni Mguild scornfully described as "savages."

49 Raynal 1960: 296.

50 The Gerouan defection was understandable; attacked at the sultan's request by lowland and mountain Berbers in October 1807, they had been relocated in the Saïs plain (El Mansour 1990: 103).

51 Arnaud 1916: 82. A. de Prémare has collected an oral satirical poem on the "Azrou incident" (1989: 1124–5) .

52 El Mansour 1990: 105.

53 This animosity at times assumed racist undertones, when Arabic-speaking members of the Cheraga and similar *jaysh* components took to seizing and murdering any Berber levy rash enough to stray near their encampments; cf. Clément 1979: 23.

54 Clément 1979: 107.

55 Also known as Abu Ahmed al-'Arabi ad-Darqawi (1760–1823); Trimingham 1971: 110; for a general account, cf. Peyron 1995a: 2279–83.

56 Peyron 1995a: 2279–83.

57 Peyron 1995a: 2279–83; Brignon et al. 1967: 267; Drouin 1975: 56. Encouraged to participate in an attempt to expand the eastern frontier, he had urged the people of Tlemcen to declare for Morocco (1805), but then Moulay Slimane caught cold feet and welshed on the deal. Moulay el-'Arabi never forgave him for this.

58 Clément 1979: 23–4; El Mansour 1990: 188.

59 Bouverot 1920: 46. In another oral-based version (Guillaume 1946: 45), Foum Kheneg, rather than Tizi L'afit, is mentioned as the route followed by the *mhalla* to reach Ras Tarsha. Possibly, Prince Ibrahim's main force went through the easy Foum Kheneg ravine, while a lightweight detachment detoured via the higher La'fit pass.

60 Oral tradition claims they were traitors, willfully leading the *mhalla* into a trap (Guillaume 1946: 45).

61 Much of the material on this page is based on Clément (1979: 24) and El Mansour (1990: 189), both drawing heavily on the *Istiqça* chronicle by Naciri and Zaïani, not to mention oral sources (Drouin 1975: 94).

62 A password, *srou*, was agreed upon, so that in the heat of battle, "your men will know that I am on their side, and my men will know that you are one of ours" (Drouin 1975: 95).

63 Bouverot 1920: 45.

64 Guillaume 1946: 45. Cannon represented the ultimate symbol of *makhzan* power.

65 Julien 1969: n.p.ref. A mercenary form of respect, as he knew he would be richly rewarded.

66 Barbour 1965: 125. Actually, the sultan was escorted to the fortress of Agouraï, near Meknès.
67 Guillaume 1946: 45. Moulay Srou (Srour) will reappear in our narrative in dramatic circumstances.
68 El Mansour 1990: 190. The "concord" referred to was a brotherly, inter-tribal pact, known as *tada*, whereby members of each group exchanged slippers with their opposite numbers.
69 El Mansour 1990: 191.
70 Drouin 1975: 57, quoting from G. Spillman 1951/2012; also Drouin 1996: 135–6.
71 Drouin 1975: 57.
72 Clément 1979: 37.
73 Clément 1979: 37. These apocalyptic beliefs, conveying hope of better times, still survive among some tribesmen in the area: "Lenda will rise again," is a phrase I heard near Tounfit, Ayt Yahya, March 2001.
74 Arnaud 1916: 83; Cambon 1952: 65.

Chapter 11

1 Arnaud 1916: 83.
2 This, incidentally, was the rationale behind the late nineteenth-century appointment of famous *qayd*s such as Moha ou Hammou Zaïani and Moha ou Saïd.
3 Guennoun 1933: 168.
4 Montagne 1930/1989: 270.
5 Montagne 1930/1989: 270. These social climbers stopped at nothing. There were cases in the Western High Atlas of a successful aspirant to local honors having his rivals quietly murdered even as they sat in his guest chamber. A disgraceful crime by any standards and certainly contrary to Muslim laws of hospitality. See also Berque 1955: 87.
6 Justinard 1954; the Filala were the 'Alawids, the Semala the Tazeroualt marabouts.
7 Jacques-Meunié 1951: 211.
8 Justinard 1928: 345; Montagne 1930/1989: 130.
9 Montagne 1930/1989: 361.
10 This was composed of Beni Mguild, Ayt Ndhir, Immejat, Gerouane, and Ayt Youssi contingents.
11 Pennell 2000: 97, quoting from the *Istiqça* chronicle. Pennell correctly points out, "Thus was political and social rivalry reduced to ethnic terms"—a legacy, incidentally, of Moulay Soulaiman's defeat at Lenda and the perception by 'Alawid sultans of Fazaz Berbers as their ultimate bane. In a related episode, when in 1883 the sultan visited Tadla to assert his authority in an area long under the influence of the Ahansal *igurramn*, the then incumbent, Si Hmad ou Moh, refused to come down and pay homage, claiming he knew no master other than God and retreating instead into Asif Melloul (Ithier 1947: 8).
12 These would have been 1871 model Snider-Enfield breech-loaders, though the Martini-Henry, one of the outstanding rifles of its day, was to find its way to Morocco in considerable numbers shortly afterwards. Some were even license-produced locally at great expense (Pennell 2000: 73). By the end of the nineteenth century the Lee-Metford of Boer War fame had briefly appeared on the local scene; cf. Simou 1994: 153.

13 Jacques-Meunié 1951: 215; Pennell 2000: 101; Schroeter 1988; Charqi and Zaki 2008: 105.

14 Berger 1929: 27; Le Glay 1922: 223–4; Guennoun 1933: 135. The last-named claims there were actually 400 troops supported by three cannon.

15 Berger 1929: 28.

16 Montagne 1930/1989: 113.

17 Bouverot 1920: 53.

18 De Segonzac 1910: 55; cf. also Tarrit 1923: 535.

19 Bouverot 1920: 47. Some confusion surrounds Moulay Hassan's campaigns. An attempt has been made here to piece together an account taken from a hotchpotch of oral and written sources.

20 Le Glay 1922: 284–7.

21 De Segonzac 1910: 57. According to another account, the *harka* behaved so badly on arriving in Aghbala, molesting local women, that the irate Ayt 'Abdi fell on them and massacred them (Ithier 1947: 9). Interestingly, Moulay Srou's tent, no doubt singled out as a worthy trophy, subsequently passed through several hands, being ultimately recovered from the Ayt Merghad sheikh 'Ali ou Benyahya during Moulay Hassan's final campaign near Tafilalt (Guillaume 1946: 49).

22 Guennoun 1933: 188.

23 This was the closest the Berbers ever came to total warfare in their own inter-tribal strife. Disemboweling, to say the least, indicates a certain thoroughness, possibly stemming from a desire to wipe out the very progeny of one's adversary, and has remained one of the ultimate weapons in the Maghribi arsenal, together with emasculation, questionable practices that were to resurface in equally distressing circumstances in the 1954–62 Algerian War.

24 The ravaged tribe sent several deputations to the sultan protesting their innocence. Though he never received them, out of consideration for his vassal, Moha ou Hammou, he finally realized they were not the real culprits (Guennoun 1933: 189; Ithier 1947: 8).

25 Guillaume 1946: 52.

26 A nomination calculated to act as a counterweight to the ambitious Moha ou Hammou.

27 Whether or not the *mhalla* actually reached Asif Melloul is a moot point. However, in 1975, during a visit to Asif Melloul, our guide, Saïd ou Haddou from Ou-Lghazi, claimed that the north bank path we were following was sometimes called *abrid n-makhzan*, or *trik 'askria* (cf. Tarrit 1923: 543), in memory of that campaign. The inhabitants of nearby Zerchan claim that from their *ighrem* they successfully defied the sultan's men about this time (Jacques-Meunié 1951: 109).

28 Guillaume 1946: 52. The place of the ambush was thereafter named Ama'arad n Sidi 'Ali ("Sidi 'Ali's cudgel"), as the marabout had predicted an Ayt Sokhman victory at that very spot.

29 De Segonzac 1910: 55–6. The bulls symbolized submission to the *makhzan*.

30 Ithier 1947: 9; *hediya*, in this case, was a ceremonial gift, a token of submission.

31 Guillaume 1946: 53–4.

32 Le Glay 1922: 287.

33 Le Glay 1922: 28

34 Cf. "La harka de Mulay el Hasan vers le Tafilâlt," 1893: 13–14 and "Mûlay el Hassan I dans le Sud," 1894: 8–9. The Derqawi marabout was famous in southeast Morocco and was venerated as a *duddjal* as far afield as among the Beni Mguild, the Zaïan, and Ayt Youssi. He had actually died a year earlier, but not before having become the

uncrowned king of the Atlas marches. Apart from being a rebel, this gentleman had been found in possession of Moulay Srou's tent.

35 See *Archives Marocaines* 8, 1906: 330; Guillaume 1946: 54.
36 See Montagne 1930/1989: 329–30.
37 Maxwell 1966: 47–8.
38 Maxwell 1966: 50, largely based on Tharaud and Tharaud 1929: 165.
39 Guillaume 1946: 54–5.
40 Guillaume 1946: 96.

Chapter 12

1   Montagne 1930: 17.
2   Montagne 1930/1989: 305–9.
3   Montagne 1930/1989: 312.
4   Montagne 1930/1989: 336–7; Bidwell 1973: 99; Stroomer 2001: 29, 35, 37.
5   Cf. Brown 2014: 4.
6   Montagne 1930/1989: 338; also Bidwell 1973: 102–3.
7   Montagne 1930/1989: 338–9; Tharaud and Tharaud 1929: 168–70; Maxwell 1966: 105–6.
8   Guennoun 1933: 305–30.
9   For a detailed account, see Al-Khalloufi 1993; also Dunn 1981: 31–48.
10 From a ballad on the Ayt Na'aman (Beni Mtir), cf. Peyron and Roux 2002: 110.
11 Cf. Maxwell 1966: 114–15; Harris 1921; also Pennell 2000: 127–9; Charqui and Zaki 2008: 153–5.
12 Concerning El-Kettani, cf. Pennell 2000: 140; à propos of Moulay Zin, see Burke III 1976: 159–60.
13 For those who can read French, one of the best eyewitness accounts of this period is Weisgerber 1947; also Arnaud 1952. For a journalistic coverage of some of these events, cf. Babin 1912.
14 Désiré-Vuillemin 1958: 29–52.
15 Saulay 1985: 1/36–9; Charqui and Zaki 2008: 114–15.
16 "Mangin broke him like a butterfly upon a wheel," Scott O'Connor 1923/1929: 122. Cf. also Charqui and Zaki 2008: 219–23.
17 Maxwell 1966: 124–33; Bidwell 1973: 103–4; El Hiba subsequently retired to Kerdous where he led an ascetic life of prayer and meditation until his death in June 1919; Charqui and Zaki 2008: 227.
18 For a detailed account, see Peyron 1997: 25–41; also Charqui and Zaki 2008: 234.
19 De Segonzac 1910: 58–9.
20 Guennoun 1933: 179–80.
21 Le Glay 1930: 125.
22 Known in French as *Officiers des Affaires Indigènes* (AI). For detailed discussion, cf. Bidwell 1973: Ch. 9.
23 Guennoun 1933: 181.
24 Guennoun 1933: 199; Berger 1929: 136; Le Glay 1930: 252; Vial 1938: 123; Charqui and Zali 2008: 241.
25 Cf. "*Sidi Raho est un as,*" Bordeaux 1935: 120; Le Glay 1921: 197.
26 Le Glay 1921: 186; Burke III 1976: 162, 190; Pennell 2000: 156. The coalition included elements from Beni Mtir, Beni Mguild, Ayt Youssi, and Ayt Seghrushen; Ayt Sadden and Beni Ouaraïn contingents were also involved at one juncture. This is an interesting

example of cooperation between spiritual (Sidi Raho) and temporal leaders (Mtiri *qayd* Aqqa Boubidmani, a recent member of Moulay Zin's bogus *makhzan*).

27 Le Glay 1921: 190.
28 Le Glay 1921: 189; Babin 1912: 200, 215; Tharaud and Tharaud 1929: 52. The Ayt Fringo and Ayt 'Arfa clans followed Sidi Raho into the hills according to Reisser and Bachelot 1918: 40.
29 Peyron and Roux 2002: 57, 59.
30 Guillaume 1946: 31.
31 Guennoun 1934: 34–5.
32 Charqi and Zaki 2008: 210–11.
33 Tharaud and Tharaud 1929: 53. *imjuhad* = "Holy War combatants."
34 Lahlimi 1978: 28–9; Simou 1994; Pennell 2000: 123.
35 Brignon et al. 1967: 324. For an admirable summary in English of this debate concerning the "Struggle for Morocco's past," cf. Gellner 1969: 22–9.
36 Lit. "One day the Christians will come [out] and attack you," Peyron 2000: 109.
37 Personal conversation with René Euloge (author of *Les Derniers Fils de l'Ombre*, etc.), summer 1972.
38 Zaouit Ahansal, May 1984. I heard similar complaints from Ayt Hadiddou tribesmen on the shuttle truck between Imilshil and Aghbala, spring 1994.
39 Peyron and Roux 2002: 141–2. From a ballad by a Tounfit bard; all the more surprising as, with this allusion to the Qarawiyin, the Ayt Yahya *amdyaz* expresses concern at the fate of Fez, a city whose inhabitants would usually have little time for uncouth, ill-clad mountaineers of his ilk!
40 For an excellent account of this, see Aouchar 2002: 80–96.
41 See Rivet 1999: Ch. 2, "Une guerre de trente ans."

Chapter 13

1   The standard work in French is Rivet's 1988; for detailed expressions of the colonial view, see Raynaud 1923, Cambon 1952: Chs. 9 and 10, and Saulay 1985: 1/34–43; for accounts in English, a well-documented volume by Gershovich 2000: 45–62. See also Pennell 2000: Ch.4; Bidwell 1973; the highly readable Porch 2005; Burke III 1976: 173–190; and the excellent Kably 2015.
2   Guillaume 1946: 147
3   Gershovich 2000: 107–11.
4   Guennoun 1933: 182–3.
5   Guillaume 1946: 138.
6   Guennoun 1933: 172.
7   Magnin 1913: 56.
8   Lines 13–16 from *tamdyazt* on the Battle of Merraman, to give the action its Berber name; Hamri 2005: 133.
9   These included some fifteen model '92 cavalry carbines (*mousquetons*), eighteen model '86–'93 magazine rifles (Lebel), 1,400 model '74 rifles (Gras, or Chassepot, *sassbu*); also some Winchester (*settashya*), Lee-Metford, Martini-Henry, and Remington rifles, the rest being outmoded flintlock muskets of the *buhaba* or *bushfer* type; Berber informant quoted by Guillaume 1946: 145.
10 Guillaume 1946: 23; Saulay 1985: 67; cf. also Gershovich 2000: 99.
11 Guennoun 1933: 210.

12 Le Glay 1930: 167–8.

13 Le Glay 1930: 241–9; Guennoun 1933: 220–4; Guillaume 1946: 162–8; a brief account in English in Scott O'Connor 1923/1929: 155–6; also Gershovich 2000: 103.

14 Peyron and Roux 2002: 176. Extract from a 54-line Ishqern ballad devoted to the battle.

15 Peyron and Roux 2002: 58. Visits from dead spirits, expressed in the nocturnal crying of an owl (*tawusht*), are considered a particularly evil omen by Berbers.

16 Peyron and Roux 2002: 173.

17 Laverdure's sword, along with one of the machine guns in perfect working order, was finally recovered near Tounfit in July 1931; Guillaume 1946: 309.

18 Peyron and Roux 2002: 92. N.B. Zaïani, "Zaïan tribesman" (Ar.) = *azayyi* (Ber.).

19 Gershovich 2000: 101; cf. also Ben Lahcen 2003: 112–20.

20 Théveney 1930–2: 490.

21 Le Glay 1930: 104–6.

22 Magnin 1913: 61–2.

23 J. Martin, *Je suis un Légionnaire*, 81–2, 171–2; R. Euloge, *Silhouettes*, 119.

24 Théveney 1930–2: 334.

25 A contemporary observer described him as "the wisest and most impartial of the Imehzan' and the most likely candidate to take over from his uncle the Zaïani"; Cne. Bendaoud 1917: 276–306. Mi'ami, Moha's son by a Fassi lady, had bushwhacked a French Native Affairs officer in highly dubious circumstances, despite which his subsequent odyssey through the Middle Atlas, across the High Atlas to Ayt Merghad territory and eventually Rio de Oro, has since been depicted by oral tradition as an epic. Cf. A. Roux archive, Aix-en-Provence, file XX; Khadaoui (n.d.), http://www.tawiza.net/Tawiza95/khadaoui.

26 An entire volume could be devoted to German involvement by proxy in the Atlas campaigns. Cf. Ben Lahcen 2003: 124, 128.

27 Théveney 1930–2: 35.

28 Cf. Le Glay 1930: viii: "The finest individuals in the opposite camp, our most worthy adversaries ... were undoubtedly those we met in the harsh hills of the Middle Atlas, where men like Sidi Raho, Moha ou Hammou, independent Berbers both ... were our resolute yet loyal opponents."

Chapter 14

1   Guillaume 1946: 131–2; Voinot 1939: 108.

2   Peyron and Roux 2002: 74.

3   < *ti mhadd it*, "the one that watches" in Ber.

4   Voinot 1939: 211; Saulay 1985: 85–6; cf. a romantic account of the siege of a French post near Tishshoukt, probably based on the Taghzout affair, in D'Agraive 1948: 148–59.

5   Ben Lahcen 2003: 137.

6   Guillaume 1946: 180–1; Voinot 1939: 174.

7   Gershovich 2000: 9–110.

8   Peyron and Roux 2002: 75

9   Voinot 1939: 175.

10 Convicts serving in the army popularly known as *Bats d'Af* (*Bataillons d'Afrique*), or *Joyeux* (hence *id juyyu* in Berber), and the lowest of the low in the *Armée d'Afrique* pecking order.

11 Voinot 1939: 175–6.
12 Guillaume 1946: 193.
13 Guillaume 1946: 197; Voinot 1939: 175–6.
14 Guillaume 1946: 198.
15 Voinot 1939: 199.
16 Saulay 1985: 114.

Chapter 15

1 Quedenfelt 1902–4: 172.
2 Dunn 1973: 85–107.
3 Colorful, picturesque bandits.
4 A tale admirably told in Porch 2005b: 226–7.
5 Dunn 1977: 235.
6 Dunn 1977: 235; cf. also Voinot 1939: 60 for another version of message: "We invite you to leave your walls and fight clean in the open, failing which the Muslim warriors will come and inflict a shameful defeat upon you."
7 Voinot 1939: 60.
8 Dunn 1977: 235.
9 Dunn 1977: 236; Voinot 1939: 60.
10 Peyron and Roux 2002: 83–4; from a ballad epic by Moulay 'Aomar of Tazrouft, one of the most famous *imdyazn* of Zaouia Sidi Hamza.
11 Manue 1930: 220.
12 Voinot 1939: 242.
13 Voinot 1939: 244.
14 Voinot 1939: 244.
15 Spillman 1936.
16 Louis 1916: 42–3, and February 1918: 53; Voinot 1939: 50.
17 Article by Moulay Ahmed 'Alaoui in *Le Matin du Sahara,* 1982 (https://fr.wiktionary.org/wiki/berbéritude).
18 Bordeaux 1931: 106–7; Peyron 1991: 1434–5; also Charqui and Zaki 2008: 246–54.
19 Bordeaux 1931: 107.
20 Vial 1938: 116.
21 Collected by myself from Aïcha 'Azzaoui, Ayt Y'azza segment of Ayt 'Atta, Ifrane, May 2002.
22 Ould Cheikh 1936: ix.
23 Vial 1938: 116 Janon 1941: 100–2.
24 Bordeaux 1931: 108; Saulay 1985: 94; Gershovich 2000: 110; Doury 2008: 310–13.
25 Vial 1938: 117.
26 Théveney 1930–2: 325–6. As proof of these attempts to achieve cohesion, according to M. Ben Lahcen (2003: 138), a high-level meeting between Moha ou Saïd, Moha ou Hammou, and Sidi Raho actually took place in 1918 at Enjil, in Ayt Youssi territory.
27 Voinot 1939: 255.
28 Voinot 1939: 245; Théveney 1930–2: 325; Vial 1938: 117.
29 Saulay 1985: 1/94.
30 Voinot 1939: 254; Guillaume 1946: 183.
31 Théveney 1930–2: 326.
32 Bordeaux 1931: 109; Ould-Cheikh 1936: xi.

33 Ould-Cheikh 1936: xi.
34 Hart 1984: 130.
35 Some Moroccan researchers are less than severe in their judgment of his exactions; cf. Charqi and Zaki 2008: 250–1.

Chapter 16

1 Montagne 1930/1989: 336; cf. also Maxwell 1966: 73–4.
2 Célérier and Charton 1924: 194.
3 Célérier and Charton 1924: 193.
4 Montagne 1930/1989: 340.
5 Spillman 1968: 50.
6 Tharaud and Tharaud 1929: 199–200.
7 I heard this story in the area, March 1982.
8 Local tradition claims that in the old days Mecca pilgrims used to climb to the summit of this hill, grow wings, and fly to the Hejaz! Information obtained in Tounfit area, at Asaka village (1981).
9 Cf. Gellner (1969) for a thorough case study of the Ahansal marabouts.
10 *képi* = *bu shemrur* in Berber. A reference to the distinctive, pillbox cap French officers usually wear.
11 Tharaud and Tharaud 1929: 200–1.
12 Louis 1916: 32–3.
13 Tharaud and Tharaud 1929: 228–32; cf. Maxwell 1966: 149. Powder-play is known as *fantasia* in tourist-brochure jargon, *tburida* in Arabic, *tafrawt* in Berber.
14 Hart 1984: 166.
15 Babin 1923: 33–4.
16 Babin 1923: 16–17.
17 Martin 1925: 93.
18 Hart 1984: 167; Babin 1923: 37 claims only twenty-two killed and fifty wounded; interestingly, Spillman 1968: 47 puts the figure at 250–300 casualties all told.
19 Hart 1984: 37.
20 Hart 1984: 144–5.
21 The onomatopoeia *taraka* means "machine gun" in Berber.
22 Tharaud and Tharaud 1929: 225; collected by M. Coliac, an interpreter stationed at the Azilal outpost.
23 Babin 1923: 157–9; Guillaume 1946: 232; Saulay 1985: 121.
24 Spillman 1968: 50.
25 Martin 1927: 277–88.
26 Voinot 1939: 367.
27 Guillaume 1946: 249.

Chapter 17

1 Guennoun 1933: 182.
2 Guillaume 1946: 207.
3 Guennoun 1933: 204–5.

4 Guennoun 1934: 82. For a romanticized picture of this character, cf. Le Glay 1923.
5 Guennoun 1933: 86.
6 M. Holmström 1930: 164.
7 Guillaume 1946: 219.
8 These included the *kerkur n-taqa* ("cairn of the juniper") at Tafessasset, the *kerkur n-umzra* at Bou Wattas, and another at Tinteghallin dating back to Bou-Bker Amhaoush.
9 Guennoun 1934: 272.
10 Guennoun 1934: 28.
11 Guennoun 1933: 256.
12 Guennoun 1933: 258.
13 Guennoun 1933: 259–60; Guillaume 1946: 210; Saulay 1985: 117–18.
14 Guennoun 1934: 267.
15 Peyron and Roux 2002: 154–5.
16 Containing tribesmen from the Ayt Sokhman, Ishqern, Ayt Ihand, Ayt Myill, and Ayt Yahya, usually at loggerheads with each other.
17 Holmström 1930: 112–14, for an eyewitness account of operations around Alemsid at this time.
18 Guillaume 1946: 221.
19 Guillaume 1946: 222; Voinot 1939: 358; see also, drawing heavily on Guillaume, the account in Saulay 1985: 118–19. While Guillaume claims victory, with only seventeen killed and twenty-seven wounded in the column, Voinot cites a higher figure: seventy-one killed and twenty-seven wounded, which tells a rather different story. There is probably a mistake over the casualty figures.
20 Le Glay 1923: 216. Cowards returning unharmed from the battle would be marked with *henna*, thus losing all credibility in the eyes of their womenfolk and fellow-tribesmen.
21 Guillaume 1946: 225–6.
22 Roux 1992: 169.
23 Guennoun 1933: 263; 1934: 272; Guillaume 1946: 230.
24 Ben 'Aomar had sworn he would cut neither hair nor beard till he had succeeded. Having failed, he was forced to shave, this in itself being his punishment and suitably shaming him in the eyes of all men.
25 Fragment of ballad collected at El Kebbab in 1932 (Roux Archive, Aix-en-Provence). The last line depicts the despair of a tribesman who, let down by his marabouts, hopes that some good will come from the arrival of the French from *azaghar*, "the plain."
26 Guillaume 1946: 220.
27 Guennoun 1933: 315.
28 Guennoun 1933: 270–2.
29 Peyron and Roux 2002: 61. From some Ichqern poetic couplets (*izlan*), Khenifra, 1934.

Chapter 18

1 This confirms local tradition, according to which *c.* 1690 Moulay Ismaïl penetrated well into the mountain fastenesses between Bou Iblan and Bou Nasser (Marcy 1929: 105).
2 Bordeaux 1935: 110.
3 These men came from Ayt Oumnasf; cf. Reisser and Bachelot 1918: 38.

4   Reisser and Bachelot 1918: 47.
5   Reisser and Bachelot 1918: 46. Sidi 'Ali ou Yahya is the tribe's patron saint and the very
     man who had petrified (*seghr*) the jackal (*ushen*), hence their name.
6   Reisser and Bachelot 1918: 50. Also Ayt Slim, possibly derived from Ayt Slimia, "son
     of the converted one." A woman from this formerly Jewish tribe converted to Islam, so
     goes an old legend.
7   Reisser and Bachelot 1918: 50. The Ayt Smah who had laid siege to Ksabi in 1919.
8   Reisser and Bachelot 1918: 50. This was the case with the Ayt Lhsseyn ou n-Zemmourt
     clan.
9   Reisser and Bachelot 1918: 50.
10   These included contingents from Ahl Tsiouant, Ahl Aïoun, and Ayt Bou Illoul.
11   Made up of several tribes such as the Beni Zeggout, the Beni Bou Zert, and Ayt
     Jellidasen (lit. "sons of their king"), not to mention their spiritual mentors, the
     Tanshraramt *shurafa*; Marcy 1929: 79–81.
12   Manue 1930: 123.
13   Letter to Albert de Mun, quoted in Maurois 1931: 226–7.
14   Rivet 1999: 25, 27.
15   These included Moulay Hmad ou Lahssen, Mouloud el-Marmoushi, and el-Chinguetti,
     together with Sidi Raho. Voinot 1939: 206.
16   The wild boar symbolizes the fighter, the mountaineer, in Berber resistance period
     poetry; see Peyron 2000: 117.
17   Voinot 1939: 206.
18   Peyré 1950: 47.
19   Voinot 1939: 190.
20   Voinot 1939: 193.
21   Voinot 1939: 193. Partisans, *lbertiza* in Beber, were local levies, usually from a clan that
     had recently surrendered, who were given back their rifles and instructed to act as
     skirmishers (actually thinly-disguised cannon fodder) ahead of French columns. Their
     wages amounted to roughly two pence a day, plus an issue of cartridges, and the right
     to pillage and plunder refractory tribesmen. They were not 100 percent reliable.
22   Scott O'Connor 1923/1929: 125.
23   Voinot 1939: 202.
24   Voinot 1939: 202.
25   Voinot 1939: 214.
26   Bordeaux 1935: 120–1.
27   Bordeaux 1935: 120; Voinot 1939: 208; Saulay 1985: 137.
28   Bordeaux 1935: 138–9.
29   Bordeaux 1935: 158.
30   Voinot 1939: 220.
31   Voinot 1939: 223.
32   Bordeaux 1935: 126. This comprised twenty infantry battalions, seven squadrons of
     cavalry (*Spahis*, *Chasseurs*, etc.), sixteen artillery batteries, and six squadrons of
     biplanes. The latter had spent the winter making photo-reconnaissance flights to
     provide ground troops with proper maps for the forthcoming campaign (Rousseau
     1923: 564).
33   Bordeaux 1935: 129.
34   If we are to believe Klose c. 1927: 241–3, some *Tirailleurs* and *Spahis* also turned tail.
     In his official version, Voinot merely observes that "around midday the situation
     became serious, reinforcements had to be called up" (1939: 215); while Saulay (1985:

139–40) states that "the partisans ... had just lost some fifty men and were showing signs of exhaustion."

35 I found an unexploded vintage model hand grenade in a stream in Bou 'Arfa vale (June 1966).

36 Klose *c.* 1927: 240. After the rout at Anoual (1921) in the Rif, the rifles had been captured from the Spaniards, subsequently finding their way south in the saddlebags of gunrunning muleteers.

37 Klose *c.* 1927: 240. There are many recorded instances of the active role played by Tamazight women in these battles, though few as vivid as this.

38 Klose *c.* 1927: 250. There is possibly some exaggeration here regarding the suggestion that Berbers were using heavy weapons.

39 Three Legionnaires deserted that night. Guilty of some misdemeanor, after an altercation with a sergeant they been made to sleep in their one-man tents *outside* the bivouac and were last seen heading towards Jbel Tishshoukt! (Klose *c.* 1927: 275). This was far from a rare occurrence, though. Given the lack of food, not to mention other hardships, their everyday life among resistance fighters was anything but pleasant; cf. Ward Price 1934: 211–12.

40 A unit of the Foreign Legion urged forward at gunpoint, *Tirailleurs* from the same unit that had deserted at Oum Jeniba, with orders from Poeymirau to open fire on them should they run away; cf. Klose (*c.* 1927: 276–7).

41 Voinot 1939: 216; Saulay puts the figure of French casualties at sixty-four dead and 170 wounded, the Moroccans having lost approximately 200 killed and 300 wounded (1985: 141).

42 Voinot 1939: 142.

43 D'Esme 1952: 91–3.

44 Bordeaux 1935: 134; Carrère (1973: 152) says the "grim carnage" at El-Mers had accounted for a total of over 300 French casualties.

45 Voinot 1939: 209. There were only fifteen casualties on the French side.

46 Voinot 1939: 209.

47 Voinot 1939: 228–9.

48 Saulay 1985: 144.

49 Bordeaux 1935: 131.

50 Voinot 1939: 219; Gershovich 2000: 116–17.

51 For the full story of Ayt Bou Slama resistance, cf. Peyron 1996: 75–95.

52 Peyré 1950: 96.

53 As one observer puts it, "The deterioration of their living conditions only enhanced their resolution to fight to the end and led them to desperate attacks on French outposts ... these pockets of resistance remained an open sore in the midst of the occupied zone, an unresolved problem which the Lyautey administration left for its successor." Gershovich 2000: 116.

Chapter 19

1 For background I have drawn mainly on Woolman 1957/1968; Hart 1976: 369–404; Pennell 2000: 188–210; Charqi and Zaki 2008: 279–88; and also the comprehensive account by Courcelle-Labrousse and Marmié 2008.

2 Kably 2015: 154.

3   Verde 2017. In the Shefshawn museum she is depicted as a helmeted lady with cuirass
    and sword.
4   Kably 2015: 407.
5   Charqi and Zaki 2008: 153–4.
6   Charqi and Zaki 2008: 55. This was General Pinto; cf. https://es.wikipedia.org/wiki/
    Desastre_del_Barranco_del_Lobo.
7   Charqi and Zaki 2008: 159.
8   Charqi and Zaki 2008: 121–46. Raissouni is chiefly famous for having kidnapped and
    held to ransom celebrities such as Perdikaris, Walter Harris, and *qayd* Maclean.
9   Courcelle-Labrousse and Marmié 2008: 47, 54.
10 Courcelle-Labrousse and Marmié 2008: 57.
11 Courcelle-Labrousse and Marmié 2008: 73–4. Cf. also https://en.wikipedia.org/wiki/
    Battle_of_Annual, quoting from Woolman 1957/1968: 96. For a recent Spanish
    account, cf. Garcia 2011.
12 Cf. Charqi 2003.
13 For a discussion of this aspect, cf. Tahtah 2000.
14 Courcelle-Labrousse and Marmié 2008: 120.
15 Courcelle-Labrousse and Marmié 2008: 134.
16 Catroux 1952: 164. Formerly with Raissouni, Kheriro (a Jebli from Beni Hazmar tribe)
    had gone over to Abdelkrim; cf. Charqi and Zaki 2008: 287.
17 Catroux 1952: 198–225; also Hubert-Jacques 1927: 221–4.
18 Catroux 1952: 175. Crop failures in the Rif and a sealed southern border with the
    French were also factors in prompting 'Abdelkrim to attack; cf. Wyrtzen 2015: 132.
19 More accounts of these desperate sieges of French forts in Belot 1946: 252–97; Celarié
    1928: 11–151; also Courcelle-Labrousse and Marmié 2008: 165–86.
20 Lyautey castigated this *sauvagerie*, sending urgent requests to Paris for shells
    containing gas to be used in retaliation for alleged Rifian atrocities. He never got them,
    though the Spaniards did get round to dropping gas canisters from aircraft;
    Courcelles-Labrousse and Marmié 2008: 203.
21 Courcelles-Labrousse and Marmié 2008: 221. Otherwise, Foreign Legion units were
    disciplined and reliable, providing the mainstay of the French forces. There were also
    Algerian soldiers deserting to 'Abdelkrim, the latter's victories arousing undisguised
    enthusiasm among Algerians in the Oran district.
22 Courcelle-Labrousse and Marmié 2008: 229–30; also Hubert-Jacques 1927: 250.
23 Catroux 1952: 202–6.
24 Catroux 1952: 207; also Hubert-Jacques 1927: 211.
25 Courcelle-Labrousse and Marmié 2008: 246.
26 Catroux 1952: 230–1.
27 Courcelle-Labrousse and Marmié 2008: 246.
28 Courcelle-Labrousse and Marmié 2008: 253–4; Hubert-Jacques 1927: 256–7
29 Courcelle-Labrousse and Marmié 2008: 255.
30 Courcelle-Labrousse and Marmié 2008: 258–9.
31 https://en.wikipedia.org/wiki/Rif_War, quoting from Perry 2005: 274.
32 Catroux 1952: 245–6. Given his success at Anoual, Abdelkrim felt obliged to attack
    France.
33 Courcelle-Labrousse and Marmié 2008: 274.
34 Catroux 1952: 259; Hubert-Jacques 1927: 335–6.
35 Courcelle-Labrousse and Marmié 2008: 267, 269; also *L'Expresse du Sud*, September 20,
    1925.

36 Courcelle-Labrousse and Marmié 2008: 272; also Catroux 1952: 26
37 Catroux 1952: 260; Pascal 2009: 319–38, https://www.cairn.info/revue-strategique-2009-1-page-319.htm.
38 Catroux 1952: 267–9.
39 Catroux 1952: 270.
40 Catroux 1952: 271; also Courcelle-Labrousse and Marmié 2008: 280–3.
41 Catroux 1952: 273–5.
42 Catroux 1952: 286.
43 Catroux 1952: 295–6. Bournazel was known as *"l'homme à la veste rouge"* ("he of the red jacket"); Bordeaux 1935: 204–8.
44 Catroux 1952: 304–5.
45 Catroux 1952: 323.
46 Courcelle-Labrousse and Marmié 2008: 326.
47 https://artsandculture.google.com/exhibit/7ALS34yVgnJIKw. For more on Millán Astray and the *Tercio*, cf. Alvarez 2001.
48 Celarié 1928: 154–99; Courcelle-Labrousse and Marmié 2008: 328–9.
49 Courcelle-Labrousse and Marmié 2008: 336; Hart 1976: 403. He was buried near the tomb of Sidi Abdesslam Ben Mchich; cf. Charqi and Zaki 2008: 288; Pascal 2009: 319–38.
50 Wyrtzen 2015: 135.

Chapter 20

1   Ward Price 1934: 62.
2   Ward Price 1934: 62; confirmed as being official policy by Guillaume 1946: 87.
3   A fact openly acknowledged by French journalist R. Janon 1941: 98.
4   Bordeaux 1935; cf. also Vial 1938.
5   Peyron 2000: 116.
6   Psichari 1920/1967.
7   Janon 1941: 49.
8   Bordeaux 1931: 55; also Manue 1930: 79.
9   Méraud 1990: 95; quote from Gal. G. Diberder's unpublished personal archive.
10 Col. Materne, in charge of Native Affairs training (1934–7); Méraud 1990: 27.
11 Voinot 1939: 246; Saulay 1985: 238. The incident, involving the Ayt Bel Lhassen segment, was sparked by two notables influenced by diehards who had escaped from the *tache de Taza*; also angry and no doubt humiliated at having to hand in their arms to the AI officer. Their attack on the outpost was beaten off, and they failed to break out into the Sahara. They were later encircled on Jbel Bouferma, south of Talsint, and forced to surrender on Christmas Day of the same year.
12 Ou-Skounti 1991: 167.
13 Based on Guennoun 1934; Janon 1941; Holmström 1930; Peyré 1950; Weygand 1954; D'Agraive 1948, etc.
14 Janon 1941: 53.
15 Scott O'Connor 1923/1929: 149.
16 Womanizing of this kind could have its downside, though Lieut. Boulet-Desbareau, while never himself succumbing to the charms of Berber women, refrained from criticizing those of his colleagues who crossed that particular bridge (Méraud 1990: 158); see also my "Entre haine and amour," *AWAL* 19 (1997): 12.

17 Weygand 1954: 176–84; also Méraud 1990: 15.

18 I interviewed some of the parties concerned: Ribat al-Kheir (Ahermoumou),
    September 1973; Tounfit, March 1982; Ayt Hadiddou n-Imedghas, November 1984;
    Anefgou, June 1998, etc. Cf. also my "Saga des Ayt Bou Slama," *EDB* 14 (1996): 75–95.

19 Méraud 1990: 171. *Bel Ma'aqul* (Raclot 1937) was actually the title of a book; this
    expression could have been the unofficial motto of the Native Affairs officer.

20 Méraud 1990: 15. Possibly apocryphal, but we have an orally recorded case of this
    actually happening southeast of Taza in 1923, after the Beni Bou Zert surrendered; see
    my "Saga des Ayt Bou Slama," *EDB* 14 (1996).

21 Manue 1934.

22 Pinon 1935: 149.

23 Janon 1941: 204; Méraud 1990: 16.

24 Scott O'Connor 1923/1929: 152; also: "Conquer, then hold out one's hand to the
    conquered; that's the way with Native Affairs officers," Weygand 1954: 101.

25 Janon 1948: 113.

26 As in the case of an irrigation channel, the *targa n-burlanj* in the Ayt Bou 'Arbi gorge,
    that a villager of Ayt Chrad showed me, not without a hint of respect in his voice (May
    1975).

27 Wielding pick and shovel was deemed unseemly by men more used to knife and rifle.
    However, participation in a *corvée* (*tiwizi*) was only expected five days a year, but even
    then you could pay somebody else to do the job; Carrère 1973: 145.

28 Méraud 1990: 15.

29 According to historian Germain Ayache; personal conversation, Rabat Faculty of
    Letters, 1975.

30 Berque 1962: 115; Monteil 1958; Gellner 1969: 19.

31 Post-1956 critics of France's alleged evangelizing ambitions should recall that she had
    become a lay republic in 1905, with the division between church and state
    unambiguously stated. Making Christians of her North African subjects, or *protégés*,
    could never, ever, have become official state policy, however much the Roman Catholic
    clergy might have wished to do so. These questions actually belong to the debate on
    the so-called "Berber dahir" of 1930.

32 Bidwell 1973: 155–98; Landau 1950: 190, 192.

33 The cover of D'Agraive 1948 shows a Berber woman gazing admiringly up at a French
    AI officer—something of a popular contemporary stereotype! Another account has a
    Berber telling a Frenchman, "We never asked for anything . . . we were happy without
    you" (Guennoun 1934: 90).

34 Peyron 2000: 115.

35 Guennoun 1934: 171; Janon 1941: 50–2; Weygand 1954: 166.

36 Guennoun 1934: 252–3.

37 Voinot 1939: 401.

38 Peyron 2000: 117. The hill of Terwillal (Tourgillal) overlooking Ayt Shaq, feels
    indignant at having had a fort built on its summit; by wedding a wild boar it conveys
    its defiance and urges Hammou ou 'Amr to fight to the finish. As a local Berber said to
    a French officer, "Your very presence on Tourgillal hill is an insult to all those who
    wear turbans!" (Guennoun 1934: 88).

39 Peyré 1950: 65.

40 Ward Price 1934: 230

41 Carrère 1973: 50.

42 Saulay 1985: 146.

43 Carrère 1973: 53.
44 Carrère 1973: 50.
45 Bordeaux 1935: 138; also Ward Price 1934: 231; Saulay 1985: 146, etc.
46 Gershovich 2000: 145.
47 Voinot 1939: 231.
48 Saulay 1985: 203.
49 Saulay 1985: 202 makes light of the day's fighting, mentioning only four killed and eight wounded among the Goums; interestingly, however, Voinot (1939: 230) speaks of forty-seven dead in the ranks of the partisans (visualized as cannon fodder anyway), including their French officer.
50 Voinot 1939: 232
51 This ordnance was conveyed to the scene by a 0.60 m railway from Sidi Harazem (just outside Fez) to Ahermoumou. Up-trains would transport various military supplies, soldiers, horses, and fodder; down-trains would be mostly laden with firewood. To this day there are vestiges of the line, including station buildings and part of a platform at Ahermoumou. Conversation with M. A. Kerouach, March 2004.
52 Saulay 1985: 204.
53 Saulay 1985: 205–6.
54 Algerian *tirailleurs* and Foreign Legionaries; Saulay 1985: 206; Voinot 1939: 232; Celarié 1928: 211–12.
55 Celarié 1928: 228.
56 Celarié 1928: 232–3 contains possibly the most detailed account of what amounted to a humiliating reverse for the French.
57 Saulay 1985: 207. Whereas there had been an anti-war movement in France over the Rif war, it failed to show undue concern over the fate of Sidi Raho and his men. A certain traitor, El-Bahlouli by name, was allegedly instrumental in the collapse of Ouaraïni resistance at this time, though he was later killed in retaliation by local people. Conversation with M. A. Kerouach, Zloul plain, February 2004.
58 Celarié 1928: 218.
59 Rivet 1999: 83.
60 *BCAF*, April 1930, contains a picture of him, along with other notables, greeting Resident Lucien Saint, during the latter's first visit to the Atlas front.
61 *BCAF*, April 1930: 209.
62 Conversation with M. Mzerd, Talzemt, May 1984.
63 Voinot 1939: 196, 231. There is a *qasida* devoted to this intrepid fighter (Alouiz 2005). According to Voinot, he was one of Moha ou Hammou Zaïani's sons, though this is discounted locally. Given his intimate knowledge of the area, he is more likely to have come from Ayt Ben 'Ali, northeast of Ahermoumou. Conversation with A. Kerouach, Zloul plain, 2 February 2004.
64 Saulay 1985: 208.
65 Saulay 1985: 208.
66 Reminiscent of General Crooks, of US 7th Cavalry fame, possibly using Mescalero or Mimbreno scouts against Chiricahua Apache.
67 Saulay 1985: 215; Gershovich 2000: 144–5. For discussion of the advantages of the "oil stain" policy over the previous massive use of *Groupes Mobiles*, cf. Guillaume 1946: 106–9.
68 Guillaume 1946: 233.
69 Guillaume 1946: 241; Voinot 1939: 360–2; Saulay 1985: 216–17.
70 The theme of several contemporary poems; see Roux 1992: 165–219.

71 Méraud 1990: 124.

72 In contemporary French currency the equivalent of 3,000,000 francs. Voinot 1939: 369; Guillaume 1946: 252; Méraud, 1990: 124 adds a rider to the effect that a quantity of "fantasia rifles" were included in the ransom.

73 Méraud, 1990: 252.

Chapter 21

1   Spillman 1936: 25.

2   "Notice sur le Tafilalet" *c.* 1930: 7.

3   Manue 1930: 221.

4   Voinot 1939: 247.

5   Voinot 1939: 247. The Doui Menia nomads who served in the Saharan companies, skillful fighters in their own right, were supposed to outdo the Ayt Hammou at their own game.

6   [Guennoun] 1932: 399.

7   Voinot 1939: 247.

8   Saulay 1985: 239–40. In a development typical of the tight-laced mindset that has often plagued the French military, Tournemire was at first reprimanded for having taken unwarranted risks; it took a visit to southeast Morocco by Marshal Franchet d'Esperey to free him of all blame.

9   Voinot 1939: 248; Saulay 1985: 239.

10 Bordeaux 1931: 61; Voinot 1939: 247; Saulay 1985: 239. A mounted company was a hybrid, mule-mounted unit, with every two soldiers taking turns to ride their one steed. A somewhat unsatisfactory arrangement when faced with highly mobile adversaries.

11 Bordeaux 1931: 110.

12 [Guennoun] 1932: 399.

13 Saulay 1985: 265–6.

14 Voinot 1939: 379.

15 Parlange 1927: 11. This was none other than the famous *burlanj*, later one of France's Native Affairs specialists, here making his début.

16 See opening chapters of Weygand 1954.

17 Voinot 1939: 385; Janon 1948.

18 Action report by Lieut. de Hauteclocque, quoted by Saulay 1985: 270.

19 Action report by Lieut. Lecomte (commanding Goum from Mzizel), Saulay 1985: 269.

20 The name *wi n-iwaliwn* ("place of the voices") probably derived from fact that the Tadighoust gorge is famous for its echo. Conversation with M. A. Kerouach, March 2004.

21 Actually Jean Boulet-Desbareau (known to the Berbers after this fight as *mulay al-lbarud*, "prince of battle"), who was replacing his brother Roger, then on leave.

22 Khettouch 1982.

23 Boulet-Desbareau 1985: 10; Voinot and Saulay mention some twenty dead for the Goum, forty-four in all.

24 Méraud 1990: 128.

25 Account based on Boulet-Desbareau 1985: 10; Janon 1948: 66–7; Voinot 1939: 390; Saulay 1985: 273; Khettouch 1982.

26 Boulet-Desbareau 1985: 11. Why indeed? Ritual mutilation of dead bodies on the field of battle appears to be part of the culture over a long swathe of territory running from Morocco and Algeria, then on across to Danakil territory (Ethiopia), up through Arabia, Iraq, and into Afghanistan.

27 Based on the fact of known alliances between Belqasm and the leading raiders of the day, whether Ayt Hammou, Ayt Khebbash, or Ayt ʿIsa Izem (Janon 1941: 100–1); also material in Ould-Cheikh 1936: 200–15.

28 Saulay 1985: 274.

29 Saulay 1985: 274.

30 Voinot 1939: 385

31 Saulay 1985: 243; Gershovich 2000: 146–47, 150.

32 [Guennoun] 1932: 403; for the couplet, cf. Peyron and Roux 2002: 60.

33 Bouverot 1920: 39–41; Guennoun 1933: 305–7.

34 An interesting toponym; *maʿasker*, lit. "owner of soldiers," an allusion to the local clan's supposed warlike prowess.

35 Guennoun 1933: 307–8.

36 Canal 1902: 49; also de Segonzac 1910.

37 Huré 1952: 6. Dissidents in the area possessed some 2,000 rifles, some 500 of them repeaters.

38 Roux archive, Aix-en-Provence, file 53.4.2/12.

39 Voinot 1939: 401; Guillaume 1946: 307.

40 Voinot 1939: 401; Guillaume 1946: 307; Huré 1952: 11.

41 Voinot 1939: 401; Guillaume 1946: 307. A timorous attitude—reminiscent of the "prestige of the hills" syndrome that had long affected French military thinking and which was duly censured by General Huré (1952: 11).

42 Huré 1952: 11.

43 Voinot 1939: 404.

44 Jews and Saharans had special skills in this profession. Some also knew how to recalibrate a rifle, cf. Guennoun 1933: 92

45 Ould-Cheikh 1936: 214–15; see a similarly inspired poem in the present volume, subsection "Rather death than dishonor." (p. 134).

46 Janon 1948: 86–95; Saulay 1985: 281–2.

47 Saulay 1985: 286–7. Bournazel, one of the most colorful characters in the *Armée d'Afrique,* had just been appointed head of the newly-created Rissani Native Affairs bureau.

48 Bordeaux 1935: 269–75.

49 Bordeaux 1935: 287.

50 Saulay 1985: 283

51 In particular, the near-annihilation of a battalion of Senegalese *Tirailleurs* in the Gaouz palm grove (1918) appeared to have been forgotten.

52 Saulay 1985: 284, 288.

53 Voinot 1939: 394.

54 Further evidence, now that dissident areas were shrinking visibly, of tardy inter-tribal co-operation.

55 Voinot 1939: 394.

56 Janon 1948: 98–9.

57 Voinot 1939: 395; Saulay 1985: 289.

58 Spillman 1936: 129.

59 Saulay 1985: 294.

60 Saulay 1985: 295
61 Saulay 1985: 295.
62 Lefébure 1986.
63 Janon 1948: 105.
64 Voinot 1939: 387; Saulay 1985: 318–19.
65 Saulay 1985: 319.
66 Méraud 1990: 118.
67 Voinot 1939: 387; Saulay 1985: 319. Regarding the actual circumstances and location of Guyetand's death, journalist R. Janon (1948: 69) appears to be mistaken when he attributes the incident to an officer named Guiétan, supposedly killed near Talsint in 1927. I well recall how, one evening in February 1992, the *muqqadam* at Ayt Sidi Mha, shifting walnuts around on a tea tray, demonstrated how Ou-Skounti had enticed the enemy into the "killing-ground."
68 Peyron 1990.
69 Voinot 1939: 387.
70 Janon 1948: 115.
71 Janon 1948: 129–30.
72 Ward Price 1934: 159.

Chapter 22

1 Guillaume devotes an entire chapter to the topic, in 1946: 261–81.
2 Sung by a poet from Zaouia Sidi Yahya ou Youssef, home base of firebrand marabout Si Mohand ou-Lhajj; collected in 1933 by one of Arsène Roux's informers (cf. Roux archive, Aix-en-Provence, file 53.4.2).
3 See poetic couplet: "O mountain of Ayt 'Ayyash, O Mother of Spring, / Were it not for you, drought would indeed be our lot!" in my *Isaffen* (1993: 209); also Turnbull (1960), though not actually quoting this couplet, likewise refers to 'Ayyashi as "Mother of Spring."
4 Peyron, *tamawayt* poem, *Post-Isaffen* corpus, unpublished, 1999.
5 Moulay Hassan I's final campaign had been partially aimed at chastising the Ayt Hadiddou for their depredations along this caravan route; see *Istiqça* chronicle; also Manue 1930: 28–9.
6 Foremost among these were the French Marquis de Segonzac, who climbed 'Ayyashi in 1901.
7 "Renseignements coloniaux," September 1928: 551.
8 "Renseignements coloniaux," September 1928: 561.
9 Cdt. Bouverot (1920), Cdt. Tarrit (1923), and Cne. S. Guennoun (1933), the last-named having penned a book on the subject, *La Montagne berbère: les Aït Oumalou et le Pays zaïan*. He also contributed regularly to the Colonial Intelligence section of the *BCAF*.
10 See p. xxx.
11 Guillaume 1946: 315.
12 Interestingly, the Ayt Tana were famous throughout the area as customary law jurists, *ayt lhaqq*: see Peyron 1990: 9–102.
13 Ward Price 1934: 65.
14 Guennoun 1933: 181–3; Guillaume 1946: 299.
15 Author unspecified, *BCAF* 7 (July 1932): 422.

16 Cf. couplet: "Other people tend to speak with forked tongues; / Our speech, alone, remains as straight and true as the shuttle of a loom!" Peyron 1992: 73–92.

17 There is much scholarship in French on the Ayt Hadiddou, including Kasriel (1989), but little in English, save by D. M. Hart, *ROMM*, and W. Kraus 1997: 16–32.

18 Lit. "white river"; originally Asif Abkhoush, "black river," due to occasional flash floods, or its dark-gray color after heavy rain and snow—a negative image subsequently exorcized by its being renamed "white river." Lack of wood today still sends Ayt Hadiddou timber-rustlers northward on nocturnal expeditions to the relatively well-forested territory of their Ayt Yahya and Sokhman neighbors.

19 Hart 1984a—the best account on this tribe in English.

20 Peyron, "Barghawata," *Le Maroc des Résistances*, IRCAM, December 2003 conference.

21 In 1978, as I was preparing to visit the Ayt Sokhman, an Ou-Hadiddou warned me that where I was going the women stank of wood-smoke (Ayt 'Ali ou Ikko, Imedhgas, November 1978).

22 Based on my on-the-spot observations (1975–2008).

23 Guillaume 1946: 323.

24 Much of this chapter is based on my own fieldwork in the Asif Melloul region, 1975–2008.

25 Saulay 1985: 389.

26 For Midelt's early history, cf. Maher 1974; Aouchar 2002; also Mouhib 2015.

27 Klose *c.* 1927: 180–1.

28 Klose *c.* 1927: 225; Manue 1930: 137; Bordeaux 1934: 33–4; also conversation with S. Marciano (an ex-Midelti), June 1972.

29 Klose *c.* 1927: 192–6; contains a detailed account of such a skirmish about this time.

30 Parlange 1927: 12–13.

31 Gershovich 2000: 147.

32 Voinot 1939: 403.

33 Voinot 1939: 381. Air support would have been provided by Bréguet 19 bombers and Potez 25 army co-operation aircraft; Kirkland 1993: 22–34.

34 Saulay 1985: 241. I was informed that Zaïd ou-Skounti headed the Ayt Merghad contingents in this campaign (from an oral source, Massou, Ayt Sliman, July 1991).

35 Janon 1948: 60.

36 Gershovich 2000: 147.

37 Voinot 1939: 382; Saulay 1985: 241; also Porcher 1948.

38 Voinot 1939: 384 mentions about 600 killed; Saulay 1985: 244; in every Hadiddou or Merghad village the next of kin mourned their dead, cf. Peyron 1995b: 8.

39 Manue 1930: 215.

40 A three-star general, Jean Vidalon (1869–1959) had been appointed commander-in-chief, Morocco, not long after the Rif war. Apparently little versed in the ways of the *Armée d'Afrique*, whose members he tended to distrust (Belot 1946: 305), what military experience he had was gained on the Western Front during the Great War.

41 Gershovich 2000: 148–50.

42 Manue 1930: 42–3.

43 Saulay 1985: 242–3; also Voinot (1939: 398), who claims the attack on Tounfit was staged on June 10.

44 Voinot 1939: 398.

45 Guillaume 1946: 261.

46 Guillaume 1946: 363.

47 Guillaume 1946: 270; Saulay 1985: 254.

48 Guillaume 1946: 280; Saulay 1985: 255.
49 Manue 1930: 218.
50 Saulay 1985: 256.
51 Gershovich 2000: 153.
52 Guillaume 1946: 300.
53 Saulay 1985: 257.
54 Guillaume 1946: 299.
55 Huré 1952: 13.
56 Huré 1952: 14; Voinot 1939: 403.
57 Guillaume 1946: 310; Saulay 1985: 258. One of the machine guns captured at El-Herri in 1914 was retrieved at this spot, together with Colonel Laverdure's sword.
58 Huré 1952: 13–14.
59 Huré 1952: 16
60 Janon 1932: 164–5.
61 Voinot 1939: 403.
62 Marcireau 1938: 29.
63 Voinot 1939: 364; Saulay 1985: 259; further details emerged from conversation between myself and Ta'adlount *moqqadam* ("headman"), November 1974.
64 Voinot 1939: 408; Huré 1952: 61.
65 As the son of one of the survivors told me, "134 men from my village fought in this terrible battle with the *irumin* but only 28 returned!"; 'AtmaneOu-Saïd, November 1975; Voinot 1939: 412–14.
66 Roux 1992: 175.
67 Guillaume 1946: 326–8.

Chapter 23

1 Compared to the relatively humdrum business of *Pacification*, the Battle of Tazizaout—to which I have devoted considerable research, both archival and in the field—deserves this separate chapter, as the entire episode lasted well over a month (August–September 1932). It also left a permanent impression on the collective psyche of the local inhabitants. The present account is based on various written sources together with eyewitness accounts by a few surviving veterans.
2 Cf. "*tayffart* contre Sidi Lmekki," Hamri 2005; also Guillaume 1946: 364.
3 Oral account by 'Ali ou-Hmad, Ikassen village (August 25, 2005).
4 Based on oral accounts by Hmad ou-Moulay, Agheddou village (August 19, 2005) and Lhajj Nasser Bouqebou, Azaghar Fal (December 2004); collected on video cassette by H. Yakobi (IRCAM, Rabat).
5 Guillaume 1946: 360.
6 Guillaume 1946: 361.
7 Oral account by 'Ali ou-Hmad, Ikassen village (August 25, 2005); *bakki* was the contemptuous nickname given to Sidi Lmekki by his brothers.
8 Guillaume 1946: 72.
9 Guillaume 1946: 67–368.
10 Guillaume 1946: 368.
11 Huré 1952: 84; Saulay 1985: 334.
12 Voinot 1939: 424.

13 Poem (*tamawayt*), 'Ali ou-Hmad (August 25, 2005). Most of the oral poetry on Tazizaout was coined by Taoukhettalt, a gifted local poetess, according to H. Yakobi (IRCAM).

14 Guillaume 1946: 370.

15 Hamri 2005: 151: "Planes daily bombard me, famine torments me, big guns shatter rocks above my head, / causing havoc amid my herds of sheep, camels, and cattle as they cross the pass!"

16 Oral account, Lhajj Nasser Bouqebbou, Azaghar Fal (December 2004).

17 Oral account, Sidi Moh Azayyi, Asaka village (August 18, 2005).

18 Oral account, Hmad ou-Moulay, Agheddou village (August 19, 2005).

19 Guillaume 1946: 376; Voinot 1939: 424–5.

20 Guillaume 1946: 382.

21 Oral account, Hmad ou-Moulay, Agheddou village (August 19, 2005).

22 Guillaume 1946: 384; Saulay 1985: 336.

23 Joubert des Ouches 1936: 42–3.

24 Roux 1992: 217. I was shown the exact spot (August 21, 2005), Tassameurt n-ou-Haqqar, on the northwest slopes of Tazizaout, where the hero set up his machine gun.

25 Oral account, 'Ali ou-Hmad, Ikassen village (August 25, 2005). Another hero was mentioned, Koujan Ou-'Azzou by name, from Lmizan n-Naour, Ayt Ouirra region; oral account by Lhajj Nasser Bouqebbou, Aghbala town (August 24, 2005).

26 According to H. Yakobi (IRCAM), Rabat.

27 Oral account, Hmad ou-Moulay, Agheddou village (August 19, 2005).

28 According to oral account by Ou Ben 'Ali, Bou Imtel (August 21, 2005), he was killed by a bullet from a Lebel rifle, near the saddle at the head of the ravine between Cedar Pinnacle and the main Tazizaout ridge, probably on September 11, 1932.

29 Oral account, Lhajj Nasser Bouqebbou, Aghbala town (August 24, 2005).

30 Guillaume 1946: 384.

31 Oral account, 'Ali ou-Hmad, Ikasen village (August 25, 2005).

32 Drouin 1975: 124.

33 Oral account, Mbarch ou Hsseïn, Agheddou village (March 1977).

34 Oral account, 'Ali ou-Hmad, Ikassen village (August 25, 2005).

35 Oral account by Mahroucha, a former resistance fighter and *goumier*, Asaka village (July 1, 1984).

36 From a *tamdyazt*, cf. Peyron and Roux 2002: 197, 199.

37 Guillaume 1946: 387.

38 Acording to H. Yakobi (IRCAM), Rabat.

39 Oral account, Hmad ou-Moulay, Aghedou village (August 19, 2005).

40 Saulay 1985: 336.

41 Oral account, Mahroucha, Asaka village (July 1, 1984).

42 Marcireau 1938: 48.

43 Lhajj Nasser Bouquebou, Aghbala village (August 24, 2005).

44 Attributed to poetess Taoukhettalt; verse taken from a *tamdyazt* ("ballad") criticizing Sidi Lmekki (cf. Hamri 2005: 152). The term *ayt bujur* refers to Berbers who have submitted and say "*Bonjour!*" to the French. The 2nd and 3rd items (*timawayin*) recited by Ou Ben 'Ali, Tazra hamlet (August 21, 2005).

45 Lhajj Nasser Bouqebbou, Azaghar Fal (December 2004). This would appear to be a long *tamawayt*; source unknown, but could be poem by Taoukhettalt. Cf. similar piece, purportedly part of a *tamdyazt*, in Drouin 1975: 28.

Chapter 24

1   Bordeaux 1935: 305; Hart 1984: 178–80.

2   Bordeaux 1934: 60.

3   Sitwell 1940: 224.

4   Spillman 1936: 38.

5   Bordeaux 1935: 307.

6   Bordeaux 1935: 308–31; Spillman 1968: 116–20; Saulay 1985: 347–83. When Morocco became independent, over twenty years later, King Mohammed V further honored 'Assou ou Ba Slam for his exemplary resistance by confirming that his descendents would retain *qayd*ship of the Ayt 'Atta for all time.

7   Guillaume 1946: 397.

8   Sergeant Major Guyot, who confirmed that the Legionaries had been drunk, was serving in the Tounfit area in 1933. In March 1969 he was Chief Forester for the Tounfit district and married to a Berber wife. Hmad ou-Moulay, an Agheddou villager, referred (August 19, 2005) to a certain *geyyu* as overseeing labor-construction gangs working on the *piste* near Tirghist in late 1932.

9   Guillaume 1946: 404.

10 Voinot 1939: 429.

11 Oral account by Mahroucha, Asaka village (July 1, 1984), and details from Tirghist villager (August 1992).

12 Huré 1952: 122; Saulay 1985: 386–8; Peyron 1988–9: 197–206.

13 Conversation with Sergeant Major Guyot, Tounfit, March 1969.

14 Guillaume 1946: 402–3; Saulay 1985: 388–92.

15 Huré 1952: 16–17.

16 Guillaume 1946: 416–22.

17 Oral account, Mahroucha, Asaka village (July 1, 1984).

18 Voinot 1939: 465–6; Guillaume 1946: 437.

19 Voinot 1939: 466.

20 Guillaume 1946: 441; Saulay 1985: 418–19.

21 Ward Price 1934: 159.

22 Peyron 1997: 33.

23 Ward Price 1934: 146.

24 Ward Price 1934: 162–4; Janon 1948: 132–4.

25 Ward Price 1934: 155.

26 Guillaume 1946: 443; Saulay 1985: 426.

27 Collected by M. Gershovich and Hamid Nouamani from El Arq Hanifa ben El Housseyn (August 2000); *badi* is Lieutenant Badie, an officer serving with the 7th Goum, based on Tinghir, who on August 11, 1933, distinguished himself by occupying the spring of Oued Ifegh (Saulay 1985: 418).

28 Ward Price 1934: 169.

29 Three *izlan* supplied by 'Aomar Taws, Igwelmimen (spring 2003).

30 Though the context is love poetry, this *tamawayt*, dictated to me by Sidi Moh Azayyi, Tounfit (spring 1988), shows to what extent the Baddou episode still figures in the collective subconsciousness of the Eastern High Atlas area.

31 Voinot 1939: 467.

32 A well-known French Berberist author based one of his short stories, "Les Portes du Ciel," on this episode (Euloge 2005: 209–50).

33 Guillaume 1946: 447–50; Saulay 1985: 426–30.

Chapter 25

1 Voinot 1939: 452; Cne. Henry, Confidential report, Goulmima, July 4, 1935; also Turnbull 1960; Hart 1987: 31–4; Ouchna 2005.

2 Saulay 1985: 90. The victorious tribesmen cut off his head and sent it to El-Hiba at Kerdous.

3 Saulay 1985: 439.

4 The Ayt Ba 'Amran have since been honored as last-ditch resistance fighters by post-independence Morocco, with a street in Casablanca bearing their name.

5 There would appear, however, to have been exceptions to the Boy Scout image of gallant tribesmen submitting to chivalrous French officers. Hmad ou-Moulay of Agheddou (August 19, 2005) claims that on surrendering after Tazizaout he and his companions were roughly handled and had their valuables stolen by partisans and mokhaznis guarding them. They were then put to work on *travaux de piste*. This drove them to take to the *maquis* again, which they did, joining other dissidents on Jbel Hamdoun.

6 Bidwell 1973: 158.

7 Saulay 1985: 442–6.

8 Rivet 1999: 77.

9 Saulay 1985: 447.

10 Gellner 1969: 23.

11 Juin 1957: 34.

12 Cf. Abehri 2002: 94. No doubt this was the fruit of the immediate post-Protectorate years with their emphasis on national unity, Islam, Pan-Arabism, and the Arabic language.

13 Bidwell 1973: 54.

14 Based on conversations between myself and tribal inhabitants of the Tounfit area, 1974–5.

15 Bidwell 1973: 183–4.

16 Bidwell 1973: 57; Gellner 1969: 18–19; Brown 1973: 206; Burke III 1973: 206; Lafuente 1984: 87.

17 See article by Duclos (1973).

18 Clérisse 1933: 185.

19 Cf. Mouklis and Mounib (1997), unequivocally described by the authors as "the biggest lie in modern Moroccan history"; also Hart 1997: 28–30.

Chapter 26

1 These include: *Itto*; *Badda fille berbère*; *le Hakem au Burnous bleu*; *Le Marco héroïque*; *Goumier de l'Atlas*; *La Légende du Goumier Saïd*; *Le Collier berbère*; *Bournazel: l'homme rouge*, etc.

2 Cf. Burke III 1973: 175–99; also Benhlal 2005.

3 With the possible exception of starvation year, 1941 (Gruner 1985: 159), when food tickets had to be issued to the starving population.

4 Gellner 1969: 19.

5 Méraud 1990: 14.

6 Berque 1962: 228–30; cf. Peyron 2013: 24.

7   Rivet 1999: 41–4; Catroux 1952: 286.

8   Peyré 1950: 119 carries a picture taken during May 1942 maneuvers at Agelmous showing a march past of Goums.

9   Boyer de Latour 1956: 16.

10 Voinot 1943: 92.

11 Boyer de Latour 1956: 15.

12 Rivet 1999: 386.

13 Cf. for accounts of this period in English, see Barbour 1965; Maxwell 1966; and Pennell 2000.

14 Rivet 1999: 315.

15 Berque 1962: 15. See Peyron 2013.

16 Boyer de Latour 1956: 168–70; Tahiri 2003: 67.

17 Boyer de Latour 1956: 170; Bidwell 1973: 172; Hart 2000: 85.

18 Boyer de Latour 1956: 173; the present writer collected the same *izli* ("poetic couplet") in the Middle Atlas in the 1980s; Peyron 1993: 81.

19 Boyer de Latour 1956: 124–92.

20 Ben Kaddour 1973: 259–67.

21 Cf. Jamai-Lahbabi 2001: 4, who actually uses the term "pacified"; Gellner 1973: 361–74; also Hart 2000: 84–102. 'Addi ou-Bihi, at the time governor of Tafilalt province, actually rebelled because of a perceived *Istiqlal* threat to the throne, was later tried and eventually died in prison (of poison, according to some oral sources).

22 Old habits die hard. To this very day, after being ostracized for years, some Berbers feel awkward when you discuss their culture in public, refusing to give definite answers to certain questions, as if they were afraid of getting into trouble if they speak out. Amazigh associations often denounce the activities of supposed *imazighen sserbis*: "Berber time-servers who toe the official line and warily work the system to the best of their advantage."

23 This self-inflicted censorship could be taken to questionable extremes. When, in the early 1970s, Ahmed Boukous published his thesis in socio-linguistics, officialdom had him describe it as being on "*Culture populaire*" rather than "*Culture berbère*." Even as late as the mid-1990s, in his admirable 400-page presentation of Al-Tadili's *Le Temps des Soufis*, on Medieval Moroccan marabouts, the majority of them Berbers, Ahmed Toufiq makes little reference to the fact.

24 *Le Matin du Sahara*, October 7, 1973; typical official-speak. Though living in very basic conditions, with good reason for dissatisfaction, the local inhabitants failed to come out strongly on the side of the rebels. Yet repression in the area was characteristically brutal.

25 Bennouna 2002: 275.

26 For the best account to date of this little-publicized episode, cf. Bennouna 2002.

27 Cf. *Le Monde Amazigh* 53, November 15, 2005, 9. Composed by *amdyaz* Mohammed ou-Lmekki and entitled *aseggwas n 1973*, this seventy-two-line ballad mourns the passing of Hammou Ben Aqqa from Khenifra, together with many others, suggesting that treachery was the prime cause of their undoing.

28 For a candid discussion of this problem, cf. the first three chapters of Bounfour 1994. This oversimplification rankles with Imazighen, with demonstrations at Agadir in April 2004 and attempts to revisit Moroccan history from a Berber angle (*Monde Amazigh*, May 2004).

29 Berber leader Mahjoubi Aherdan also grasped the positive significance of the Green March as far as Berbers were concerned; cf. Khettouch 2001.

30 Brett and Fentress 1997: 1, 275.
31 This chapter is a slightly reworked version of a paper published in *Proceedings of Amazigh Days Conference*, 2003 (M. Peyron, ed.).

Chapter 27

1   *Agraw* 124, May 2004: 23; H. Aourid founded the Tariq Ibn Zyad research center in Rabat.
2   See *Actes du colloque du Grand Meknès* (1988: 413–27); contributions by Med Taifi and M. Peyron.
3   *Identité culturelle au Maghreb* (1991), 59–70.
4   J. Donnet, *Le Monde Diplomatique*, January 1995: 18.
5   Willis 2012: 215. Iken was famous for having just penned *asekkif n inzaden*, an award-winning first-ever novel in Tamazight.
6   Crawford 2002.
7   *Littérature Orale Arabo-Berbère*, a quality publication with Lacoste-Dujardin, Jeanine Drouin, Claude Lefébure, Arlette Roth as chief contributors, unfortunately phased itself out in the late 1990s, as many of its members reached retirement age.
8   Lecestre-Rollier and Garrigues-Creswell 1997.
9   Kraus 1991.
10 After staying in a Marrakesh High Atlas village, D. Crawford penned several articles. Likewise, H. Hagan visited the Ministry of Culture in Rabat in 1981, only to be told deadpan that there were no Berbers left in Morocco, that she would be watched, possibly deported, if she did fieldwork on them!
11 At end-of-term meetings, Rabat faculty members would compare notes, remarking in terms of headgear, for example, "Have you noticed? Miss So-and-So has joined the Muslim Sisters!"
12 This paragraph is based on on-the-spot observations over the past twenty years.
13 The Egyptian-inspired *hijab*, or *foulard islamique*—a major issue in France, where girls provoked the authorities by insisting on wearing it in class—is definitely not an indigenous Maghribi creation; *hayk* and *litham* ("veil") were traditionally the main items in Moroccan women's attire.
14 Cf. Kassim and Zenn 2017; also Woodward et al. (n.d.).
15 S. Chaker, interview on January 18, 2004, available on http://www.tamazgha.fr/imprimer.php3?id.
16 Flexibility, however, remained the watchword, with computers specially equipped to switch, at the mere pressing of a button, into Latin script (al-Hussein al-Mujahid, IRCAM, June 2003).
17 These were officially presented by IRCAM members Youssef Ait Lemkadem and Absslam Khalafi during "Amazigh Day 2004" (March 25), at Al-Akhawayn University in Ifran. Concurrently, similar textbooks were shown; these had been devised by Moha Ennaji and Fatima Sadiqi thanks to funding from 'Athman Benjelloun of the BMCI.
18 An international conference devoted to this topic was held at the Rabat FLSH in December 2003.
19 Many of these conferences actually took place towards the close of 2003.
20 Above three paragraphs based on on-the-spot observation (2006–8).

21 Cf. Circular letter, March 14, 2019, "*Comment l'Union Européenne contribue à la radicalisation des jeunes au Maroc?*", by R. Raha, Pdt. World Amazigh Congress (AMA; www.amadalpresse.com/RAHA). Also A. Assid, article in *Telquel*: "*Le PJD est un danger pour la monarchie*," February 7, 2019.

Chapter 28

1 Willis 2012: 222; cf. also http://www.amazighworld.org/human_rights/index_show. php?id=1429.
2 Since then, of course, Benkiran has been replaced at the head of the PJD government of moderate Islamists by the more amenable Abdesslam Othmani.
3 Gellner 1969: 88.
4 Gellner 1969: 41.
5 The above pages have provided frequent examples of this sort of potentate, from the Hintati emirs of the fourteenth century to El-Glaoui of the Protectorate Period. For a recent discussion of this problem, cf. Belkziz and Pennell 2017: 125–47.
6 Peyron 1993: 205.
7 Adventure trekking has become a growth industry over the past twenty years, providing jobs as guides, porters, and muleteers for dozens of Toubkal and Mgoun area locals.
8 Cf. M. Ennaji and F. Sadiqi, *Amazigh Days Proceedings (2003)*, for insightful comments on this topic, based on their 2004 and 2003 publications.
9 *Conseil National des Langues et de la Culture Marocaine.* This is yet another instance of passive resistance by an "Arabist" diehard element aiming to hamper influence of the IRCAM.

Bibliography

Abbreviations

AUI	Al-Akhawayn University in Ifran
AFEAM	Association Française d'Études sur le Monde Arabo-Musulman
BCAF	*Bulletin du Comité de l'Afrique Française*
BESM	*Bulletin économique et social du Maroc*
BRISMES	British Institute for Middle East Studies
BSGA	*Bulletin de la Société de Géographie d'Alger*
BSGM	*Bulletin de la Société de Géographie du Maroc*
CHEAM	Centre de Hautes Études d'Administration Musulmane
EB	*Encyclopédie Berbère*
EDB	Études et Documents Berbères
FMAV	French Military Archive Vincennes (SHAT in Fr.)
IREMAM	Institut de Recherche sur le Monde Arabo-Musulman
IRCAM	Institut Royal de la Culture Amazighe
JNAS	*Journal of North African Studies*
LOAB	*Littérature Orale Arabo-Berbère*
OUP	Oxford University Press
PUF	Presses Universitaires de France
RA	*Revue Africaine*
REMMM	*Revue du Monde Musulman et de la Méditerranée*
RGM	*Revue de Géographie Marocaine*
RIRHM	Royal Institute for Research on the History of Morocco
ROMM	*Revue de l'Occident Musulman et de la Méditerranée*
WOCMES	World Conference of Middle East Studies.

Theses and reports

Brown, H. (2014), *Cunninghame Graham in the Atlas*, unpub. notes.
Chevallier, Cdt. (1927), "L'organisation militaire du Maroc," *Affaires Indigènes*, Rabat, May 30.
Ennahid, S. (2001), "Medieval Northern Morocco," Arizona State University.
Garcia, V. (2011), *The Campaigns for the Pacification of the Spanish Protectorate in Morocco: A forgotten Example of Successful Counterinsurgency*. Fort Leavenworth, KS: General Staff College; www.dtic.mil/dtic/tr/fulltext/u2/a545164.pdf.
Gruner, R. (c. 1985), "Mon métier au Maroc, 1938–1956," unpublished thesis.
Hamri, B. (2005), "La poésie amazighe de l'Atlas central marocain," doctoral dissertation, Faculty of Letters, Beni Mellal.
Henry, Cdt. (1936), "Zaid ou Ahmed' (confidentiel)," *Affaires Indigènes*, Bureau, Asoul, July.
Henry, Cdt. (1937), *Une tribu de transhumants du Grand Atlas: les Ait Morghad*. Paris: CHEAM.
Henry, Cdt. (1937a), "Note sur les Ait Sidi Bou Yacoub," Paris: CHEAM.
Ithier, Cne. (1947), "Résumé chronologique de l'histoire du pays," *Affaires Indigènes*, Anergui Archives, 8/ BE 1 file, in Roux Archive, Aix-en-Provence.
Jacquet, Cdt. (1926), "Étude sur les Ait Yahia et la région de Tounfit," Cercle, Itzer, January (FMAV).
Jamai-Lahbabi, F. (2001), "Tradition et Modernisme chez Hassan II," Ph.D thesis, Paris.
Parlange, Lieut. (1927), "Résumé succinct des renseignements intéressant l'avant-pays de Rich," *Affaires Indigènes*. Bureau, Rich, July (FMAV).
Peyron, M. (1975), "Tounfit et les Ait Yahia," Doctoral dissertation, IGA, Grenoble.
Ruet, Cdt. (1952), "La transhumance dans le Moyen Atlas et la Haute Moulouya," Paris: CHEAM.

Unsigned reports

"La *harka* de Mûlay el Hassan vers le Tâfilalt," *BCAF* 10 (October 1893): 13–14.
"Mûlay el Hassan I dans le Sud," *BCAF* 1 (1894): 8–9.
"La Pacification du Maroc: les opérations de 1923," *L'Illustration* 4193 (July 1923): 30–4.
"La Pacification du Maroc en 1923," *L'Illustration* 4224 (10 February 1924): 155–6.
"Renseignements coloniaux: l'Assif Melloul," *BCAF* 9 (September 1928): 550–67.
"Notice sur le Tafilalet," *c.* 1930, 7 (FMAV).
[Guennon, S. (1932),] "La Pacification dans la région des confins algéro-marocains," *BCAF* 7 (July 1932): 398–425.
"Renseignements sur l'origine des Ait Hadiddou," Imilchil Bureau archives (December 1938).

Books and articles

Abehri, M. (2002), *Être ou ne plus être, séquences de vie de petites gens exilés dans leur peau: Essai romancé*. Rabat: Centre Tarik Ibn Zyad.
Abès, M. (1917), "Les Aith Ndhir (Beni Mtir)," *Archives berbères* 2, fasc. 2. Paris: Leroux, 149–94.

Abun-Nasr, J. M. (1971), *A History of the Maghrib*. Cambridge: Cambridge University Press.

Africanus, L. (aka Hassan al-Wazzan) (1897), *Description de l'Afrique du Nord*. Paris: E. Leroux.

Agnouche, A. (2002), "Maroc: Charte des revendications amazighes à propos de la révision du texte constitutionel," *Tawiza* 57.

Aherdan, M. (1997), "Les berbères et la politique," *Tifinagh* 10 (February): 55–62.

Allati, A. (2002), *Diachronie tamazighte ou berbère*. Tangier: Abdelmalek Essaâdi University.

Alouiz, R. (2005), *Actes du colloque: le Maroc des Résistances*. Rabat: IRCAM.

Alvarez, J. E. (2001), *The Betrothed of Death: The Spanish Foreign Legion During the Rif Rebellion, 1920–1927*. Westport, CT, and London: Greenwood Press.

Aouchar, A. (2002), *Colonisation et campagne berbère au Maroc*. Casablanca: Afrique Orient.

Arberry, A. J. (1950/1969), *Sufism: An Account of the Mystics of Islam*. London: George Allen and Unwin.

Arnaiz-Villena, A. (ed.) (2002), *Prehistoric Iberia: Genetics, Anthropology and Linguistics*. New York: Kluwer-Plenum.

Arnaud, Cdt. (1916), "La region de Meknès," *BSGM* 2: 70–105.

Arnaud, L. (1952), *Au temps des Mehallas ou le Maroc de 1860 à 1912*. Casablanca: Atlantides.

Ayache, G. (1979), "La fonction d'arbitrage du Makhzen," *Actes de Durham: recherches récentes sur le Maroc moderne, BESM* 138–9: 5–21.

Azaykou, A. S. (2001), *Histoire du Maroc ou les interprétations possibles*. Rabat: Centre Tarik Ibn Zyad.

Babin, G. (1912), *Au Maroc: par les camps par les villes*. Paris: Grasset.

Babin, G. (1923), *La mystérieuse Ououizert: chronique d'une colonne au Maroc*. Casablanca: Faraire.

El-Baidaq (1928), *Documents inédits de l'histoire almohade*, Lévi-Provençal trans. fragments of MS in "Legajo," Escurial, 1919. Paris: Geuthner.

Al-Bakri, A. (1963), *Description de l'Afrique septentrionale*, trans. W. Mac Guckin de Slane. Algiers: A. Jordan.

Barbour, N. (1965), *Morocco*. London: Thames & Hudson.

Beaudet, G. (n.d.), "Les Beni Mguild du Nord," *RGM* 15: 7–9.

El-Bekri, Abou Obeïd (1913), *Description de l'Afrique Septentrionale*, trans. W. Mac Guckin de Slane. Paris: n.p., 1068.

Belhoucine, J. (1981), "Les Berbères et la Colonisation, mythes et réalités," *Amazigh* 7: 22–9.

Belkziz, N. and C. R. Pennell (2017), "Family Loyalties and Oppression in Morocco and Libya," *Journal of Mediterranean Studies* 26, no. 2: 125–47.

Belot, P. (1946), *Trente Ans de Baroud (Histoire militaire du Général Colombat)*. Paris: Arthaud.

Bendaoud, Cne. (1917), "Notes sur le pays Zaïan," *Archives berbères* 2, fasc. 3. Paris: Leroux, 276–306.

Benhlal, M. (2005), *Le collège d'Azrou*. Paris: Karthala-IREMAM.

Ben Kaddour, A. (1973), "The Neo-Makhzan and the Berbers", in E. Gellner and A. Micaud (eds.), *Arabs and Berbers: From Tribe to Nation in North Africa*, 259–67. London: Duckworth.

Ben Lahcen, M. (2003), *Moha ou Hamou Zayani*. Fès: Info-Print.

Bennouna, M. (2002), *Héros sans gloire*. Casablanca: Tarik éditions.

Berger, F. (1929), *Moha ou Hammou le Zaïani: un royaume berbère contemporain au Maroc, 1877–1921*. Marrakesh: Atlas.

Berque, J. (1955), *Structures sociales du Haut-Atlas*. Paris: PUF.

Berque, J. (1958/2001), *Al-Youssi: problèmes de la culture marocaine au XVIIème siècle*. Paris: Mouton.

Berque, J. (1962), *Le Maghreb entre deux guerres*. Paris: Seuil.

Berque, J. (1978), *De l'Euphrate à l'Atlas*. Paris: Sindbad.

Berrada, T. (1994), "Quelques aspects de la question militaire au Maroc au XIXe siècle," *L'Armée marocaine à travers l'histoire, Maroc-Europe* 7: 293–311.

Bertrand, A. (1977), *Tribus berbères du Haut Atlas*. Lausanne: Vilo.

Bidwell, R. (1973), *Morocco under Colonial Rule: French Administration of Tribal Areas*. London: Frank Cass.

Blunt, W. (1951), *Black Sunrise*. London: Methuen.

Bonjean, F. (1950), *Au Maroc en roulotte*. Paris: Hachette.

Bordeaux, H. (1931), *Un printemps au Maroc*. Paris: Plon.

Bordeaux, H. (1934), *Le Miracle du Maroc*. Paris: Plon.

Bordeaux, H. (1935), *Henry de Bournazel (L'Épopée marocaine)*. Paris: Plon.

Boudhan, M. (1995), "L'Arabisation de l'enseignement: un subterfuge pour préserver les privilèges de classe!" *Tifinagh* 7 (September): 19–26.

Boudhan, M. (1995a), "Tamazight, entre le culturel et le linguistique," *Tifinagh* 8 (December): 51–3.

Boulet-Desbareau, J. (1985), "Baptême du feu: Tarda–31 août 1930," *Revue Brutionne*, Prytanée de la Flèche: 8–11.

Bounfour, A. (1994), *Le Nœud de la Langue*. Aix-en-Provence: Édisud.

Bounfour, A. (1997), "Où en est le berbère au Maroc?" *Tifinagh* 10 (February): 75–6.

Bournazel, G. (1979), *Le Cavalier rouge: Henry de Bournazel*. Paris: France-Empire.

Bourqia, R. and S. G. Miller (eds.) (1999), *In the Shadow of the Sultan: Culture, Power, and Politics in Morocco*. Cambridge, MA: Harvard University Press.

Boutet, R. (*c.* 1935), *La Dame de Bou-Laouane*. Casablanca: Editions du Moghreb.

Bouverot, Cdt. (1920), "Ras Moulouya," *BSGM*: 44–58.

Bovill, E. W. (1958/1999), *The Golden Trade of the Moors*. Princeton, NJ: M. Wiener.

Boyer de la Tour, P. (1956), *Vérités sur l'Afrique du Nord*. Paris: Plon.

Brett, M. (1999), *Ibn Khaldun and the Médieval Maghrib*. Abingdon: Taylor & Francis.

Brett, M. and E. Fentress (1997), *The Berbers*. Oxford: Blackwell.

Brignon, J. et al. (eds.) (1967), *Histoire du Maroc*. Paris: Hatier.

Bromberger, C. and B. Nouvel (eds.) (1997), *Jacques Berque: La Méditerranée, le Haut Atlas*. Aix-en-Provence: Université de Provence.

Brown, H. (2012), *The Mountains look on Marrakech*. Caithness: Whittles Publishing.

Brown, K. (1973), "The impact of the Berbr dahir in Salé," in E. Gellner and C. Micaud (eds.), *Arabs and Berbers: From Tribe to Nation in North Africa*, 201–15. London: Duckworth.

Burke III, E. (1973), "The Image of the Moroccan State in French Ethnological Literature: A New Look at the Origin of Lyautey's Berber Policy," in E. Gellner and C. Micaud (eds.), *Arabs and Berbers: From Tribe to Nation in North Africa*, 175–99. London: Duckworth.

Burke III, E. (1976), *Prelude to Protectorate in Morocco: Pre-colonial Protest and Resistance*. Chicago: University of Chicago Press.

Byrne, C. (2009), "Edward I and Moulay Ismaïl," in M. Peyron (ed.), *Contemporary Amazigh issues in Morocco*, 126–33. Ifran: AUI.

Cambon, H. (1952), *Histoire du Maroc*. Paris: Hachette.

Camps, G. (1980), *Les Berbères aux marges de l'histoire*. Toulouse: Hespérides.

Canal, J. (1902), *Géographie générale du Maroc*. Paris: Challamel.

Carrère, J.-D. (1973), *Missionaires en burnous bleu*. Paris: Charles-Lavauzelle.

Catroux Gal. (1952), *Lyautey le marocain*. Paris: Hachette.

Celarié, H. (1928), *L'Épopée marocaine*. Paris: Hachette.

Célérier, J. (1931), *Le Maroc*. Paris: Armand Colin.

Célérier, J. and A. Charton (1924), "Dans les vallées du Haut Atlas central. Goundafa et Tifnout," *BSGM* 4, Fasc. 1–3: 10–22.

Chafik, M. (1996), "Trente-trois siècles de l'histoire des Imazighen," *Tifinagh* 9 (Spring).

Chafik, M. (1996/2000), *Pour un Maghreb d'abord Maghrébin*. Rabat: Centre Tarik Ibn Zyad.

Chapelle, F. de la (1931), *Le Sultan Moulay Ismaïl et les Berbères Sanhaja du Maroc central*, Archives marocaines 28. Paris: Champion.

Charqi, M. (2003), *Abdelkrim El Khattabi: l'Emir guerillero*. n.p.p.: Coll. Histoire & politique.

Charqi, M. and M. Zaki (2008), *Maroc: Colonisations and Résistances 1830–1930*. Salé: Imprimerie Beni Snassen.

Chiapuris, J. (1979), *The Ait Ayash of the High Moulouya Plain: Rural Social Organization in Morocco*. Ann Arbor: University of Michigan Press.

Clément, J.-F. (1979), "Révoltes et répressions au Maroc," Salé, *Al-Asas* 13 (January–February): 20–6, 35–40.

Clément, J.-F. (1981), "Zaid u Ah'mad: héros méconnu de l'histoire marocaine," *Lamalif* 130 (November–December): 43–5.

Clérisse, H. (1933), *Du Grand Nord à l'Atlas*. Paris: Tallandier.

Colin, G. S. (n.d.), "Fazaz," in P. Bearman et al. (eds.), *Encyclopaedia of Islam*, 2nd edition, vol. 2, 894–5. Leiden: Brill; https://www.google.com/search?client=firefox-b-d&q=G.S.+Colin,+Islamic+Encycl.+Volume.II,+(894–95).

Cook, Jr., W. F. (1993), "Warfare and Firearms in 15th century Morocco, 1400–1492," *War and Society* 11, no. 2, http://www.deremilitari.org/RESOURCE/SARTICLES/COOK.htm.

Cornell, V. J. (1998), *Realm of the Saint: Power and Authority in Moroccan Sufism*. Austin: University of Texas Press.

Courcelle-Labrousse, V. and N. Marmié (2008), *La guerre du Rif*. Paris: Tallandier.

Couvreur, G. (1968), "La vie pastorale dans le Haut Atlas central," *RGM* 13: 3–54.

Crawford, D. (2002), "Morocco's Invisible Imazighen," *JNAS* 7, no. 1 (Spring): 53–70.

Crawford, D. and K. E. Hoffman (2000), "Essentially Amazigh: Urban Berbers and the Global Village," in R. K. Lacey and R. M. Coury (eds.), *The Arab, African and Islamic Worlds*, 117–33. New York: Peter Lang.

Crucy, F. (1928), "La Pénétration pacifique dans le Grand-Atlas: au pays des Ida ou Tanan qu'aucun sultan n'avait soumis," *L'Illustration* 4478/28 (December): 785–9.

D'Agraive, J. (1948), *Le Collier berbère*. Paris: Editions de Flore.

Daoud, Z. (2004), *Zaynab, reine de Marrakech*. La Tour-d'Aigues: Éd. de Laube.

De Elvira, M. R. (1996), "Basques, Imazighen ... une même origine ?" *Tifinagh* 9 (Spring): 31–2.

De Gorgoza Fletcher, M. (1988–9), "The Anthropological context of Almohad history," *Hespéris-Tamuda* 26–27: 27–50.

De Gorgoza Fletcher, M. (1996), "Mystique et politique: traditions étiologique d'une fondation maraboutique au Maroc," *LOAB*, UPR 414/ CNRS 24: 129–46.

Delanoë, G. (1988), *Lyautey, Juin, Mohammed V: fin d'un Protectorat*, Paris: L'Harmattan.

Désiré-Vuillemin, G.-M. (1958), "Cheikh Ma El Aïnin et le Maroc, ou l'échec d'un moderne Almoravide," *Revue d'Histoire Outre-Mers* 158: 29–52.

D'Esme, J. (1952), *Bournazel, l'homme rouge*. Paris: Flammarion.

Despois, J. (1949), *L'Afrique du Nord*. Paris: PUF.

Doury, P. (2008), *Un échec occulté de Lyautey: L'affaire du Tafilalet*. Paris: L'Harmattan.

Drouin, J. (1975), *Un cycle oral dans le Moyen-Atlas marocain*. Paris: Sorbonne.

Drouin, J. (1996), "Mystique et politique: Traditions étiologiques d'une fraction maraboutique au Maroc," *LOAB* 24: 135–6.

Duclos, L.-J. (1973), "The Berbers and the rise of Moroccan Nationalism," in E. Gellner and C. Micaud (eds.), *Arabs and Berbers: From Tribe to Nation in North Africa*, 217–29. London: Duckworth.

Dufourcq, C. E. (1968), "Berbérie et Ibérie médiévales: un problème de rupture," *Revue Historique* 240, no. 2: 293–324.

Dunn, R. E. (1973), "Berber imperialism: the Ait Atta expansion in Southeast Morocco," in E. Gellner and C. Micaud (eds.), *Arabs and Berbers: From Tribe to Nation in North Africa*, 85–107. London: Duckworth.

Dunn, R. E. (1977), *Resistance in the Desert*. Madison: University of Wisconsin Press.

Dunn, R. E. (1981), "The Bu Himara Rebellion in Northeast Morocco: Phase I," *Middle Eastern Studies* 17, no. 1: 31–48.

Eickelman, D. F. (1976), *Moroccan Islam: Tradition and Society in a Pilgrimage Center*. Austin and London: University of Texas Press.

Ennaji, N. (2004), *A Grammar of Amazigh (Berber)*. Fez: University of Fez Publications (in co-authorship with Fatima Sadiqi).

Epton, N. (1958), *Saints and Sorcerers: A Moroccan Journey*. London: Cassell.

Euloge, R. (1952), *Les Derniers Fils de l'Ombre*. Marrakesh: Tighermt.

Euloge, R. (2005), *Des Fils de l'Ombre aux Chants de la Tassaout*. Marrakesh: Youssef Impressions.

Felze, J. (1936), *Au Maroc inconnu: dans le Haut Atlas et le Sud marocain*. Paris and Grenoble: Arthaud.

Ferhat, H. and H. Triki (1988–9), "Faux prophètes et mahdis dans le Maroc médiéval," *Hespéris-Tamuda* 26–27: 5–24.

Fletcher, Richard, A. (2006), *Moorish Spain*. Oakland: University of California Press.

Flint, B. (1997), "La Culture arabo-berbère face aux pressions méditerranéennes et proche-orientales," *Tifinagh* 11–12 (August): 111–25.

Gautier, E. F. (1927), *Les siècles obscurs du Maghreb*. Paris: Payot.

Gélard, M.-L. (1998), "Le droit coutumier, l'honneur et la tribu," *AWAL, Cahiers d'études berbères*. Paris: MSH 17: 65–81.

Gellner, E. (1969), *Saints of the Atlas*. London: Weidenfeld and Nicolson.

Gellner, E. (1973), "Patterns of rural rebellion in Morocco during the early years of independence," in E. Gellner and C. Micaud (eds.), *Arabs and Berbers: From Tribe to Nation in North Africa*, 361–74. London: Duckworth.

Gellner, E. and C. Micaud (eds.) (1973), *Arabs and Berbers: From Tribe to Nation in North Africa*. London: Duckworth.

Gershovich, M. (2000), *French Military Rule in Morocco: Colonialism and its Consequences*. London and Portland, OR: Frank Cass.

Guennoun, S. (1933), *La Montagne berbère: les Aït Oumalou et le Pays zaïan*. Rabat: Éd. Omnia.

Guennoun, S. (1934), *La Voix des Monts: mœurs de guerre berbères*. Rabat: Éd. Omnia.

Guennoun, S. (1990), "Les Berbères de la Haute-Moulouya," *EDB*. Paris: Boîte à documents 7: 136–76.

Guennoun, S. (1991), "Littérature des Berbères de la Haute Moulouya," *EDB*. Paris: Boîte à documents / Édisud 8: 113–34.

Guillaume, A. (1946), *Les Berbères marocains et la Pacification de l'Atlas central*. Paris: R. Julliard.

Hachid, M. (2000), *Les Premiers Berbères: entre Méditerranée, Tassili et Nil*. Aix-en-Provence: Edisud.

Hammoudi, A. (1999), "The reinvention of *dar al-mulk*: the Moroccan political system and its legitimation," in R. Bourquia and S. G. Miller (eds.), *In the Shadow of the Sultan: Culture, Power and Politics in Morocco*, 129–75. Cambridge, MA: Harvard University Press.

Hannoum, A. (2003), "Translation and the Colonial Imaginary: Ibn Khaldûn Orientalist," *History & Theory* 42, no. 1 (February).

Harris, W. B. (1895), *Tafilet: The Narrative of a Journey of Exploration in the Atlas Mountains and the Oases of the North-West Sahara*. London: Blackwood and Sons.

Harris, W. B. (1921), *The Morocco That Was*. Edinburgh and London: Blackwood and Sons.

Harrison, J. (1613), *Latest News out of Barbary*. London: Arthur Johnson.

Hart, D. M. (1976), *The Aith Waryaghar of the Moroccan Rif: An Ethnography and History*. Tucson: University of Arizona Press.

Hart, D. M. (1981), *Dadda 'Atta and his Forty Grandsons: The Socio-political Organisation of the Ait'Atta of Southern Morocco*. Wisbech, UK: Menas Press.

Hart, D. M. (1984), *The Ait 'Atta of Southern Morocco: Daily Life and Recent History*. Wisbech, UK: Menas Press.

Hart, D. M. (1984a), "The Ait Sukhman of the Moroccan Central Atlas," *ROMM* 38: 137–52.

Hart, D. M. (1987), *Banditry in Islam*. Wisbech, UK: Menas.

Hart, D. M. (1993), "Four centuries of history on the hoof: the North-West passage of Berber sheep transhumants across the Moroccan Atlas, 1550–1912," *Morocco: JSMS* 3: 21–55.

Hart, D. M. (1997), "The Berber Dahir of 1930 in Colonial Morocco: then and now (1930–1996)," *JNAS* 2, no. 2 (Autumn): 11–33.

Hart, D. M. (2000), *Tribe and Society in Rural Morocco*. London and Portland, OR: Frank Cass.

Himmich, B. (1997), *Au Pays de nos crises: essai sur le mal marocain*. Casablanca: Afrique-Orient.

Holmström, M. (1930), *Un pays de gel et de soleil*. Paris: Berger-Levrault.

Hubert-Jacques, ? (1927), *L'aventure riffiane et ses dessus politiques*. Paris: Bossard.

Huré, A. (Général) (1952), *La Pacification du Maroc (Dernière étape: 1931–34)*. Paris: Berger-Levrault.

Ibn al Zayyât al Tâdilî (1995), *Regard sur le temps des Soufis: vie des saints du Sud marocain desVe, VIe, VIIe siècles de l'hégire*, ed. and trans. A. Toufiq and M. de Feyol. Casablanca: EDDIF/UNESCO.

Ibn Khaldoun (1925/1999), *Histoire des Berbères*, 4 vols., trans. De Slane. Paris: Geuthner.

Al-Idrissi, M. (1836–40), *Livre de la récréation de l'homme désireux de connaître les pays (Kitab nuzhat al-mushtaq fi'khtiraq al-'afaq)*, 2 vols, trans. Pierre Amédée. Paris: Jaubert.

Idriss, H. R. (1962), *La Berbérie oriental sous les Zirides, Xe–XIIe siècles*. Paris: Adrien-Maisoneuve,

Ihrai-Aouchar, A. (1988–9), "Communautés rurales de la Haute Moulouya," *Hespéris-Tamuda* 26–27: 171–96.

Jacques-Meunié, D. (1951), *Greniers-Citadelles au Maroc*, 2 vols. Paris: Arts & Métiers graphiques.

Jacques-Meunié, D. (1958), "Hiérarchie sociale au Maroc pré-saharien," *Hespéris* 41: 239–64.

Janon, R. (1932), "À l'assaut du Haut Atlas, sur les pentes du Djebel Ayachi," *Monde Colonial Illustré* (September): 164–5.

Janon, R. (1941), *Les Salopards*. Algiers: Edmond Charlet.

Janon, R. (1948), *Pillafort*. Casablanca: Fontana.

Jaulin, R. (1994), "Le mythe de l'identité," *Tifinagh* 3–4 (April–July): 43–6.

Joffé, G. (1996), "Walter Harris's vision of Morocco," *JNAS* 3 (Winter): 248–65.

Joubert des Ouches, Lieut. (1936), *L'Adieu au Bled*. Published by author.

Juin, A. (1957), *Le Maghreb en feu*. Paris: Plon.

Julien, Ch.-A. (1969), *Histoire de l'Afrique du Nord*. Paris: Payot.

Justinard, Col. (1940), *La Rihla du Marabout de Tasaft: Sidi Mohammed ben el Haj Brahim ez Zerhouni: notes sur l'histoire de l'Atlas: texte arabe du XVIIIe siècle*. Paris: Geuthner.

Justinard, Col. (1954), *Un petit royaume berbère, le Tazeroualt; un saint berbère: Sidi Ahmed ouMoussa*. Paris: Maisonneuve–Max Besson.

Kably, M. (ed.) (2015), *History of Morocco*. Rabat: RIRHM.

Kasriel, M. (1989), *Libres femmes du Haut-Atlas? Dynamique d'une micro-société au Maroc*. Paris: Harmattan.

Kassim, A. and J. Zenn (2017), "Justifying war: the Salafi-Jihadi appropriation of Sufi Jihad," *Hudson Institute*, March, https://www.hudson.org/research/13480-justifying-war-the-salafi-jihadi-appropriation-of-sufi-jihad-in-the-sahel-sahara.

Khadaoui, A. (n.d.), "L'histoire de la résistance armée dans les Atlas racontée par la poésie," http://www.tawiza.net/Tawiza95/khadaoui.

Al-Khalloufi, M. E. (1993), *Bouhmara, du Jihad à la compromossion: Le maroc orientale de 1900 à 1909*. Rabat: Al Jadida.

Khettouch, M. (1982), "Ouine Iwalioune," *Lamalif* 137 (June–July): 46.

Khettouch, M. A. (1991), *Azour Amokrane ne meurt jamais . . .* Casablanca: API.

Khettouch, M. A. (2001), *La Mémoire de Tamazight: l'œuvre d'Aherdan*. Casablanca: Marsam, 40–1.

Kilito, A. (1999), "Speaking to princes: Al-Yusi and Mawlay Isma'il," in R. Bourqia & S. G. Miller, eds.), *In the Shadow of the Sultan: Culture, Power and Politics in Morocco*, 30–46. Cambridge, MA: Harvard University Press.

Kirkland, F. R. (1993), "French Air Strength in May 1940," *Air Power History*: 22–34; https://en.wikipedia.org/wiki/History _of_the_Armée_de_l'Air.

Klose, F. (*c.* 1927), *The Legion Marches: The Woes and Wrongs of the Foreign Legion*, trans. C. W. Sykes. London: John Hamilton.

Kraus, W. (1997), "Tribal land rights in central Morocco," *JSMS* 2: 16–32.

Kraus, W. (1991), *Die Ayt Hdiddu. Wirtschaft und Gesellschaft im zentralen Hohen Atlas*. Vienna: Österreichischen Akademie des Wissenschaft.

Lafon, M. (1992), "Regards croisés sur le capitaine Saïd Guennoun (1887–1940)," *EDB*, Paris: Boîte à documents / Édisud 9: 93–120.

Lafon, M. (1992a), "Quelques aspects de l'œuvre et de la personnalité de Maurice Le Glay," *Visages du Maroc*, Alliance Franco-Marocaine de Rabat: 53–63.

Lafuente, G. (1984), "Dossier marocain sur le Dahir berbère de 1930," *ROMM* 38, Aix-en-Provence: 83–116.

Lagardère, V. (1998), *Les Almoravides*. Paris: L'Harmattan.

Lahlimi, A. (1978), "Collecitivités rurales traditionnelles," *Études Sociologiques*.

Lakhdar, M. (1971), *La vie littéraire au Maroc sous la dynastie 'alawide (1075–1311 = 1664–1894)*. Rabat: Éd. Techniques nord-africaines.

Landau, R. (1950), *Invitation to Morocco*. London: Faber & Faber.

Landau, R. (1969), *The Kasbas of Southern Morocco*. London: Faber & Faber.

Laoust, E. (1932/1934), "L'habitation chez les transhumants du Maroc central," *Hespéris* 2: 137–90, 123–200.

Laoust, E. (1939), *Cours de berbère marocain. Dialecte du Maroc central*, 3rd edition. Paris: P. Geuthner.

Laroui, A. (1975), *L'histoire du Maghreb*, 2 vols. Paris: F. Maspero.

Laroui, A. (1977), *Les origines sociales et culturelles du Nationalisme marocain*. Paris: F. Maspero.

Last, H. (1932), "The wars of the age of Marius," in S. A. Cook et al. (eds.), *The Cambridge Ancient History*, vol. 9, 125–30. Cambridge: Cambridge University Press.

Lawless, R. I. (1972), "The concept of *tell* and *sahara* in the Maghreb: a reappraisal," *Transactions of the Institute of British Geographers* (Nov): 125–37.

Lawless, R. I. (1973), "Population, resource appraisal and environment in the pre-Saharan zone of the Maghreb," *Mélanges Despois*: 229–37.

Leblanc, Adjt. (1939), *Au Pays de la Peur et du Mensonge*, preface M. Binet-Valmer. Compiègne: n.p.

Lecestre-Rollier, B., M. Garrigues-Creswell et al. (1997), *La Méditerranée, le Haut Atlas*. Aix-en-Provence (France): Publications de l'Université de Provence.

Lefébure, C. (1986), "Ayt Khebbach, impasse sud-est: l'involution d'une tribu marocaine exclue du Sahara," *Désert et montagne au Maghreb (Hommage à Jean Dresch)*, *ROMM* 41–42: 136–57.

Le Glay, M. (1921), *Badda, fille berbère et autres récits marocains*. Paris: Plon.

Le Glay, M. (1922), *Récits marocains de la Plaine et des Monts*. Paris: Berger-Levrault.

Le Glay, M. (1923), *Itto, récit marocain d'Amour et de Bataille*. Paris: Plon.

Le Glay, M. (1930), *Les Sentiers de la Guerre et de l'Amour: récits marocains*. Paris: Berger-Levrault.

Lesur, ? (1920), "Note sur la Zaouïa de Sidi Hamza," *BSGM* 2–3: 141–7.

Loubignac, V. (1924), *Étude sur le dialecte berbère des Zaïan et Aït Sgougou*, 2 vols. Paris: Leroux.

Louis, G. (1916), "Le sud-est marocain," *BSGM* (October–December).

Lugan, B. (2012), *Histoire du Maroc, des origines à nos jours*. Paris: Ellipses.

Magnin, Col. (1913), *Campagne du Tadla*, Paris: Lavauzelle.

Maher, V. (1974), *Women and Property in Morocco*. Cambridge: Cambridge University Press.

El-Manouar, M. (2012), *Dads, De l'organisation sociale traditionnelle à la domination coloniale (XIXème–XXème siècles)*, 2 vols. Rabat: IRCAM.

El-Mansour, M. (1990), *Morocco in the Reign of Mawlay Slayman*. Wisbech, UK: MENAS Press.

Mansouri, H. A. (1995), "Carthage en Berbérie," *Tifinagh* 5–6 (May): 47–54.

Manue, G. R. (1930), *Sur les marches du Maroc insoumis*. Paris: Gallimard.

Manue, G. R. (1934), *Le Hakem au burnous bleu*. Paris: Portiques.

Marçais, G. (1947), *La Berbérie musulmane et l'Orient au Moyen Âge*. Paris: Aubier.

Marcireau, R. (1938), *Souvenirs d'un goumier: Grand Atlas 1932–1933*. Poitiers: L'Action intellectuelle.

Marcy, G. (1929), "Une tribu berbère de la confédération Aït Waraïn: les Aït Jellidasen," *Hespéris* 9: 79–142.

Marcy, G. (1988), "Les Berbères.—Vie intellectuelle—Littérature—Croyances—Religion," *EDB*, Paris: Boîte à documents 4: 143–56.

Martin, Cdt. (1925), "D'Azilal au Dadès," *BSGM*: 85–115.

Martin, Cdt. (1927), "En pays Aït Abbès et Aït Bou Guemmez au Tizi n'Aït Imi," *RGM*: 277–88.

Martin, J. (1938), *Je suis un Légionnaire*. Paris: A. Fayard.

Massignon, L. (1906/2018), *Le Maroc dans les premières années du XVI siècle*. n.p.p: L. G. Binger; London: Forgotten Books.

Maurois, A. (1931), *Lyautey*. Paris: Plon.

Maxwell, G. (1966), *Lords of the Atlas*. London: Longmans.

Mazel, J. (1971), *Enigmes du Maroc*. Paris: Robert Laffont.

Mazières, M. de and J. Goulven (1932), *Les Kasbas du Haut Atlas*. Casablanca: Imprimeries Réunies, 1932.

Méraud., M. (1990), *Histoire des AI: Le Service des Affaires Indigènes du Maroc, Histoire des Goums marocains*, vol. 3. Paris: Koumia.

Mercier, E. (1867), "Sidjilmassa selon les auteurs arabes," *RA* 11: 233–42, 274–83.

Mercier, E. (1871), "Notes sur l'origine du people berbère," *RA* 15: 420–33.

Merrakushi, Al- Ibn 'Idhari (1951), *Histoire de l'Afrique du Nord et de l'Espagne musulmmane*, trans. G. S. Colin and E. Léci-Provençal. Leiden: Brill.

Mezzine, L. (1987), *Le Tafilalt: contribution à l'Histoire du Maroc aux XVIIe et XVIIIe siècles*. Rabat: Faculté des lettres.

Michaux-Bellaire, E. (1927), *Les Confréries religieuses au Maroc, Archives marocaines* 27. Paris, 1927.

Michaux-Bellaire, E. (ed.) (1917), "Note sur les Amhaouch et les Ahansal," *Archives berbères* 2, Paris: Leroux: 209–18.

Michel, N. (1991), "L'approvisionnement de la *mhalla* au Maroc au XIXe siècle," *Hespéris-Tamuda* 29, fasc. 2: 313–40.

Michel, N. (1994), "Itinéraires de la mhalla, L'Armée marocaine à travers l'histoire," *Maroc-Europe* 7: 81–115.

Montagne, R. (1930), *Villages et Kasbas berbères: tableau de la vie sociale des berbères sédentaires dans le Sud du Maroc*. Paris: F. Alcan.

Montagne, R. (1930/1989), *Les Berbères et le Makhzen dans le Sud marocain*. Casablanca: Afrique-Orient.

Montagne, R. (1973), *The Berbers: Their Social and Political Organisation*, trans. and intro. D. Seddon. London: Frank Cass.

Monteil, V. (1958), *Les Officiers*. Paris: Éditions du Seuil.

Morsy, M. (1967), "Moulay Ismaïl et l'Armée de métier," *Revue d'Histoire moderne et contemporaine* 14 (April–June): 97–122.

Morsy, M. (1972), *Les Ahansala: examen du rôle historique d'une famille maraboutique de l'Atlas marocain*. Paris and The Hague: Mouton.

Morsy, M. (1979), "Comment décrire l'histoire du Maroc," *Actes de Durham: recherches récentes sur le Maroc moderne, BESM* 138–139: 121–43.

Morsy, M. (1984), *North Africa 1800–1900*. London: Longmans.

Morsy, M. (1986), "Ahansal," in G. Camps (ed.), *Encyclopédie Berbère*, vol. 3: 1–5.

Morsy-Patchett, M. (1963), "La longue captivité et les aventures de Thomas Pellow," *Hespéris-Tamuda* 4: 289–311.

Mouhib, M. (2015), *Midelt: Esquisses historiques et culturelles*. Fez: Infoprint.

Moukhlis, M. S. (1994), "Discours dominants et culture tamazight," *Tifinagh* 2 (February–March): 11–14.

Moukhlis, M. S. (1997), "Le mouvement national et Tamazight: le kidnapping de l'histoire," *Tifinagh* 11–12 (August): 55–8.

Moukhlis, M. (1999), "Le Mouvement National et Tamazight," *Tifinagh* 11–12 (May): 55–8.

Moukhlis, M. S. and M. Mounib (1997), "Dahir berbère: grand bluff politique dans le Maroc contemporain," *Tifinagh* 11–12 (August): 85–8.

Mtouggui, L. (*c.* 1935), *Vue générale de l'histoire berbère*. Paris: Larose.

Naciri, A. (1906–7), *Kitab al-Istiqça*, trans. E. Fumey, *Archives marocaines* 8, 9, and 10. Paris: n.p.

Naciri, A. (1923), *Kitab al-Istiqça*, trans. A. Graulle, *Archives marocaines* 30. Paris: n.p.

Naciri, A. (1925), *Kitab al-Istiqça*, trans. A. Graulle and G. S. Colin, *Archives marocaines* 31. Paris: n.p.

Naciri, A. (1927), *Kitab al-Istiqça*, trans. I. Hamet, *Archives marocaines* 32. Paris: n.p.

Neuville, J.-J. (1927), *Sous le Burnous bleu*. Paris: Charpentier & Fasquelle.

Norris, H. T. (1975), *The Tuaregs—Their Islamic Legacy and its Diffusion in the Sahel*. Warminster: Aris & Phillips.

Norris, H. T. (1982), *The Berbers in Arabic Literature*. London and New York: Longmans.

Noyce, W. (1962), "Climbing solo in the High Atlas," *Alpine Journal*: 65.

Ouachrine, L. (1999), "Anthologie d'Aït M'guild," *La Tribune de Meknès-Tafilalet* 37: 20–4.

Ouchna, Z. (2005), *Zaid Ouhmad: Un honneur debut*. Errrachidia: Medaghrap.

Ougrour, J. (1962), "Le fait berbère (essai de démystification)," *Confluent* 23–24 (September–October): 617–34.

Ould-Cheikh, M. (1936), *Myriem dans les Palmes*. Oran: Éditions Plaza.

Ouriachi, K.-M. (1988), "Éléments pour la compréhension de la problématique tamazight," *AWAL, Cahier d'études berbères*, Paris: MSH: 1–6.

Pascal, J. (2009), "L'Armée française face à Abdelkrim ou la tentation de mener une guerre conventionnelle dans une guerre irrégulière 1924–1927," *Stratégique*: 319–38; https://www.cairn.info/revue-strategique-2009-1-page-319.htm.

Pellow, T. (1890), *Adventures*, intro. and notes Robert Brown. London: T. Fisher Unwin.

Pennell, C. R. (2000), *Morocco since 1830: A History*. London: Hurst.

Perry, J. M. (2005), *Arrogant Armies: Great Military Disasters and the Generals Behind Them*. Edison, NJ: Castle Books.

Peyré, J. (1950), *La Légende du goumier Saïd*. Paris: Flammarion.

Peyron, M. (1984), "Contribution à l'histoire du Haut Atlas oriental: les Ayt Yafelman," *ROMM* 38, no. 2: 117–35.

Peyron, M. (1988–9), "Un regard nouveau sur le combat du Msedrid (Premier Mai 1933)," *Hespéris-Tamuda* 26–27: 197–206.

Peyron, M. (1989/1990), *Great Atlas Traverse*, 2 vols. Reading: West Col Productions.

Peyron, M. (1990), "Chronique orale sur la vie des Ayt Merghad," *LOAB* 21: 93–102.

Peyron, M. (1991), "Belgassem Ngadi," *Encyclopédie Berbère* 9: 1434–5.

Peyron, M. (1992), "Proverbes de l'Atlas marocain de Taza à Azilal," *EDB* 9: 73–92.

Peyron, M. (1992a): "Ben Barakat," *Encyclopédie Berbère* 9: 80–3.

Peyron, M. (1993), *Isaffen Ghbanin/Rivières profondes: poésies du Moyen–Atlas marocain traduites et annotées*. Casablanca: Wallada.

Peyron, M. (1995a), "Derkaoua," *Encyclopédie Berbère* 15: 2279–83.

Peyron, M. (1995b), "Tradition orale et résistance armée: la bataille des Ayt Yâqoub (Haut-Atlas)," *EDB* 12: 5–16.

Peyron, M. (1996), "La saga des Ayt Bou Slama," *EDB* 14, Paris: Boîte à Documents/Édisud: 75–95.

Peyron, M. (1997), "Combattants du Maroc central: une résistance morcelée (1912–33)," *AWAL* 16: 25–41.

Peyron, M. (1998), "La femme tamazight du Maroc central," in C. Lacoste-Dujardin and M. Virolle (eds.), *Femmes et Hommes au Maghreb et en immigration: la frontière des genres en question*, 109–125. Paris: Éd. Publisud.

Peyron, M. (1999), "Entre haine et amour: officiers des Affaires Indigènes et tribus dissidentes (Atlas marocain, 1914–56)," *Awal* 19: 9–18.

Peyron, M. (2000), "Amazigh poetry of the Resistance period (Central Morocco)," *JNAS* 5, no. 1 (Spring): 109–20.

Peyron, M. (2000a), "Berka, Ou-," *Encyclopédie Berbère* 23: 3614.

Peyron, M. (2001), "Imihiwach," *Encyclopédie Berbère* 24: 3694–703.

Peyron, M. (2005), "Barghawata et résistance," *Le Maroc des resistances*. Rabat: IRCAM: 165–81.

Peyron, M. (2010), *Berber Odes: Poetry from the mountains of Morocco*. London: Eland.

Peyron, M. (2013), "Hostilités académiques: approches conflictuelles à propos des Imazighen du Maroc central," in *La culture amazighe: réflexions et pratiques anthropologiques du temps colonial à nos jours*, 13–31. Rabat: IRCAM.

Peyron, M. (2020), *Contes et légendes de la montagne amazighe; Maroc*. Rabat: IRCAM.

Peyron, M. and A. Roux (2002), *Poésies berbères de l'époque héroïque: Maroc central (1908-1932)*. Aix-en-Provence: Édisud.

Philippe, F. (1911), "Voyage d'El Hadj El Bachir au Tafilala en 1867," *RA*, Algiers: 255–73.

Pinon, R. (1935), *Au Maroc, fin des temps héroïques*. Paris: Berger-levrault.

Planhol, X. de (1962), "Caractères généraux de la vie montagnarde dans le Proche-Orient et dans l'Afrique du Nord," *Annales de Géographie* 384: 113–30.

Poncet, L. (1967), "Le mythe de l'invasion Hilalienne," *Annales ESC* 5: 1099–120.

Porch, D. (2005a), *The Conquest of Morocco*. New York: Farrar, Straus & Giroux.

Porch, D. (2005b), *The Conquest of the Sahara*. New York: Farrar, Straus and Giroux.

Porcher, L. (1948), *Baroud d'honneur*. Casblanca: Imprimerie rapide.

Prémaré, A. de (1989a), "Affaire d'Azrou", *RMMM* 51: 1124–5.

Prémaré, A. L. de (1989b), "L'expression littéraire en langue régionale au service de causes politiques ou religieuses contestataires dans le Maroc d'autrefois," *Les Prédicateurs profanes au Maghreb*, *REMMM* 51. Aix-en-Provence: Édisud: 121–6.

Psichari, E. (1920/1967), *Les Voixqui crient dans le Désert*. Paris: L. Conard.

Quedenfeldt, M. (1902–4), "Division et répartition de la population berbère au Maroc," *Revue Africaine*.

Raclot, G. (1937), *Bel Maaqoul: scènes de la vie des Partisans marocains*. Casablanca: Éd. Inter-Presse.

Raha, A. R. (1995), "Tamazight commune? Elle existe déjà!" *Tifinagh* 7: 43–6.

Ranger, T. O. (1968), "Connexions Between 'Primary Resistance' Movements and Modern Mass Nationalism In East and Central Africa," *Journal of African History* 9: 437–53.

Raynal, R. (1960), "La terre et l'homme en Haute Moulouya," *BESM* 86–87: 281–346.

Raynaud, Rober (1923), *En marge du livre jaune: le Maroc*. Paris, Plon.

Reisser, Cne. and Cne. Bachelot (1918), "Notice sur le cercle de Sefrou," *BSGM* (February–March): 29–51.

Reyniers, F. (1930), *Taougrat, ou les Berbères racontés par eux-mêmes*. Paris: P. Geuthner.

Rinn, L. (1882–9), "Essai d'études linguistiques et ethnologiques sur les origines des Berbères," *RA*.

Rivet, D. (1988), *Lyautey et l'Institution du Protectorat*, 3 vols. Paris: L'Harmattan.

Rivet, D. (1999), *Le Maroc de Lyautey à Mohammed V: le double visage du Protectorat*. Paris: Denoël.

Robichez, J. (1946), *Maroc central*: Grenoble and Paris: Arthaud.

Rousseau, G. (1923), "Au Maroc inconnu," *BSGM*: 560–6.

Roux, A. (1942), *Récits, contes et légendes berbères dans le parler des Beni-Mtir*. Rabat: n.p.

Roux, A. (1992), "Quelques chants berbères sur les opérations de 1931–1932 dans le Maroc central," EDB. Paris: Boîte à documents/Édisud 9: 165–219.

Sadiqi, F. (2003), *Women, Gender and Language in Morocco*. Leiden and Boston: Brill.

Sadki, A. (1988–9), "La zawiya de Tasaft," *Hespéris-Tamuda* 26–27: 67–92.

Saulay, J. (1985), *Histoire des Goums*, vol. 1. Paris: La Koumia.

Schroeter, D. (1988), *Merchants of Essouira: Urban Society and Imperialism in Southwestern Morocco, 1844–1886*. Cambridge: Cambridge University Press.

Scott O'Connor, V. C. (1923/1929), *A Vision of Morocco: The Far West of Islam*. London: Thornton Butterworth.

Segonzac, R. de (1910), *Au cœur de l'Atlas, Mission au Maroc (1904–1905)*. Paris: Larose.

Shatzmiller, M. (1983), "Le mythe d'origine berbère: aspects historiographiques et sociaux," *ROMM* 35, no. 1: 45–156.

Shatzmiller, M. (2000), *The Berbers and the Islamic State*. Princeton, NJ: M. Wiener.

Simoneau, A. (1967), "Gravures rupestres du Yagour," *RGM* 11: 67–76.

Simou, B. (1994), "L'apport des pays européens aux réformes militaires au Maroc: le cas de l'Italie," *L'Armée marocaine à travers l'histoire*, in *Maroc-Europe* 7: 139–75.

Sitwell, S. (1940), *Mauretania: Warrior, Man, and Woman*. London: Duckworth.

Skounti, M. Ou- (1991), "Trois poèmes en tamazight," *AWAL* 8: 167.

Slouschz, N. (1908), "Les origines des Berbères," *Archives marocaines* 14. Paris: E. Leroux: 311–77.

Spillman, G. (1936), *Les Aït Atta du Sahara et la Pacification du Haut Dra*. Rabat: F. Moncho.

Spillman, G. (1951/2012), *Confréries et Zaouïas*. Rabat: Faculty of Letters.

Spillman, G. (1968), *Souvenirs d'un Colonialiste*. Paris: Presses de la Cité.

Stroomer, H. (2001), *Tashelhiyt Berber Folktales (Southern Morocco)*, Koln: Rudiger Koppe Verlag, 2001.

Stroomer, H. (2001a), *Textes berbères des Guedmioua et Goundafa (Haut-Atlas, Maroc)*. Aix-en-Provence: Edisud.

Swanson, L. (2000), "Mosque at Ait Isman: Todra gorge, Morocco," *JNAS* 5, no. 1: 147–64.

Tadili, Ibn, Al, Z. al Tâdilî (1995), *Regard sur temps des Soufis, vie des saints du Sud marocain des Ve, VIe, VIIe siècles de l'hégire*, trans. M. de Fenyol, ed. A. Toufiq. Rabat: EDDIF/UNESCO.

Tahiri, B. (2003), *Le Temps des Anciens: mémoires—clandestinité—récits Armée de Libération marocaine*. Rabat: Omnia.

Tahtah, M. (2000), *Entre Pragmatisme, Réformisme et Modernisme: Le Rôle Politico-Religieux des Khattabi dans le Rif (Maroc) Jusqu' à 1926*, Orientalia Lovaniensia Analecta. Leuven: Peeters.

Taifi, M. (1991), *Dictionnaire Tamazight-Français (Parlers du Maroc central)*. Paris, Awal / L'Harmattan.

Talton, B. (2011), "African Resistance to Colonial Rule," *Schomburg Center for Research in Black Culture*.

Tarrit, Cdt. (1923), "Étude sur le front chleuh: le pays des Aït Seri et des Aït Chokmane," *BSGM* 2–4: 517–59.

Tauxier, H. (1862), "Examen des traditions grecques, latines et musulmanes relatives à l'origine du peuple berbère," *RA*, Algiers: 353–63, 453–72.

Terrasse, H. (1938), *Kasbas berbères de l'Atlas et des oasis*. Paris: Horizons de France.

Terrasse, H. (1952), *History of Morocco*, trans. Hilary Tee. Casablanca: Ed. Atlantides.

Tharaud, J. and J. Tharaud (1929), *Marrakech, ou les Seigneurs de l'Atlas*. Paris: Plon.

Theveney, Gal. (1930, 1931, 1932), "Devant le bloc zaïan irréductible (1914–1917)," *BSGA* 124, 127, 129.

Torres, D. de (1650), *Histoire des Chérifs*, trans. Duke of Angoulème. n.p.p.: n.p.

Trimingham, J. S. (1971), *The Sufi Orders of Islam*. Oxford: Oxford University Press.

Turnbull, P. (1960), *The Hotter Winds*. London: Hutchinson.

Van den Boogert, N. (1997), *The Berber Literary Tradition of the Sous, with an Edition and Translation of "The Ocean of Tears" by Muhammad Awzal*. Leiden: NIVHNO.

Van den Boogert, N. (1998), "La Révélation des Énigmes," *Lexiques arabo-berbères des XVIIᵉ et XVIIIᵉ, siècles*. Aix-en-Provence: IREMAM.

Venema, B. and A. Mguild (2003), "Access to Land and Berber ethnicity in the Middle Atlas, Morocco," *Middle Eastern Studies* 39, no. 1 (October): 35–53.

Verde, T. (2017), "Mailika VI: Sayyida al-Hurra," *Aramco World*, January–February.

Vermeren, P. (2001), *Le Maroc en transition*. Paris: La Découverte.

Véronne, C. de la (2002), *Yaghmurasan, premier souverain de la dynastie berbère des Abd-al-Wadides de Tlemcen*. Saint-Denis: Bouchène.

Vial, J. (1938), *Le Maroc héroïque*. Paris: Hachette.

Vinogradov, A. R. (1974), *The Aith Ndhir of Morocco: A Study of the Social Transformation of A Berber Tribe*. Ann Arbor: University of Michigan Press.

Voinot, L. (1939), *Sur les traces glorieuses des Pacificateurs du Maroc*. Paris: Charles-Lavauzelle.

Voinot, L. (1943), "L'Evolution moderne du Maroc," in *Maroc*, 6th ed., 109–32. Paris: Encyclopédie coloniale et maritime.

Walraven, K. Van and J. Abbink (n.d.), "Rethinking resistance in African history: An introduction"; https://openaccess.leidenuniv.nl/bitstream/handle/1887/9605/ASC_1267345_085.pdf?sequence=1 http://exhibitions.nypl.org/africanaage/essay-resistance.html.

Ward Price, G. (1934), *In Morocco with the Legion*. London: Jarrold Publishers.

Watt, W. Montgomery (1965/1967), *A History of Islamic Spain*. Edinburgh: Edinburgh University Press.

Weisgerber, F. (1947), *Au Seuil du Maroc moderne*. Rabat: La Porte.

Wellard, J. (1967), *Lost Worlds of Africa*. London: Hutchinson.

Weygand, J. (1954), *Goumier de l'Atlas*. Paris: Flammarion.

Wharton, E. (1920/1927), *In Morocco*. London: Jonathan Cape.

Willis, M. J. (2012), *Politics and Power in the Maghreb: Algeria, Tunisia and Morocco from Independence to the Arab Spring*. London: Hurst.

Woodward, M. et al. (n.d.), "Salafi Violence and Sufi tolerance?" *Perspectives on terrorism*, http://www.terrorismanalysts.com/pt/index php/pot/article/view/311/html.

Woolman, D. S. (1957/1968), *Rebels in the Rif: Abd El Krim and the Rif Rebellion*. Stanford, CA: Stanford University Press

Wyrtzen, J. (2015), *Making Morocco: Colonial Intervention and the Politics of Identity*. Ithaca, NY, and London: Cornell University Press.

Zar', Ibn Abu (1918/1999), *Rawd al-Qirtas*, trans. A. Beaumier, 2nd ed. Rabat: La Porte.

Index

Abou 'Abdallah Mohammed Lhajj, Dila'i leader, 49

Abou-Bekr, Almoravid leader, 19

Abou-Bekr ben Mohammed El-Mejjati Es-Senhaji, founder of Dila', 47, 53

Abou 'Aam, market, southeast Morocco, 69

Abou Debbous, Almohad prince, 31

Abou Inan, Merinid amir, 32, 37

Abou l-Hassan, Merinid amir, 32, 37

Abou Mahalli, Ahmed Ibn 'Abdallah ('Bum Hully'), 41

Abou Ma'arouf, Merinid leader, 30

Abou Saïd 'Athman Ibn 'Abdelhaqq, Merinid amir, 28

Abou Thabet, Merinid sultan, 37

Abou Yahya, Merinid amir, 30

Abraray, Tazizaout veteran, 220

Ab'abou, rebel officer, Skhirat coup, 246

Adaroush, village, Middle Atlas, 85, 109

Adekhsan, village near Khenifra, 55, 56, 65, 67, 71, 73

Adgherni, Ahmed, Amazigh politician, 255

Adrar n-Dern (Marrakesh High Atla), 123

Adrar n-Siwan, peak, Middle Atlas, 172

Aedemon, rebelled against Rome, 10

AFEMAM, French-organized research conference, 250

Agadir, city southwest Morocco, 84, 249, 253

Agelbi (aka Aqebli), Mohammed, Ayt Sgougou qayd, 84, 111

Agerd n-Oulghoum, hill, near Tazizaout, 215–16

Agerssif, town, east Morocco, 29

Agerssif, village, Middle Atlas, 73

Aghbala, town, Middle Alas, 62, 69, 82, 85, 86, 102, 134, 177, 206

Aghbalou n-Kerdous, southeast Morocco, 190, 227, 230, 232, 242

Aghbalou n-Serdan, village, Moulouya region, 72, 86

Aghbar, upper Nfis, 59

Aghembo n-Masko, cliff, Ahansal region, 201

Aghembo n-Mestfran, ("la Grande Cathédrale"), High Atlas, 125, 228

Aghembo n-Shinzer, peak, Kousser, 233

Aghfour, Oued, battle site, 31

Aghfour, Oued, site of Almohad defeat, 33

Aghmat, former capital city near Marrakesh, 19, 20, 31

Aghzaz, cavalry, 30

Agoudal, village, Hadiddou region, 230

Agouddim, site of Zaouia Ahansal, 125, 130

Agouddim Ikhf n-Ouaman, village, 192–3

Agouraï, village, Meknes region, 99

Ahansal, Oued (asif n-ouhansal), 43, 47, 201

Ahansal, Zaouia (zaouit n-ouhansal), 43, 63, 99, 125–7, 129–30, 166, 201, 211

Ahansala (ihansalen), marabouts of Zaouit Ahansal, 43, 45, 97, 125, 130, 201, 206, 233, 246

Aherdan, Mahjoubi, (amghar) political leader, Oulmes (Zaïan), 246–7

Aherdan, Ouzzin, Berber activist, 247, 249

Ahermoumou (Ribat El-Khayr), foot-hill town, Middle Atlas, 141, 172, 175

Ahlil, village, Middle Atlas, 71

Ahnou, site of makhzan defeat, Sokhman region, 87

Ahmed, Ba, famous vizir, 90

Ahmed, Idrissi prince, 15

Aïn El-Ouirra, village, southeast Morocco, 180

Aïn Leuh, town, Middle Atlas, 17, 55

Aïn Shayr, palm-grove, southeast Morocco, 116, 180

Aïn Tisigdelt, spring, Middle Atlas, 19

Aïnin, Ma el-, saintly leader, W. Sahara, 94, 101, 163

Aïsha, ou-, ou-'Ali, nineteenth-century loyalist Sokhman *qayd*, 87 Akhawayn, Al-, University (AUI), Ifran, 250

Aix-en-Provence, city, France, 250

Ajdir, 'Abdelkrim's village, Rif, 152, 156–7

Ajjou, Jbel, Bou Iban, 172

Alegmou, hill, west of Tazizaout, 214, 217

Alemsid, outpost, Moulouya region, 86, 134, 136

Alhoceima, Bay, Rif, 151–2, 156–7

Al-Jazeera, TV channel, 253

Almis n-Gigou, village, Middle Atlas, 110

Almis-Marmousha, village, Middle Atlas, 142–3

Almohads (*al-muwahidun*), Berber dynasty, 3, 19–21, 24, 25, 27, 30, 31, 35, 36, 41, 48

Almoravids (*al-murabitun*), Berber dynasty, 18–21, 22, 23, 24, 26, 27, 43, 94

Almou n-Tarselt, pasture, near Waouizaght, 130

Al-Sakhrat, battle site near Fez, 30

Amalou n-Mansour, mountain, Jbel Saghro, 225

Amalou n-Tmezra, French outpost, near Tounfit, 209

Amdghous, region, High Atlas, 43, 198–9, 227

Amekla, district, Middle Atlas, 96

Amellago, village, Oued Ghriss, 192–3

Ameqran, Air Force pilot, 1972 coup, 246

Amezian, Mohand, religious leader, Rif, 150

Amgernis, village, Ida ou Msattog, 61

Amhaoush, Bou-Bker, Middle Atlas marabout, 68, 72, 73–5, 79, 82, 85, 256

Amhaoush, maraboutic lineage, 194

Amhaoush, Sidi Hmad, Sidi Lmekki's grand-son, 203

Amhaoush, Sidi Mohammed ou Nasser, eighteenth-century saint, 66

Amhaoush, Sidi Mohammed ou Nasser, marabout, Jbel Fazaz, 62

Amhaoush, Sidi 'Ali, religious leader, 84–8, 95, 117, 131–2, 134, 177, 185–6, 194, 199, 213, 222

Amharoq, Zaïan chief, 106, 208, 217, 221

Amir, Beni, Arabic-speaking Tadla tribe, 11

Amjot, Derqaouia zaouia, Beni Zeroual, 157

Ammougger, village, Oued Ziz, 182, 192

Andalucia, 21, 27, 28, 29, 30, 150

Anefgou, *qsar*, Hadiddou region, 211, 252–3

Anergui, village, High Atlas, 35, 69, 88, 99, 125, 130, 200, 211

ANLCA (*Agence Nationale de Lutte contre l'Analphabétisme*), 253

Anoual, battle site, Rif, 151–3

Anoual, French outpost, southeast Morocco, 180

Annosser, Sidi Raho's home village, 96, 161, 174

Anzegmir, (*asif n-ounzegmir*), Moulouya tributary, 70, 72, 186

Aoufous, village, Oued Ziz, 180

Aoujja, hill, Bou Iblan, 172

Aoulay, French outpost, N Morocco, 154

Aousan, Sidi, El-, zaouia, 121

Aoutat, n-Ayt Izdeg, (Midelt), town, 19, 88, 201

Aoutat, river, (Midelt), 201

Aqebli, 'Ali Ben Ichou, *qayd* in Jbel Fazaz under Moulay Ismaïl, 55, 56

Aqqa, ou-, Mimoun, resistance fighter, Marmousha, 244

Aqqa Bou Tafersit, Ghriss region, 194

Aqqa n-Oushlou, ravine, Tazizaout, 214–15-217, 220–2

Aqqa n-Tassent, ravine, 228

Aqqa n-Tefza, ravine, Tazizaout, 214, 216

Aqqa n-Zebzbat, river, near Tazizaout, 213–16, 220–1

Arafa, Ben, Moulay, puppet sultan (1953–1955), 221

Aroudan, mountain, High Atlas, 125

Arruit Monte, Spansih outpost, Rif, 151–2

Arsalan, Shakib, Syrian Salafist leader, 242

Arsène Roux, French Berberist, 17, 250

Asif n-Ougheddou, (Agheddou river) High Atlas, 209, 213–17

Asif n-Oukhashan, river, High Atlas, 233

Asker, Zaouia, Ahansal order, 125, 206

Askjour, outpost, Oued Dra'a, 191–2

Asoul (Sidi Bou Ya'qoub), town, upper Ghriss, 44, 48, 62, 193, 231
Assarag, High Atlas village, 124
Assatour, hill east of Tounfit, 187
Astray, Milan, Spanish officer, *Tercio*, 159
Atchana, French outpost, southeast Morocco, 181
Attia, Ayt Bou, section of Ayt 'Arfa tribe, 72
Aubert, French general, Tishshoukt, 142–3
Awraba, Berber tribe, 15
Ayard (*ayar*), officer in charge, *Affaires Indigènes* (AI), 165
Azaghar Fal, plain near Aghbala, 69, 205, 213
Azaghar Irs, plateau, Hadiddou region, 230
Azaykou, 'Ali Sedki, Berber historian and militant, 249
Azerkan, Riffian Foreign Secretary, 159
Azeroual, Sidi Mohand Belqasm, marabout, Berkin, 144, 172
Azerzou, village, Moulouya region, 134
Azgin, village, southeast Morocco, 190
Azigza, Agelmam, lake, Middle Atlas, 112
Azila, coastal town, north Morocco, 150
Azilal, town, High Atlas 126, 127, 129–30, 177, 233
Azinous, outpost, Middle Atlas, 142–3
Azlag n-Tzemmourt, Middle Atlas, site of Moha ou-Hammou's death, 95
Azourki, Jbel, 47, 198, 201, 211
Azrou, Berber College, 241
Azrou, Middle-Atlas town, 15, 17, 24, 25, 55, 66, 72, 101, 105, 109, 251
'Abbas, Ayt, High Atlas tribe, Azilal region, 124
'Abdallah, Abou Mohammed Lhajj, Dila'i leader, 53
'Abdallah, Seksawa magician, 37, 38
'Abdallah, Sidi, local Merghad saint, 184
'Abdallah, Sidi Mohammed Ben, 'Alawid sultan, 66, 67, 68
'Abdallah Dila'i, Ahmed ben, Dila'yin pretender, 50
'Abdallah Ibn Yassin, Almoravid preacher, 18–19
'Abdelkrim (el-Khattabi), Rifi resistance leader, 151–61, 170, 175–6, 178, 246
'Abdelmalek, pro-German agitator, northeast Morocco, 93, 111

'Abdelmoumen, Almohad sultan, 22, 23, 24, 25, 26, 27
'Abdelouadids, Zenata Berbers, medieval rulers of Tlemcen, 30
'Abd el-'Aziz, Merinid sultan, 39
'Abdi, Ayt, Beni Mguild clan, 103
'Abdi, Ayt, Beni-Mguild clan, Bekrit, 110
'Abdi, Ayt, Sokhman clan, 87–8, 162, 200, 213, 227
'Abdi n-Kousser, Ayt, Sokhman clan, 98, 149, 227, 233, 246
'Affan, Ayt, upper Tassaout tribe, 125
'Alawid *shurafa* (Filala), reigning dynasty, 48, 49, 51, 52, 65, 67, 68, 76–7, 79, 82–3, 139
'Ali, *amghar* of Tamdakht, 123–4
'Ali, Oulad, Berber tribe, Middle Atlas, 172–3, 175
'Ali, Sidi 'Ali, Seghroushen clan, 93, 140
'Ali Ibn Youssef, Almoravid sultan, 23, 24
'Amr, Ayt, Hadiddou clan, 209–10
'Amr, Hammou ou-, 156
'Amr, Moulay, Idrissid sharif, 8
'Amran, Ayt Ba, Berber tribe, southwest Morocco, 235–7
'Aomar, Ben, false Ayt Sgougou sharif, 135
'Aouam, Jbel, silver mines near Mrirt, 15, 24, 30, 31
'Aousan, Sidi El-, Derqaoua zaouia, Ferkla region, 113
'Aqqa, Moha ou, nephew of Zaïan notable Ou-Laïdi, 106
'Arfa, Ayt, Berber tribe, Middle Atlas, 73–4
'Atman, Sidi Bou, battle site, 94, 102
'Atta, Ayt, super-tribe, southeast Morocco, 35, 44, 45, 46, 53, 54, 67, 68, 69, 115–16, 118–19, 121, 124, 126–8, 162, 179, 191, 192, 225–6
'Atta, Dada, founding father of Ayt 'Atta, 46
'Atta n-Oumalou, Ayt, northerly component of Ayt 'Atta, 94
'Attab, Ayt, Berber tribe, High Atlas, 63
'Ayad, Sidi, site of Idrassen defeat, 72
'Ayyad, Jbel, Marmousha region, 170
'Ayyash, Ayt, Idrassen tribe, 44, 49, 52, 70, 71, 72, 197
'Ayyashi, El-, 'Abdallah Ibn Hamza, nineteenth-century marabout, 75

'Ayyashi, El-, Abou Salim, famous marabout, Zaouia Sidi Hamza, 45

'Ayyashi, Jbel, el-, 24, 44, 45, 49, 55, 69, 70, 133, 187, 197–8

'Ayyashi, El-, marabout, north morocco, 48, 150

'Aziz, -ou, Ould-Mohammed, Idrassen *qayd*, 67

'Aziz, Sidi Ben Nasser, mid-nineteenth-century Mtiri *qayd*, 10

'Aziza (Seksawiya), Lalla, famous holy woman, 38, 39

Ba Slam, 'Assou ou-, resistance leader, Jbel Saghro, 162, 225–6

Bab Ftouh, gate, Fez, 99

Bab Lguissa, gate, Fez, 99

Bab n-Ouyyad, mountain, Imilshil region, 228

Babin, Gustave, French journalist, 128

Badie, (*badi*) French lieutenant, 232

Badis, Spanish outpost, Rif, 150

Baddou, Jbel, High Atlas, 3, 162, 194, 230–3, 247

Bani, Jbel, southwest Morocco, 102, 161, 236

Bani, Ou-, Mohammed, Khebbash chief, 191–2

Banu Salih (Nekkour), medieval state, Rif, 149

Barakat, (aka Ou-Barka), 'Ali Ben, *makhzan qayd*, upper Moulouya, 56, 62

Barbary, 63

Barranco del Lobo, Rif, 150

Batn El-Roumman, Dila'yin defeat, 51

Beht, Oued, battle site, 16

Bejaia (Bougie), Algerian city, 22

Bekrit, village, Middle Atlas, 73, 101, 110–12

Ben Bou-Bker Dila'i, 46

Benasser, Sidi Mohammed, nephew of 'Ali Amhaoush, 134

Benchtiya, el-Guedmioui, eighteenth-century Makhzan *qayd*, Western High Atlas, 9

Beni Behloul, site of Almohad defeat, 30

Beni Bou Zert, Ouaraïni clan, 142

Beni Derkoul, Frech outpost, Rif, 153

Beni Hassan, Arabic-speaking tribe, Gharb, 46, 71

Beni Hassan, Middle Atlas tribe, 172–3, 175

Beni Hilal, Arabic-speaking nomads, 27, 28

Beni Idjfashi, Zenata tribe, 17

Beni Ifran, Zenata tribe, 17

Beni Mellal (Day), city, Tadla region, 2, 126, 130, 177, 211, 251

Beni Mestara, tribe, Ouezzan region, 160

Beni Mkoud, Arabic-speaking tribe, 25

Beni Midrar, Berber dynasty, Tafilalt, 16

Beni Ouattas (Ouattasid), Berber dynasty, 32, 39

Beni Tadjit, village, southeast Morocco, 181

Beni Tarif, Berghaouati tribe, 16

Beni Yazgha, tribe, Middle Atlas, 25

Beni Zeroual, Arabic-speaking tribe, north Morocco, 153, 156–7

Benkiran, PJD politician, 255

Berber anarchy (*al fitna al barbariyya*), 256

Berber dahir, 238–9

Berber *diaspora*, 250

Berber problem, 256

Berber spring (*tafzut n imazighen*), 247

Berberism, (*Berbéritude*; *timuzgha*), 199, 246–7, 255, 257

Berenguer, Spanish general, 151

Berghaouata, Berber heretics, 2, 15, 16, 17, 19, 85, 149, 200

Berkin, village, Middle Atlas, 47, 172, 245

Bernat, Asif, 117, 130

Berque, Jacques, distinguished Arabist, ex-*contrôleur civil*, 38, 166, 244, 250

Bessam, valley, Tishshoukt, 168

Biban, French outpost, Beni Zeroual, 157

Bidwell, Robin, British writer, 167

Bihi, ou-, 'Abdallah, nineteenth-century *qayd*, Haha region, 81, 82, 91

Bihi, ou-, 'Addi, *makhzan qayd*, Ayt Izdeg, 192, 230, 245

Billotte, French general, 155

Bindeq, Ayt, Sokhman clan, Kousser region, 233

Bocchus I, Mauretanian king, 10

Bordeaux, Henri, member, *Académie française*, 163

Bou Adian, French outpost, Aghbala region, 205

Bou Attia, Ayt, section, Ayt 'Arfa, 74

Bou Bernous, wells, southeast Morocco, 180

Bou-Bker, Sidi Hmad ben, head of Tamgrout zaouia, southeast Morocco, 121

Bou-Bker, ou-, Sidi Mohammed, Idrissid sharif, 44

Bouaboud, residence of *qayd* El-mtouggui, 92

Bouasidi, railway terminus near Midelt, 202Boudenib, town, southeast Morocco, 10, 95, 116–17, 119–21, 161, 181, 203

Boogert, van den, Nico, Dutch Berberist, 250

Bougafer, Jbel Saghro, 225

Bou Genfou, Jbel, west of Tazizaout, 214, 220

Bou Guemmez, Ayt, Berber tribe, High Atlas, 45, 127, 129, 161

Bou Haddou, Ayt, Zaïan clan, 107

Bou Hadi, French outpost, Oued Ziz, 180

Bou Hayati, Jbel, hill near Khenifra, 106

Bou Hmara, *rogui,* (aka Jilali Zerhouni), 93, 150

Bou Iblan, Jbel, Middle Atlas, 102, 139–40, 142, 146, 161, 171–3, 175, 238, 245

Bou Illoul, Ayt, Ouaraïni clan, 172, 175

Bou Khamouj, plateau, Marmousha region, 145, 146

Bou Leggou, Ghriss region, 184

Bou Nasser, culminating point, Middle Atlas, 139–40, 146, 172

Bou Regreg, river, 9

Bou Tarrisen, hill, southeast Morocco, 190

Bou Wattas, village, 85, 131–2, 136, 177

Bou Wlli, Ayt, Berber tribe, 124

Bou Yahya, village, 126, 128

Bou Zeitouon, Jbel, near Tetouan, 159

Bou 'Arfa, ridge, Tishshoukt, 144

Bou'azza, Moulay, famous medieval holy man, 4

Bou'azza, son of Moha ou Hammou Zaïani, 106, 133, 137–8

Bou'inaniya, a Fez *madrassa*, 48

Bougrin, rebel officer, Skhirat coup, 224

Bouhassous, cousin of Moha ou Hammou Zaïani, 83

Boukous, Ahmed, Amazigh intellectual, second rector of IRCAM, Rabat, 251

Boula'joul, village, Moulouya region, 70

Boulet-Desbareau (*mulay lbarud*), Jean, Lieutenant, Tarda battle (1930), 184–5

Boulman, village, Middle Atlas, 109, 139, 144

Boumaln, town, Dadds, 125, 226

Bournazel, Henri, De, captain, 143–4, 146, 158, 189, 226

Bouseqqour, river near Khenifra, 104

Boutferda, Ayt Sokhman village, 87

Bouverot, French officer, Moulouya region, 198

Bouzid, Ayt, Berber tribe, Tadla region, 89

Brahim, Ayt, Hadiddou clan, High Atlas, 44, 199

Brahim, Moulay, son of Moulay Slimane, killed, Lenda (1819), 10

Brans, Arabic-speaking tribe, Taza region, 154, 156, 158, 226

Brenier-Estrine, Claude, French researcher, 250

Briand, Aristide, French politician, 159

Burnol, French Spahi officer, 173

Caligula, Roman emperor, 10

Cambay, French officer, Rif front, 154

Camerone, Foreign Legion site of memory, Mexico, 227

Canary Islands, 250

Canning, Gordon, English negotiator, Rif war, 159

Capua of the borderlands, 201–2

Casablanca, coastal city, 242–3

Catroux, French officer, Lyautey's staff, 157

"Cattle Herder" period, 7

Cauvin, French colonel, 172

Cedar Pinnacle, Tazizaout, 218–20

Ceuta (Sebta), Spanish-held town, 150–1

Chafik, Mohammed, Berber militant and writer, first rector, IRCAM, 229, 251

Chaker, Salem, professor at INALCO, Paris, 252

Chardon (*shardu*), French Lieutenant-Colonel, Native Affairs, 190–1

Chebli, ould-, Hammou, mid-nineteenth-century Mtiri *qayd*, 80

Cheikh, Mohammed, penultimate Sa'adi sovereign, 46

Cherarga, Arabic-speaking *jaysh* tribe, 71, 85

Cherqaoui, Sidi Ben Daoud, marabout, Bouj'ad, 78

Chettou, ou-, *makhzan qayd*, N'tifa tribe, 127, 129

Chinguetti, El-, Seghrouchen resistance leader, 130

Churchill, Winston, British Prime Minister, Marrakesh, 243

Clavery, French general, 185

CNLCM (*Centre National des Langues et Cultures Marocaines*), 257

Colomb-Beshar, town, Algeria, 116

Colombat, French general, Middle Atlas and Rif front, 154

Cooper, Fennimore, 244

Cordoba, city, Islamic Spain, 17

Corsica, place of exile, 244

Courtine de l'Oued el Abid, 197, 205

Crawford, David, American anthropologist, 250

Crusoe, Robinson, 166, 244

Cunningham-Graham, Robert, British traveler, 92

Curtiss, British trader, Sous area, nineteenth-century, 83, 84

Dadds, Oued, southeast Morocco, 45, 47, 54, 120, 125, 125, 127, 130

Damsira, Berber tribe, High Atlas, 40

Daoud, ou 'Ali, Ayt, Sokhman clan, 200, 211

Daoud, -Ou, Moha, independent 'Atta *amghar*, 128

Dar Oubarran, site of Spanish defeat, 151

Dar Oubarran, Spanish outpost, Rif, 151

Day (Beni Mellal), 19, 24

Debray, French lieutenant, 209

Dechra el-Oued, French outpost, 133

Demnat, foothill town, High Atlas, 24, 94, 123–4, 126

Denis, French commandant, 172–3

Derqawi, 'Abderrahman, religious leader, Beni Zeroual, 153, 157

Derqawi, ed-, Moulay el-'Arabi, Derqawi leader, 72, 75, 76

Derqawi, Mohammed, el-'Arabi el-Medghari, rebel marabout southeast Morocco, 83

Despax, French lieutenant, 163

Dila', Dila'yin, zaouia, marabouts, Fazaz region, 3, 47, 49, 51, 55, 62, 63, 66, 85, 97, 150

Dila'i, ben Bou-Bker, Mohammed, 48

Djorf, battle site, southeast Morocco, 116

Douirat, Middle Atlas, 142

Doukkala, Atlantic coastal region, 16, 40

Doukkali, ed-, 'Abd es-Salam, 'Alawid general, 63

Doury, French colonel, 119

Dra'a, Bou, outpost, Moulouya region, 136

Dra'a, valley, 5, 7, 24, 30, 40, 46, 49, 54, 83, 88, 102, 115, 122, 124, 189, 191–2, 194, 236, 243

Dubuisson, French general, Tazizaout, 214

Durand, French officer, Rif front, 158

Durosoy, French officer, Middle Atlas and southeast Morocco, 170

El-Baidaq, author, 25

El-Bordj, outpost, Ziz region, 202–3

El-Ghazzali, famous philosopher, 22

El-Guedmioui, thirteenth-century Atlas sheikh, 30

El-Mourtadi, governor of Tangier, 15

El-Mortada, Almohad amir, 30, 31

El-Mou'atamid, king of Sevilla, 20

El-Qahira, Merinid fortress, 37, 39

El-Rashid, Almohad amir, 29

El-'Arabi, Mohammed, Derqawi marabout, 84

Elias, Berghaouati prince, 16

Emmanuel, French officer, 7th Moroccan *Tirailleurs*, 203

Enjil, Ayt Youssi village, 109, 144

Erdouz, Jbel, High Atlas, 59

Erfoud, Jbel, Tafilalt, 118

Erfoud, town, Tafilalt, 120–1

Fadel, El, Mohammed, Saharan leader, 94

Fahd, king, Saudi Arabia, co-founder with Hassan II of Al-Akhawayn University in Ifran (AUI), 250

Faska, Mou Haddach, pro-*makhzan* 'Atta notable, 16, 23, 204

Fassi, El-, Abbas, Istiqlal politician, 253

Fassi, El-, Allal, Istiqlal leader, 242

Fassiyin (sing. Fassi), inhabitants of Fez, 237

Fatimids, Arab dynasty, Tunisia, 17

Fazaz, Jbel (Middle Atlas), 12, 15, 16–18, 20, 28–30, 48, 52–3, 55–6, 61, 65–70, 72–4, 76, 79, 82, 84–5, 88, 107, 109, 113, 131, 161, 246

Fazaz, Jbel, Imilshil High Atlas, 209

Feqran, Oued, Meknes area, 85

Ferkla, Oued, southeast Morocco, 56, 69, 119–20, 127, 189–90, 225, 233

Ferouan, Imi n-, village, 83

Fez, city, xiv, 2, 15, 17, 25, 30–1, 48–9, 51, 54, 65, 68, 70–3, 75, 76, 83, 85, 88, 90–4, 96, 115, 120, 141, 154, 156, 161, 201, 238

Figuig, town, southeast Morocco, 246

Filala, 82, 88, 188–9

Flilou, Ayt, 'Atta component, 226

Foum Anagam, gorge, Ktaoua, 192

Foum Asefti, locality, near Gourrama, 117

Foum Kheneg, canyon, Middle Atlas, 86, 88

Foum Taghzout, valley near Ksiba, 103

Foum Taouerda, Bani region, 236

Foum Zabel, southeast Morocco, 117

Franco, Francisco, Spanish officer, *Tercio*, 157

Freydenberg, Henri, French officer, Atlas front, 144, 146, 172–3, 180, 204–5

Fringo, Ayt, Youssi clan, 140

Gabrielli, French negotiator, Rif war, 156, 159

Gafsa, Tunisia, (Capsian man) found, 7

Galand, Lionel, French Berberist scholar, 249

Galand-Pernet, Paulette, specialist, Berber oral literature, 249

Gaouz, palm-grove, southeast Morocc, 119–20

Gates of Heaven, Kousser, 233

Gautier, E. F., French geographer, 29

Gelaya, Rif tribe, 151

Gellner, Ernest, British anthropologist, with Charles Micaud, co-edited book on Berbers (1972), 26

Gerouan (*iyerwan*), Middle Atlas tribe, 46, 65, 66, 67, 71, 72, 84

Gerioun, Ida, highland Seksawa clan, 9

Gerssif, town, east Morocco, 139–40, 161, 202

Gharb, Atlantic coastal region, 61, 64, 143, 156

Ghazi, el-, Ibn, leader, Zemmour tribe, 72, 73, 74, 76

Ghiata, tribe, Taza region, 25, 30

Ghomara, region in western part of Rif, 5

Ghoufaïr, Abou, prominent Berghaouati prince, 3, 27

Ghriss, river, 44, 47, 48, 56, 62, 68, 88, 181, 186–7, 192, 194, 230

Gigou, Oued, 55, 66–7, 71, 73, 86, 110

Giraud, French general, 155, 181–2, 185–6, 189–90, 192, 232

Glaoui, El-, Hajj Thami, brother of Si Madani, pasha of Marrakesh, 80, 123, 125, 127–30, 161, 226, 244–5

Glaoui, El-, Mohammed (*tibibit*), nineteenth-century gate-keeper, Tizi n-Telouat, 89

Glaoui, El-, Si Madani, his son, great *qayd*, Marrakesh region, 88–90, 92–3, 120, 123–4, 126, 243

Glaoui, El-, Si 'Abdelmalek, Si Madani's son, 126

Glaoui, gate-keeper, Tizi n- Telouat, 54

Glaoua (pl. of Glaoui), Berber tribe, 84, 86, 115, 117–18

Goliath (*jalut*), mythical ancestor of the Berbers, 6, 50

Goudot, French general, 208

Goulmima, town, southeast Morocco, 232, 246, 249

Goundafi, -el, Si Taïb, great *qayd*, Western High Atlas, 80, 92, 123, 235

Gourara, desert region, Algeria, 28, 69

Gourrama, village, southeast Morocco, 117

Granada, city, Andalucia, 150

Gra', Jbel, Bou Iblan outlier, 172

Green March (*tawada taizawt*), 247

Guedmioua, Berber tribe, High Atlas, 22, 31, 38, 59, 92

Guenfissa, medieval tribe, High Atlas, 22

Guennoun, Saïd, AI officer, Kabylian origin, 79, 132, 198

Guerouan (*iyerwan*), Berber tribe, 7, 10, 11, 61–2

Guillaume, French officer, Atlas front, resident-general, 96, 134, 176–7, 216, 218–19, 227, 243–4

Guir, river, southeast Morocco, 10, 118, 181

Guyetand (*jida*), French captain, soputheast Morocco, 192–4, 232

Haddash, Mou, Ayt 'Atta chief, 128, 225

Haddious, Ayt, highland Seksawa clan, 37, 41, 92

Haddou, *qayd*, negotiator, Rif war, 156

Haddou Ben Youssef, Seksawa prince, 36, 37

Hadi Ibn Hanin, rebel chief (Fazaz), 28

Hadiddou, Ayt, Berber tribe, High Atlas, 44, 48, 88, 120, 133, 162, 177, 184, 186, 190, 198–200, 202–3, 205, 209, 211, 213–14, 217, 222, 225, 227, 230–1, 233, 246, 250

Hadiddou n-Midoul, Ayt, 44

Hadiddou n-Zoulit, Ayt, 44

Hadramaut, 10, 11

Haddou, Mi'ami Ou-Lhajj, relative of Moha ou-Hammou Zaïani, 101

Haddou Ben Youssef, Seksawa dynast, 36

Hagan, Helene, American Berberist, 250

Hagenbeck's Zoo, 199

Haha (pl. of Hahi), Berber tribe, Mogador region, 82, 91

Haidar, 'Ali Ben, Tazerualt prince, 52

Hakem, Beni, Arabic-speaking *jaysh* tribe, 56

Hakmaoui, el-, eighteenth-century *qayd*, 71

Halli, Ayt, Youssi clan, 140

Hamara, Bou, pretender in N. Morocco, early-twentieth century, 87–8, 110, 137

Hamdoun, mountain, southeast Morocco, 162, 222, 230

Hammam, Jbel, Rif, 159

Hammou, Ayt, Bel-Hsseyn, Seghroushen clan, 116–17, 161, 163, 178–81, 184, 186, 189, 191, 194, 203, 205, 225, 236

Hammou, ou-, 'Amr, resistance fighter, 168

Hammou, ou-, Hassan, Idrassen *qayd* at Lenda, 74, 76

Hammou, ou-, Moha, Zaïani, Zaïan leader, 80, 83–7, 94, 96, 103, 99, 105, 107, 133, 137, 236, 251

Hammou, ou-, Saïd, Zaïan tribesman, brother of Moha, 78

Hammou, Mohand ou-, Ouaraïni resistance fighter, 171, 175

Hammou, Moroccan general, Skhirat coup, 246

Hamza, Si, Zaouia, 44, 48, 75, 197, 202

Hamzaoui, marabout, Za. Si Hamza, 75

Hana, ou-, Hrou, resistance leader, Hadiddou, Imilshil, 232

Hani, Ayt, Hadiddou clan, High Atlas, 184

Hansali, El-, Sidi Mah, Ahansal marabout, 102, 125–6, 127–30, 201, 233

Hansali, El-, Sidi Saïd (Dadda Saïd), 43

Haouz, plain around Marrakesh, 24, 36, 38, 62, 73, 85, 92, 101

Hargha, Masmouda tribe, Anti-Atlas, 22

Harkat, Ayt, section, Zaian tribe, 83

Harris, Walter, British journalist, 159

Haskoura, defunct tribe, High Atlas, 30, 31, 40

Hassan, l-, Abou, Merinid sultan, 5, 6

Hassan, l-, Abou 'Ali Ben Brahim, seventeenth-century Fazaz holy man, 8

Hassan, brother of Sidi Raho, 96

Hassan, Zaïan chief, 106, 208

Hassi El-Kerma, wells, Dra'a region, 192

Hassine, Ba, Zaïan auxiliary, Khenifra, enemy of Moha ou Hammou, 13

Hassoun, Abou, Sidi 'Ali, Tazerualt marabout, 48, 49, 51, 52

Hautecloque, De (*laqluq*), French officer (Marshal Leclerc), southeast Morocco, 182, 236

Hayyan, Jbel, 73, 110–12

Hemama, Ayt, Sokhman clan, Aghbala region, 200, 213

Heroic Age, 241

Herri, El-, battle of, near Khenifra, 3, 95, 101, 104–5, 120, 134, 184, 203

Herriot, French politician, 153
Hiba, El-, ("Blue Sultan") son of Ma el-Aïnin, resistance leader, 94, 131, 235
Hkim, Ayt, village, Ayt Bou Guemmez, 128–9
Himyarite, (Beni Himyar), from Yemen, 11, 247
Hintata, defunct tribal grouping, Marrakesh High Atlas, 3, 22, 37
Hintati, Mohammed Ibn Wanoudin, 30
Hintati, 'Amr, Ibn Mohammd, Atlas warlord, 37, 38, 39
Hintati, Moulay Driss, Atlas warlord, 40
Hiraq, unrest in Rif, 255
Hmad, Ben Sidi (*ou-sidi*), Ayt Hadiddou leader, Tilmi, 199, 203, 209, 227–8, 231
Hmad, Ben, Sidi Taïb, his brother, 228, 231
Hmad, ou-, Zaïd, raider and gun-runner, Ayt Merghad, 179, 235
Hmad, ou-Haqqar, Ishqern resistance fighter, Tazizaout, 220
Hmad, Sidi, Sidi Lmekk's grandson, 222
Hnini, Ayt, Yahya clan, Moulouya, 208
Hoffman, Katherine, US researcher, 250
Houant, El-, forest, Sokhman region, 200, 211
Houari, El-, Sidi, Derqaoui saint, southeast Morocco, 121
Hourra, El-, Sayyida, warrior princess, Rif, 150
Houwwara, Berber tribe of northern Morocco, 3
Hsseyn, ou-, Sidi 'Ali, Sokhman marabout, Anergui, 125, 211, 228, 233
Huré, general, commander-in-chief, 189, 217, 226, 228

Ibn Abou Bekr, chief *murabit*, Dila' zaouia, 41
Ibn Houd, ruler of Andalucia, 29
Ibn Khaldoun, medieval scholar, 5, 6, 27, 28, 36
Ibn Mimoun Ibn Midrar, Midrarid ruler, 17
Ibn Qounfoudh, Muslim scholar, 39
Ibn Roshd (Averroes), physician, 25
Ibn Toufail, prominent thinker under the Almohads, 25
Ibn Toumert, Almohad *mahdi*, 21, 22, 35

Ibn Tunart, author of Arabic-Berber lexicon, 25
Iboqqoyen, Rif tribe, 151
Ida Gerioun, Seksawa clan, 57
Ida ou Izimmer, tribe, High Atlas, 86
Ida ou Mahmoud, tribe, High Atlas, 37
Ida ou Msattog, tribe, High Atlas, 60, 61
Ida ou Semlal, tribe, Anti-Atlas, 118
Ida ou Tanan, tribe, High Atlas, 84
Idlan, hill, Marmousha region, 146
Idmouma, *qsar*, east of Amellago, 192–3
Idrassen, Ayt, defunct Berber super-tribe, 55, 56, 66, 67, 70, 71, 74, 80
Idriss el-Ma'moun, Almohad amir, 29
Idriss I, founder, Idrissid dynasty, 15
Ifegh, village, southeast Morocco, 189–92, 232
Ifkern, village, Marmousha region, 145
Ifni, Spanish enclave, southwest Morocco, 235
Ifou, hill, Sokhman region, 209
Ifran, town, Morocco, 250
Ifriqiya (Tunisia), 7, 28, 32
Igezzouln (Gezzoula), Berber tribe, southwest Morocco, 40
Igherriben, Spanish outpost, Rif, 151
Ighezran, Ouaraïni clan, 172
Ighrem n-Tihouna n-Ouwejjal, cliff-side fortress, 87
Igli, *qsar*, Oued Ziz, 202
Igzennayn, Rif tribe, 158
Ihand, Ayt, Berber tribe, Moulouya, 70, 85
Ijanaten, Berber clan, upper Nfis, 59
Ijberten, mountain, Imilshil rgion, 228
Ijoukak, village, High Atlas, 59
Ikassen, valley, north of Imilshil, 214
Ikkis, valley, Tishshoukt north slope, 168
Iknifen, Ayt Bou, Ayt 'Atta component, 7
Iknioun, village, Jbel Saghro, 225
Ilemshan, 'Atta component, 225
Iligh, capital of Tazeroualt, Semlala marabouts, 49, 52, 83
Imdghas, Asif n-, upper part of Dadds river, 44, 68, 125, 230
Imelouan, *qsar*, southeast Morocco, 192–3
Imejjat, Berber tribe, Meknes region, 82
Imghal, Jbel, High Atlas, 88, 217
Imhazan (pl. of Amhazoun), Zaïan clan, 83, 106

Imilshil, town, High Atlas, 199, 211, 214, 227, 235, 246–7

Imi n-Tanout, foothill town, High Atlas, 41

Imlil n-Oughbar, village, 59

Immouzzer-Marmousha, village, Middle Atlas, 143, 145–6, 170, 172–3, 175, 245

Imsaden, Jbel Saghro, 225–6

Imsifern, tribal coalition (*leff*), High Atlas, 57

Imtchimen, Ayt Yahya clan, 19, 20, 172, 186–7

Indghertit, tribal coalition (*leff*), High Atlas, 57

Irbiben, Ayt Merghad clan, 44, 199

IRCAM, Royal Institute for Amazigh Culture, Rabat, 251, 257

Irklaoun, Beni Mguild clan, 72

Iseha, Ayt, Messat clan, 211, 228

Isellaten, upper Ziz, 199

Ish n-Tili, Bou Iblan, 171–2

Ishaq, last Almohad prince, 35

Ishqern, Middle Atlas tribe, 43, 66, 82, 85–6, 95, 113, 131, 133, 136, 208, 214, 220

Isir, Abou, mythical ancestor of Berbers (sometimes confused with Goliath), 50

Isrouta, plateau, Sokhman region, 87, 201

Issouka, hill, Marmousha region, 146

Istiqlal, Moroccan Nationalists, 96–7, 237–9, 243–6, 253, 255

Ithier (*iti*), Native Affairs officer, Zaouit Ahansal and Ahermoumou, 163, 166

Itto, oupost, Middle Atlas, 109

Itto Fezzou, village, Merghad region, 230

Itzer, town, Moulouya region, 86, 120–1

Izdeg, Ayt, Berber tribe, Ayt Yaflman confederation, 47, 69, 88, 230

Izimmer, Ida ou, Berber tribe, High Atlas, 92

Iznassen, Ayt, Berber tribe, estern Morocco, 98

Izoughar, lake and/or pastures, High Atlas, 46, 47, 128, 201

'Isa Izem, Ayt, clan of Ayt Merghad, 44, 179, 181–2, 185–6, 192–4, 231–2

Jama, Ouled, Arabic-speaking *jish* tribe, 71

Jawhar el-Roumi, Fatimid general, 17

Jazouli, -el, religious scholar, 48

Jbala (pl. of Jebli), tribe, north Morocco, 9, 150, 153–4, 156, 159, 257

Jellidasen, Ayt, Berber tribe, Beni Ouaraïn, 144, 172

Jesus (*sidna 'isa*), Mouminid amir el-Ma'amoun, 30

Jihani, SE Morocco, 167

Juba II, a king of Mauretania under Roman empire, 9

Jugurtha (Yugurten), early Amazigh hero, 9, 10

Julien, Charles-André, French historian, 166

Juin, Alphonse, French officer, Resident-General, 185, 237, 243

Justinard, (*qebtan shluh*), French officer, Souss, 49, 235

Kabylia, Kabyle, 247, 252

Kadoussa gorge, Oued Guir, 117–18

Kairouan (Qayrawan), Tunisian city, 32

Kasba El-Farah, village, Middle Atlas, 141

Kasba Tadla, town, 56, 83, 105, 131–2, 206

Kasbat al-Makhzan (Lqsabi), town, Moulouya, 88

Kauffman, captain, French aviator, 198

Kebbab (*lqbab*), village, Middle Atlas, 132

Kemkemia, Tafilalt region, 181

Kenitra (ex-Port Lyautey), 165

Kerdous, Anti-Atlas, 235–6

Kerdous, region, southeast Morocco, 3, 69, 162, 230

Kert, Oued, Rif region, 156, 158

Kerrando, village, Oued Ziz, 117

Kettani, el-, Moulay Hai, rebel sharif, 94

Khachan, Asif n-, Anergui region, 211

Kharijites, anti-Arab rebels, 12, 15

Khattabi, M'hmmed, 'Abdelkrim's brother, 140

Khebbash, Ayt, Ayt 'Atta component, 46, 69, 115, 119, 178–9, 181, 189, 191–2, 194, 225, 236

Khemisset, town, Zemmour region, 242

Khenifra, Middle Atlas town, 55, 84, 95, 103–5, 111, 131, 217, 251

Kheriro (Jeriro), Ahmed, Jebli leader, 153, 157, 159

Khorifla, Oued, site of Ibn Yassin's tomb, 19

Kiffan, village north of Taza, 157

Klose, Foreign Legion Sergeant, 144

Konrad Adenauer Foundation, 249

Koubbat, Jbel, near Bekrit, 73, 111, 112

Koudiat 'Abdelmoumen, 24

Kousser (*qusr*), Jbel, High Atlas, 3, 69, 98, 125, 162, 201, 212, 227, 233

Ksabi, town, Moulouya region, 83, 112, 120–1

Ksar es-Souk (Rachidiya, *imteghren*), city, southeast Morocco, 88, 117, 120

Ksiba (*taqsibt n muha u saïd*), town, Middle Atlas, 3, 62, 85, 87, 101–3, 117, 133, 206

Ktaoua, Dra'a region, 191–2

Kudia Tahar, hill near Tetouan, 157

Labonne, Eric, Resident-General, 243

Laffitte (*la'afrit*), French captain, Tishshoukt, 168–70

Lahssen, Ahmed ou-, resistance fighter, Marmousha, 244

Lahssen, Ayt, Seksawa clan, High Atlas, 57, 92

Lahssen ou 'Athman, Sidi, saint of Zaouit Si Hamza, 45

Laïdi, Ou-, Zaïan notable, 106–7, 120

Lakes Plateau, Imilshil region, 211, 214–215, 217, 227

Lamothe, French general, Souss, 213

Landau, Rom, British writer, 167

Laou, Oued, Rif, 151, 156

Lapeyre, Pol, French officer, 141

Larache, coastal town, 41, 56, 150

Latour, Boyer de, Pierre (*muha w latur*), AI officer, last Resident-General, 166, 211, 233, 243, 245

Las Navas de Tolosa (El-Ouqab), Almohad defeat, 30

Laverdure, French colonel, 104

La'abid, Oued, 24, 56, 87, 90, 127, 129, 130, 134, 176, 197, 205–6, 211

Lbaz, ou-, Mohammed, anti-*makhzan* Sokhman *qayd*, 87

Lebel, French rifle, 173, 177, 230

Lemtouna, Saharan tribes, early supporters of Almoravids, 18

Lenda, battle site, Middle Atlas, 73, 76, 77, 86

Lgara, battle site, 49

Lhajb, Middle Atlas, 65, 80, 82, 84, 99, 109

Lhajj, ou-, Haddou, Mi'ami, relative of Zaïan notable Ou-Laïdi, 106

Lhajj, ou-, Sidi Mohand, Tounfit region, 120, 132, 136, 186, 203, 207–8

Lhousseyn Sidi, late-nineteenth-century Tazeroualt marabout, 81–3

Linguistic resistance, (*muqawama lughawiyya*), 246, 253

Ljoua, valley, Tishshoukt, 168

Lmal, Asif, river, High Atlas, 40

Lmehdi, Sidi Mohand, brother of Sidi Lmekki, 215, 219–22

Lmekki (*bakki*), Sidi, 'Ali Amhaoush's eldest son, 131, 177, 186, 199, 208, 214–15, 217, 220, 222

Lmortada, Sidi, brother of Sidi Lmekki, 219–20, 222

LOAB (*Littérature Orale Arabo-Berbère*), 250

Louqqout, Meghraoui amir, 19

Loustal, De, French general, Atlas front, 176, 206–8, 214, 216–17

Lqroun, Jbel, peak of Kousser, 233

Lqsabi, town, Moulouya region, 55

Lrba', Ayt 'Attab, Wednesday market at Ayt 'Attab, 126

Lugan, B., French historian, xv

Lyautey, Hubert, Marshall, resident-general, 52, 94, 102, 111, 119, 120, 139, 139–44, 146, 153, 155–6, 158, 166, 176, 178

Mackenzie, Donald, British trader, Sous area, late-nineteenth-century, 83, 84

Madagascar, place of exile, 244–5

Madrid, 156, 159

Maginot, French Minister for War, 206

Magnin, Colonel, French officer, 103

Mahalli, Abou, Ahmed ou 'Abdallah Ibn ('Bum Hully'), pretender, southeast Morocco, 41, 106, 115

Mahomet's mule, 194

Mangin, French general, victor of El-Hiba, 94, 102–3, 131, 167

Mansour, Ahmed, Sa'adi sultan, 41

Mansour, 'Abdelkrim, Ben, eighteenth-century pasha of Marrakesh, 58, 60, 61

Maokayn, hill, Sokhman region, 206

Marcireau, Sergeant-Major, Goums, Atlas front, 222

Marçais, Jean, early-twentieth-century French historian, 29

Marghiti, El-, Mohammed Ben Saïd, astronomer, 48

Marin, Spanish negotiator, Rif war, 159

Marmousha (*imermushen*), Berber tribe, Middle Atlas, 90, 111–12, 120–1, 140-2-145, 171, 238, 244

Marrakesh, city, xiv, 1, 17, 19–22, 29, 30, 31, 37–41, 48, 54, 58–9, 68, 73, 82–3, 88–92, 94, 123, 128, 130, 211, 226, 243–4, 253

Masmouda, Berber founding tribe, 19, 21, 27, 31, 35, 36, 40, 43, 57, 61

Massa, Oued, southwest Morocco, 78, 83

"Master of the Hour", Tilmirat, 147

Matterne, French commandant, Bou Iblan, 172

Mauretania (Tingitana), Roman province, 9

Mauri, early Moroccans, 9

Maysara, leader of Kharijite revolt, 2, 15, 16

Mazel, French writer, 11

Mazigh, ancestor of the Berbers, 6

Meghraoua, Berber dynasty, 17, 18

Ma'adid, -El, village, Tafilalt, 118–20

Ma'ammar, village, Tadla region, (Dila' zaouia), 47, 52

Ma'qil, Beni, Arabic-speaking nomad tribe, 27, 28, 49

Ma'asker, Jbel, High Atlas, 69, 186, 209

MCA (*Mouvement Culturel Amazigh*), 253

Meknes, city, central Morocco, 15, 17, 30, 46, 51, 53, 61–2, 65–8, 72, 75–6, 82–4, 110, 161, 186, 204, 207, 214, 216–17, 219, 249, 253

Mentagga, Berber tribe, High Atlas, 37

Merinid (Beni Merin), Berber dynasty, 27, 28, 29, 30, 31, 32, 35, 36, 37, 39

Mdez, tributary of Oued Seghina, 146

Mecca, holy city, 67

Mecissi, village, southeast Morocco, 110, 112, 177, 191

Medboh, Moroccan general, pre-Rif, killed during Skhirat coup, 246

Medghara, district, southeast Morocco, 88

Medghari, El-, Mohammed el-'Arabi, 88

Mehdi, el-, Moulay, sultan's representative in Tafilalt (1918), 119

Mehdi Ibn Taoula Idjfashi, Zenata prince, 17, 18

Melilla, Spanish-held town, Rif, 93, 150–2, 156

Melloul, Asif, 47, 62, 87, 186, 198–203, 214, 227–8

Melloulou, river, Middle Atlas, 141

Merghad, Ayt (*ayt melghad*), Berber tribe, High Atlas, 44, 47, 48, 69, 120, 162, 178–179, 182, 184, 189–91, 193–4, 199, 203, 227, 230, 235, 246, 249

Merghadi, el-, 'Ali Ben Yahya, Derqaoui rebel chief, 88

Mers, El-, sacred village, 140, 143, 145–7

Mers-el-Kebir, French naval base, 156

Merzouga, village, Tafilalt, 185

Mesissi, village, Tafilalt, 119, 121

Meskeddal, pastures, Bou Iblan, 146, 172, 175

Meski, village, southeast Moroco, 117

Mesnaoui, el-, Mohammed el-'Arabi, seventeenth-century writer, 48

Mesri, Ayt, Ayt Merghad clan, 44

Messad Ayt, (*ayt messat*), High Atlas tribe, 83

Mess'aoud Ibn Gelidasen, Haskouri sheikh, 31

Mess'aoud Wanoudin el-Meghraoui, eleventh-century ruler of Sijilmassa, 18

Mexican War, 227

Mezouari, el-, 'Abd el-'Aziz, fourteenth-century Atlas *qayd* under Sa'adi sultans, 41

Mgoun, Ayt, Tassaout valley, Berber tribe, 124

Mgoun, Ighil, mountain, 129

Mguild, Beni (*ayt myill*), Berber tribe, Middle Atlas, 35, 72, 73, 82, 84, 85, 86, 95, 101, 110–11, 112, 120, 132, 136, 214, 221

M'hammed, Ayt, foothill town, High Atlas, 43, 201

M'hammed, Riffian Minister for War, 152

Midelt (Aoutat), town, Moulouya region, 21, 55, 101, 120–1, 136, 168, 180, 186, 197, 201–3

Midrar El-Montassir, founded Midrarid dynasty, Sijilmassa, 16

Midrarid, Berber dynasty, 17

Midrassen, hill, near Aghbala, 176

Mismental, plateau near Berkin, 144

Missour, town, Moulouya region, 142–3

MLA (Moroccan Liberation Army), 244–6

Mogador (Essaouira, *tassurt*), Atlantic coastal city, 67

Moha n-Ifrouten, *see* Semlali

Mohammed, Sidi, nineteenth-century 'Alawid sultan, 80, 91

Mohammed Ibn Wanoudin, Hintati sheikh, 31

Mohammed V, (sultan Ben Youssef), 242–5

Mohammed V University, Rabat, 250

Mohammed VI, Morocco's present king, 251

Mohammed XIII, last Sa'adi sultan, 51

Mohand, Ayt, Messad clan, Azilal region, 206

Monteil, Vincent, French writer, ex-A.I. officer, 166

Morsy, Magali, twentieth-century French researcher, 63

Moudden, Bel, military leader under Moulay Hassan I, 87

Moughfir, village in Retteb region, 49

Mouiz, ou-, Haïda, pasha of Taroudannt, 235

Moulay Ahmed 'Alaoui, press magnate, 247

Moulay 'Abdallah, 'Alawid sultan, 62, 63, 65

Moulay 'Abdel'aziz, 'Alawid sultan, 90, 92–4, 106

Moulay 'Abd er-Rahaman, 'Alawid sultan, 79

Moulay 'Ali Sharif, ancestor of 'Alawid dynasty, 49, 51, 189

Moulay, Ben 'Arafa, puppet sultan, 244

Moulay Brahim, Moulay Sliman's son, 72, 74

Moulay Brahim, son of Moulay Yazid, 76

Moulay Bou'azza, famous Moroccan saint, 21

Moulay Hafid, last sultan of pre-Protectorate Morocco, 92–3, 101, 106

Moulay Hassan ben Ismaïl, Filali sharif, 67

Moulay Hassan I, late-nineteenth-century 'Alawid sultan, 80, 82–6, 90, 92–3, 97, 123, 212, 237

Moulay Hassan II, king of Morocco, 246–7, 249–51

Moulay Hisham, 'Alawid prince, 68

Moulay Ismaïl, 'Alawid sultan, 49, 52, 53, 54, 55, 56, 57, 58, 61, 62, 63, 65, 67, 80, 113

Moulay Mohammed, son of Moulay 'Ali Sherif, 49, 50

Moulay Mohammed Seghroushni, war-chief, 128

Moulay Rashid, 'Alawid sultan, 51, 52

Moulay Sliman, 'Alawid sultan, 68, 70, 72–3, 74, 76–7

Moulay Srou, 'Alawid sharif, killed, Aghbala (1888), 75, 86, 88

Moulay Tahar, Belqasm Ngadi's brother, 189

Moulay Yazid, pro-Berber 'Alawid sultan, 66, 68, 76

Moulay Youssef, 'Alawid sultan under Lyautey, 121, 153–4

Moulay Zidan, Sa'adi ruler, 41

Moulouya (*asif n-melwiyt*), river, 1, 3, 10, 19, 24–5, 28, 30, 48–9, 52–3, 55, 66, 69–72, 84, 86, 88, 93, 109, 117, 120, 130–2, 134, 136, 140–2, 144, 155, 173, 175–6, 186, 197, 200–2, 205, 220

Moulid, Hmad ou-, last independent *amghar*, Seksawa, 92

Moulid, Lhajj, *amghar* of Ayt Haddious clan, Seksawa, 92

Mouminids, Almohad rulers, sons of 'Abd el-Moumen, 29

Mounadir el-Berbri, Midrarid ruler, 17

Mouriq, Jbel, above Anergui, 201, 211

Mourtadi, el-, governor of Tangier, killed by Kharijites, 15

Moussa, -ou, Sidi Hmad, holy man, Souss region, 40

Mouvement Populaire, Aherdan's political party, 246

Mou'attamid, el-, king of Sevilla, imprisoned by Almoravids, 21

Mrirt, town, Middle Atlas, 17

Mschitt, hamlet, Tounfit region, 209

Msedrid, Jbel, Lakes plateau region, 3, 162, 227–8

Msemrir, village, Dadds valley, 99, 253
Mtir, Beni (*ayt ndhir*), Berber tribe,
　　Middle Atlas, 62, 66, 70–2, 79, 80, 82,
　　84, 93, 109–10
Mtiri, el-, Ibn Nasser, tribal leader, 71
Mtouggui, el-, Sidi 'Abdelmalek, great *qayd*,
　　Marrakesh region, 80, 82, 92–4, 123
Mzab, Amazigh-speaking Algerian region,
　　115
Mzizel, village, Oued Ziz, 182

Nador, city, Rif, 150, 160
Nador, plateau, Midle Atlas, 143
Nafzaouiyya, Zineb bint Ishaq, Ibn
　　Tashfin's bride, 19
Naour, village, Middle Atlas, 133
Nasser, Ibn Bou'azza, Idrassen leader, 71
Naudin, lieutenant, cartographer, 198
Naulin, French general, 155–6
Nfis, Oued, 22, 24, 36, 58, 59, 60
Ngadi, Belqasm, resistance leader,
　　southeast Morocco, 118–21, 127,
　　131–2, 162, 178, 181, 185, 187, 189,
　　191–2, 236, 256
Nieger, French general, Midelt, 187, 203–4,
　　207
Nkob, village, Saghro, 226
Noguès (*nugis*), French officer, later
　　Resident-General, 154, 185
Norris, H.T., historian specialised in the
　　Tuareg, 10
Noun, Oued, southwest Morocco, 51, 82
N'tifa, lowland tribe, High Atlas, 94, 127
Numidia, ancient Algeria, 9, 15

O'Connor, Scott, V.C., British writer, 26
Ogdemt, valley, High Atlas, 59
Oil stain policy, 176, 228
Ou-Brouz, Ayt Merghad chief, Baddou,
　　232
Ou-Khnouch, Merghad leader, Baddou,
　　232
Ou-Terbat, village, Hadiddou region, 232
Ouakrim, Yahya, eighteenth-century
　　Western High Atlas sheikh, 9
Ouabzaza, Asif, High Atlas, 128
Ouali, el-, marabout, 206
Oualili (Volubilis), 15
Ouallal, Ayt, Berber tribe, High Atlas, 43, 51

Ouanir, Ayt, Ayt 'Atta component, 35
Ouanshrigh, Seksawa village, 38
Ouaraïn, Beni (*ayt warayn*), Berber
　　super-tribe, Middle Atlas, 93, 140, 142,
　　146, 155, 155, 161, 171
Ouassar, Ayt (*ayt waster*), defunct High
　　Atlas tribe, 45
Ouattasi, Ahmed, El-, sixteenth-century
　　sultan, 150
Ouazzan, town, north Morocco, 154, 156,
　　159
Oubaoui, 'Ali, Ishqern warrior, 133
Ouches, Joubert des, French lieutenant,
　　fought at Tazizaout (1932), 22
Oudaïa, Arabic-speaking *jaysh* tribe, 66,
　　74, 85
Oudghes, river near Tounfit, 136
Ouergha, River, north Morocco, 153,
　　156–7
Ouezzan, Sharif of, 75
Oufella, Ayt, Berber tribe, Mouoouya, 70,
　　86
Ouiksen, Jbel, mine near Melilla, 150
Ouirin, Asif, upper Oued L'abid, 177, 208–9
Ouirra, Ayt, Berber tribe, 85, 87, 102, 133
Oujda, city, east Morocco, 118, 159
Ouksersou, culminating point, Jbel
　　Baddou, 231
Oulghes, plain near Khenifra, 98, 104
Oulmes, village, central Morocco, 16
Oum er-Rbia' (Wansifen), river, 30, 94, 131,
　　133
Oumalou, Ayt, defunct tribal
　　confederation, Fazaz, 55–6, 66–8, 71–3,
　　79, 84
Oumeyyad, dynasty, Islamic Spain, 17
Oumeyyads, Arab dynasty, Cordoba, 17
Oum Jeniba, pass, Middle Atlas, 109, 144,
　　145
Ouriaghel, Ayt (*ayt waryaghar*), Rif tribe,
　　138–40, 146
Ourika, tribe, Marrakesh High Atlas, 38
Oussikis, Ayt, Ayt 'Atta clan, Dadds valley,
　　47
Ousikis, Asif n-, upper Dadds, 125
Oustry, Lieutenant, 119
Outat El-Haj, town, Moulouya region, 141
Outrouzou, Sokhman region, 205
Ou'aziz, Mohamed, Mtiri notable, 71, 72

Pacification, 146, 175–6, 178, 237–8, 246

Painlevé, French politician, 153, 155, 159

Paris, 155, 158, 176, 185, 206, 252

Pan-Berberism, 250

Parlange (*burlanj*), French officer, E. High Atlas, 166, 181, 202, 209, 221, 227

Paulin (*bulan*), French AI officer, Tinghir, 166, 190, 233, 235

Paulinus, Suetonius, Roman general, 2

Pax Gallica, 242

PDA (*Parti Démocratique Amazigh*), short-lived Berber party, 255

Pellow, Thomas, English renegade, served under Moulay Ismaïl, 63

Pétain, Philippe, French marshal, 155–8

Picardy, 182

Picquart, French cavalry officer, 102–3

Pillafort, French officer, Baddou, 231–2

PJD, moderate Islamists, 251–3, 255

Poeymirau, general, Tafilalt and Middle Atlas, 110, 103, 111, 119, 121, 144–5, 201

Polisario, independence movement, Sahara (ex-Rio de Oro), 247

Post-Independence Moroccan Vulgate, xv, 245

Poulaine, Robert, French journalist, 158

Primo de Rivera, Spanish dictator, 156

Prioux, French colonel, 173

Protectorate Vulgate, 241

Psichari, Ernest, French officer turned mystic, 163

Ptolemy, Mauretanian king, 10

Qala'at el-Mehdi, Fazaz fortress, 17, 18, 19, 20, 24

Qala'at Mgouna, town, Dadds valley, 2

Qarawiyin, mosque, Fez, 48, 99

Qsar beni Mtir, 'Alawid fortress on Oued Gigou, 55

Rabat, city, 98, 139, 142, 155–6, 162, 176, 198, 204, 217, 245–6, 249–52

Rabat-Salé airport, 222

Raba', captain Laffitte's Berber concubine, 170

Rahman, er-, Moulay 'Abdallah, nineteenth-century 'Alawid sultan, 74–5

Raho (*rehhu*), Sidi, ou-Mimoun, marabout, Ayt 'Arfa, 95, 102, 106, 109–10, 112, 120, 132, 140–1, 143, 145, 170–5

Raissouni, Moulay Ahmed, 138, 140, 151, 153

Ras Ashkourn, hill, Marmousha region, 170

Ras Tarsha, hill near Bekrit, 73, 80, 85, 86, 111, 112

Rat, Jbel, High Atlas, 124

Rebbo, Merebbi, Saharan resistance leader, son of Ma el-Aïnin, 131, 189, 235–6

Regg, valley, southeast Morocco, 118–19, 189, 191, 225–6

Renault, tanks, 172, 191, 231

Reunion, place of exile, 159

Reverter the Catalan, Christian renegade under Almoravids, 19, 25

Rif, region, north Morocco, xiv, 9, 51–2, 93, 102, 110, 115, 147, 149–51, 153–61, 170, 175–7, 179, 237, 244–6, 255, 257

Rio de Oro, (aka Western Sahara), 177–8, 189, 236, 249

Rish, town, Oued Ziz, 108, 112, 117, 120

Rissani, town, Tafilalt, 113, 181, 185, 189

Rivet, Daniel, French historian, xv

R'nim, Jbel, 63, 125, 130

Roi de la Bière, restaurant, Midelt, 202

Rokba, Si 'Ali Bou, Rif village, 158

Rome, 163

Roubaix, city, France, 250

Rousseau, Jean-Jacques, 244

Sadden, Ou-, 'Abdelmalek, Berber militant, 249

Safi, coastal town, 39, 41

Saghro, Jbel, 46, 53, 119, 162, 191, 216, 225–6

Saharan Company of the Guir, 180–1

Saharan Company of the Ziz, 180–1

Saïd, brother of Sidi Raho, 96

Saïd, Dadda, founding marabout, Zaouit Ahansal, 125

Saïd, Moha ou-, *makhzan qayd*, Ayt Ouirra, 87, 94, 96, 102, 103, 105–6, 131, 132

Saïd, ou-Hammou, brother of Moha ou-Hamou, 83

Saïd El-Fazazi, rebel chief, 28

Saïd El-Ma'moun, Almohad amir, 29, 30

Saint, Lucien, French Resident-General, 185, 189, 202

St. Cyr, French military academy, 168

Saint-Rome de Dolan, town, France, 250

Salafi, Salafism, (*Al-Salafiyya Al-Jihadiyya*), Moslem fundamentalist ideology, 152, 242, 251, 253, 257

Salih, Berghaouati prince, 16

Santa Cruz (Agadir), Portuguese outpost, 39

Saoura, desert region, Algerian border, 41, 106, 115

Saulay, Jean, French officer, historian of Goums, 175

Sa'adi, Moroccan dynasty, 40, 41, 48, 99

Sbaï, es-, Moulay Lahssen, Sehghroushen marabout, 102, 115–18

Sbaï, ou-, Moulay 'Abdallah, 118

Sebbah, Arabic-speaking tribe, south-east Morocco, 56

Sebou, Oued, 139–40

Sefrou, town, Middle Atlas, 25, 73, 96, 99, 109, 139–40

Seghina, Oued, Middle Atlas, 140, 143, 146

Seghroushen, Ayt, Middle Atlas Berber tribe, 93, 95, 110, 116, 120–1, 141–3, 145, 168–9, 171, 180, 221

Seghroushni, Moulay Mohammed, Seghroushen war-chief, 140

Seghroushni, El-, Saïd ou Mohand, Seghrouchen war-chief, Jbel Tishshoukt, 144–6, 168, 170

Seguiat El-Hamra, Saharan coastal region, 94, 102

Seksawa, Berber tribe, High Atlas, 35, 36, 37, 38, 39, 40, 41, 57, 92

Seksawi, 'Aomar ('Amr ou-Haddou), Seksawa chief, 36, 37

Seksawi, 'Abdallah, rebel leader, 40

Seksawi, el-, Mokhtar, tribal chief, 92

Seksawiya, woman from Seksawa, 59

Selwan, village, Rif, 93, 150

Semgat, district of Ghriss region, 44

Semlal, Ida ou, Berber tribe, Anti-Atlas, Semlali / Semlala, family of marabouts, Tazeroualt, 40, 81, 82

Semlali, es-, (aka Moha n-Ifrouten), resistance leader, Tafilalt region, 102, 106–7, 118, 120–1, 125

Senghor, Léopold, Senegalese leader, 247

Senhaja, one of Berber founding families, 17, 19, 25, 28, 35, 43, 44, 46, 47, 53, 55, 62, 63, 65, 66, 70

Senoual, village, Middle Atlas, 73

Serdrar, Sidi, saint's tomb, near Amellago, 194

Serri, Ayt, Middle Atlas ribe, 56

Sgatt, plateau, near Waouizaght, 130, 206

Sghir, es-, Sidi Mohammed, war minister under Moulay Hassan I, 87

Sgougou, Ayt, Zaïan clan, 84, 111–12, 136

Shah (of Iran), 251

Shaq (Ishaq), Ayt, town, Tadla region, 47, 66

Shawia, Atlantic coastal region, 101

Shefshawn (Xauen), town, Rif, 150–2

Shegg El-'Ard, valley, Middle Atlas 172–3

Sheikh, -esh, Mohammed, Sa'adi monarch, 48

Sheikh, Sidi, son of Sidi 'Ali Amahoush, 131, 134

Shelouati, officer, Skhirat coup, 246

Sherqawi, Sidi Ben Daoud, 84

Shinguetti, el-, Seghroushen leader, 141

Shiker, Jbel, Middle Atlas, 130, 142

Shouf esh-Sherg, valley, Middle Atlas, 142

Sidi, Ayt Sidi 'Ali (children of Amhaoush), 203

Sidi Mha, Ayt, Merghad clan, Oued Ghriss, 193

Sidi, Ou-, *see* Hmad, Sidi Ben

Sidi Saïd ou 'Abdnaïm, Seksawa holy man, 41

Sidi Salah, Tadla region, 94

Sidi Yahya Abou Zakary, tribal leader, High Atlas, 41

Sidi 'Abdallah ou Saïd, Seksawa holy man, 41

Sidi 'Ali, Ayt, Seghroushen clan, 128

Sidna 'Isa (Jesus), 29

Sijilmassa, ancient city, southeast Morocco, 2, 16, 17, 18, 19, 29, 30, 31, 41, 48, 49, 67, 69

Silvestre, Spanish general, 150–2

Siroua, Jbel, extinct volcano, 124

Skhirat, attempted military coup, 246

Skounti, ou-, Zaïd, chief, Ayt 'Isa Izem, 178, 181–2, 184–8, 192–4, 207, 228, 231–2

Skoura, n-Ayt Seghroushen, village, 102, 140–1, 143, 146, 168, 170

Slama, Ayt Bou, Ouaraini clan, 146–7

Slane, de, Baron de, translator of Ibn Khaldoun and el-Bekri, 27

Smara, sacred town, Sahara, 94

Sokhman, Ayt, super-tribe, High Atlas, 35, 62, 69, 85–7, 103, 131, 136, 177, 198, 200, 205, 209, 212–14, 217, 220, 222, 227

Souf Ifeltasen, river, Middle Atlas, 139

Soufouloud, river, Middle Atlas, 172

Souk El-'Arba, Middle Atlas, 141–2

Sountat, village, Imilshil region, 246

Souss, region, southwest Morocco, 5, 19, 36, 40, 43, 49, 51, 52, 61, 81–2, 84–5, 94, 257

Spillman, Georges (*sliman*), French officer, 130, 179, 191–2

Sraghna, region east of Marrakesh, 243

Srou, Oued, 62, 73, 132

Steeg, French Resident-General, 177, 185

Stroomer, Harry, Dutch Berberist, Leiden University, 250

Suetonius Paulinus, Roman general, 10

Tabou'asamt, *qsar* in Tafilalt, 48, 49

Tadafelt, *qsar*, Todgha region, 235

Taddart, Ayt, Hadiddou clan, Ziz, 199

Tadighoust, village, Oued Ghriss, 88, 178, 184, 185

Tadla, region, central Morocco, 15, 17, 19, 40, 63, 71, 83, 87, 90, 94–5, 102–3, 121, 125, 130, 197–8, 205–6, 211, 214, 216–17, 231, 246

Tadout, plateau, Tishshoukt, 146

Tafessasset, battle site, Moulouya region, 134, 136

Taffert, cedar forest, Bou Iblan, 172–3, 175

Tafgourt, Jbel, Middle Atlas, 131

Tafilalt, oasis, southeast Morocco, 3, 16, 29, 41, 46, 48–9, 51, 53, 67–71, 76, 88, 102, 115, 117–18, 120–1, 123, 127, 161–2, 178–81, 184–5, 188–90, 201, 225, 236

Tafrant, village, Jbala region, 157

Tafza, village, Tazizaout, 213, 221

Tagendoust, village, southeast Morocco, 182

Tagerroumt, *qsar*, near Tafilalt, 189

Taghia, distric, Oued Ghriss, 193

Taghzout, French fort, Oued Gigou, 110, 143

Tagouzalt, hill near Moulouya sources, 136

Tagountaft, Goundafi stronghold, 92

Tagzirt, foothill town near Beni Mellal, 62

Tahiant, village, High Atlas, 203

Taïbi, Oulad Sidi, family of marabouts, Tadla area, 131–2

Taïbi, Sidi Mohammed, Ishqern marabout, Moulouya, 131, 205

Taïbi, Si 'Abdelmalek, marabout, Naour, 131, 132

Takbalt, village, near Ksiba, 87

Takoushtamt, ridge, Tazizaout, 213, 217

Talat n-Irshi, ravine, southeast Morocco, 230

Talat n-Ou'arab, village, near Tounfit, 208

Talat Oukidar, gorges, 73

Talat n-Ya'qoub, site of Goundafi kasbah, 92

Talmest, Ayt 'Atta pastures, 46

Talsinnt, village, southeast Morocco, 117–18, 161, 163, 180

Talzemt, village, Bou Iblan, 146

Tamalout, village, Yahya region, 214

Tamayoust, village, Moulouya region, 86

Tamdakht, village, southern Morocco, 123

Tamgrout, zaouia, Oued Dra'a, 121

Tamesna, Atlantic coastal region, 2, 15, 16, 19, 39

Tamjilt, village, Middle Atlas, 139

Tamnousht, female resistance fighter, Hamdoun/Kerdous, 232

Tana, Ayt Merghad village, 199

Tanant, Atlas foot-hill town, 127

Tanchraramt, village, Bou Iblan, 172

Tanfit, Oued, Moulouya region, 72

Tangier, port city, north Morocco, 15, 150, 159

Taniat Msamir, Missour region, 142

Tanneghrift, village, High Atlas, 202, 204

Tanout n-Bou Wourgh, well, Sokhman region, 211

Tansmakht, battle site, Fazaz, 67

Tanzim, revolt, spring 1973, 246

Taoujja'aout, hill, Tazizaout, 216–17

Taounat, town, north Morocco, 154, 157

Taourirt, kasbah, Warzazat, 89

Taouz, *qsar*, Tafilalt, 185

Tarda (*wi n-iwaliwn*), French outpost and battle site, southeast Morocco, 162, 184

Tarfaya, Saharan coastal region, 84

Targuist, town, Rif, 159

Tarif el-Berghaouati, founder of Berghaouta dynasty, 16

Taroudannt, town, Souss region, 19, 48, 82, 92, 94

Tarrit, French colonel, Atlas front, 198

Tarselt, Almou n-, pasture, 120

Tasaft, zaouia, High Atlas, 58, 59, 60

Tashfin, Ibn ʿAli, Almoravid sultan, 22

Tassa, Seksawa village, 92

Tassaout, river, High Atlas, 125

Tassaount n-Ouidammen, hill, Tazizaout, 215–16

Tassent, village, Imilchil region, 214, 228

Tassemit, Jbel, above Beni Mellal, 130, 197

Taswiqt Square, Tounfit, 253

Tata, pre-Saharan oasis, 192

Taza, city, north Morocco, 25, 30, 93, 102, 123, 139–42, 144, 154–6, 158, 161, 253

Taza, *tache de*, resistance area, 139–40, 142–3, 146, 161, 171, 175, 177

Tazarout, village, north Morocco, 150

Tazememart, prison, southeast Morocco, 247

Tazeroualt, region, southwest Morocco, 3, 40, 48, 52, 81–4

Tazibout, female resistance fighter, Baddou, 231

Tazizaout, Jbel, High Atlas, 3, 162, 194, 197–8, 208, 213–14, 216–17, 219–22, 226, 231–2, 247

Tazougguert, battle site, southeast Morocco, 116–17

Tazouta, outpost near Sefrou, 93, 96, 141

Tazra, Asif, Tazizaout, 196

Tazra, hamlet, Tazizaout, 215–17, 221–3

Tazra n-Ismekh, cliff, Tazizaout, 216

Tazrouft, *qsar* Zaouit Si Hamza, 44

Tazzarin, village, Jbel Saghro, 119

Taʿadlount, village, High Atlas, 95, 177, 208–9

Taʾazzount, princess, sister of Saïd el-Almohad, 30

Telagh, Oued near Tlemcen, 31

Telouat, village, residence of El-Glaoui, 89, 123, 128, 243

Temga, Asif, Kousser region, 198, 233

Temga, ou-, Si Lhousseyn, Ahansal marabout, 102, 125, 129–30, 206, 211

Temga, Zaouia, 125, 130, 211, 234

Temsaman, Rif tribe, 151

Termoun, Aïcha, influential woman, early-eighteenth-century, upper Moulouya, 62

Termoun, ou-, ʿAli, leader, Ayt Hadiddou, 228, 231

Temzezdekt, ʿAbdelouadid fortress, 30

Terrasse, Henri, Protectorate period historian, 10, 27, 31, 32, 54, 70

Terwillal, hill, Tadla region, 168

Tetouan, city, north Morocco, 90, 150, 153, 156–7, 159

Tfassiyt, oul-, Miʾami, son of Moha ou Hammou, 106, 236

Tharaud, J., French writer, 128

Théveney, French General, Tafilalt and Tadla regions, 121, 134

Tidikelt, desert region, Algeria, 69

Tifinagh, Berber script, 251–2, 255

Tifnout, valley, High Atlas, 124

Tiffert n-Ayt Hamza, village, Oued Laʿabid, 206

Tigleft, village, Oued Lʾabid, 206

Tigrigra, plain near Azrou, 15, 66, 85

Tighmart, village, Tafilalt, 119–20, 189

Tignamas, village, Middle Atlas, 143

Tikhedouin, village, Imilshil region, 227

Tillougouit, village, High Atlas, 129, 211

Tilmi, Asif n-, river Hadiddou region, 228

Tilmi (*tilmi n-ayt sidi*), Hadiddou village, 199, 227, 230

Tilmirat, village, Marmousha region, 147, 172

Timghazin, Jbel, 43, 125

Timhadit, Middle Atlas village, 73, 86, 88, 109–10, 112, 144

Timimoun, oasis, Touat, Algeria, 116

Tingerft, plateau, Sokhman region, 83, 201

Tinghir, city, southeast Morocco, 15, 125, 166, 222, 233, 235

Tinjdad, town, Merghad region, 213, 235

Tinmel, cradle of Almohad dynasty, 21, 22, 24, 29, 31, 35, 36, 58, 61

Tinteghallin, Middle Atlas village, 56, 73, 133

Tintorfa, mountain, Imilshil region, 228

Tirghist, *qsar*, Hadiddou region, 209, 227

Tisigdelt, plateau, Middle-Atlas, 17, 18

Tishka, plateau, High Atlas, 57, 92

Tishshoukt, Jbel, Middle Atlas, 3, 93, 102, 110, 138–45, 161, 168, 170, 180

Tissekt n-Temda, mountain, Imilshil, 228, 230

Tiydrin, *qsar*, southeast Morocco, 182

Tizgui, village, High Atlas, 60

Tizi, Ba 'Amran region, 236

Tizi Adni, col, Tishshoukt, 143, 146

Tizi n-Ayt Imi, High Atlas, 128

Tizi n-Ayt Ouirra, col near Ksiba, 87

Tizi n-Bibaoun, col High Atlas, 19, 36, 92

Tizi Hamri, Middle Atlas, 173

Tizi La'fit, col near Jbel Koubbat, 73

Tizi n-Hamdoun, col, Ghriss region, 230

Tizi n-Ighil, col west of Tounfit, 209, 215

Tizi n-Islit, above Beni Mellal, 130

Tizi n-Issoual, Imilshil region, 227–8

Tizi n-Maoutfoud, col, High Atlas, 202

Tizi n-Meshfraoun, col near Tounfit, 185

Tizi n-Mesfergh, col, Tazizaout, 214, 219

Tizi n-Midjider, southeast Morocc, 192

Tizi n-Inouzan, Imilshil region, 228

Tizi n-Oughroum, Imilshil region, 230

Tizi n-Ouichden, col south of Nfis valley, 59

Tizi n-Talghemt, col SE of Midelt, 69, 88

Tizi n-Taghzeft, col Middle Atlas, 86, 88, 101, 109–10, 144

Tizi n-Tagnanaït, col, Middle Atlas, 141

Tizi n-Telouat, col, High Atlas, 54, 68

Tizi n-Test, col, High Atlas, 21, 92

Tizi Ouidal, Bou Iblan, 171, 173

Tizi Tagzart, col, 24

Tizi n-Tantatart, Bou Iblan, 172

Tizi n-Telouat, 51, 64, 84, 88–9

Tizi n-Test, col, High Atlas, 35, 86

Tizi n-Tighanimin, col, near Aghbala, 86

Tizi Tigoulmamin, Tishshoukt, 146, 170

Tizi n-Timezdarin, col, southeast Morocco, 182

Tizi n-Timezjalin, col, southeast Morocco, 182

Tizi n-Tkoushtamt, col, Tazizaout, 214

Tizimi, village, Tafilalt, 121

Tiznit, town, southwest Morocco, 83, 235

Ti'allalin, district, Oued Ziz, 88

Tlemcen, town, Algeria, 25, 29, 30, 31, 32

Todgha, river, southeast Morocco, 15, 56, 69, 119, 120–1, 125, 194, 235

Touat, desert region, Algeria, 28, 46, 69, 98, 115

Toubkal, Jbel, Marrakesh High Atlas, 41

Toujjit, Jbel, Moulouya sources, 69, 86, 88, 134, 208

Toulal, village, southeast Morocco, 116

Touli (Taoula), founded Qala'at el-Mehdi, 17

Toumert, Ibn, Almohad mahdi, 20, 22, 23

Tounfit, foothill town, High Atlas, xiv, 47, 62, 79, 85–6, 93, 102, 113, 120, 132, 136, 161, 164, 166, 178, 185, 188, 194, 199, 203, 205–9, 221, 253

Tournemire, French lieutenant, Middle Atlas and southeast Morocco, 166, 180

Touzin, Ayt, Rif tribe, 151

Triq *es-Seltan*, 'sultan's road' Fez-Tafilalt, 139

Tsoul, Arabic-speaking tribe, Taza region, 154, 156

Vandals, 12

Verdun, battle site, Great War, 155

Vernois, French general, Bou Iblan, 172

Victor Hugo, 194

Vidalon, Jean, general, commander-in-chief, Morocco, 1929–31, 204, 206

Voinot, French military historian, 227

Volubilis (*walili*), Zerhoun region, 2, 82

Wahhabism, Saudi-inspired Islamic philosophy, 251

Waoumana, village, Tadla region, 15

Waoumshash, battle site, Middle Atlas, 147

Wanergui, Ayt, Sokhman clan, Anergui region, 206, 211, 227, 233

Wansifen (*see* Oum er Rbia'), river, 15–16, 24, 55–6, 73, 112

Waouizaght, town, 24, 127–9, 177, 205–6, 211

Warzazat, town, 89, 123–4

Waouzgit, Ayt, Berber tribe, Warzazat area, 41, 124

Ward Price, G., British correspondent, Jbel Baddou, 231

Waryaghar, Ayt, Rif tribe, 151–2, 159

Weygand, French general, 155

Weygand (*biga*), French lieutenant, Amellago region, 192–3

Wharton, Edith, American writer, 202

World Amazigh Congress (WAC; *Agraw Amadil Amazigh*), 250

Yaflman, Ayt, tribal confederation, High Atlas, 43, 48, 56, 67, 68, 69, 198, 201

Yaghmourasn, thirteenth-century 'Abd el-Ouadid ruler of Tlemcen, 30–2

Yagour, plateau, High Atlas, 7

Yahya, Almoravid amir, 19

Yahya, 'Abdelouadid prince, 31

Yahya, Ayt, Berber tribe, Yaflman component, High Atlas, 69, 79, 85–6, 93, 132, 134, 166, 168, 185, 190, 197, 203, 205–6, 209, 211, 213–14

Yahya, ou-, Sidi 'Ali, Seghroushen marabout, 140

Yahya, Sidi 'Ali, famous early Ayt Seghroushen chief, 128

Yahya Aghoual, Almohad leader, 25

Yahya Ben Ta'afouft, Berber chieftain, ally of Portuguese, 39

Yahya Ibn Nasser, Almohad prince, 29

Yahya Ibn Sir, Almoravid governor, 24

Yahya Ibn Wanoudin, Almohad leader, 30

Yahya ou Youssef, Sidi, Atlas saint, 208

Yahya ou Youssef, Sidi, zaouia, Tounfit region, 132, 136, 186, 203, 207–8

Yassin, Tassadit, Kabylian, Paris-based researcher, Mammeri's successor, 249

Ya'qoub, Ayt, High Atlas battle site, 3, 180–1, 185, 197, 202–4, 207

Ya'qoub, Ayt, section of Zaian, 83

Ya'qoub, Ayt Sidi Bou, *shurfa*, Assoul, upper Ghriss, 20, 179, 193

Ya'qoub el-Mansour, Almohad amir, 28, 29

Ya'qoub, ou- 'Isa, Ishqern clan, 87

Ya'qoub Ibn 'Abdelhaqq, Merinid amir, 30, 31

Y'azza, 'Atta clan, 119, 225

Y'azza, Hadiddou clan, 44, 199

Yemen, 6, 10, 28

Youb, Ayt, Ayt Merghad clan, 44

Youb, Jbel, last resistance hide-out, Ghriss region, 233

Yoummour, Ayt (*ayt immur*), High Atlas Berber tribe, 56, 62, 72

Youns (Waryawara), famous Berghaouati prince, 16

Youssef, Ben Mohammed, 'Alawid prince, Morocco's first independent king as Mohammed V (1956–1961), 219, 221–2

Youssef, Sidi, (aka Joseph Haunsell) Ahansal marabout, 63

Youssi, Ayt, Berber tribe, Middle Atlas, 70–2, 85, 95–6, 110

Youssi, El-, seventeenth-century scholar, Fazaz, 48

Youssi, 'Aomar, *makhzan qayd*, 93

Youssef, Abou Ya'qoub, Merinid sultan murdered near Tlemcen, 5

Youssef Ibn Tashfin, Almoravid sultan, 17, 21, 23, 27, 36

Zafzafi, Nasser, civil rights militant, Rif, 255

Zagora, town, Oued Dra'a, 191

Zaïan (*iziyyan*), Berber tribe, central Morocco, 73–4, 83–4 95, 101, 103–7, 111–12, 120, 131, 133, 136, 161, 177, 208, 214, 216–17, 221

Zaouia (Had) Ifran, religious centre, Middle Atlas, 18

Zaouit esh-Cheikh, town, 133

Zeggout, Beni, Ouaraïn clan, 175

Zemmour, Berber tribe, 46, 55, 56, 65, 67, 71, 72, 74, 84, 242

Zenata, Berber founding family, 16, 29, 32, 35

Zerban, Ahmed, one of Belqasm Ngadi's lieutenants, 191

Zerban, Ou-Hdiddou grenade-thrower, 227

Zerhoun, Jbel, mountain near Meknes, 15, 94, 99

Zerhoun, Moulay Driss, Idrissid sharif, 58, 82

Zerhouni, ez-, Lhajj Brahim Ben Mohamed, marabout of Tasaft, High Atlas, 58–61

Zidan, Moulay, Sa'adi sultan, 41

Zidouh, Dar Ould, town, Tadla region, 177

Zin, Moulay, brother of Moulay Hafid, short-lived puppet sultan, 93

Zinit, site of Lalla 'Aziza's tomb, 39

Ziz, river, 28, 44, 47, 88, 116–18, 120–1, 180–1, 186, 192, 199, 202–3

Zloul, river, Middle Atlas, 141

Zouggat, Ben, Itto, Berber courtesan, Ishqern, 209

Zouggati, *makhzan qayd* (Zemmour origin), 84